A Devil and Her Love Song

Story & Art by
Miyoshi Tomori

Volume 7

A Devil and Her Love Song

Volume 7
CONTENTS

Song 41 5

Song 42 31

Song 43 59

Song 44 85

Song 45 111

Song 46 137

Song 47 163

The devil makes me LOVELY!!!

STORY THUS FAR

Anna Mouri, whom Maria had considered her best friend at her old school St. Katria, reveals that their friendship had always been painful for her. The revelation shocks Maria and makes her realize that their relationship is in desperate need of repair.

Anna, on the other hand, tries to tear Maria down further by telling Shin a secret from Maria's past—a secret that leaves Shin feeling he has no choice but to distance himself from Maria for her own good.

Meanwhile, Yusuke, who's been supporting Maria all along, reaches a turning point...

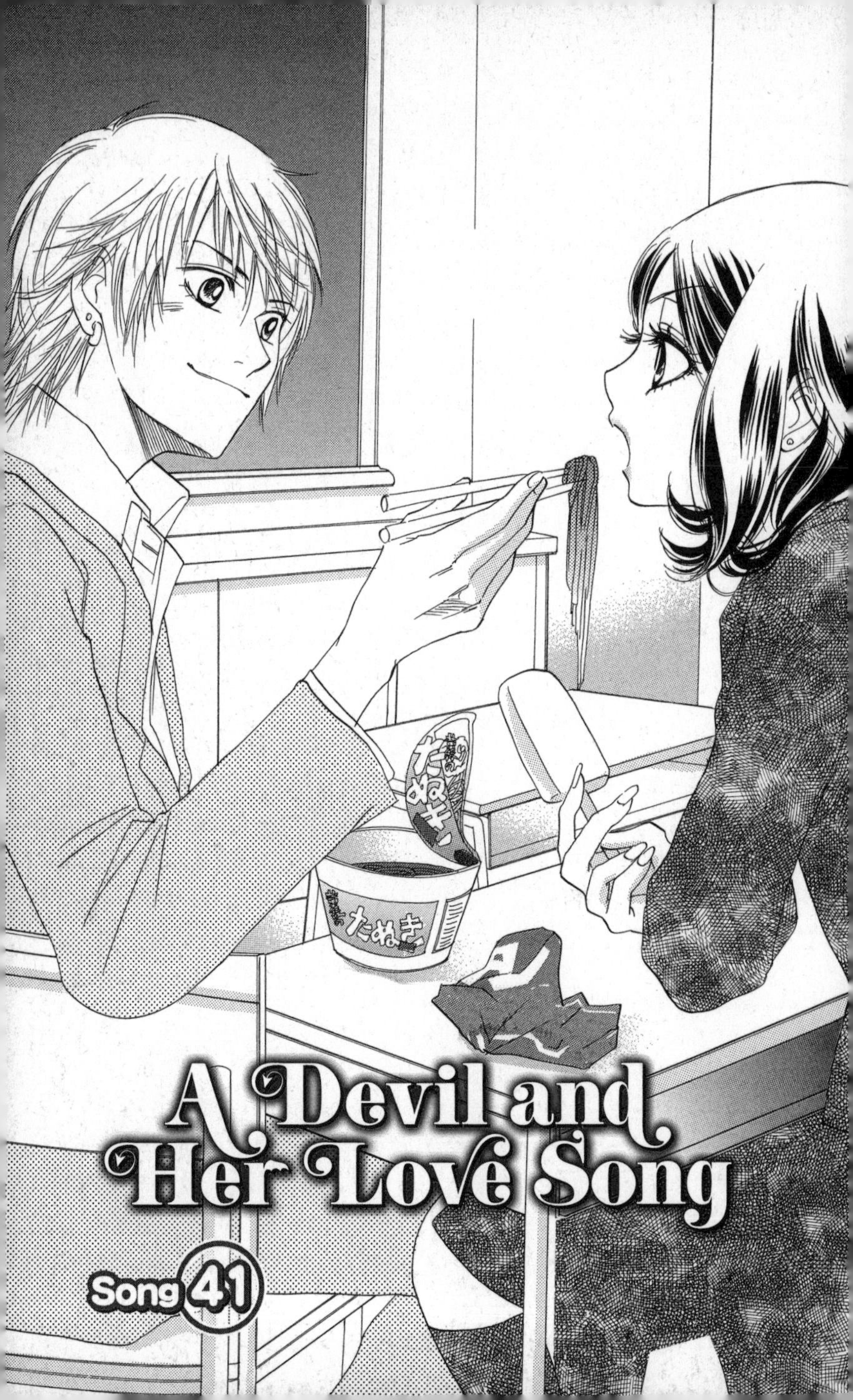
A Devil and Her Love Song
Song 41

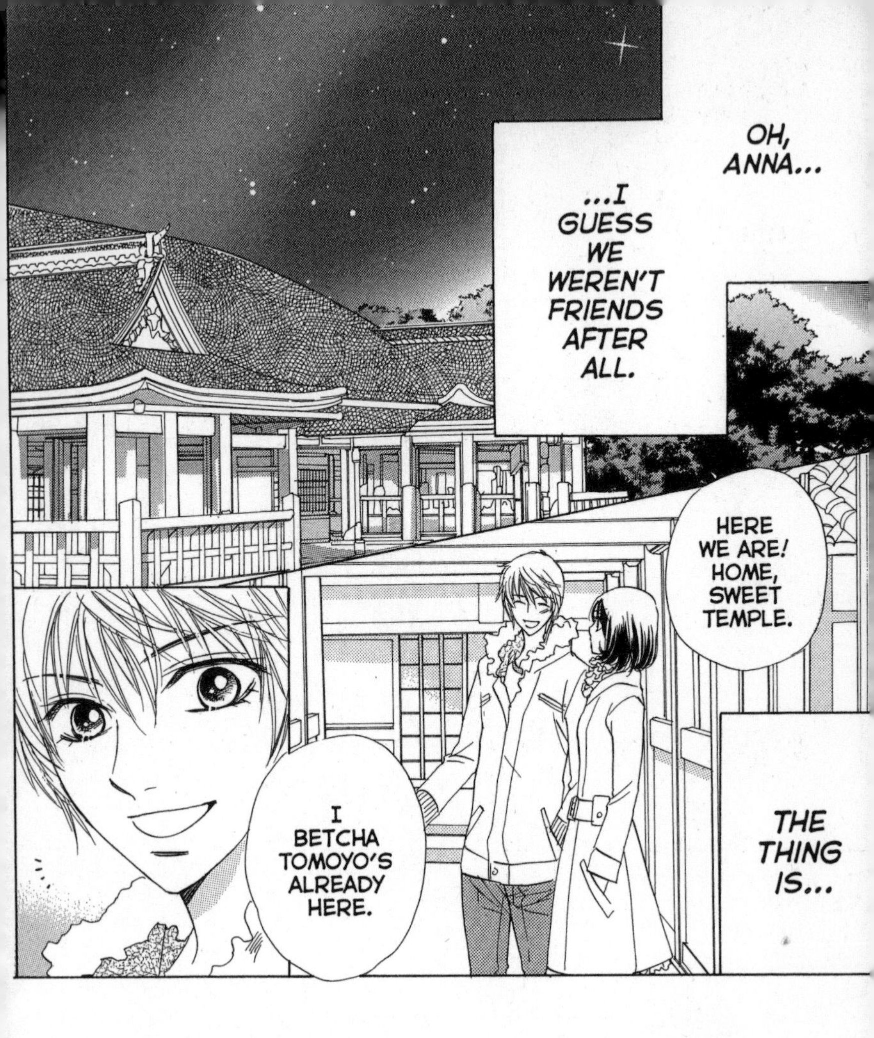
OH, ANNA...
...I GUESS WE WEREN'T FRIENDS AFTER ALL.
HERE WE ARE! HOME, SWEET TEMPLE.
THE THING IS...
I BETCHA TOMOYO'S ALREADY HERE.

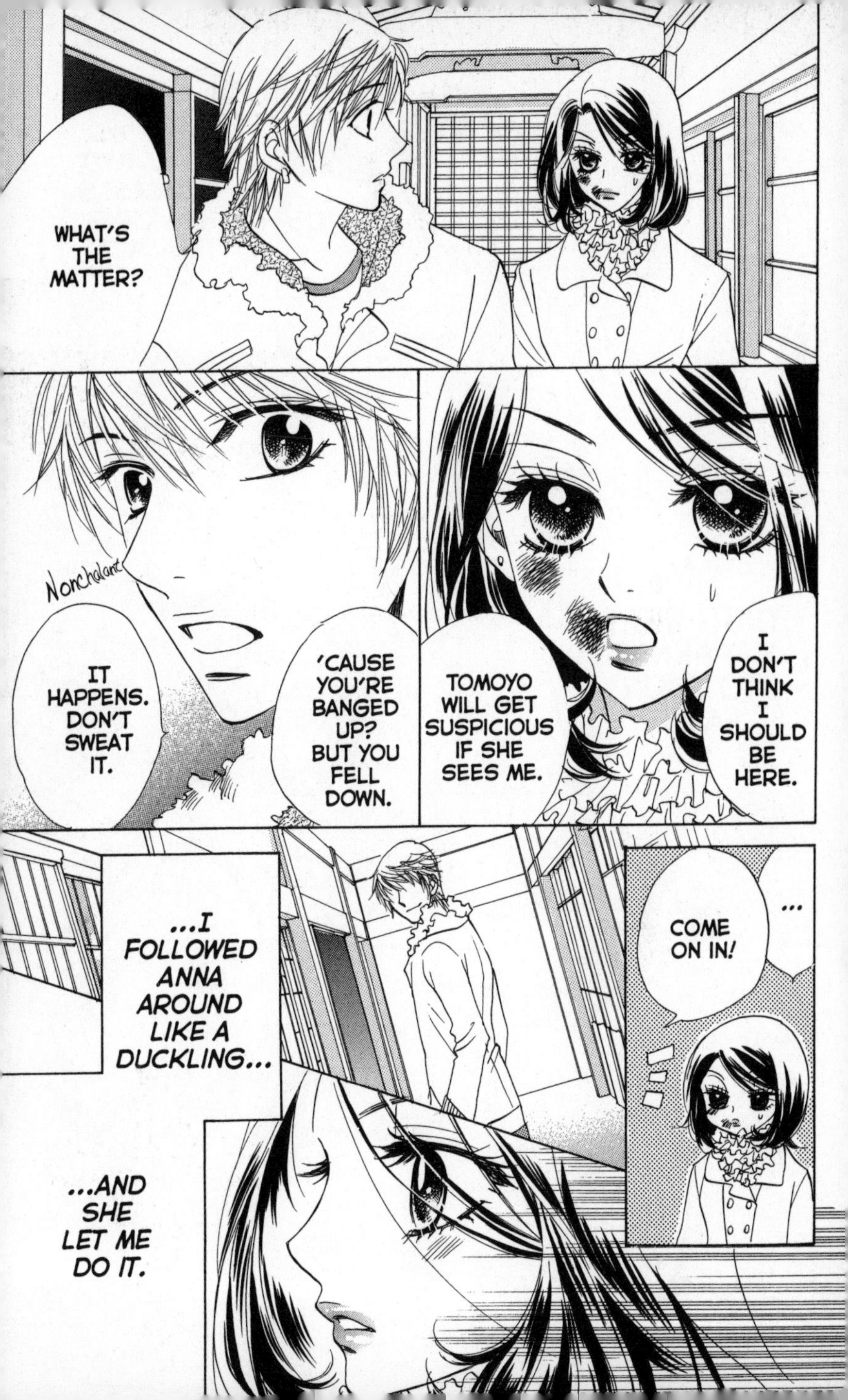
WHAT'S THE MATTER?
I DON'T THINK I SHOULD BE HERE.
TOMOYO WILL GET SUSPICIOUS IF SHE SEES ME.
'CAUSE YOU'RE BANGED UP? BUT YOU FELL DOWN.
Nonchalant
IT HAPPENS. DON'T SWEAT IT.
...
COME ON IN!
...I FOLLOWED ANNA AROUND LIKE A DUCKLING...
...AND SHE LET ME DO IT.

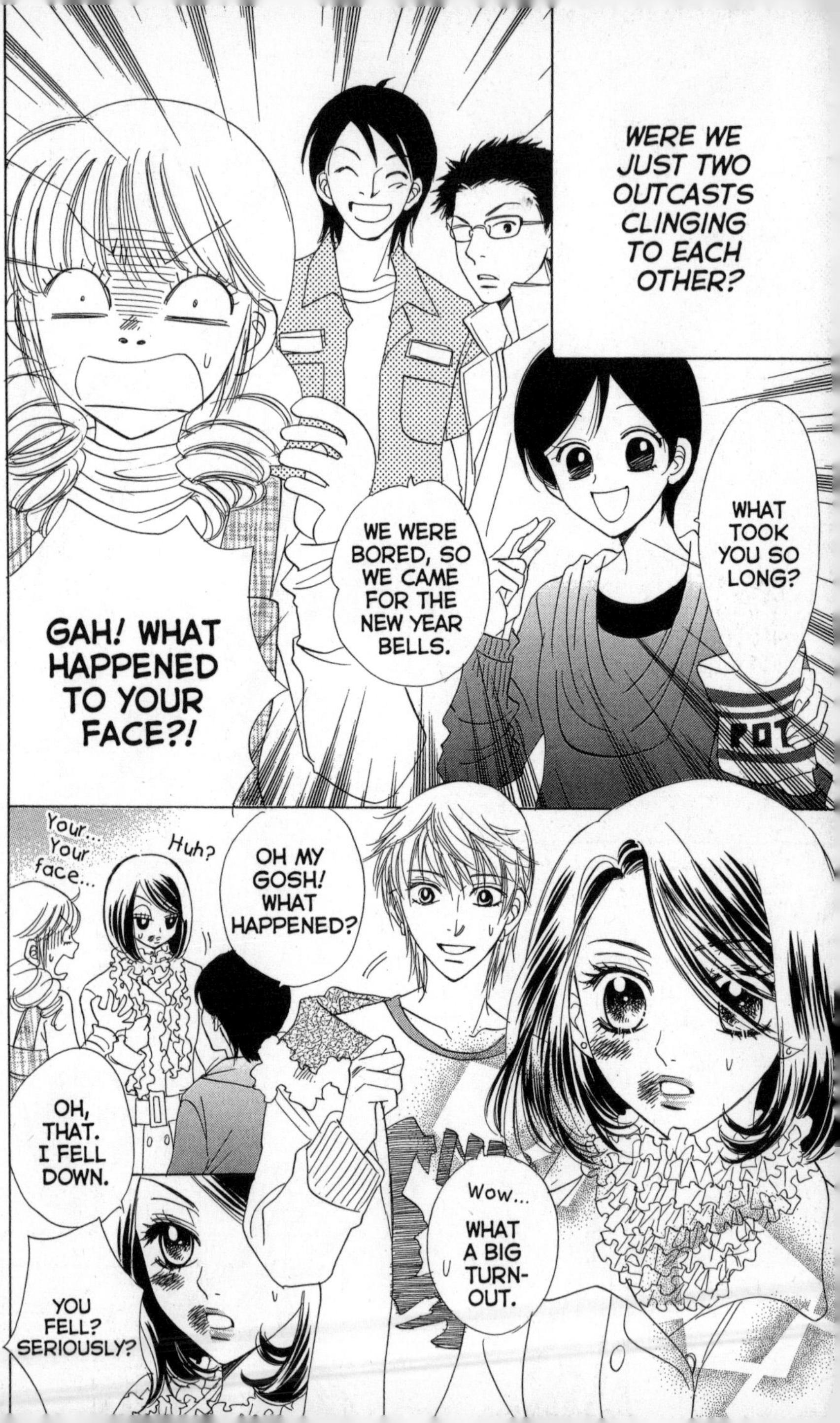
WERE WE JUST TWO OUTCASTS CLINGING TO EACH OTHER?
WHAT TOOK YOU SO LONG?
WE WERE BORED, SO WE CAME FOR THE NEW YEAR BELLS.
GAH! WHAT HAPPENED TO YOUR FACE?!
OH MY GOSH! WHAT HAPPENED?
Huh?
Your... Your face...
OH, THAT. I FELL DOWN.
Wow... WHAT A BIG TURN-OUT.
YOU FELL? SERIOUSLY?

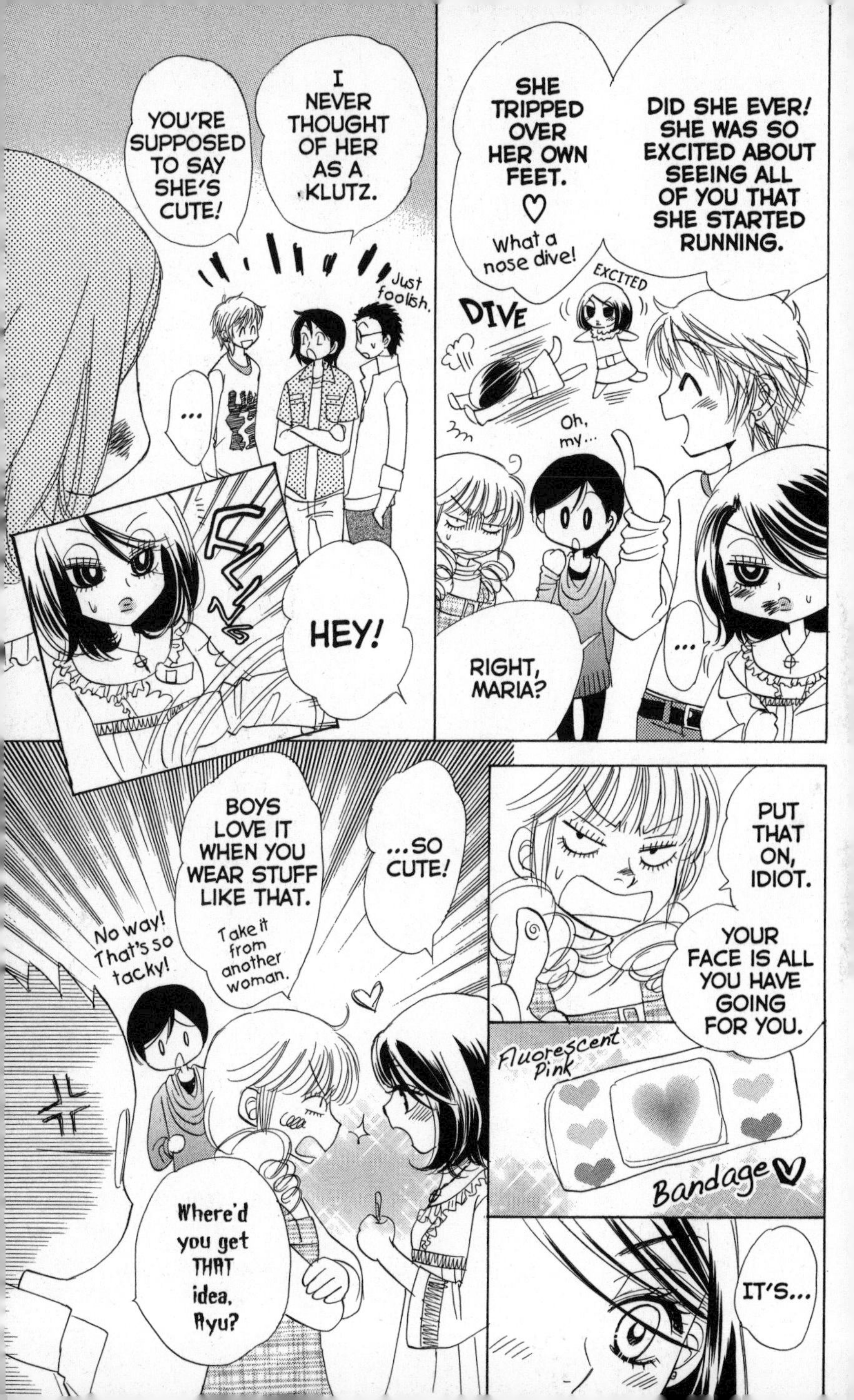
DID SHE EVER! SHE WAS SO EXCITED ABOUT SEEING ALL OF YOU THAT SHE STARTED RUNNING.
SHE TRIPPED OVER HER OWN FEET. ♡
What a nose dive!
EXCITED
DIVE
Oh, my...
...
RIGHT, MARIA?
I NEVER THOUGHT OF HER AS A KLUTZ.
YOU'RE SUPPOSED TO SAY SHE'S CUTE!
Just foolish.
...
HEY!
PUT THAT ON, IDIOT.
YOUR FACE IS ALL YOU HAVE GOING FOR YOU.
Fluorescent Pink
Bandage ♡
IT'S...
...SO CUTE!
BOYS LOVE IT WHEN YOU WEAR STUFF LIKE THAT.
Take it from another woman.
No way! That's so tacky!
Where'd you get THAT idea, Ayu?

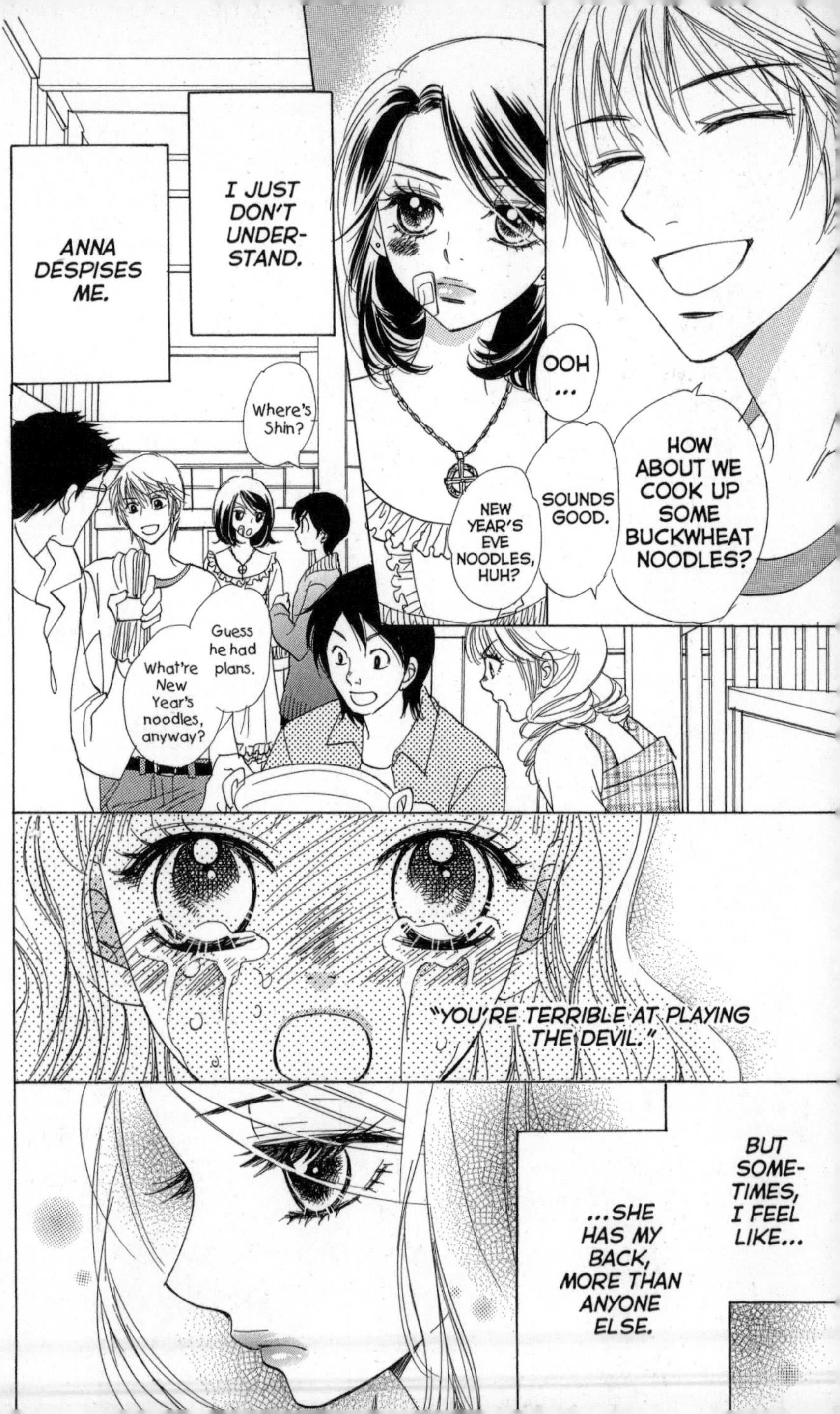
HOW ABOUT WE COOK UP SOME BUCKWHEAT NOODLES?
SOUNDS GOOD.
OOH ...
NEW YEAR'S EVE NOODLES, HUH?
I JUST DON'T UNDER-STAND.
ANNA DESPISES ME.
Where's Shin?
Guess he had plans.
What're New Year's noodles, anyway?
"YOU'RE TERRIBLE AT PLAYING THE DEVIL."
BUT SOME-TIMES, I FEEL LIKE...
...SHE HAS MY BACK, MORE THAN ANYONE ELSE.

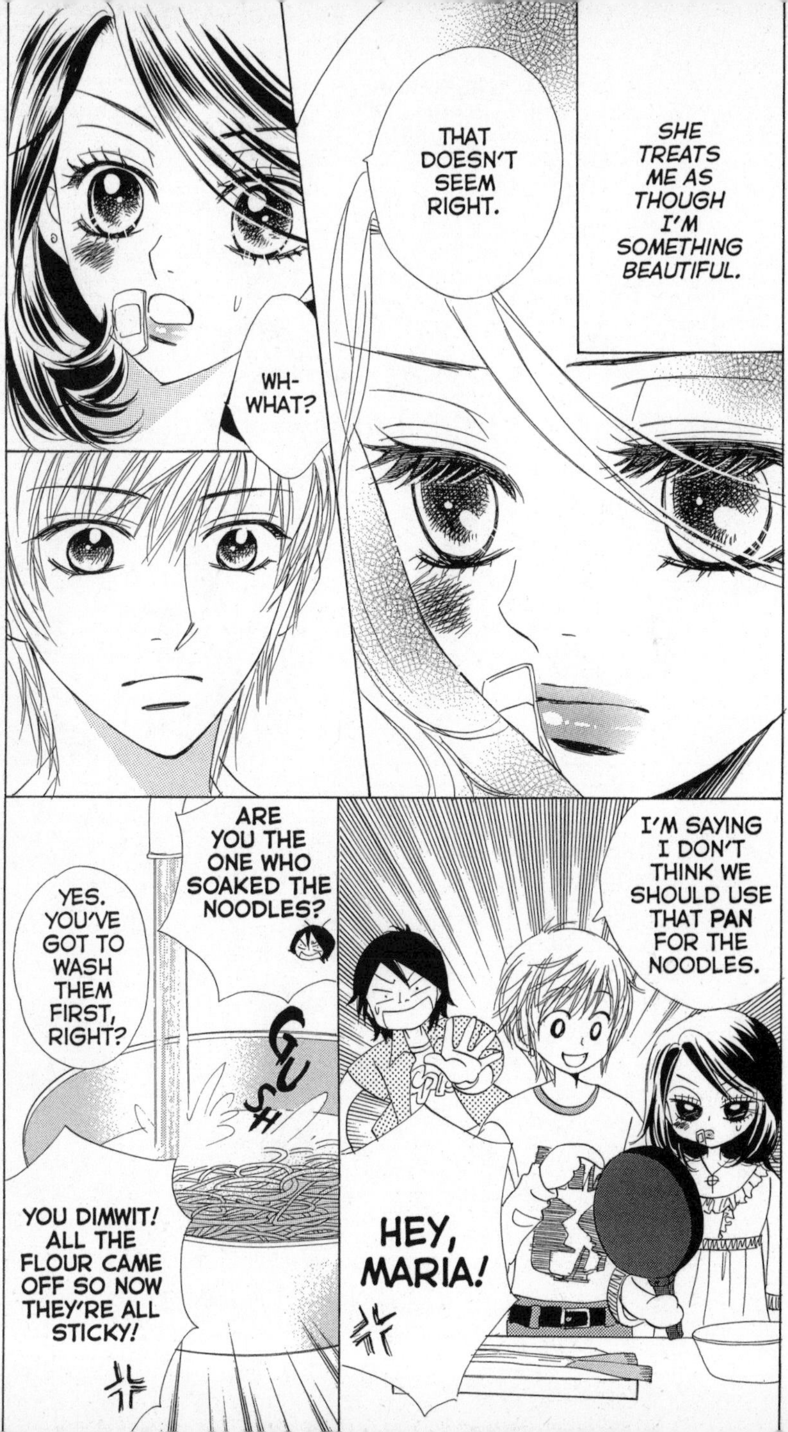
SHE TREATS ME AS THOUGH I'M SOMETHING BEAUTIFUL.
THAT DOESN'T SEEM RIGHT.
WH-WHAT?
I'M SAYING I DON'T THINK WE SHOULD USE THAT PAN FOR THE NOODLES.
HEY, MARIA!
ARE YOU THE ONE WHO SOAKED THE NOODLES?
YES. YOU'VE GOT TO WASH THEM FIRST, RIGHT?
GUSH
YOU DIMWIT! ALL THE FLOUR CAME OFF SO NOW THEY'RE ALL STICKY!

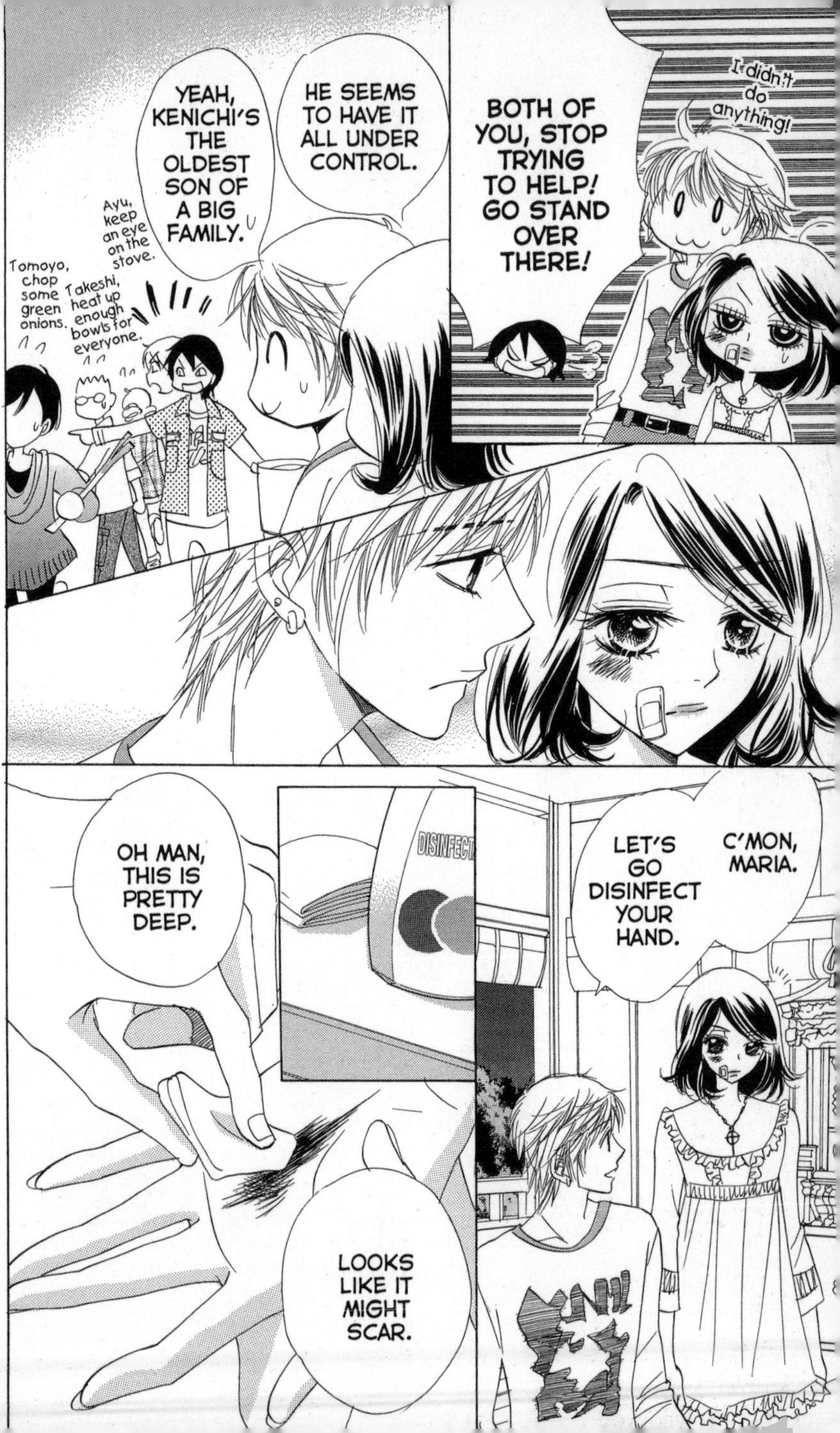
BOTH OF YOU, STOP TRYING TO HELP! GO STAND OVER THERE!
I didn't do anything!
HE SEEMS TO HAVE IT ALL UNDER CONTROL.
YEAH, KENICHI'S THE OLDEST SON OF A BIG FAMILY.
Ayu, keep an eye on the stove.
Takeshi, heat up enough bowls for everyone.
Tomoyo, chop some green onions.
C'MON, MARIA.
LET'S GO DISINFECT YOUR HAND.
DISINFECT
OH MAN, THIS IS PRETTY DEEP.
LOOKS LIKE IT MIGHT SCAR.

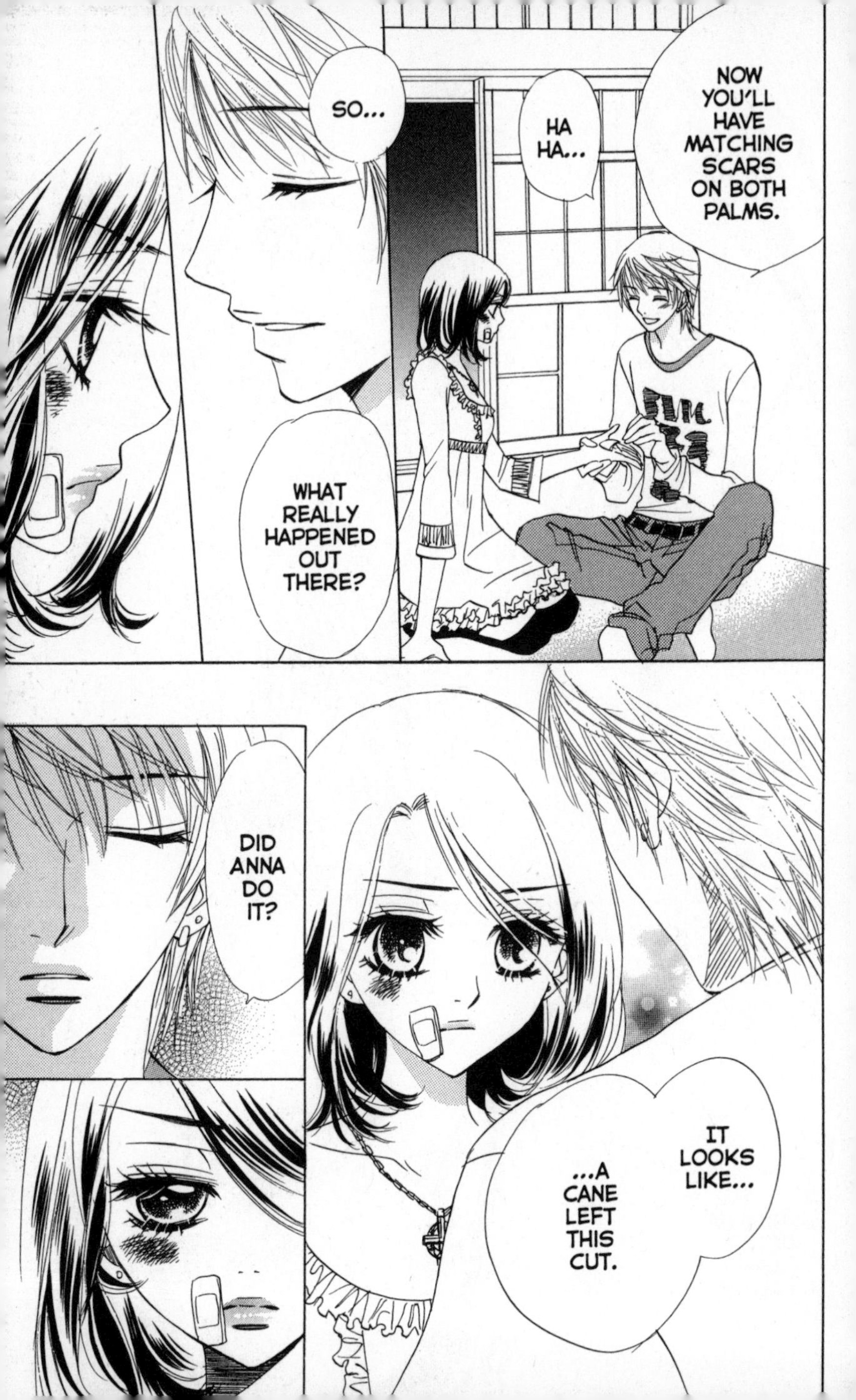
NOW YOU'LL HAVE MATCHING SCARS ON BOTH PALMS.
HA HA...
SO...
WHAT REALLY HAPPENED OUT THERE?
IT LOOKS LIKE...
...A CANE LEFT THIS CUT.
DID ANNA DO IT?

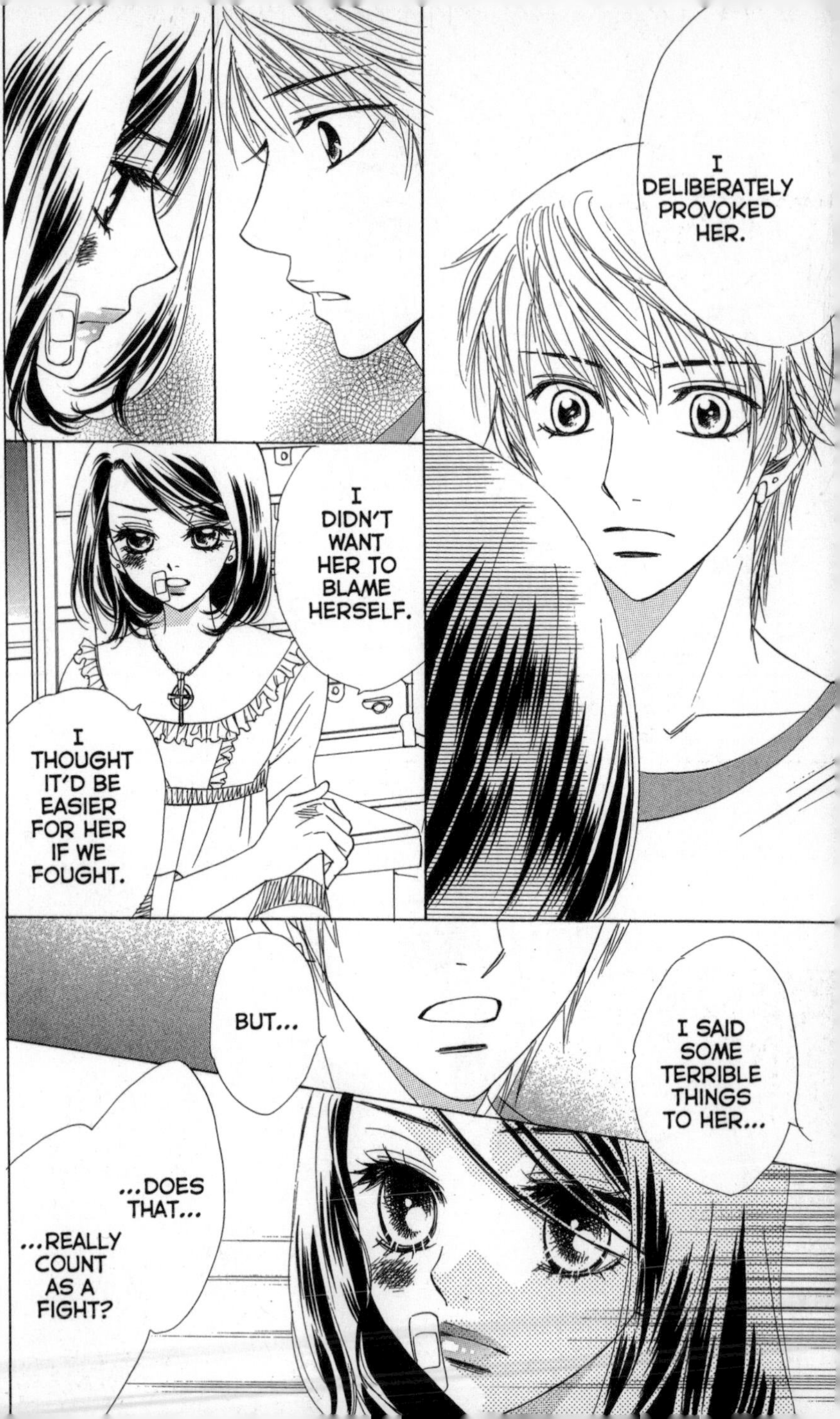
I DELIBERATELY PROVOKED HER.
I DIDN'T WANT HER TO BLAME HERSELF.
I THOUGHT IT'D BE EASIER FOR HER IF WE FOUGHT.
I SAID SOME TERRIBLE THINGS TO HER...
BUT...
...DOES THAT...
...REALLY COUNT AS A FIGHT?

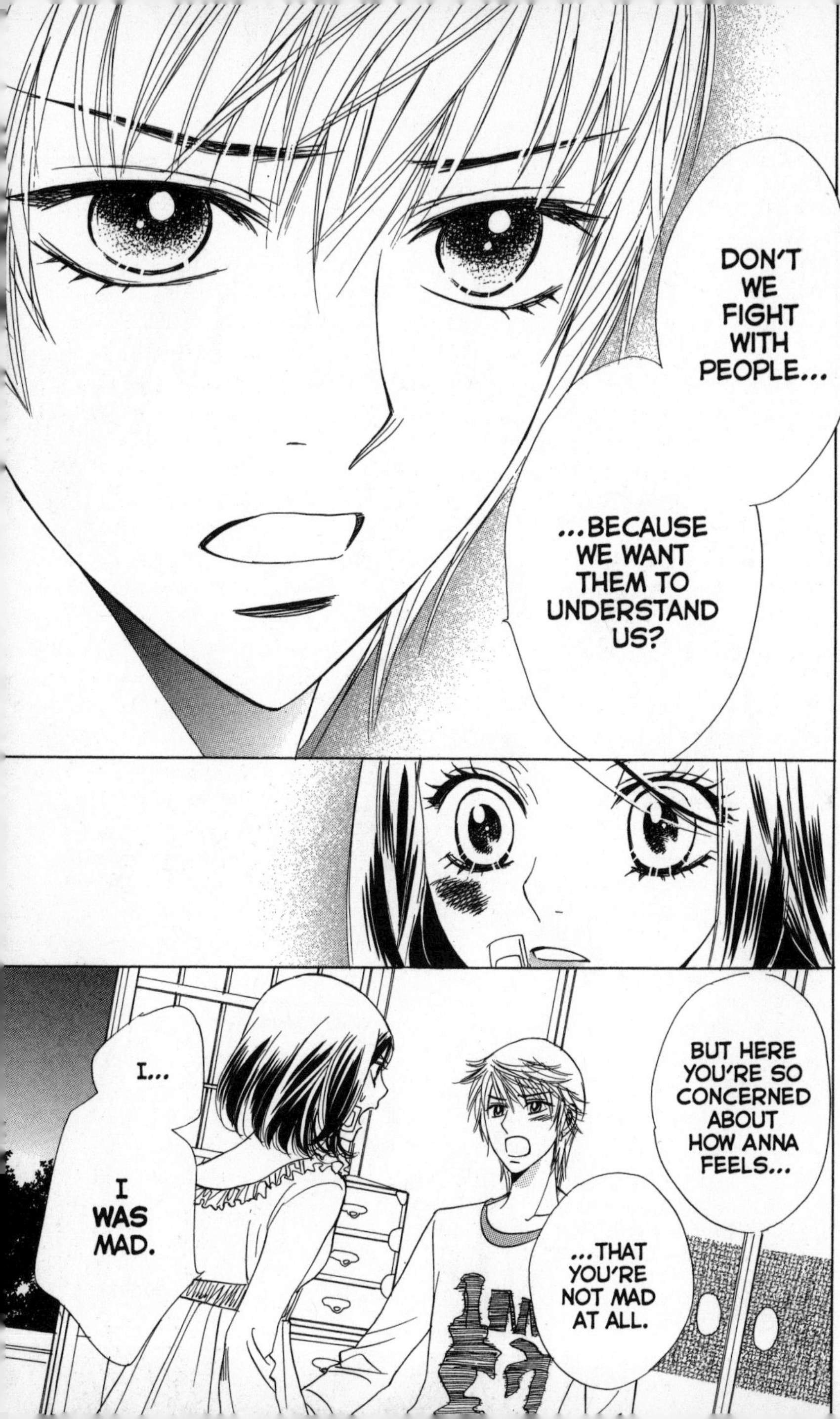
DON'T WE FIGHT WITH PEOPLE...
...BECAUSE WE WANT THEM TO UNDERSTAND US?
BUT HERE YOU'RE SO CONCERNED ABOUT HOW ANNA FEELS...
...THAT YOU'RE NOT MAD AT ALL.
I...
I WAS MAD.

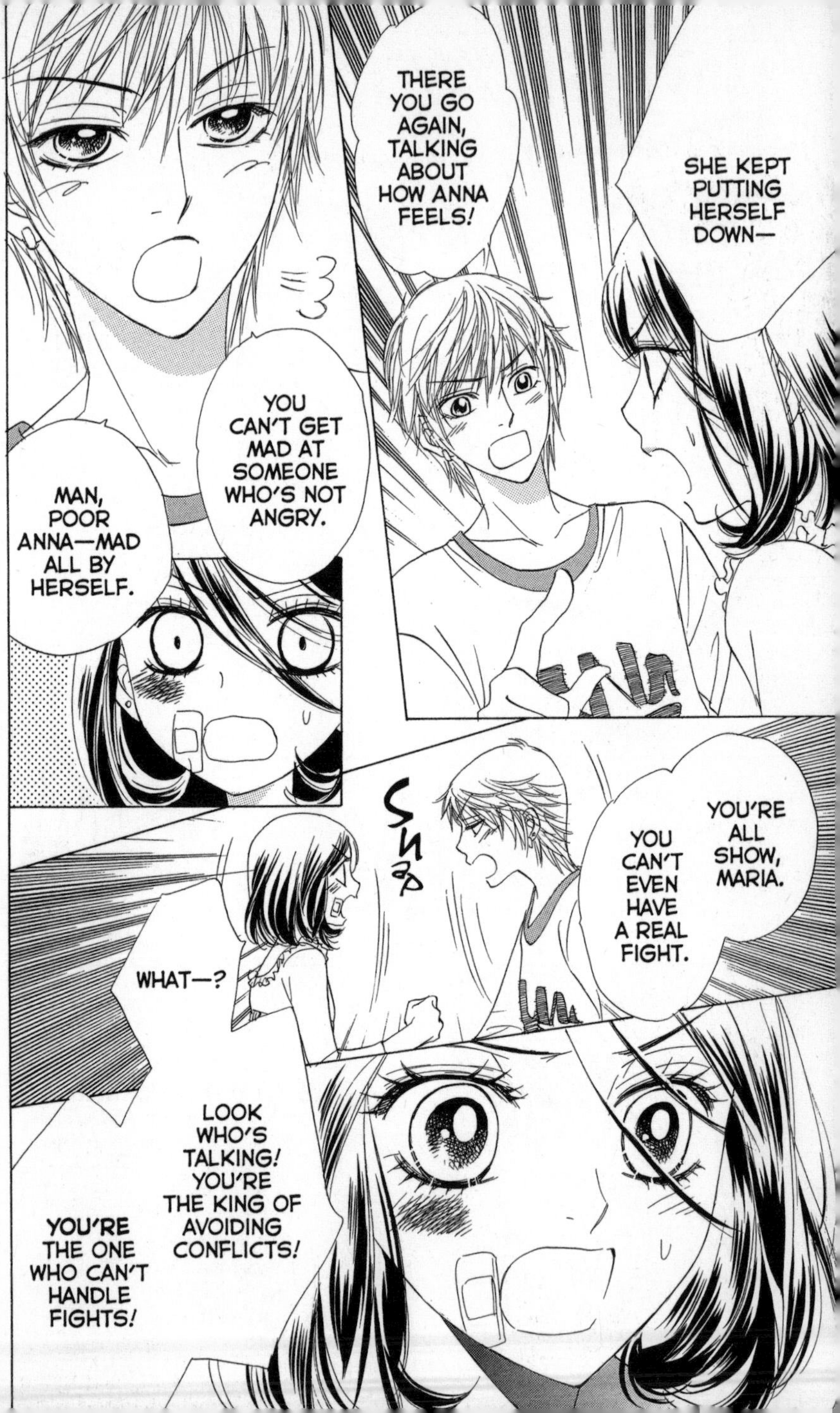
SHE KEPT PUTTING HERSELF DOWN—
THERE YOU GO AGAIN, TALKING ABOUT HOW ANNA FEELS!
YOU CAN'T GET MAD AT SOMEONE WHO'S NOT ANGRY.
MAN, POOR ANNA—MAD ALL BY HERSELF.
YOU'RE ALL SHOW, MARIA.
YOU CAN'T EVEN HAVE A REAL FIGHT.
Snap
WHAT—?
LOOK WHO'S TALKING! YOU'RE THE KING OF AVOIDING CONFLICTS!
YOU'RE THE ONE WHO CAN'T HANDLE FIGHTS!

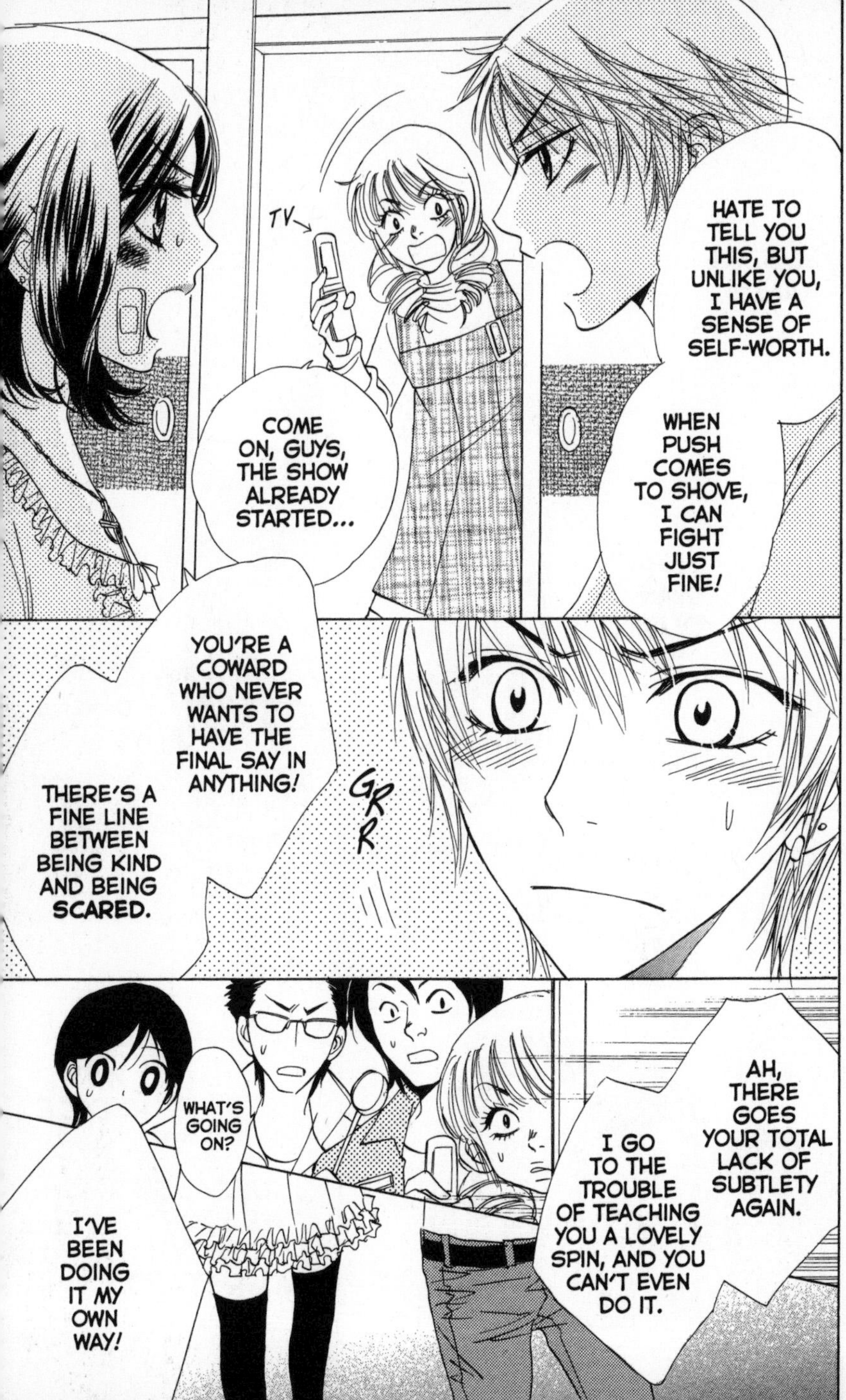

HATE TO TELL YOU THIS, BUT UNLIKE YOU, I HAVE A SENSE OF SELF-WORTH.
WHEN PUSH COMES TO SHOVE, I CAN FIGHT JUST FINE!
TV→
COME ON, GUYS, THE SHOW ALREADY STARTED...
YOU'RE A COWARD WHO NEVER WANTS TO HAVE THE FINAL SAY IN ANYTHING!
GRR
THERE'S A FINE LINE BETWEEN BEING KIND AND BEING SCARED.
AH, THERE GOES YOUR TOTAL LACK OF SUBTLETY AGAIN.
I GO TO THE TROUBLE OF TEACHING YOU A LOVELY SPIN, AND YOU CAN'T EVEN DO IT.
WHAT'S GOING ON?
I'VE BEEN DOING IT MY OWN WAY!

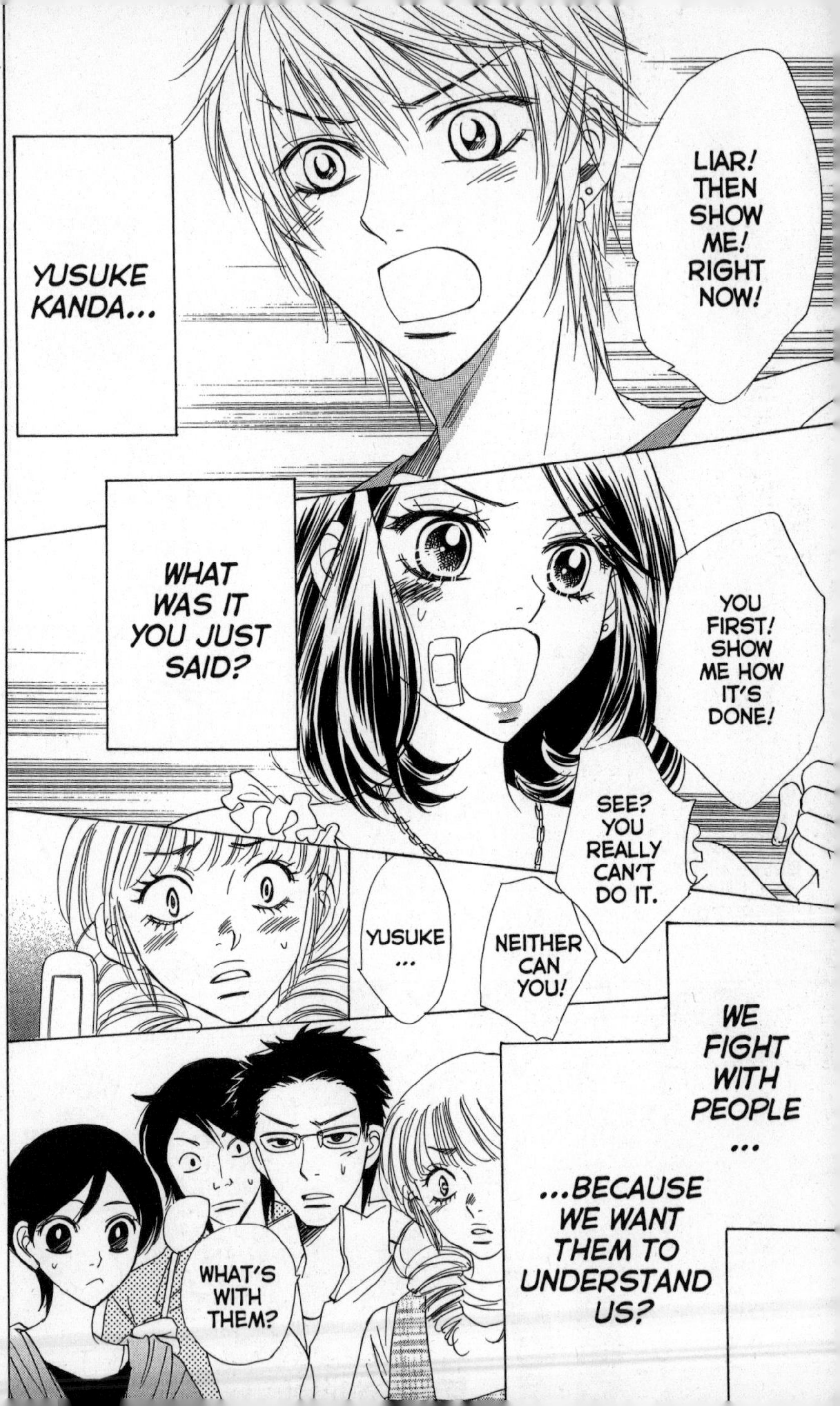
LIAR! THEN SHOW ME! RIGHT NOW!
YUSUKE KANDA...
YOU FIRST! SHOW ME HOW IT'S DONE!
WHAT WAS IT YOU JUST SAID?
SEE? YOU REALLY CAN'T DO IT.
NEITHER CAN YOU!
YUSUKE...
WE FIGHT WITH PEOPLE...
...BECAUSE WE WANT THEM TO UNDERSTAND US?
WHAT'S WITH THEM?

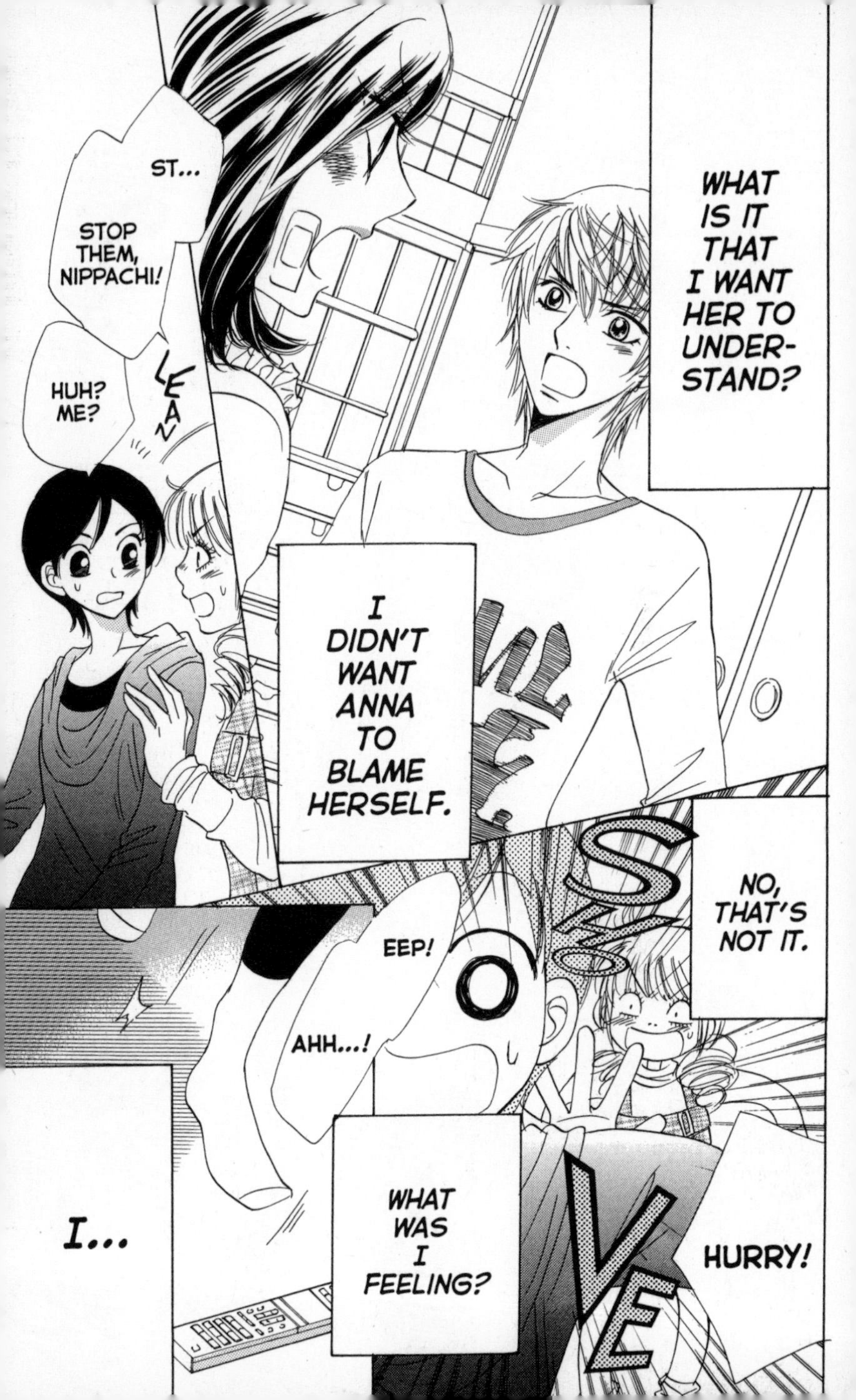
WHAT IS IT THAT I WANT HER TO UNDER-STAND?
I DIDN'T WANT ANNA TO BLAME HERSELF.
ST...
STOP THEM, NIPPACHI!
LEAN
HUH? ME?
NO, THAT'S NOT IT.
SWOO
EEP!
AHH...!
HURRY!
VE
WHAT WAS I FEELING?
I...

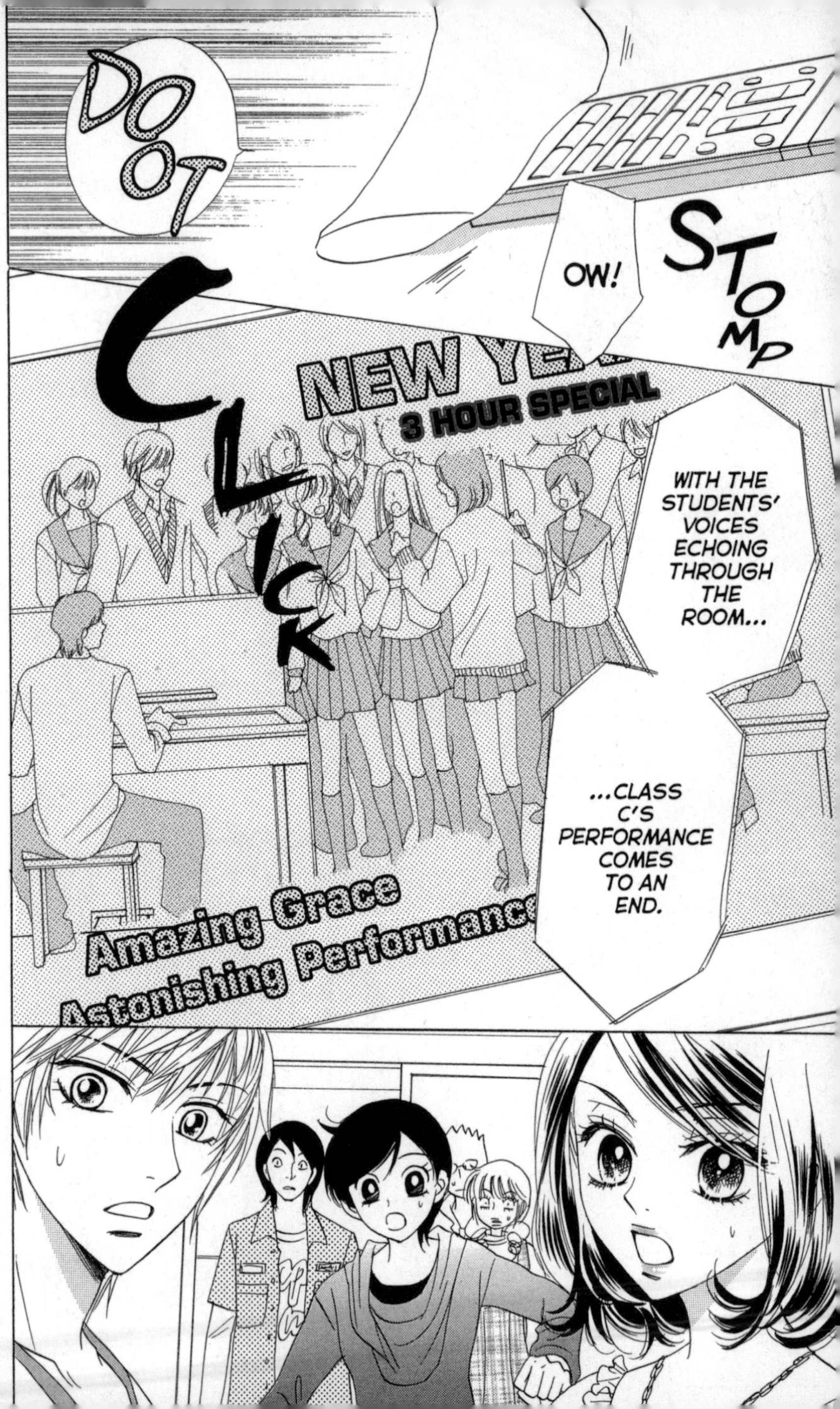
STOMP
OW!
DOOT
WITH THE STUDENTS' VOICES ECHOING THROUGH THE ROOM...
CLICK
NEW YE
3 HOUR SPECIAL
...CLASS C'S PERFORMANCE COMES TO AN END.
Amazing Grace
Astonishing Performance

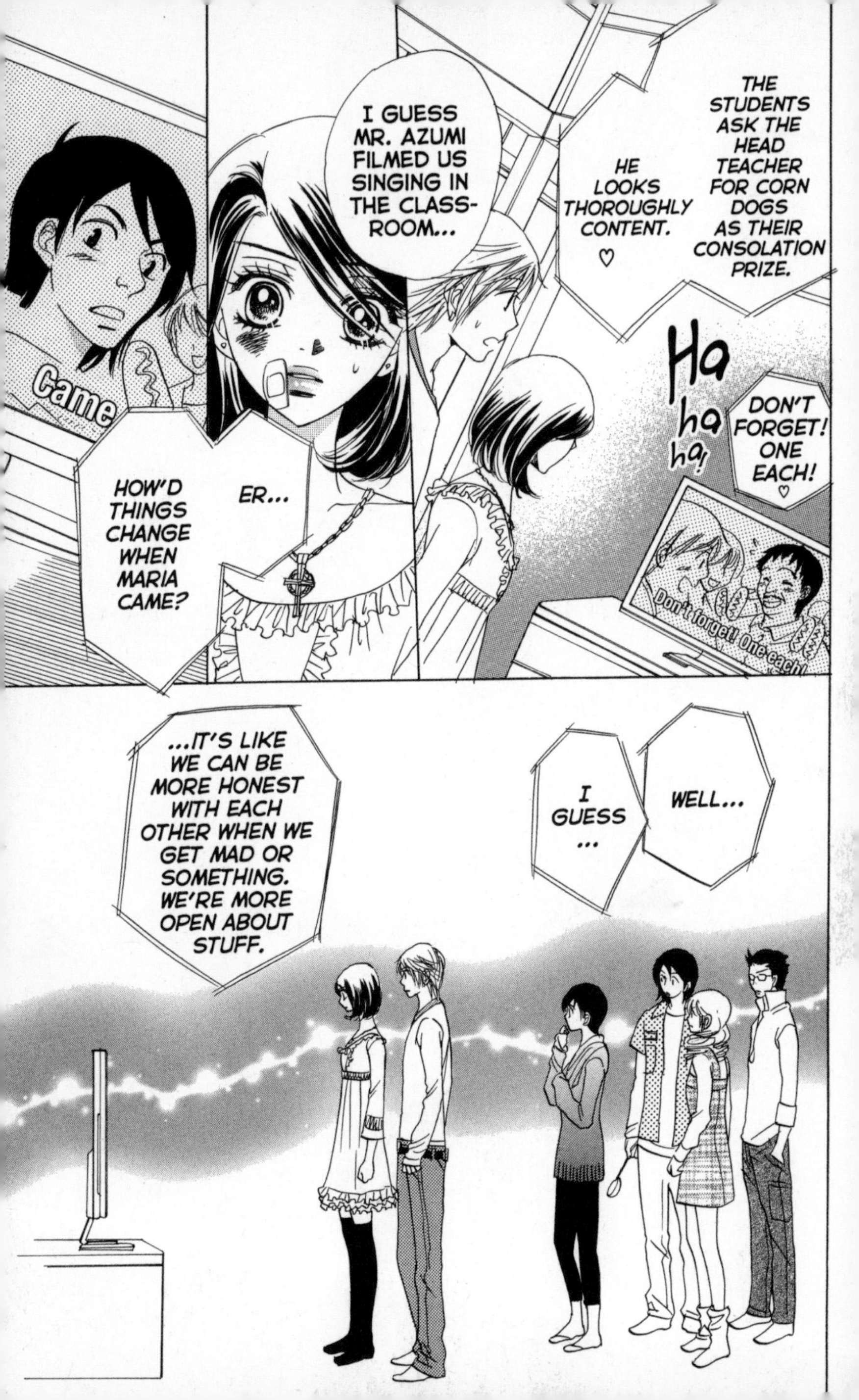
THE STUDENTS ASK THE HEAD TEACHER FOR CORN DOGS AS THEIR CONSOLATION PRIZE.
HE LOOKS THOROUGHLY CONTENT. ♡
Ha ha ha!
DON'T FORGET! ONE EACH! ♡
Don't forget! One each!
I GUESS MR. AZUMI FILMED US SINGING IN THE CLASS-ROOM...
ER...
Came
HOW'D THINGS CHANGE WHEN MARIA CAME?
WELL...
I GUESS...
...IT'S LIKE WE CAN BE MORE HONEST WITH EACH OTHER WHEN WE GET MAD OR SOMETHING. WE'RE MORE OPEN ABOUT STUFF.

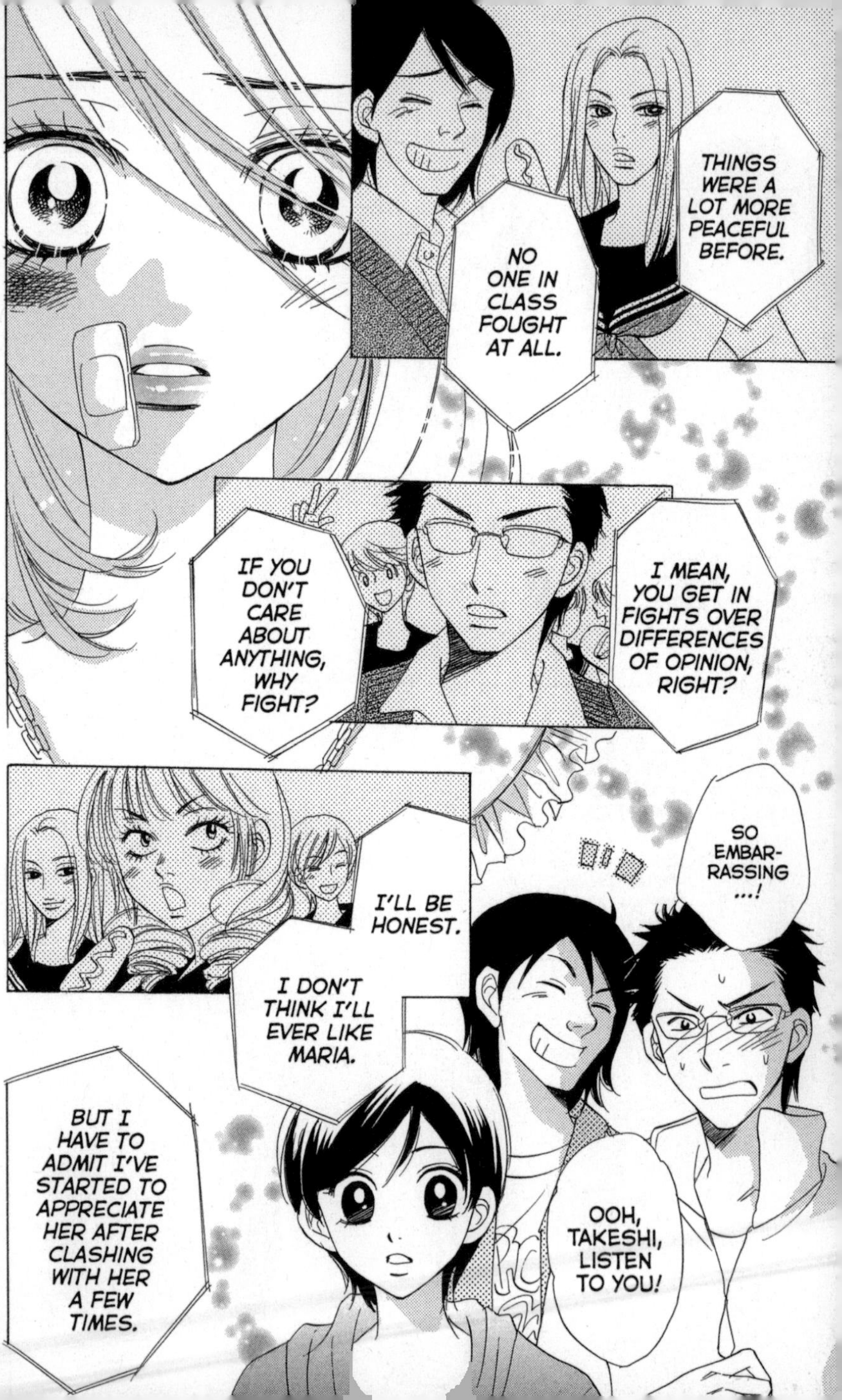
THINGS WERE A LOT MORE PEACEFUL BEFORE.
NO ONE IN CLASS FOUGHT AT ALL.
I MEAN, YOU GET IN FIGHTS OVER DIFFERENCES OF OPINION, RIGHT?
IF YOU DON'T CARE ABOUT ANYTHING, WHY FIGHT?
I'LL BE HONEST.
I DON'T THINK I'LL EVER LIKE MARIA.
BUT I HAVE TO ADMIT I'VE STARTED TO APPRECIATE HER AFTER CLASHING WITH HER A FEW TIMES.
OOH, TAKESHI, LISTEN TO YOU!
SO EMBARRASSING ...!

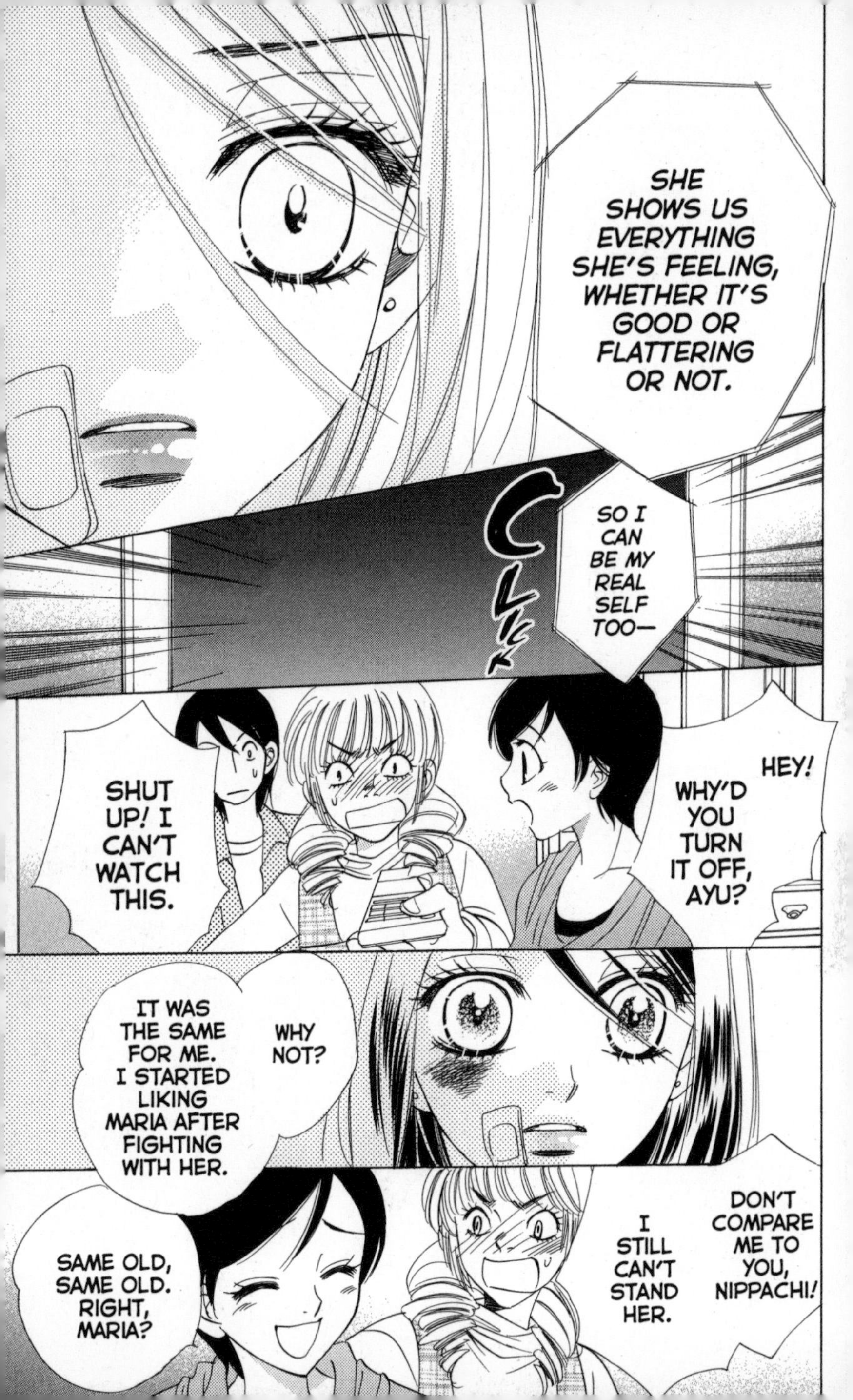
SHE SHOWS US EVERYTHING SHE'S FEELING, WHETHER IT'S GOOD OR FLATTERING OR NOT.
SO I CAN BE MY REAL SELF TOO—
CLICK
HEY!
WHY'D YOU TURN IT OFF, AYU?
SHUT UP! I CAN'T WATCH THIS.
WHY NOT?
IT WAS THE SAME FOR ME. I STARTED LIKING MARIA AFTER FIGHTING WITH HER.
DON'T COMPARE ME TO YOU, NIPPACHI!
I STILL CAN'T STAND HER.
SAME OLD, SAME OLD. RIGHT, MARIA?

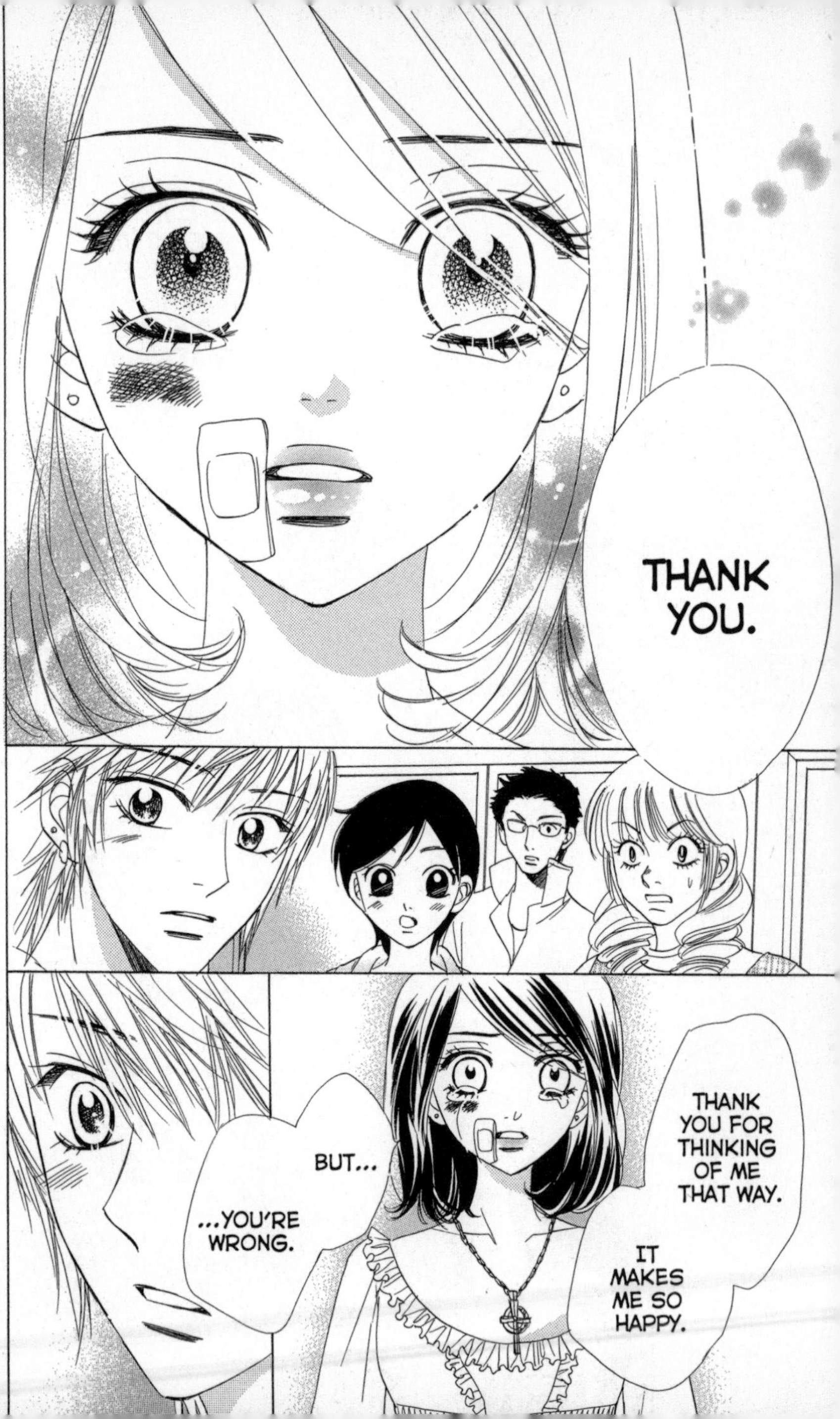
THANK YOU.
THANK YOU FOR THINKING OF ME THAT WAY.
IT MAKES ME SO HAPPY.
BUT...
...YOU'RE WRONG.

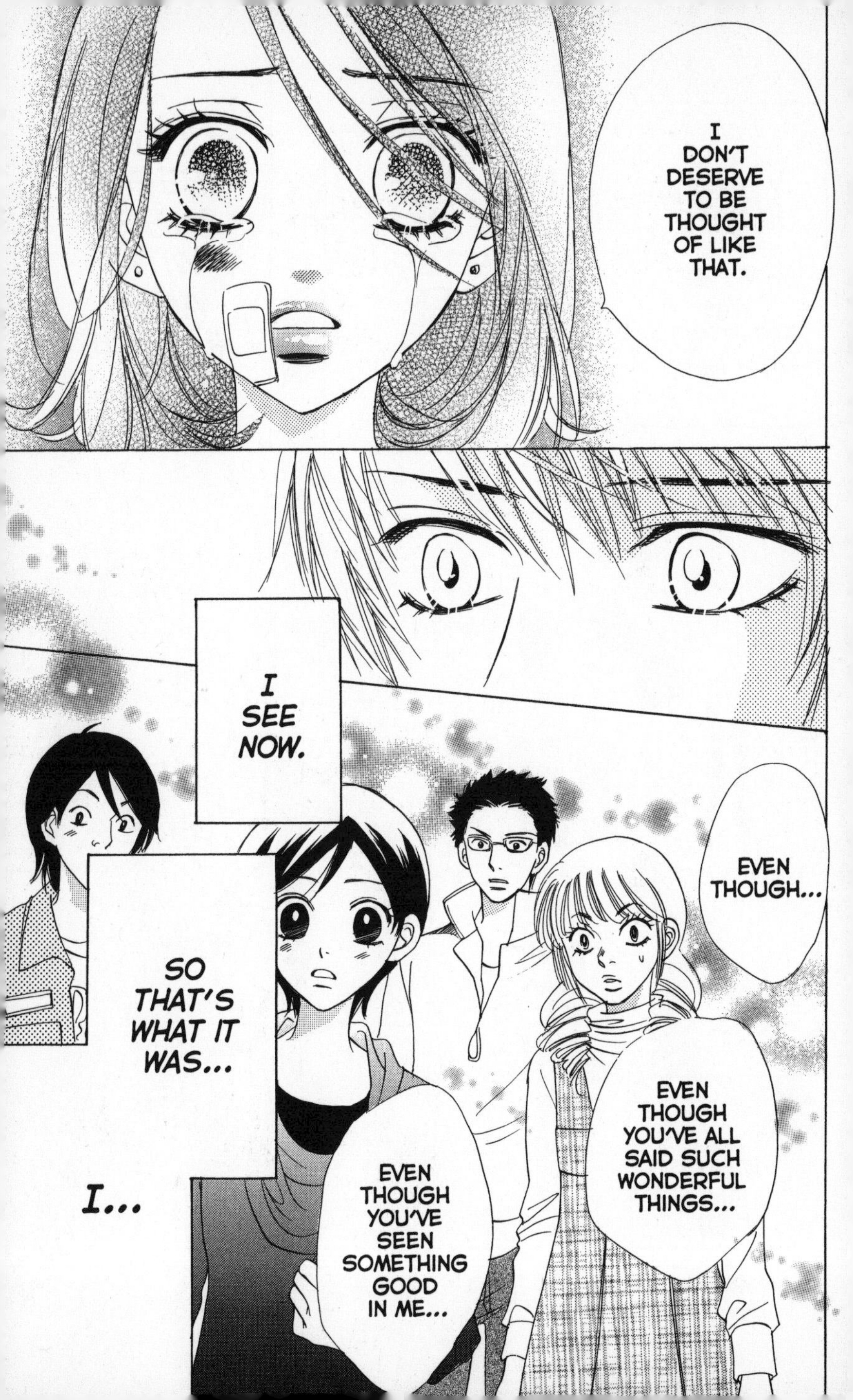
I DON'T DESERVE TO BE THOUGHT OF LIKE THAT.
I SEE NOW.
SO THAT'S WHAT IT WAS...
EVEN THOUGH...
EVEN THOUGH YOU'VE ALL SAID SUCH WONDERFUL THINGS...
EVEN THOUGH YOU'VE SEEN SOMETHING GOOD IN ME...
I...

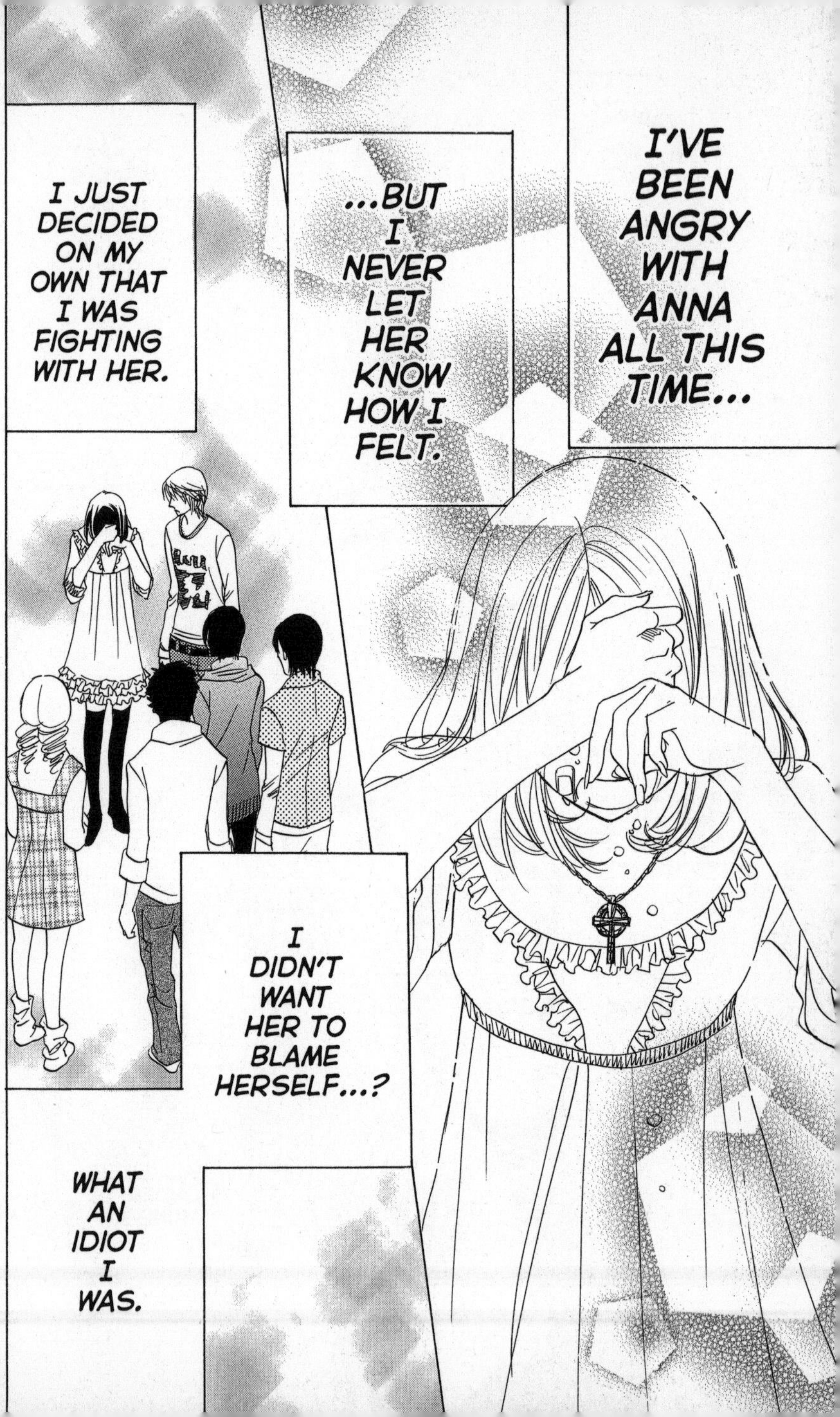
I'VE BEEN ANGRY WITH ANNA ALL THIS TIME...
...BUT I NEVER LET HER KNOW HOW I FELT.
I JUST DECIDED ON MY OWN THAT I WAS FIGHTING WITH HER.
I DIDN'T WANT HER TO BLAME HERSELF...?
WHAT AN IDIOT I WAS.

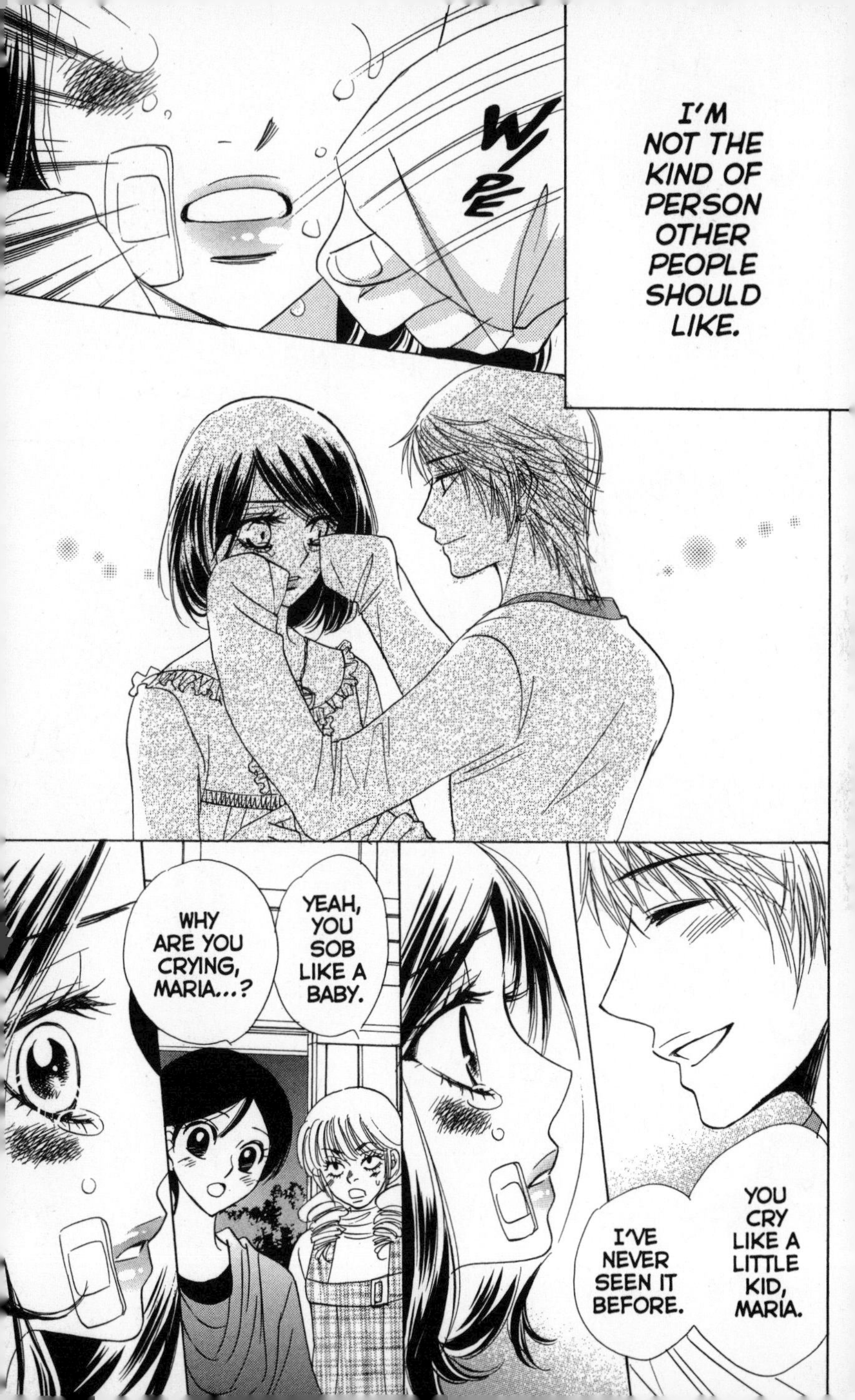
I'M NOT THE KIND OF PERSON OTHER PEOPLE SHOULD LIKE.
WIPE
YOU CRY LIKE A LITTLE KID, MARIA.
I'VE NEVER SEEN IT BEFORE.
YEAH, YOU SOB LIKE A BABY.
WHY ARE YOU CRYING, MARIA...?

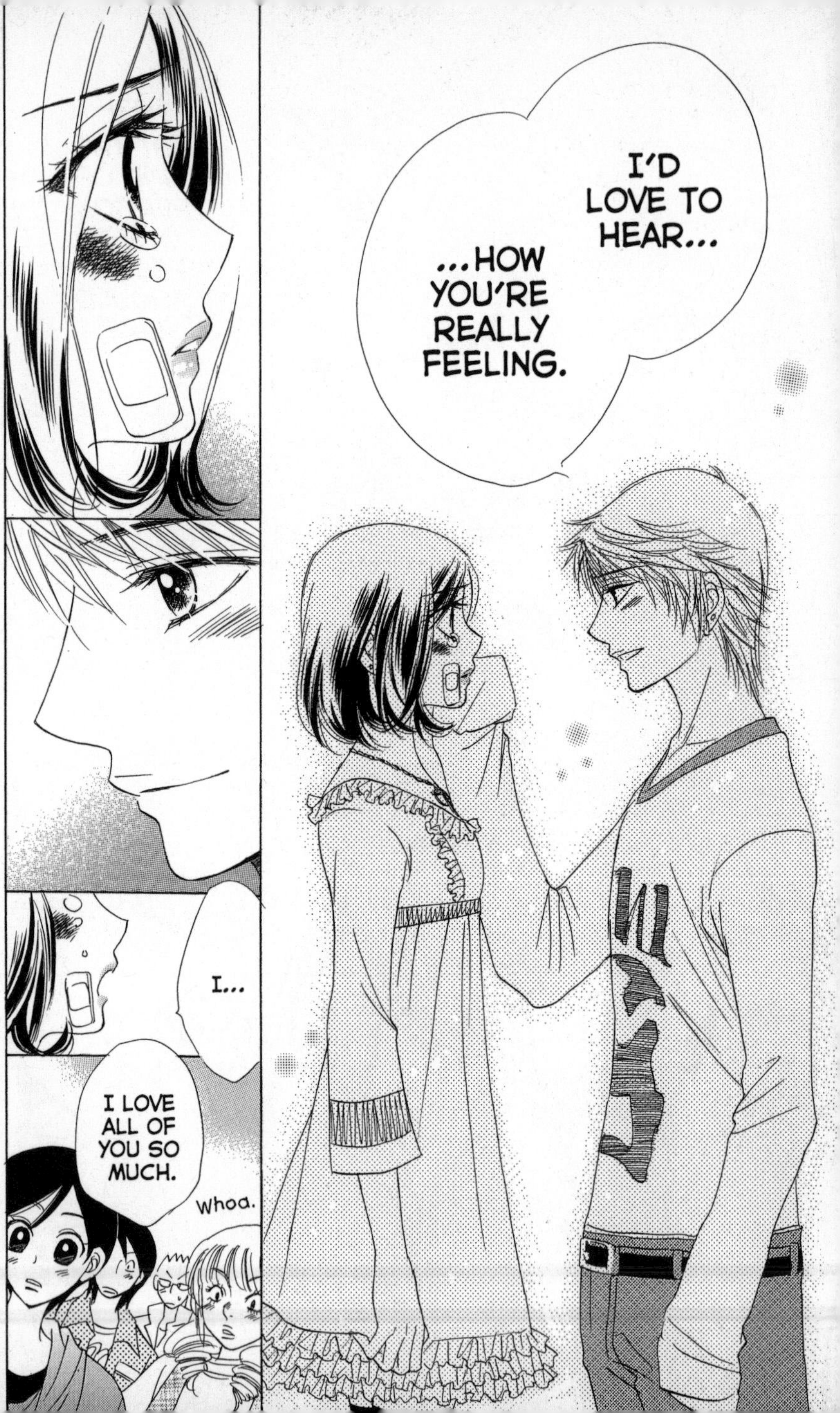
I'D LOVE TO HEAR...
...HOW YOU'RE REALLY FEELING.
I...
I LOVE ALL OF YOU SO MUCH.
Whoa.

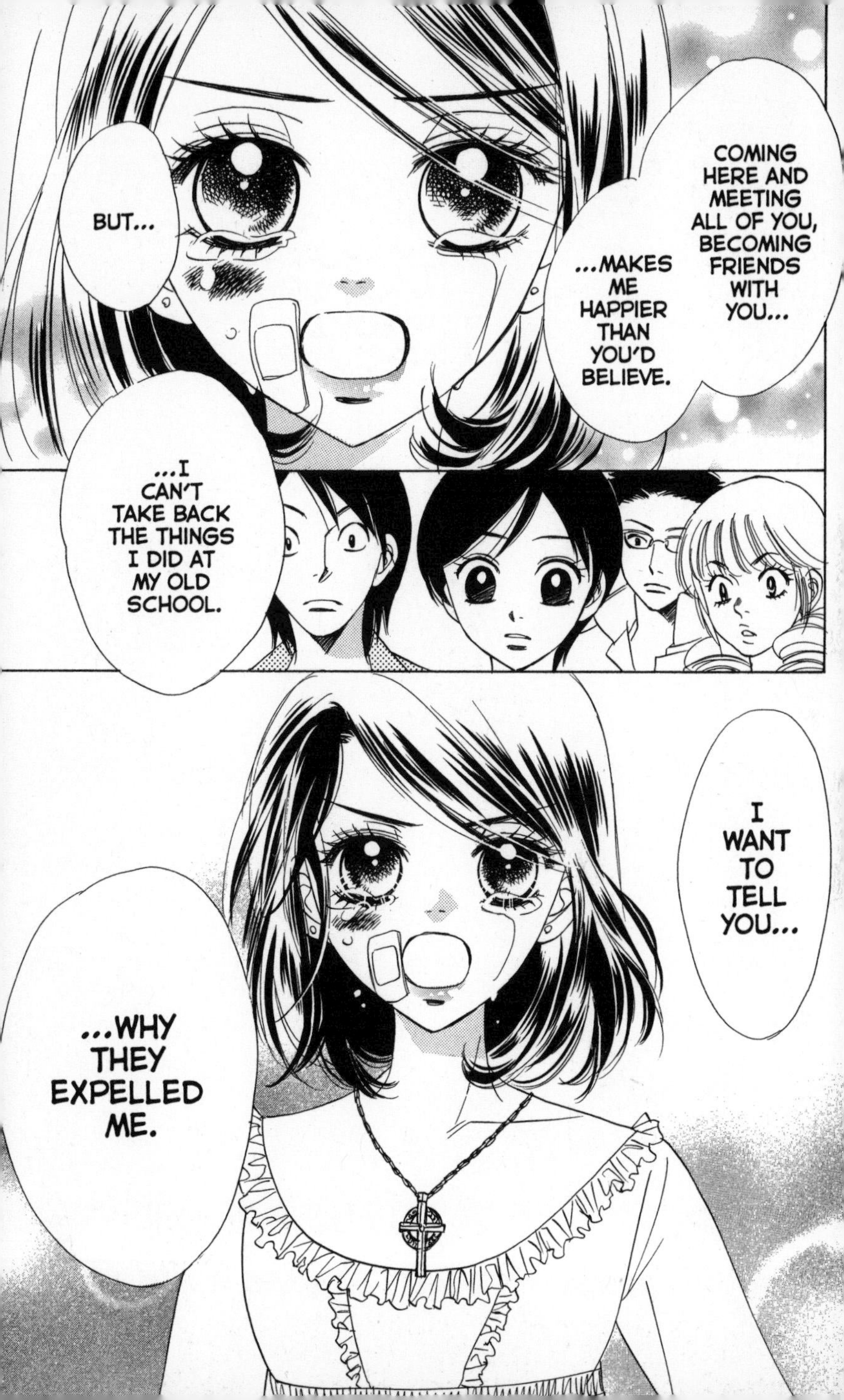
COMING HERE AND MEETING ALL OF YOU, BECOMING FRIENDS WITH YOU...
...MAKES ME HAPPIER THAN YOU'D BELIEVE.
BUT...
...I CAN'T TAKE BACK THE THINGS I DID AT MY OLD SCHOOL.
I WANT TO TELL YOU...
...WHY THEY EXPELLED ME.

A Devil and
Her Love Song

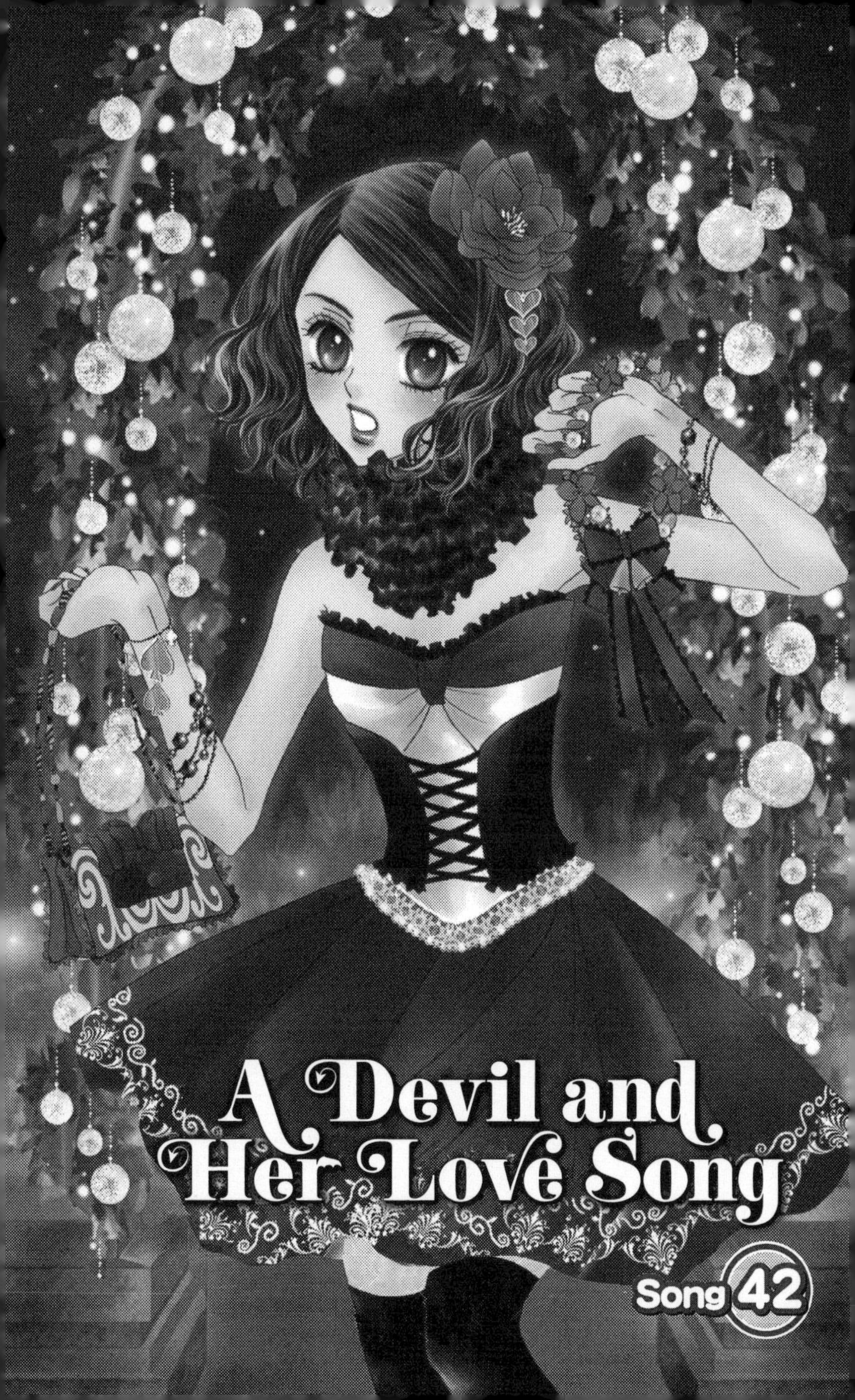
A Devil and Her Love Song
Song 42

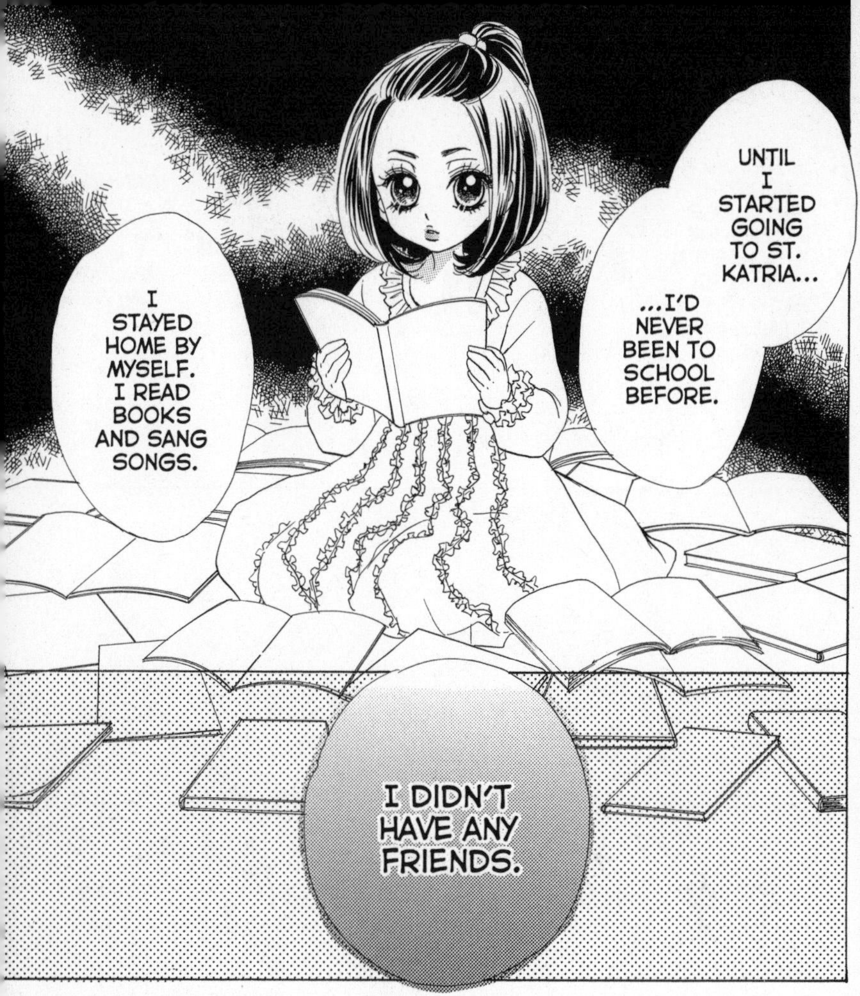
UNTIL I STARTED GOING TO ST. KATRIA...
...I'D NEVER BEEN TO SCHOOL BEFORE.
I STAYED HOME BY MYSELF. I READ BOOKS AND SANG SONGS.
I DIDN'T HAVE ANY FRIENDS.

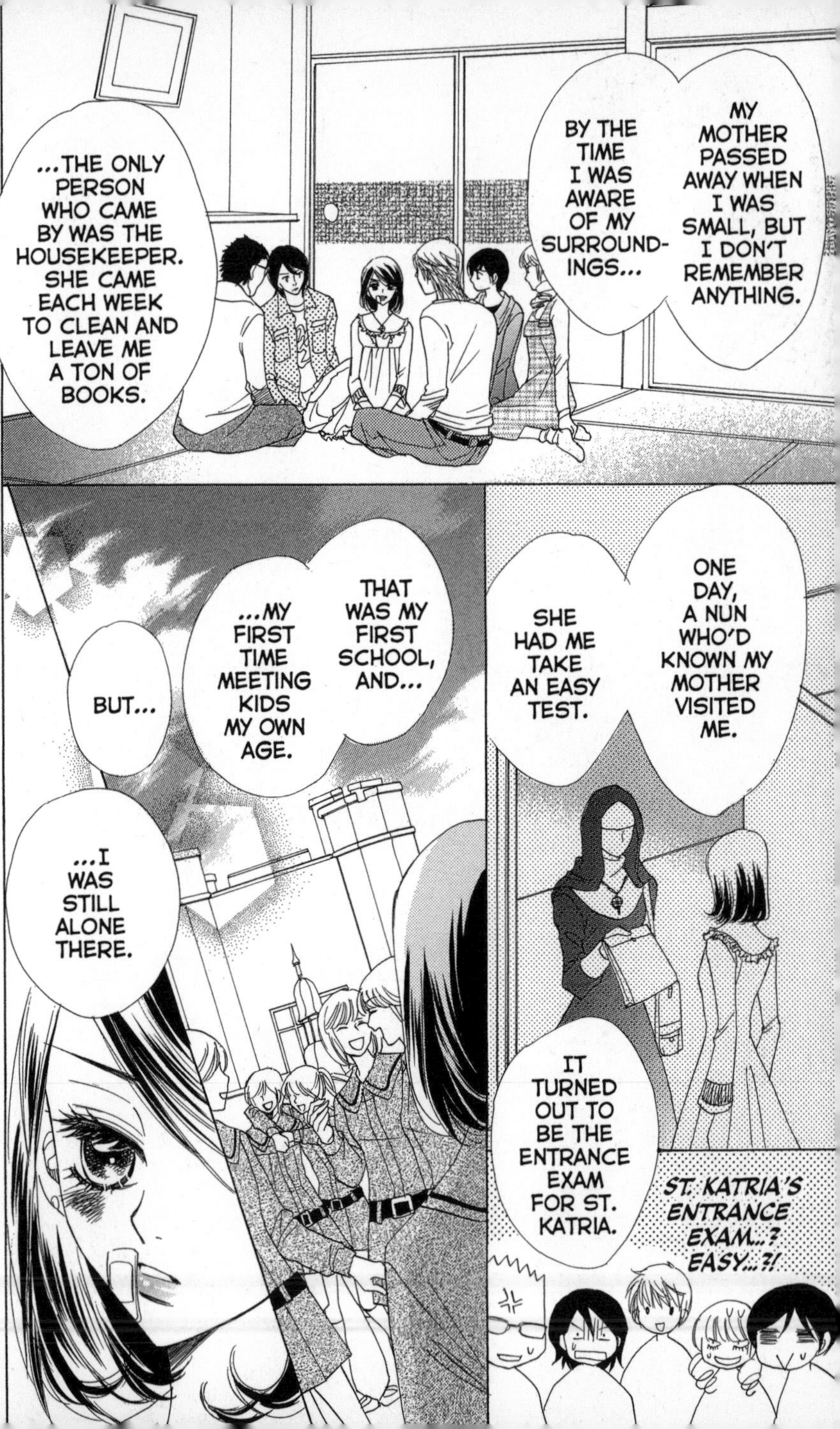
MY MOTHER PASSED AWAY WHEN I WAS SMALL, BUT I DON'T REMEMBER ANYTHING.
BY THE TIME I WAS AWARE OF MY SURROUNDINGS...
...THE ONLY PERSON WHO CAME BY WAS THE HOUSEKEEPER. SHE CAME EACH WEEK TO CLEAN AND LEAVE ME A TON OF BOOKS.
ONE DAY, A NUN WHO'D KNOWN MY MOTHER VISITED ME.
SHE HAD ME TAKE AN EASY TEST.
IT TURNED OUT TO BE THE ENTRANCE EXAM FOR ST. KATRIA.
ST. KATRIA'S ENTRANCE EXAM..?
EASY...?!
THAT WAS MY FIRST SCHOOL, AND...
...MY FIRST TIME MEETING KIDS MY OWN AGE.
BUT...
...I WAS STILL ALONE THERE.

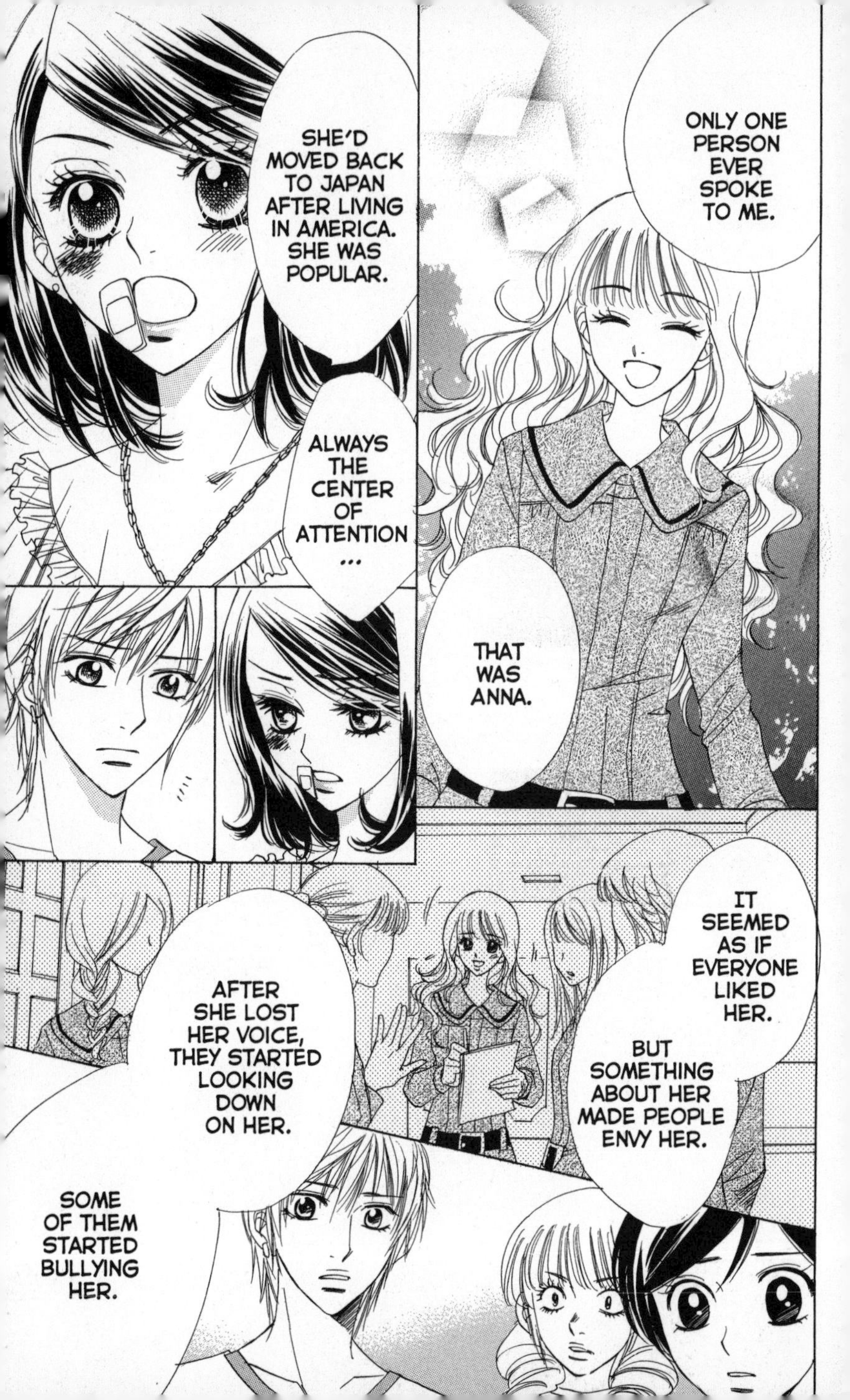
ONLY ONE PERSON EVER SPOKE TO ME.
THAT WAS ANNA.
SHE'D MOVED BACK TO JAPAN AFTER LIVING IN AMERICA. SHE WAS POPULAR.
ALWAYS THE CENTER OF ATTENTION...
IT SEEMED AS IF EVERYONE LIKED HER.
BUT SOMETHING ABOUT HER MADE PEOPLE ENVY HER.
AFTER SHE LOST HER VOICE, THEY STARTED LOOKING DOWN ON HER.
SOME OF THEM STARTED BULLYING HER.

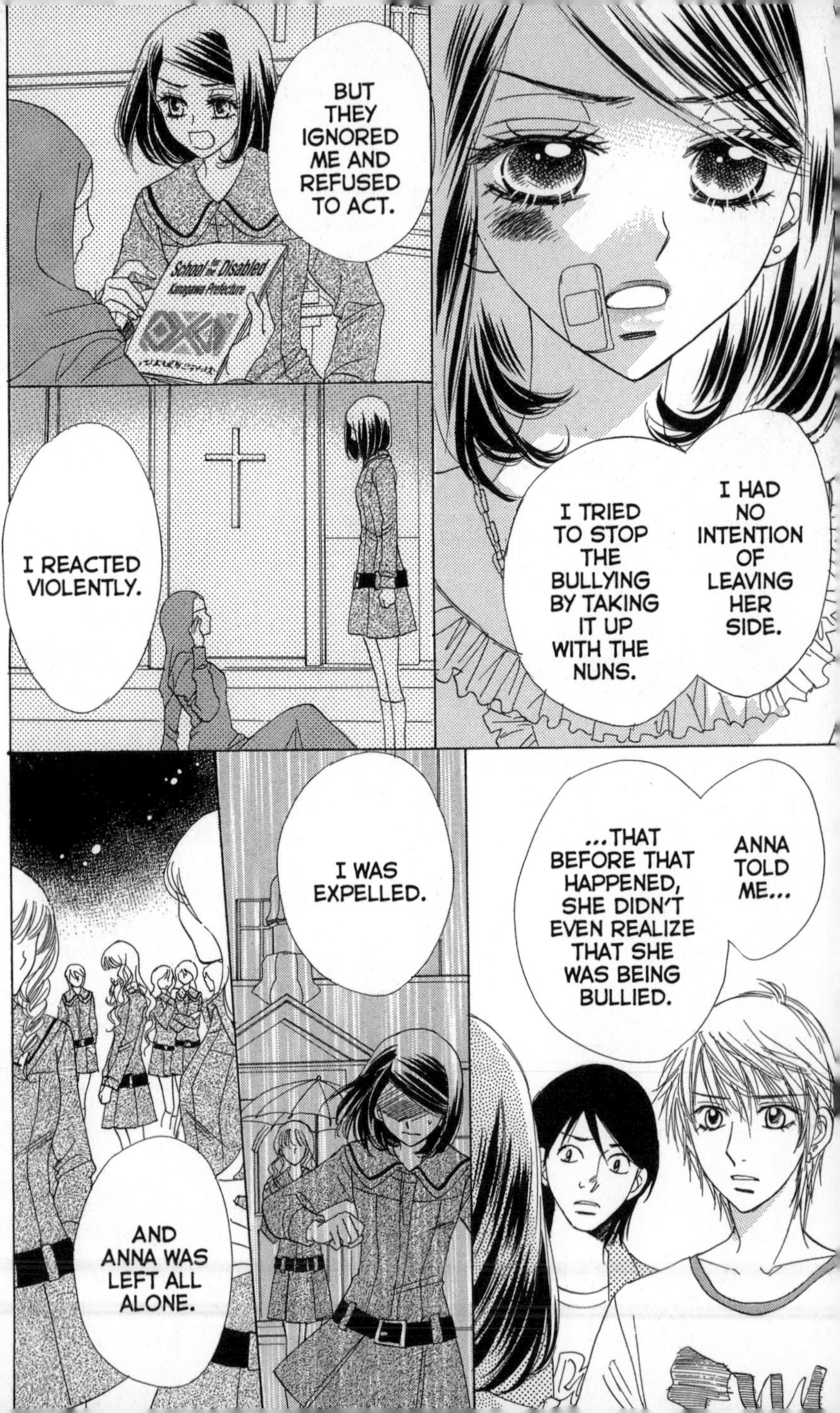
I HAD NO INTENTION OF LEAVING HER SIDE.
I TRIED TO STOP THE BULLYING BY TAKING IT UP WITH THE NUNS.
BUT THEY IGNORED ME AND REFUSED TO ACT.
School for the Disabled
Kanagawa Prefecture
I REACTED VIOLENTLY.
ANNA TOLD ME...
...THAT BEFORE THAT HAPPENED, SHE DIDN'T EVEN REALIZE THAT SHE WAS BEING BULLIED.
I WAS EXPELLED.
AND ANNA WAS LEFT ALL ALONE.

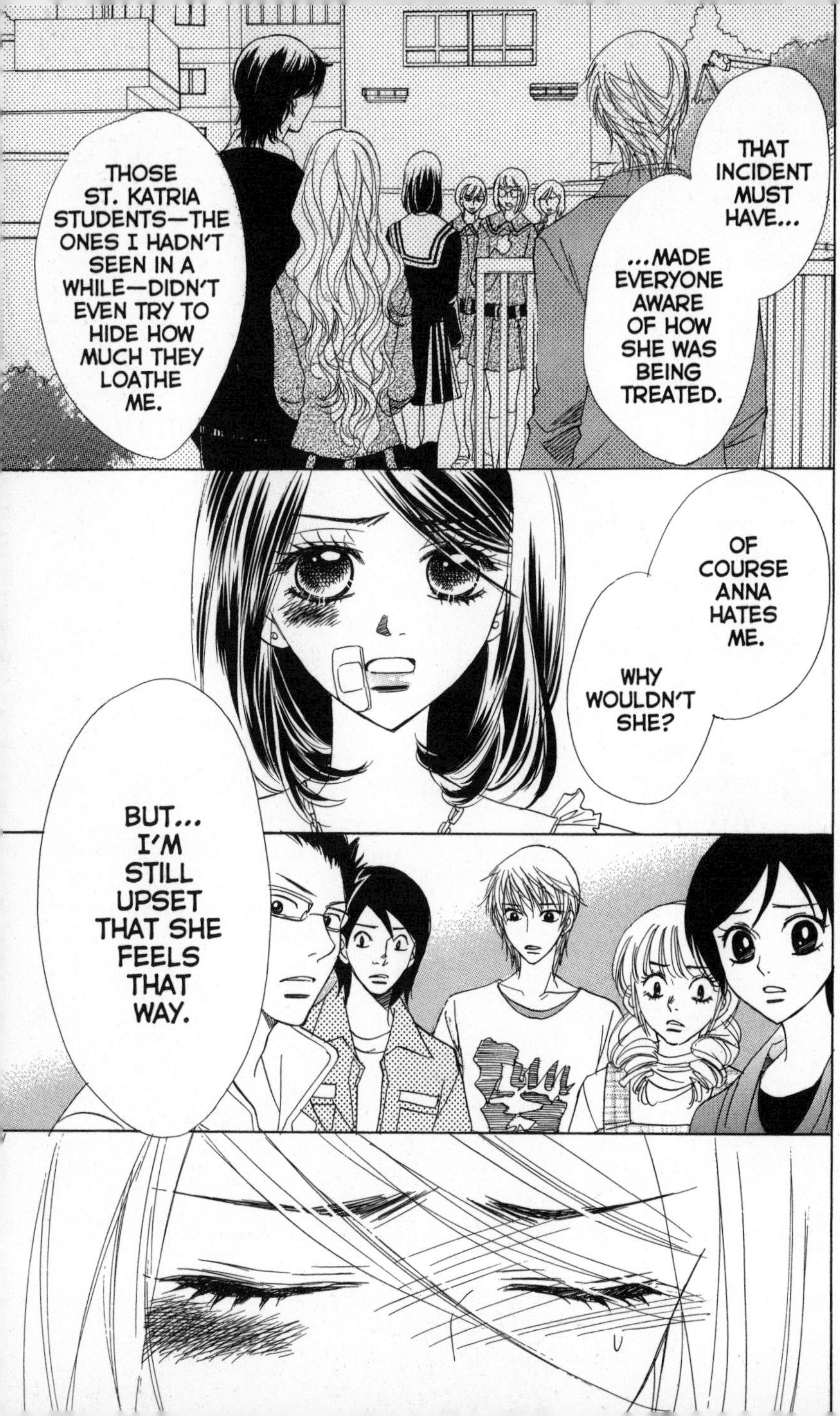
THAT INCIDENT MUST HAVE...
...MADE EVERYONE AWARE OF HOW SHE WAS BEING TREATED.
THOSE ST. KATRIA STUDENTS—THE ONES I HADN'T SEEN IN A WHILE—DIDN'T EVEN TRY TO HIDE HOW MUCH THEY LOATHE ME.
OF COURSE ANNA HATES ME.
WHY WOULDN'T SHE?
BUT... I'M STILL UPSET THAT SHE FEELS THAT WAY.

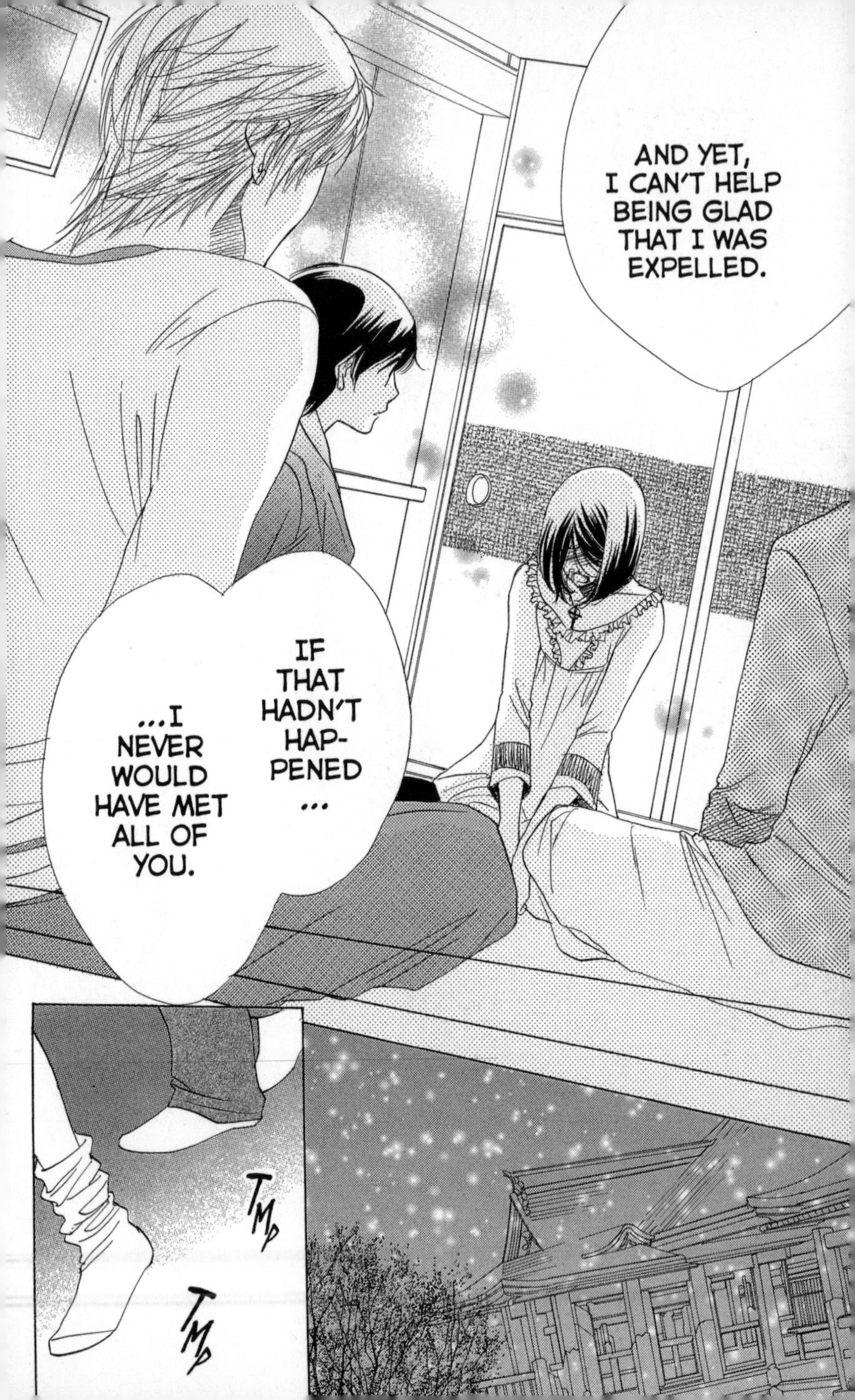
AND YET, I CAN'T HELP BEING GLAD THAT I WAS EXPELLED.
IF THAT HADN'T HAP-PENED...
...I NEVER WOULD HAVE MET ALL OF YOU.
TMP
TMP

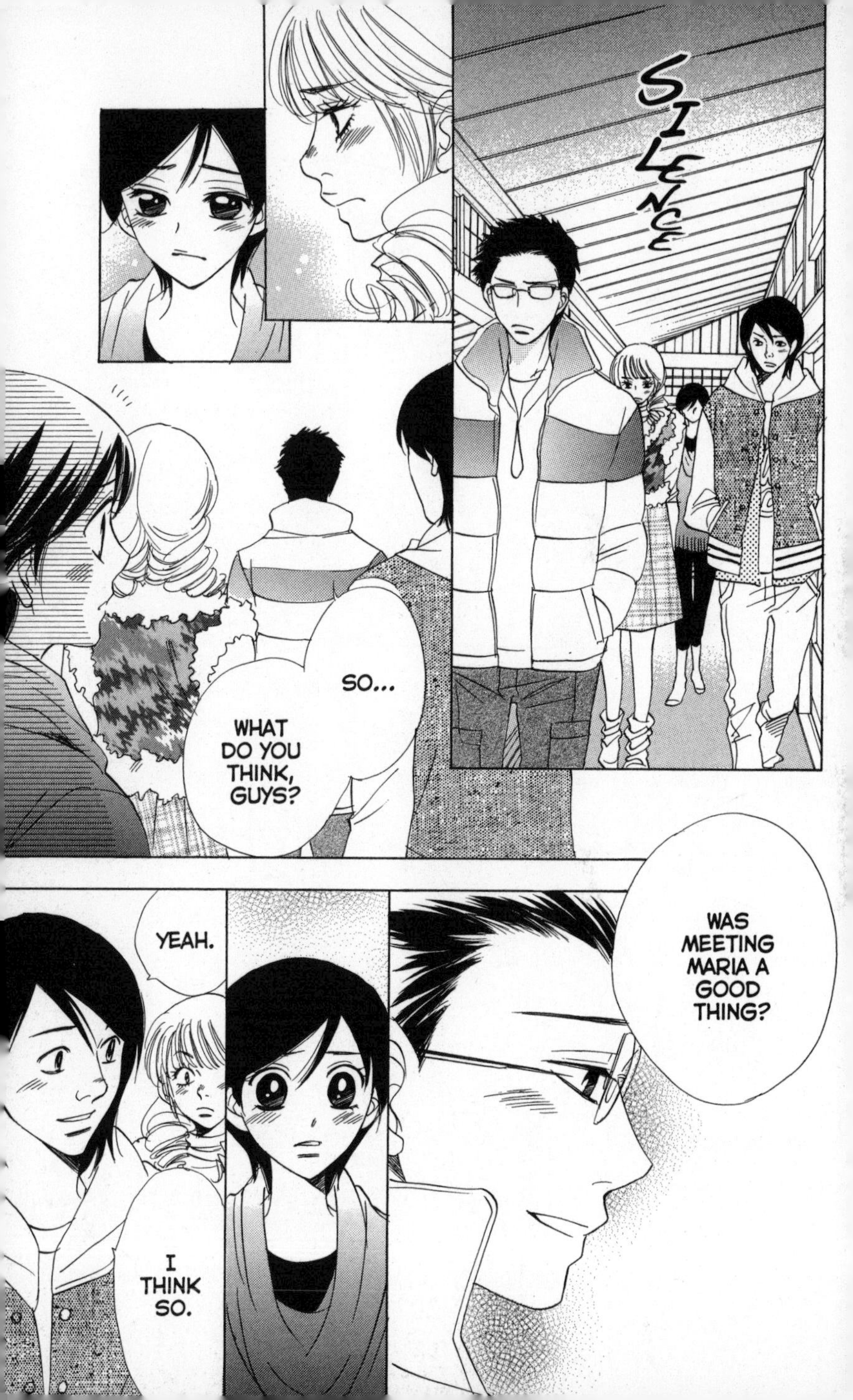
SILENCE
SO...
WHAT DO YOU THINK, GUYS?
WAS MEETING MARIA A GOOD THING?
YEAH.
I THINK SO.

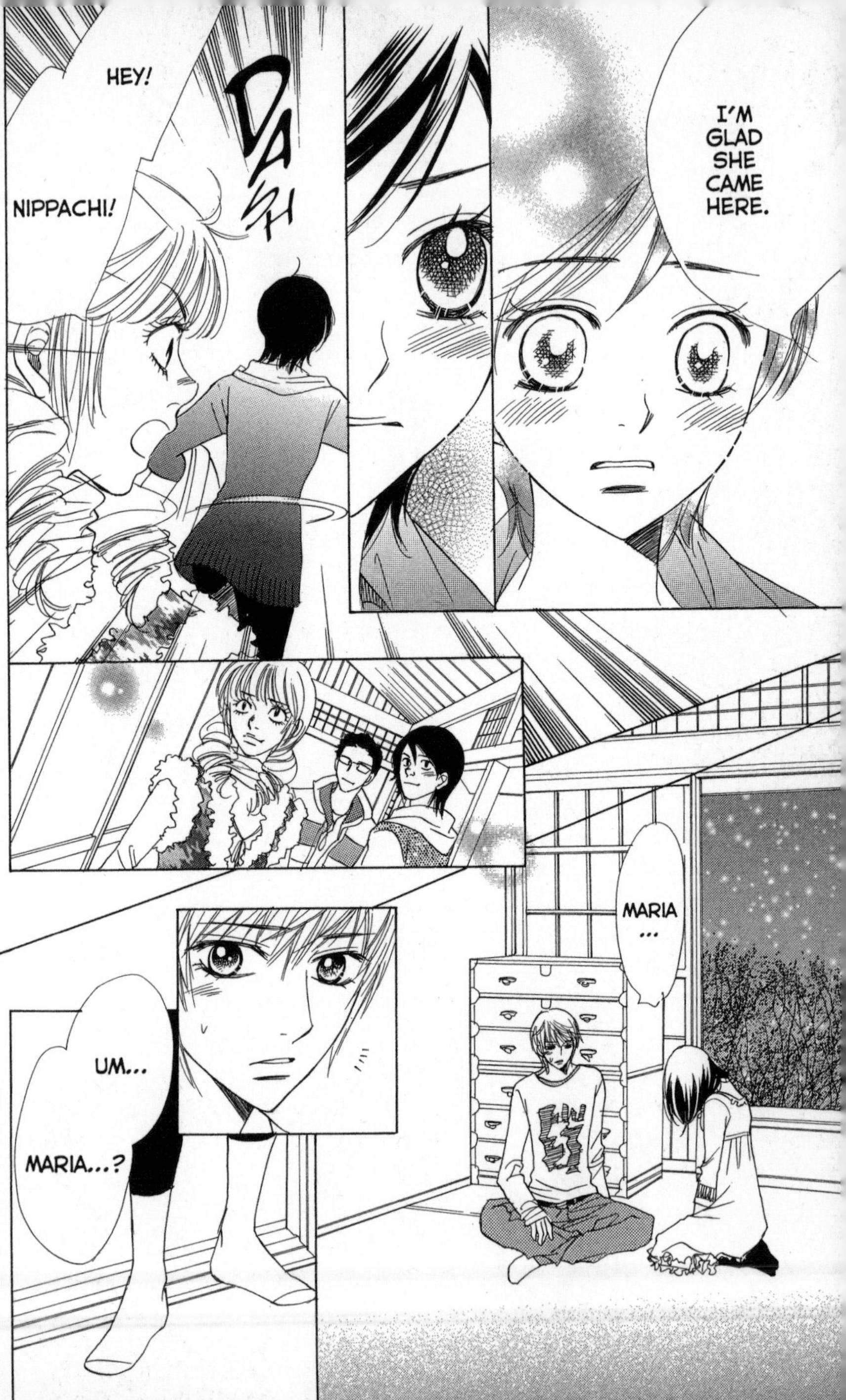
I'M GLAD SHE CAME HERE.
HEY!
NIPPACHI!
DASH
MARIA ...
UM...
MARIA...?

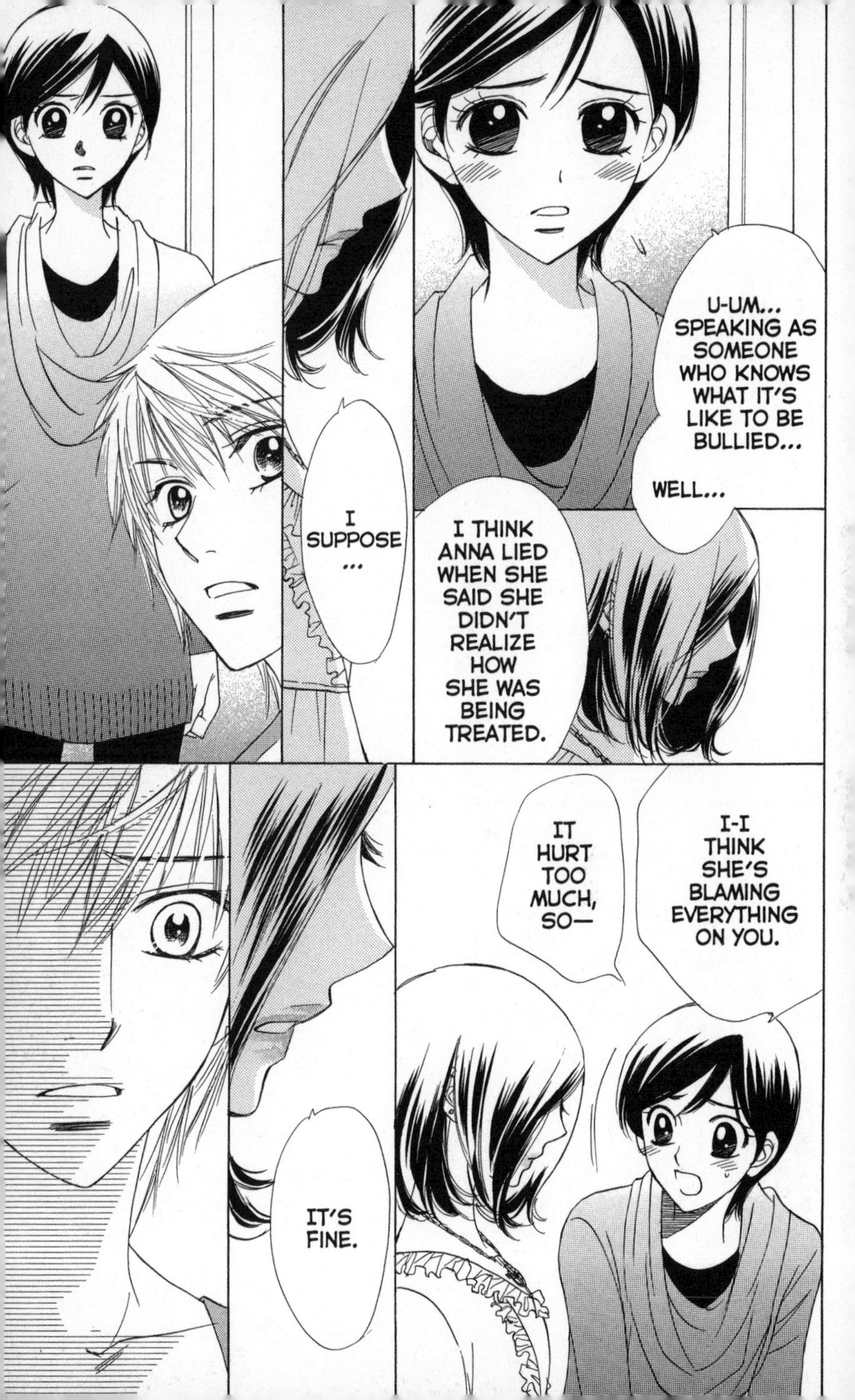

U-UM... SPEAKING AS SOMEONE WHO KNOWS WHAT IT'S LIKE TO BE BULLIED...
WELL...
I THINK ANNA LIED WHEN SHE SAID SHE DIDN'T REALIZE HOW SHE WAS BEING TREATED.
I SUPPOSE...
I-I THINK SHE'S BLAMING EVERYTHING ON YOU.
IT HURT TOO MUCH, SO—
IT'S FINE.

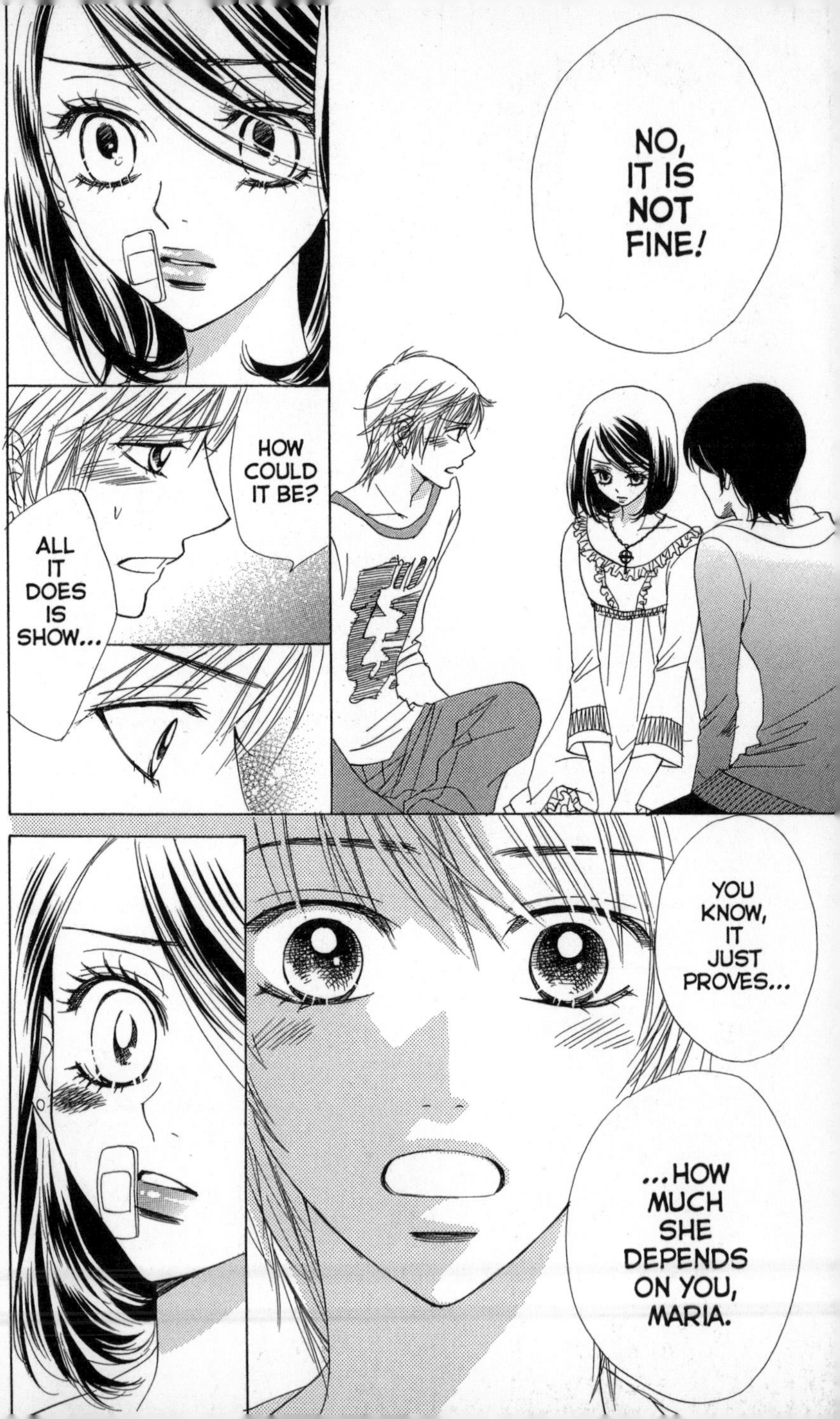
NO, IT IS NOT FINE!
HOW COULD IT BE?
ALL IT DOES IS SHOW...
YOU KNOW, IT JUST PROVES...
...HOW MUCH SHE DEPENDS ON YOU, MARIA.

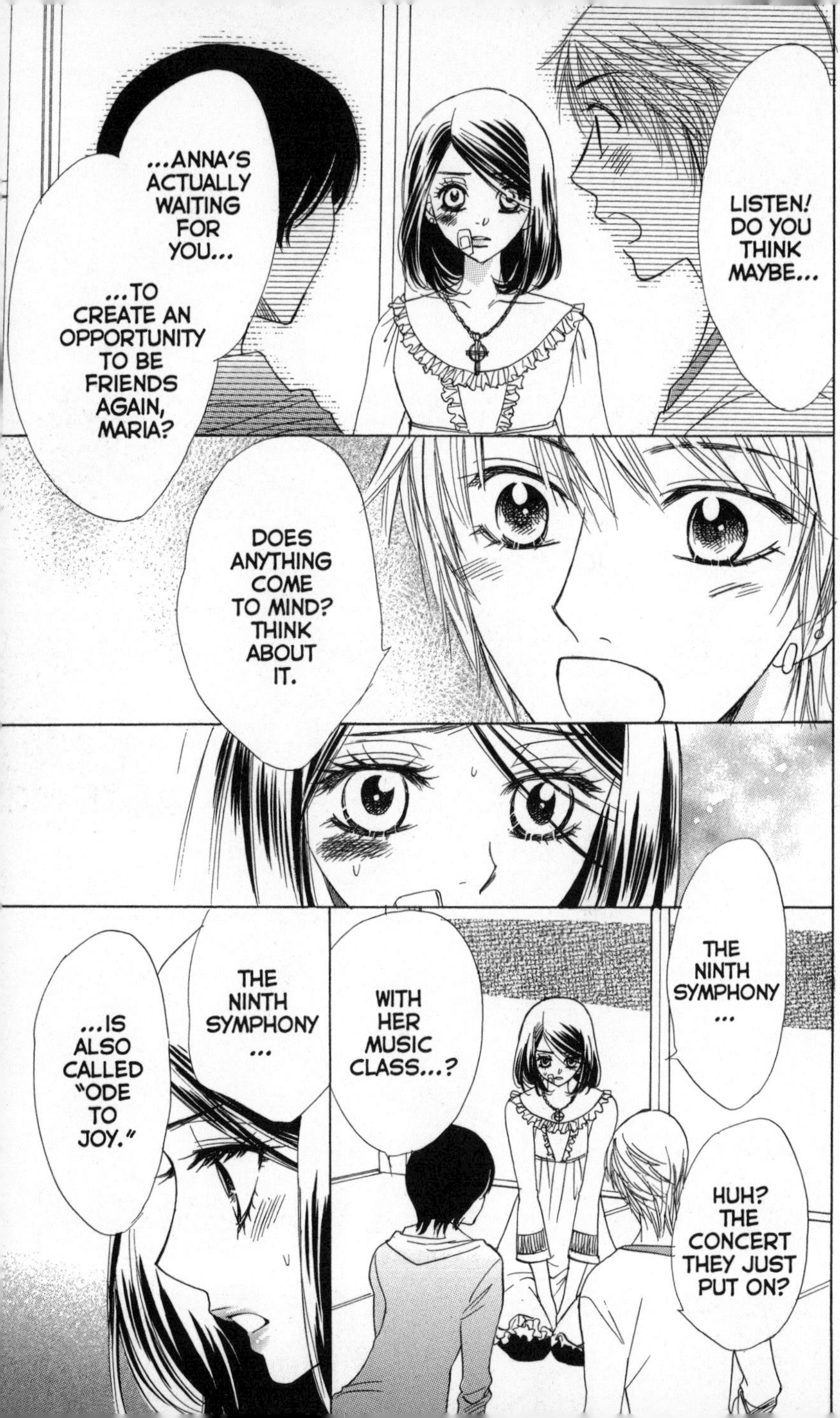

LISTEN! DO YOU THINK MAYBE...
...ANNA'S ACTUALLY WAITING FOR YOU...
...TO CREATE AN OPPORTUNITY TO BE FRIENDS AGAIN, MARIA?
DOES ANYTHING COME TO MIND? THINK ABOUT IT.
THE NINTH SYMPHONY...
HUH? THE CONCERT THEY JUST PUT ON?
WITH HER MUSIC CLASS...?
THE NINTH SYMPHONY...
...IS ALSO CALLED "ODE TO JOY."

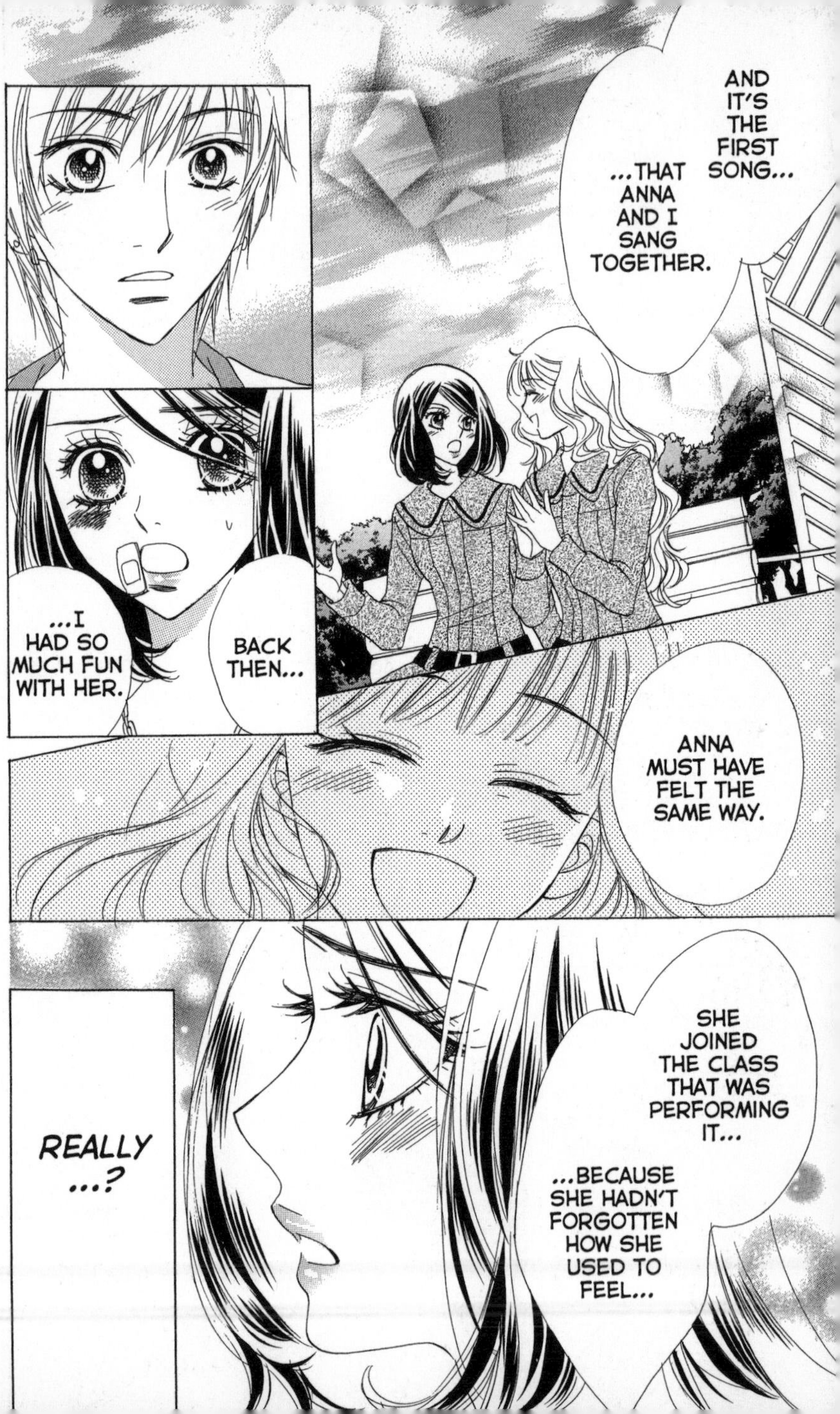
AND IT'S THE FIRST SONG...
...THAT ANNA AND I SANG TOGETHER.
BACK THEN...
...I HAD SO MUCH FUN WITH HER.
ANNA MUST HAVE FELT THE SAME WAY.
SHE JOINED THE CLASS THAT WAS PERFORMING IT...
...BECAUSE SHE HADN'T FORGOTTEN HOW SHE USED TO FEEL...
REALLY ...?

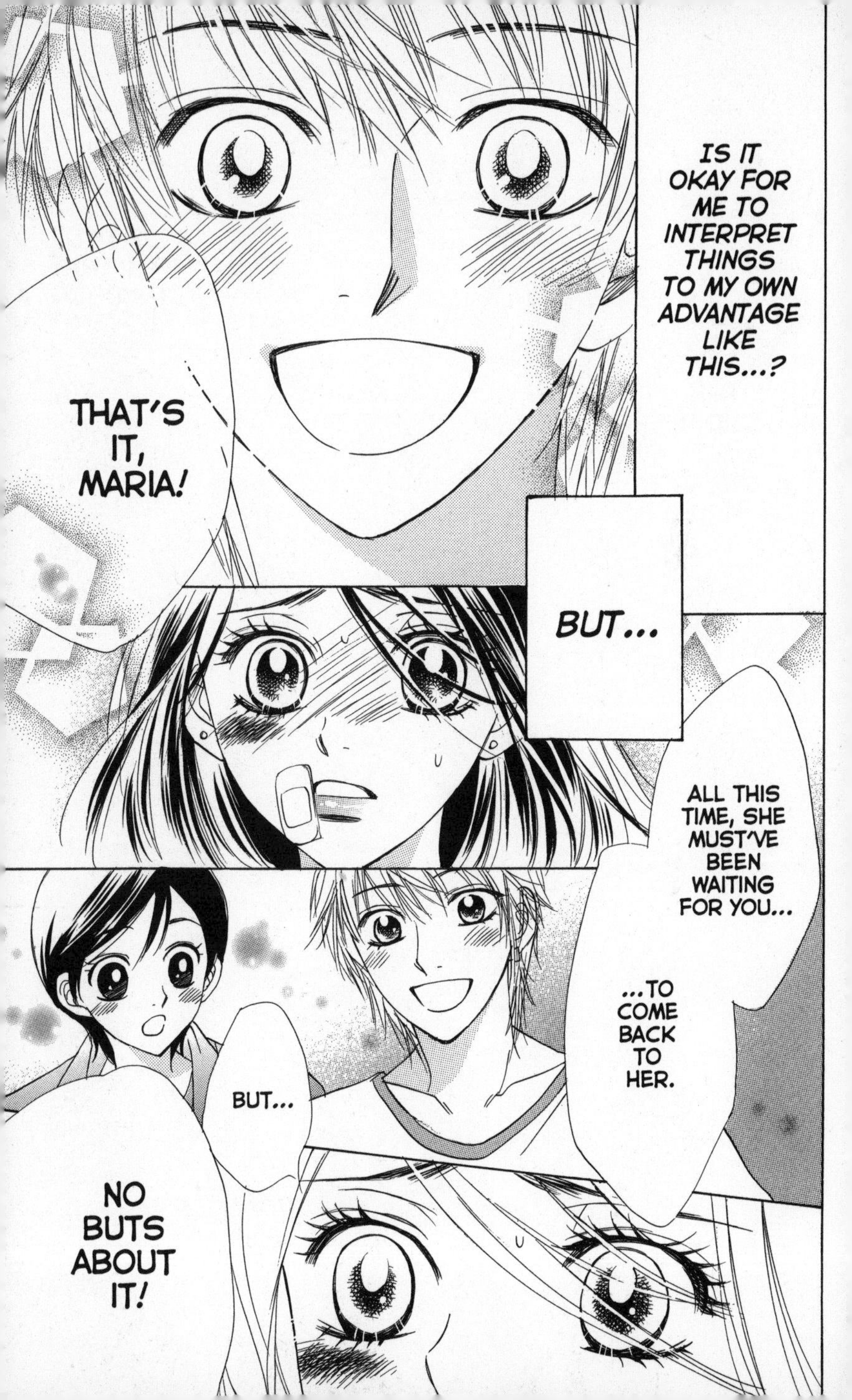
IS IT OKAY FOR ME TO INTERPRET THINGS TO MY OWN ADVANTAGE LIKE THIS...?
THAT'S IT, MARIA!
BUT...
ALL THIS TIME, SHE MUST'VE BEEN WAITING FOR YOU...
...TO COME BACK TO HER.
BUT...
NO BUTS ABOUT IT!

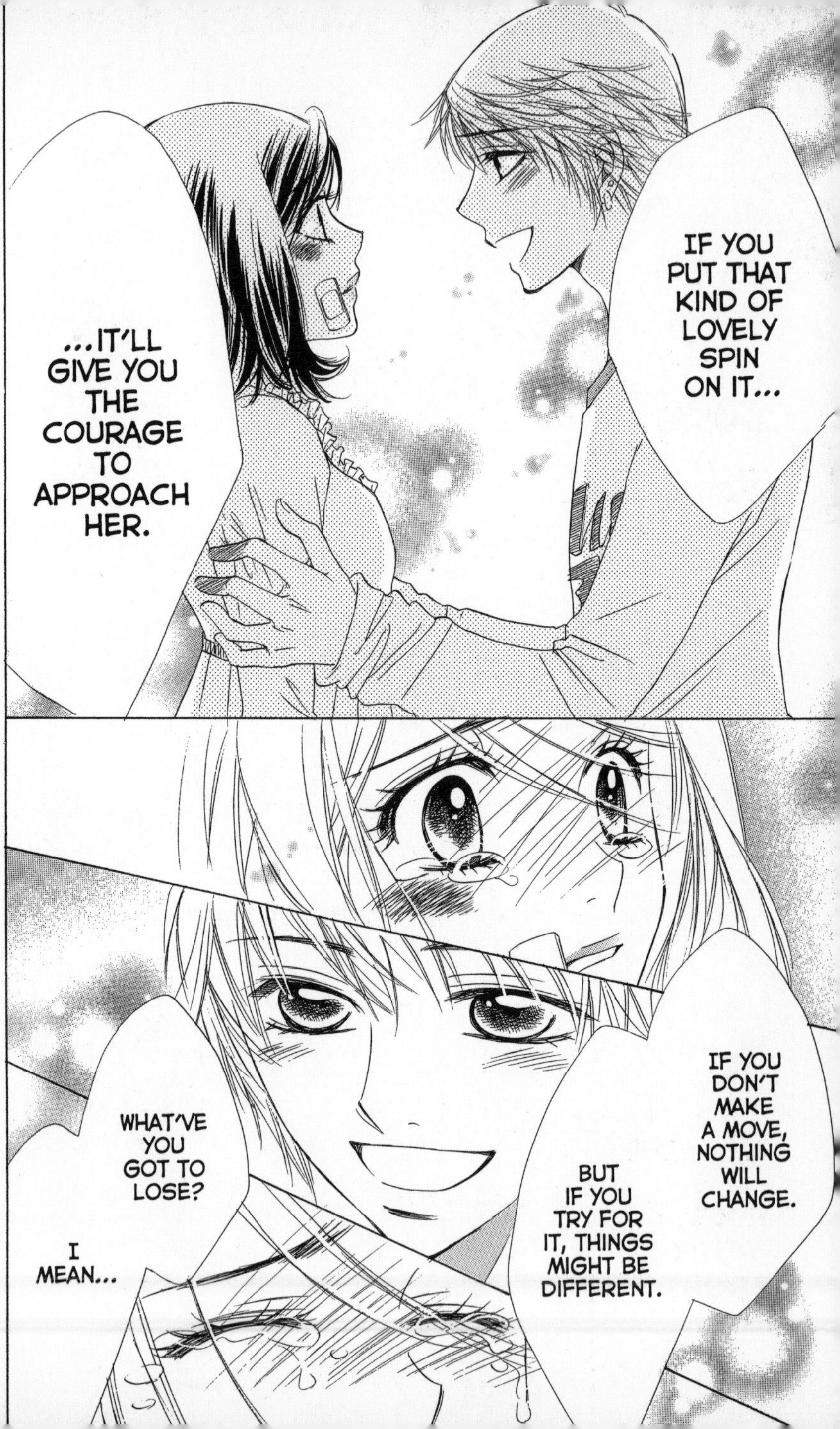
IF YOU PUT THAT KIND OF LOVELY SPIN ON IT...
...IT'LL GIVE YOU THE COURAGE TO APPROACH HER.
IF YOU DON'T MAKE A MOVE, NOTHING WILL CHANGE.
BUT IF YOU TRY FOR IT, THINGS MIGHT BE DIFFERENT.
WHAT'VE YOU GOT TO LOSE?
I MEAN...

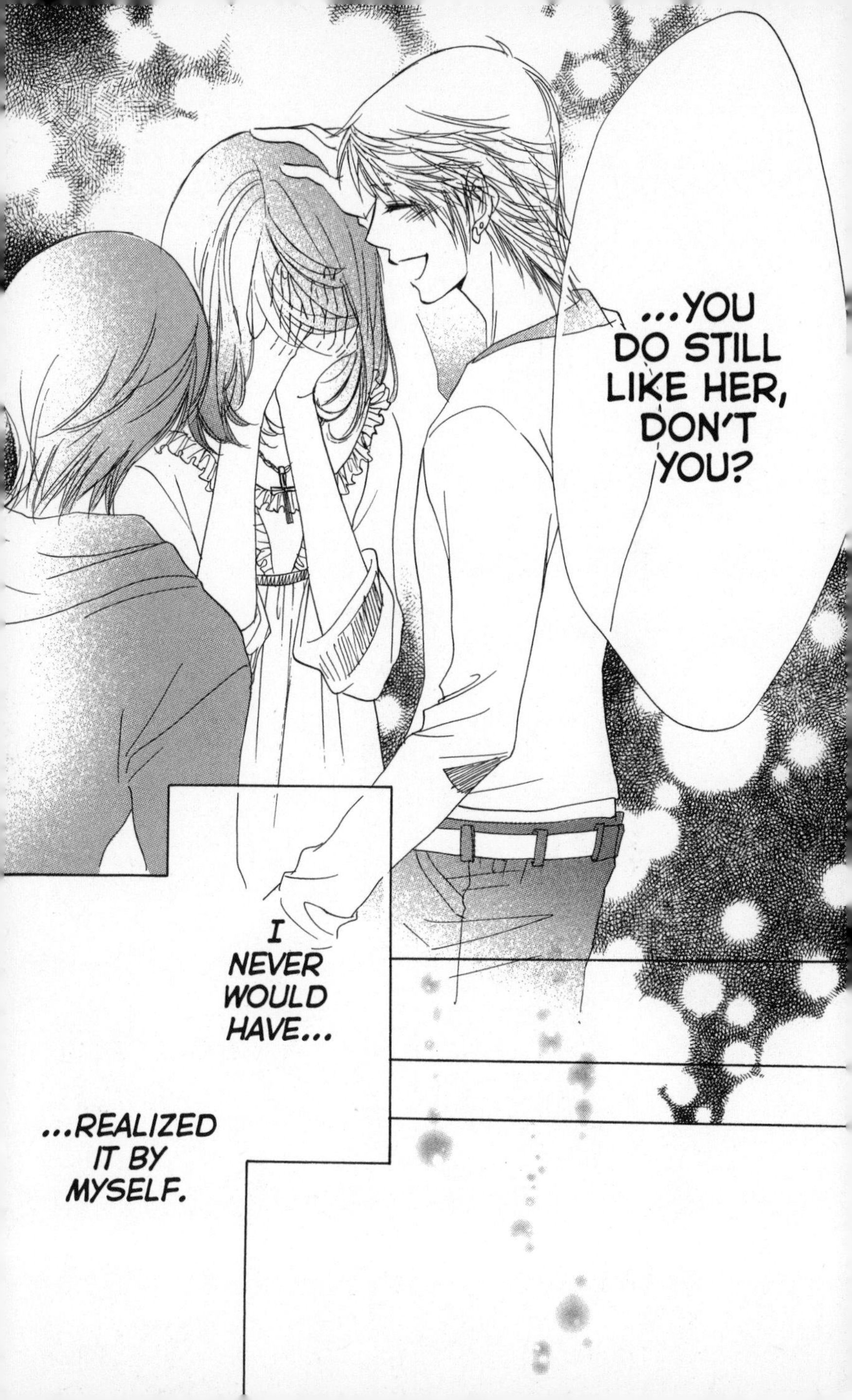
...YOU DO STILL LIKE HER, DON'T YOU?
I NEVER WOULD HAVE...
...REALIZED IT BY MYSELF.

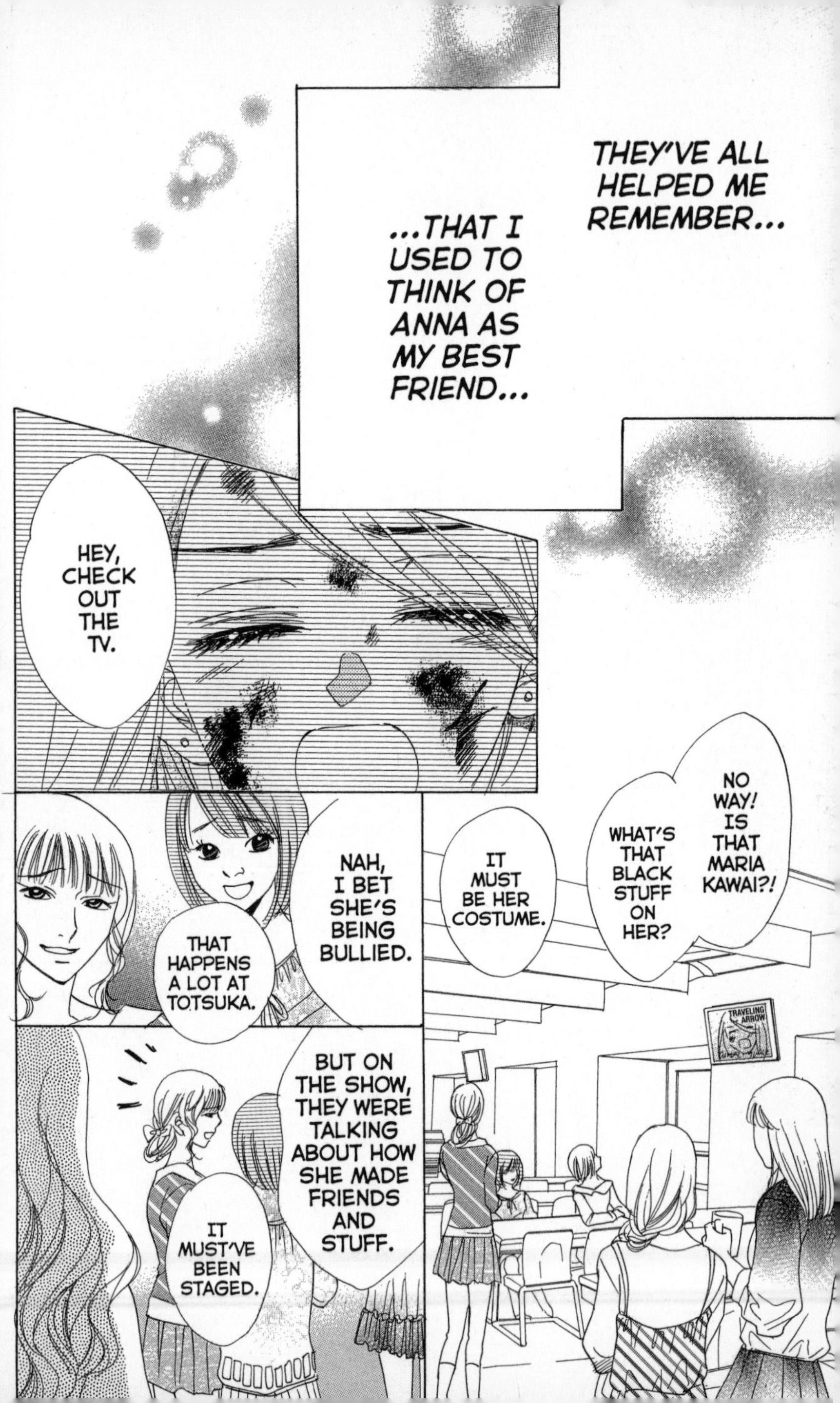
THEY'VE ALL HELPED ME REMEMBER...
...THAT I USED TO THINK OF ANNA AS MY BEST FRIEND...
HEY, CHECK OUT THE TV.
NO WAY! IS THAT MARIA KAWAI?!
WHAT'S THAT BLACK STUFF ON HER?
IT MUST BE HER COSTUME.
TRAVELING ARROW
NAH, I BET SHE'S BEING BULLIED.
THAT HAPPENS A LOT AT TOTSUKA.
BUT ON THE SHOW, THEY WERE TALKING ABOUT HOW SHE MADE FRIENDS AND STUFF.
IT MUST'VE BEEN STAGED.

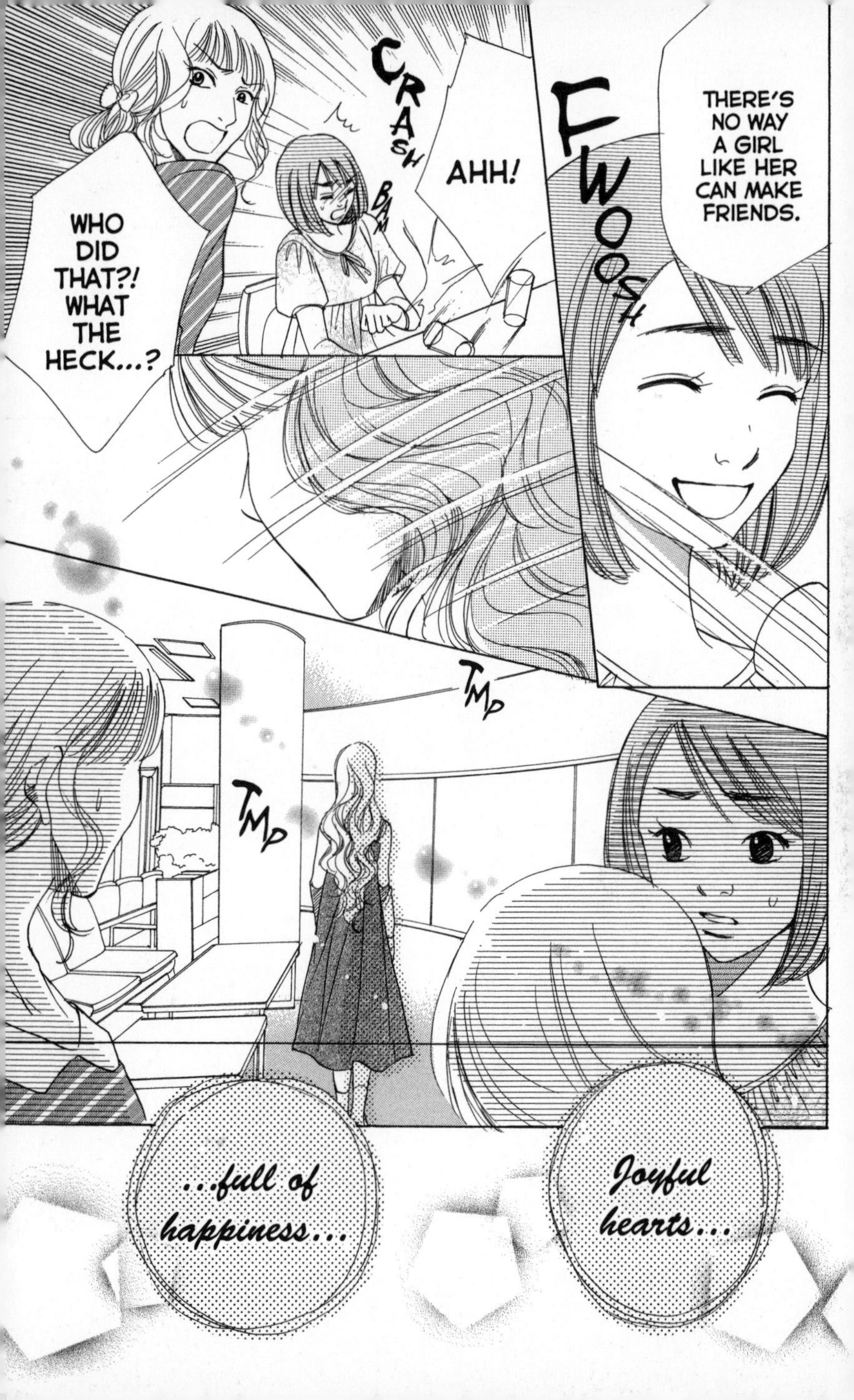
THERE'S NO WAY A GIRL LIKE HER CAN MAKE FRIENDS.
FWOOSH
CRASH
BAM
AHH!
WHO DID THAT?! WHAT THE HECK...?
TMP
TMP
Joyful hearts...
...full of happiness...

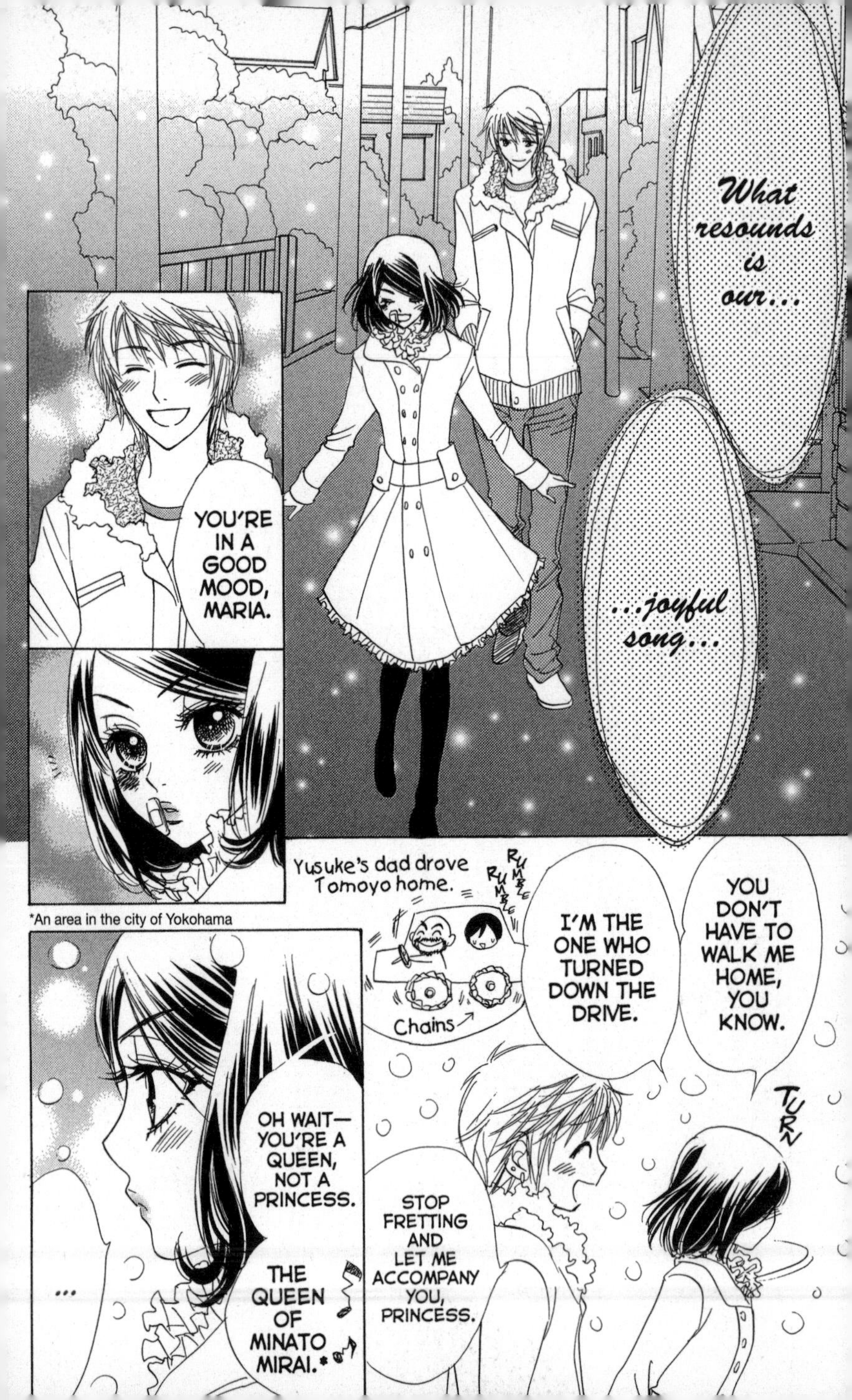
What resounds is our...
...joyful song...
YOU'RE IN A GOOD MOOD, MARIA.
YOU DON'T HAVE TO WALK ME HOME, YOU KNOW.
TURN
I'M THE ONE WHO TURNED DOWN THE DRIVE.
Yusuke's dad drove Tomoyo home.
RUMBLE RUMBLE
Chains
STOP FRETTING AND LET ME ACCOMPANY YOU, PRINCESS.
OH WAIT— YOU'RE A QUEEN, NOT A PRINCESS.
THE QUEEN OF MINATO MIRAI.*
...

*An area in the city of Yokohama

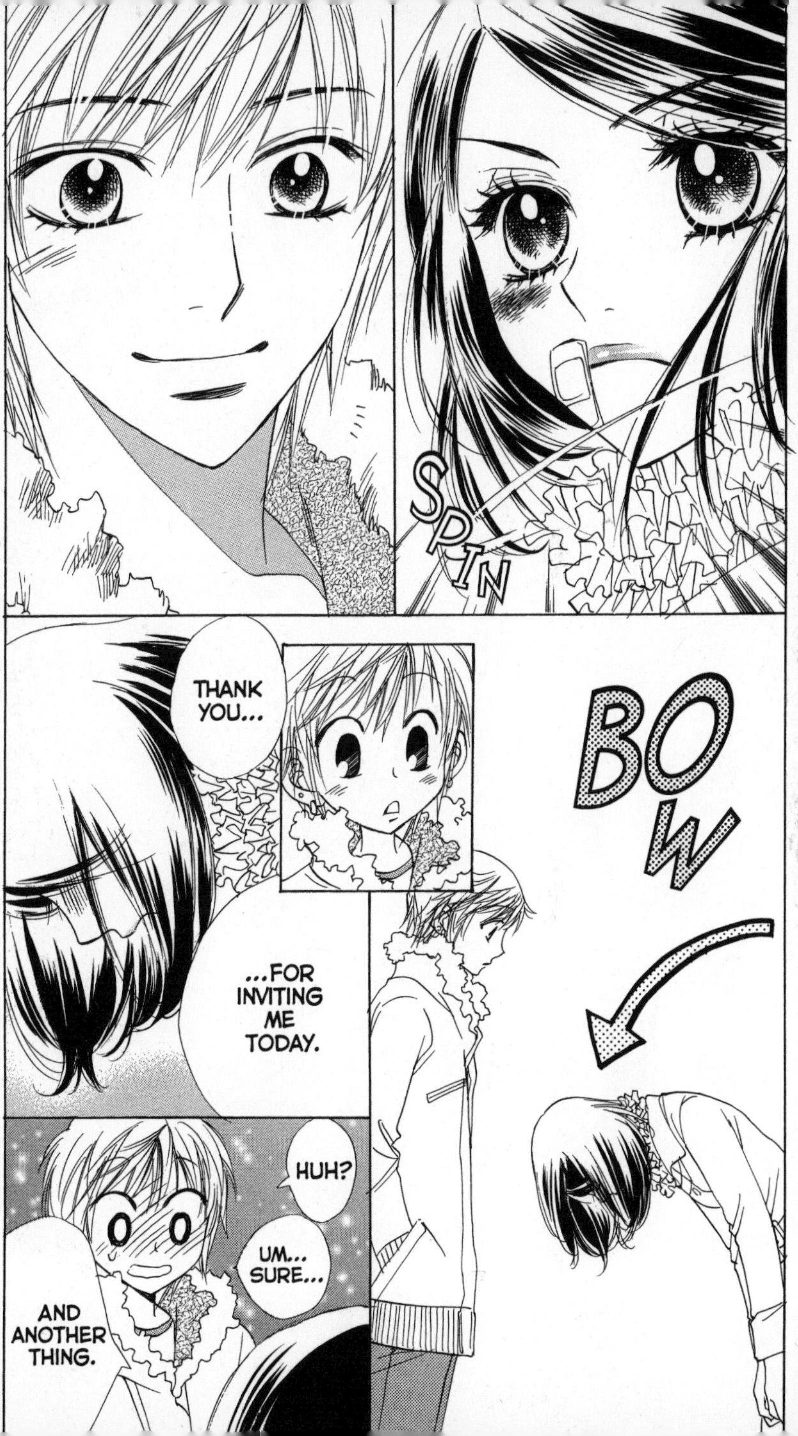
SPIN
BOW
THANK YOU...
...FOR INVITING ME TODAY.
HUH?
UM... SURE...
AND ANOTHER THING.

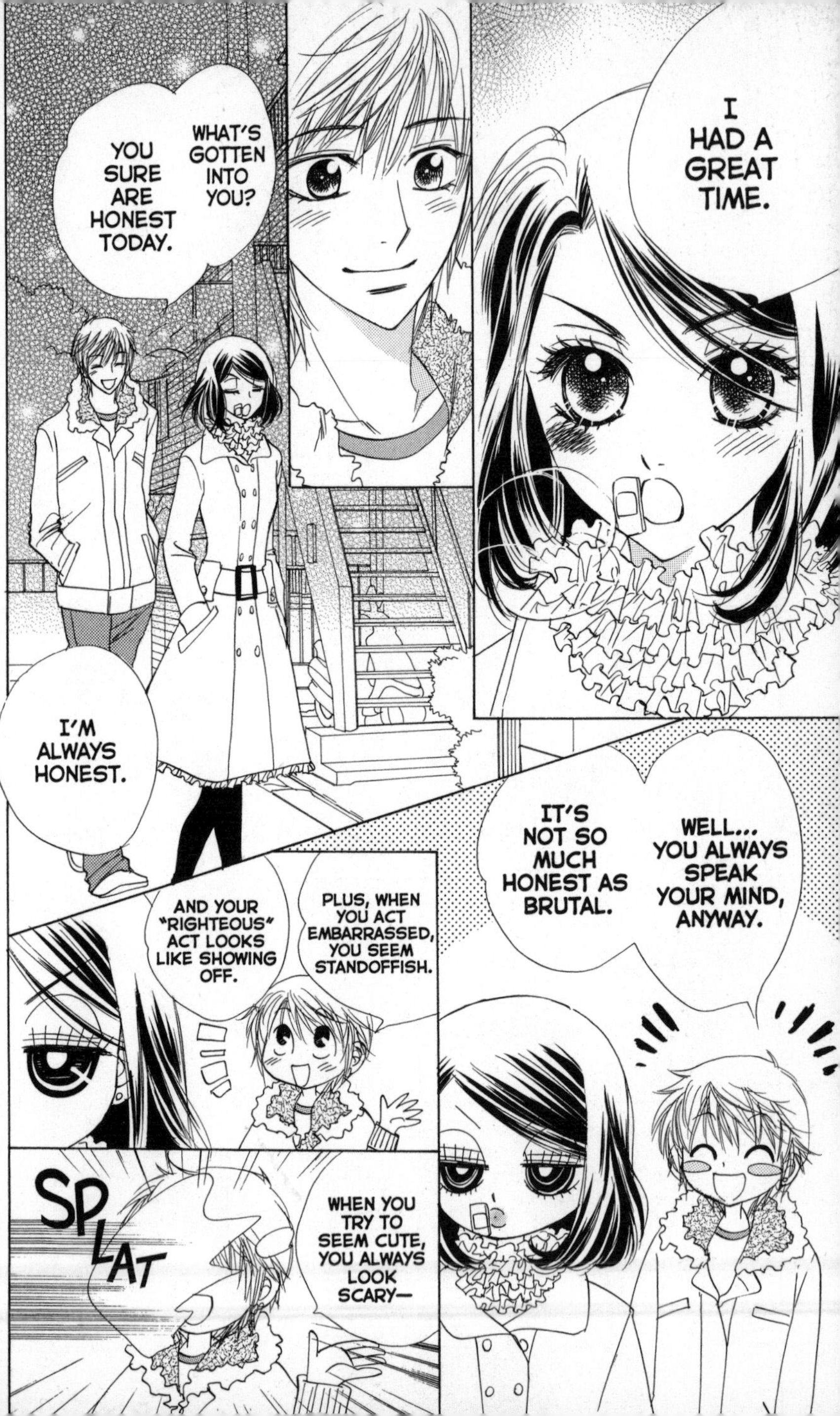
I HAD A GREAT TIME.
WHAT'S GOTTEN INTO YOU?
YOU SURE ARE HONEST TODAY.
I'M ALWAYS HONEST.
WELL... YOU ALWAYS SPEAK YOUR MIND, ANYWAY.
IT'S NOT SO MUCH HONEST AS BRUTAL.
PLUS, WHEN YOU ACT EMBARRASSED, YOU SEEM STANDOFFISH.
AND YOUR "RIGHTEOUS" ACT LOOKS LIKE SHOWING OFF.
WHEN YOU TRY TO SEEM CUTE, YOU ALWAYS LOOK SCARY—
SPLAT

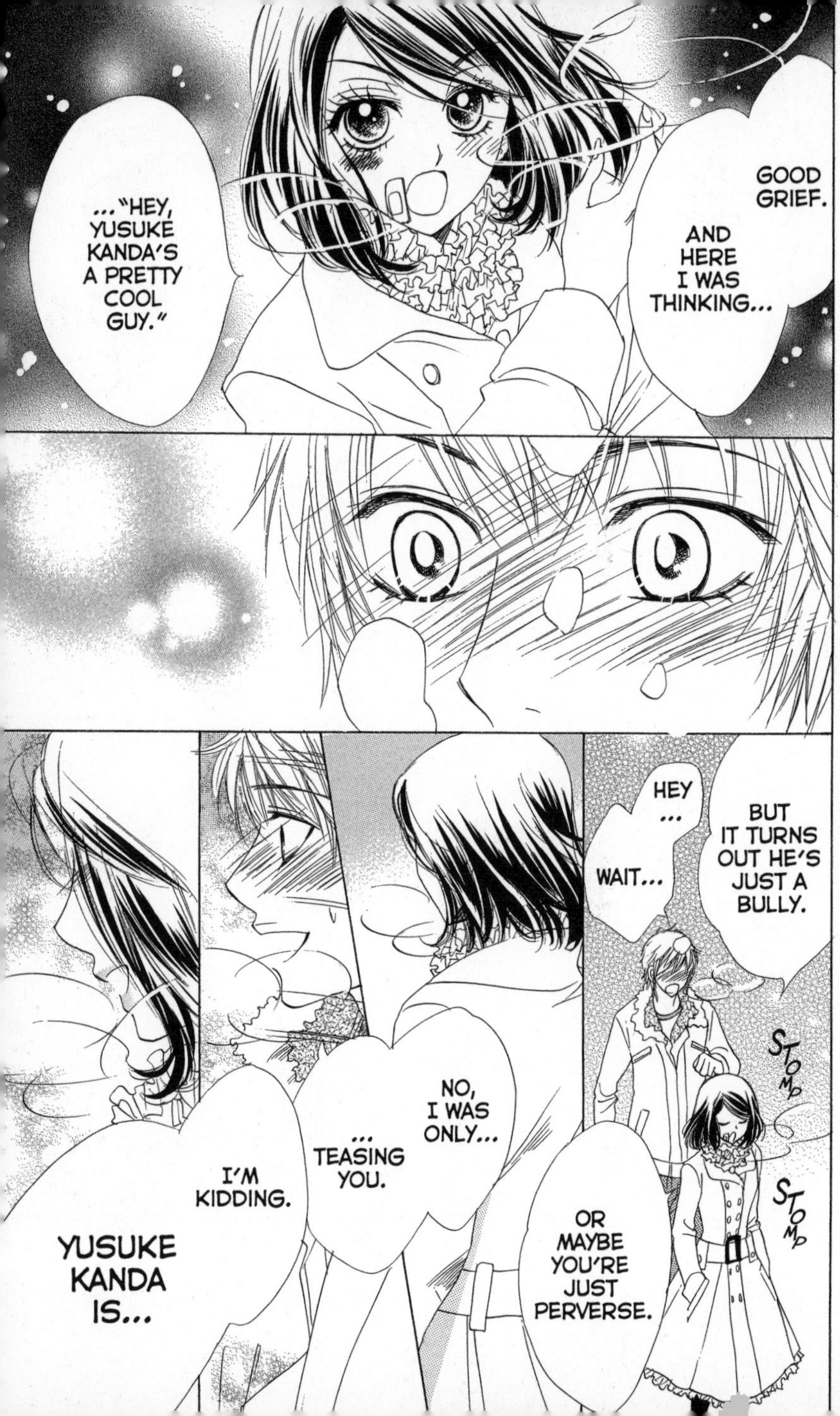
GOOD GRIEF.
AND HERE I WAS THINKING...
..."HEY, YUSUKE KANDA'S A PRETTY COOL GUY."
BUT IT TURNS OUT HE'S JUST A BULLY.
HEY ... WAIT...
STOMP
STOMP
OR MAYBE YOU'RE JUST PERVERSE.
NO, I WAS ONLY...
...TEASING YOU.
I'M KIDDING.
YUSUKE KANDA IS...

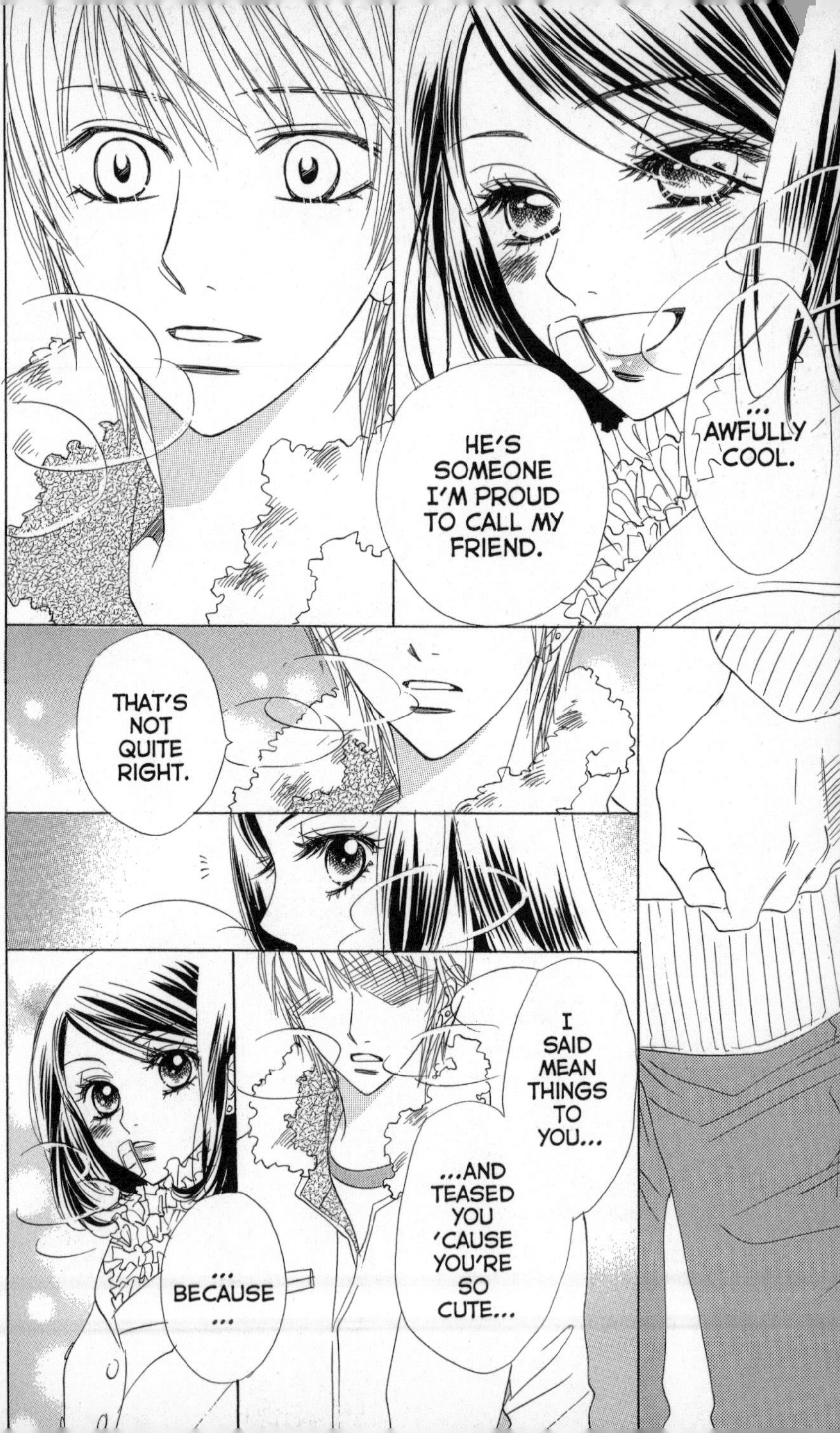
...AWFULLY COOL.
HE'S SOMEONE I'M PROUD TO CALL MY FRIEND.
THAT'S NOT QUITE RIGHT.
I SAID MEAN THINGS TO YOU...
...AND TEASED YOU 'CAUSE YOU'RE SO CUTE...
...BECAUSE ...

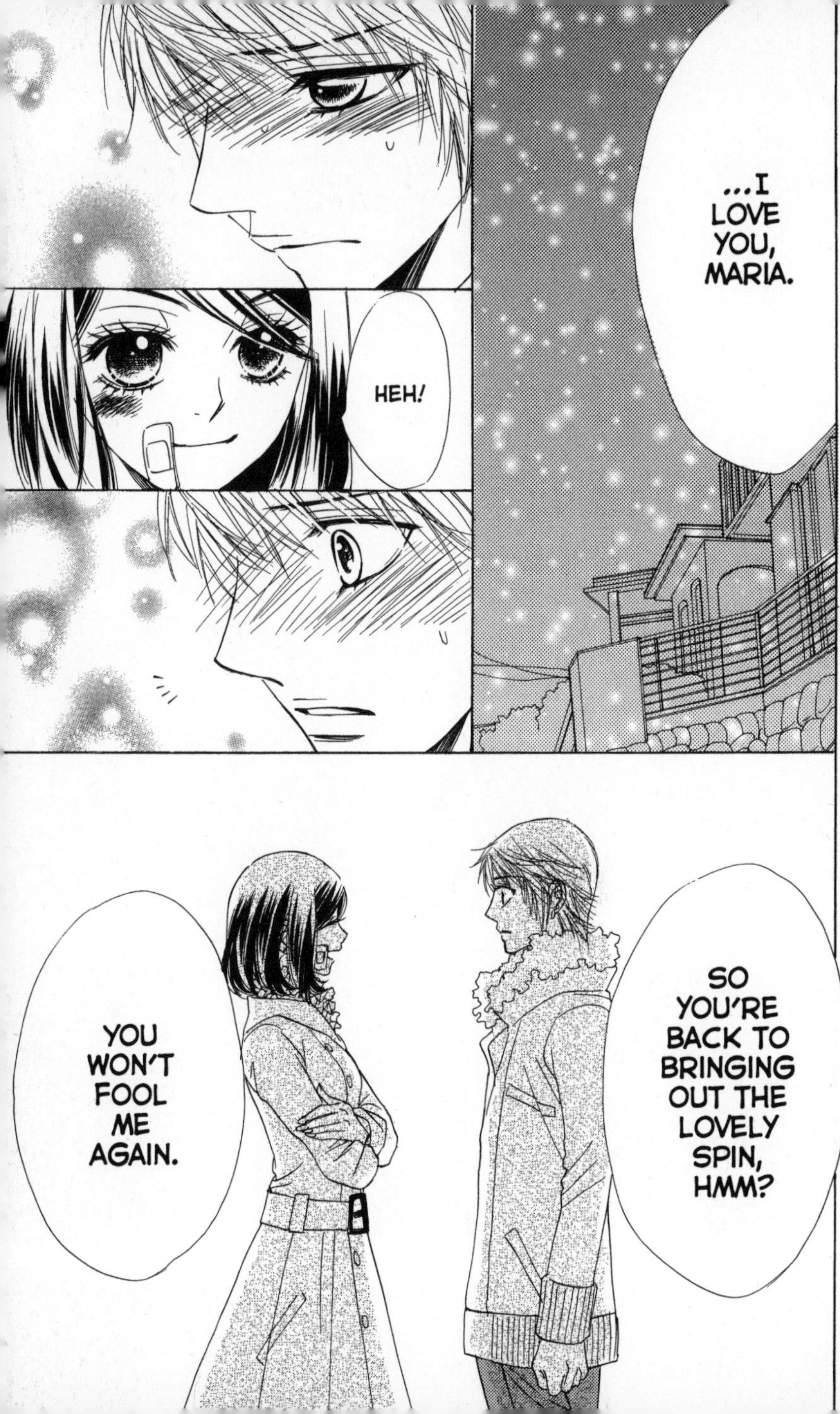
...I LOVE YOU, MARIA.
HEH!
SO YOU'RE BACK TO BRINGING OUT THE LOVELY SPIN, HMM?
YOU WON'T FOOL ME AGAIN.

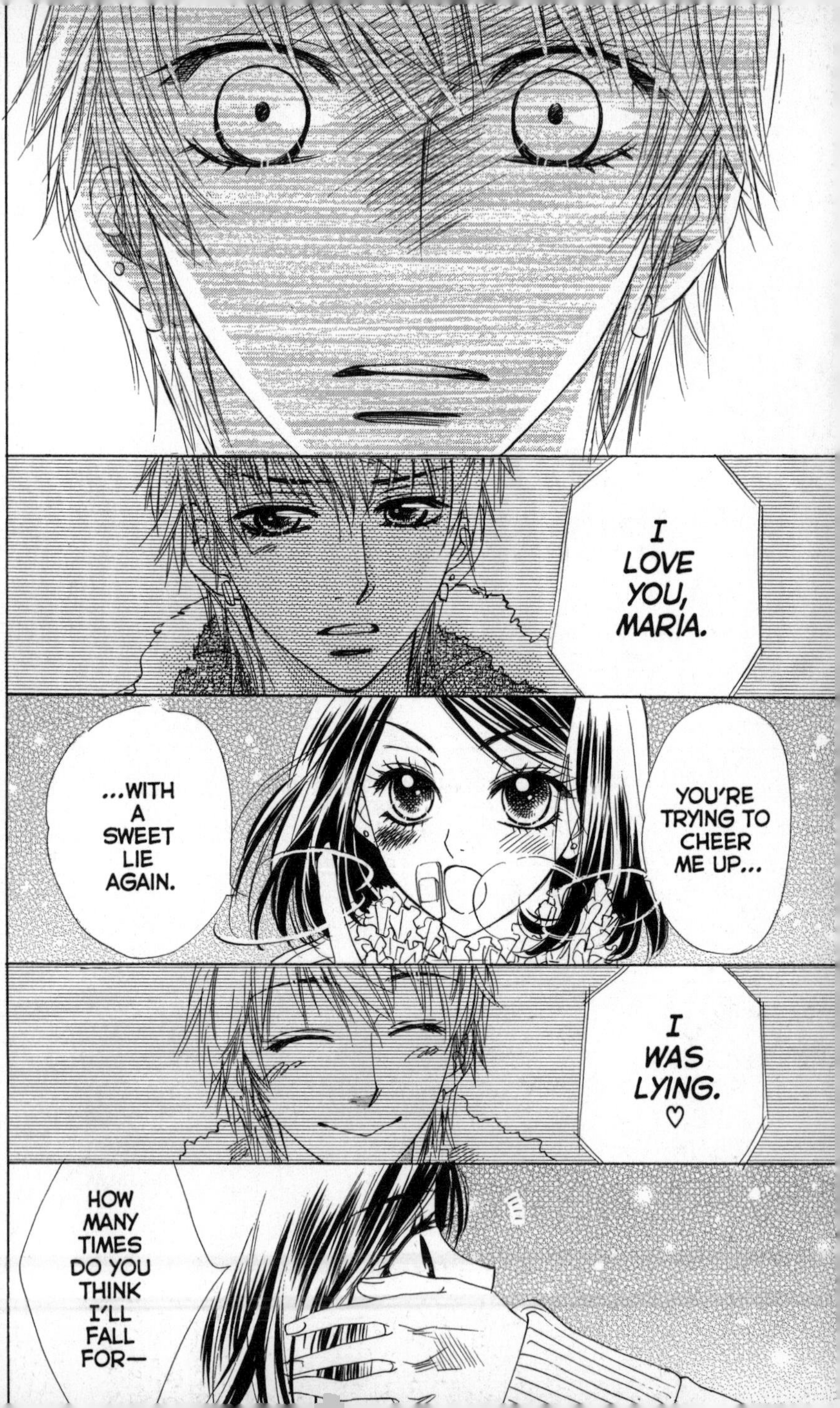
I LOVE YOU, MARIA.
YOU'RE TRYING TO CHEER ME UP...
...WITH A SWEET LIE AGAIN.
I WAS LYING. ♡
HOW MANY TIMES DO YOU THINK I'LL FALL FOR—

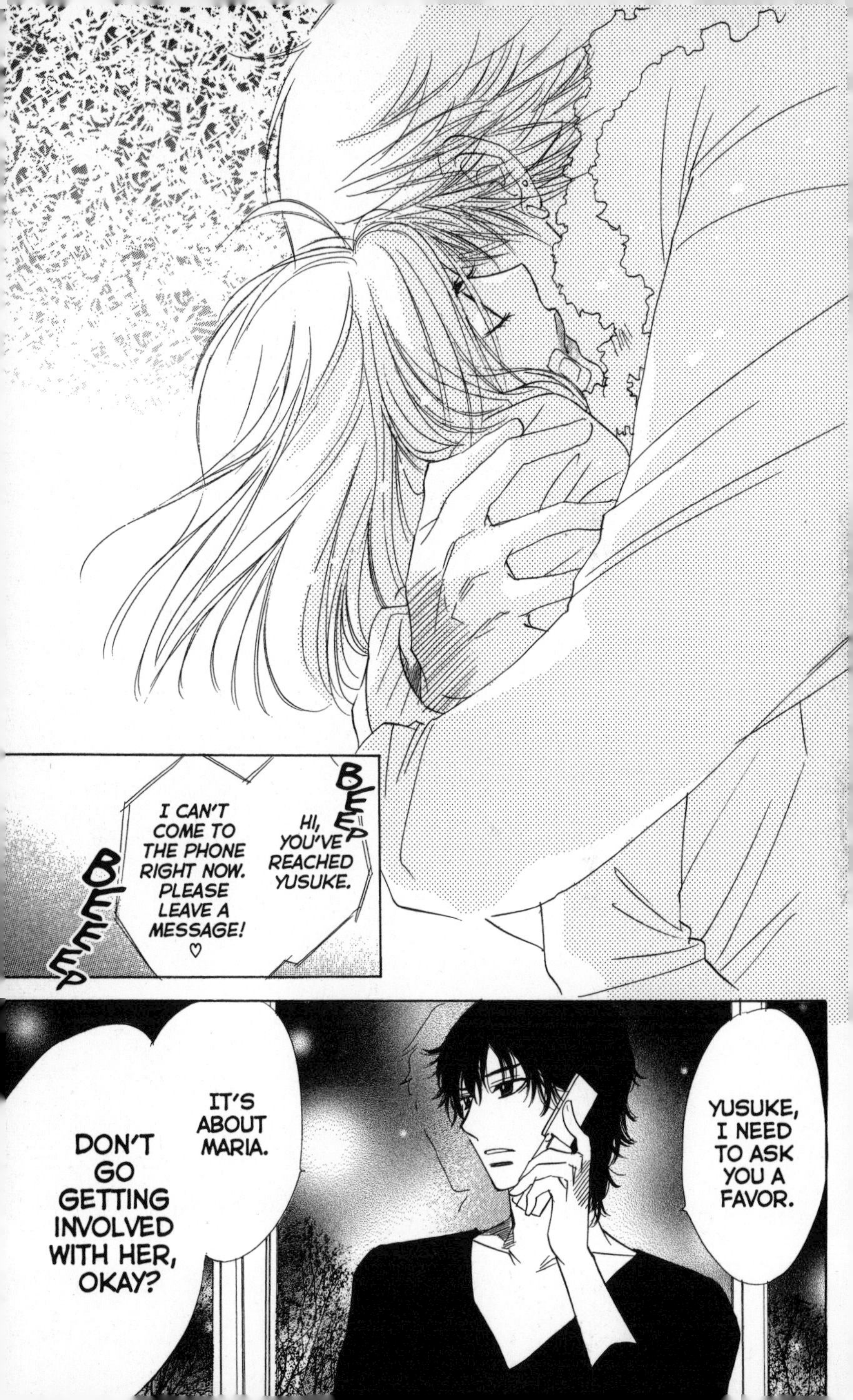
BEEP
HI, YOU'VE REACHED YUSUKE.
I CAN'T COME TO THE PHONE RIGHT NOW. PLEASE LEAVE A MESSAGE! ♡
BEEEEP
YUSUKE, I NEED TO ASK YOU A FAVOR.
IT'S ABOUT MARIA.
DON'T GO GETTING INVOLVED WITH HER, OKAY?

A Devil and
Her Love Song

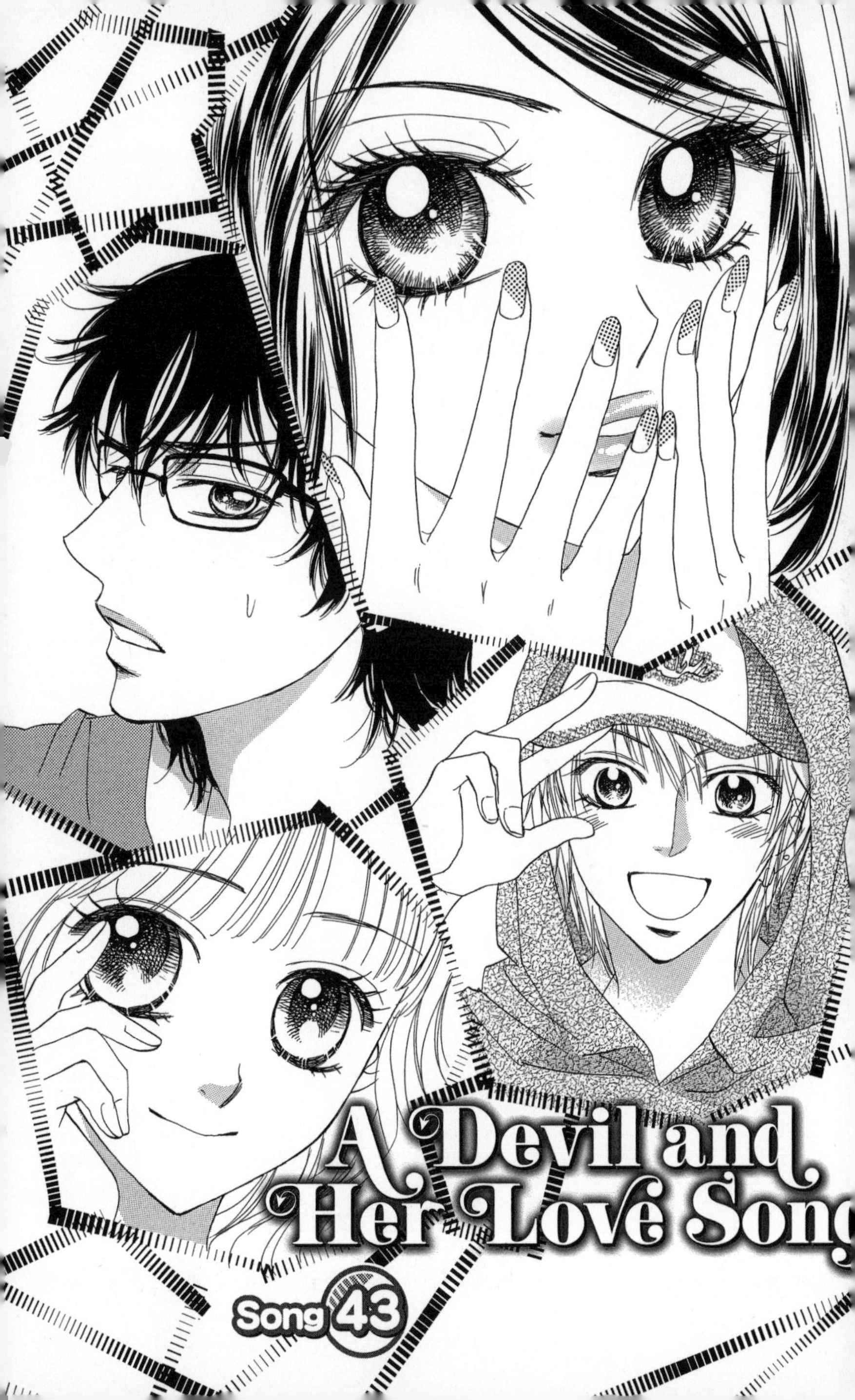
A Devil and Her Love Song
Song 43

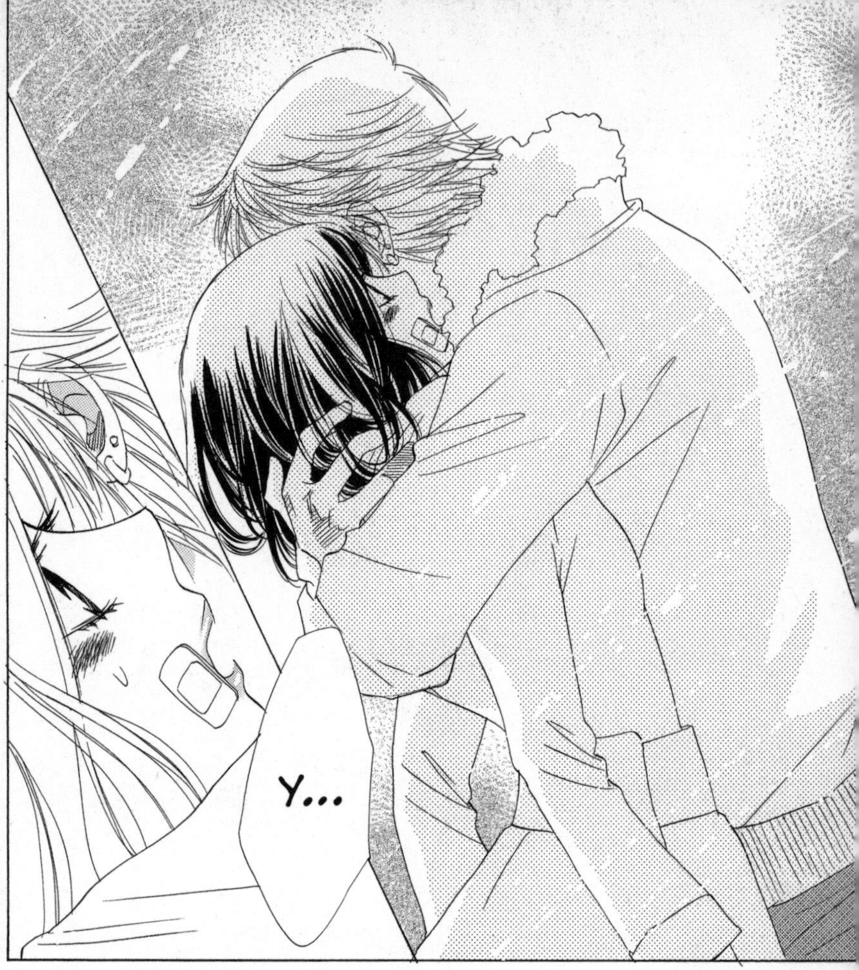
Y...

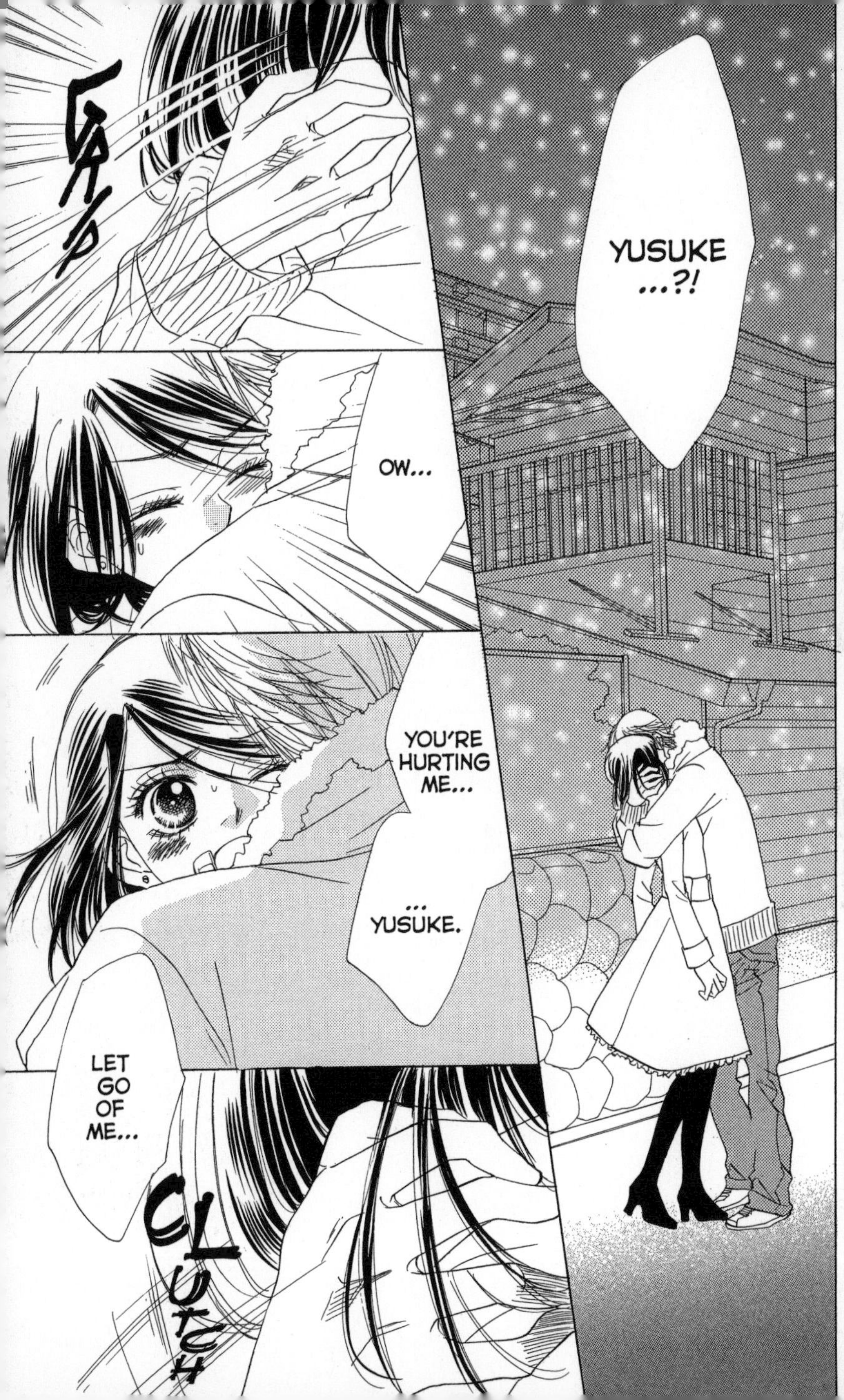
YUSUKE ...?!
OW...
YOU'RE HURTING ME...
... YUSUKE.
LET GO OF ME...
CLUTCH

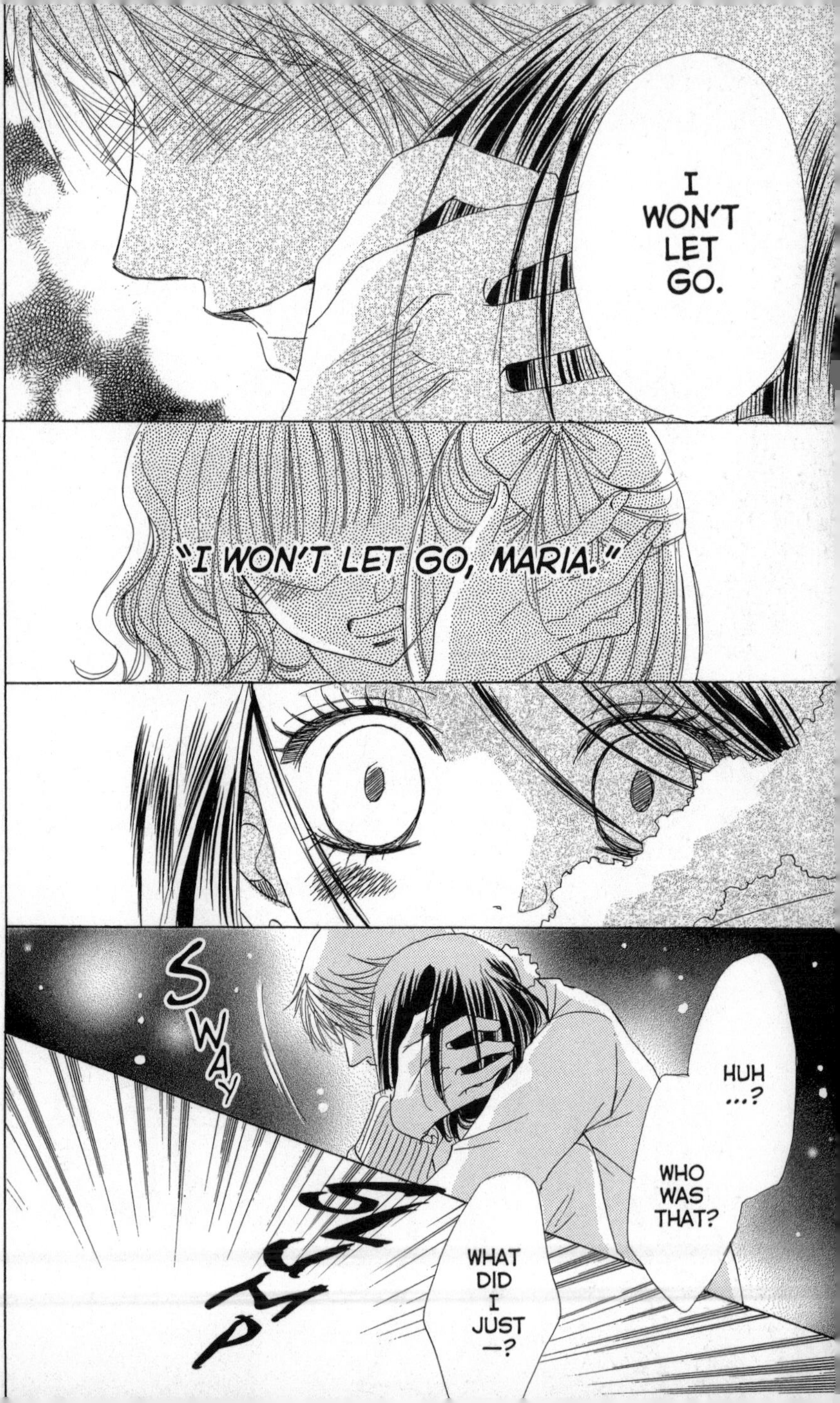
I WON'T LET GO.
"I WON'T LET GO, MARIA."
HUH ...?
WHO WAS THAT?
SWAY
WHAT DID I JUST —?
SLUMP

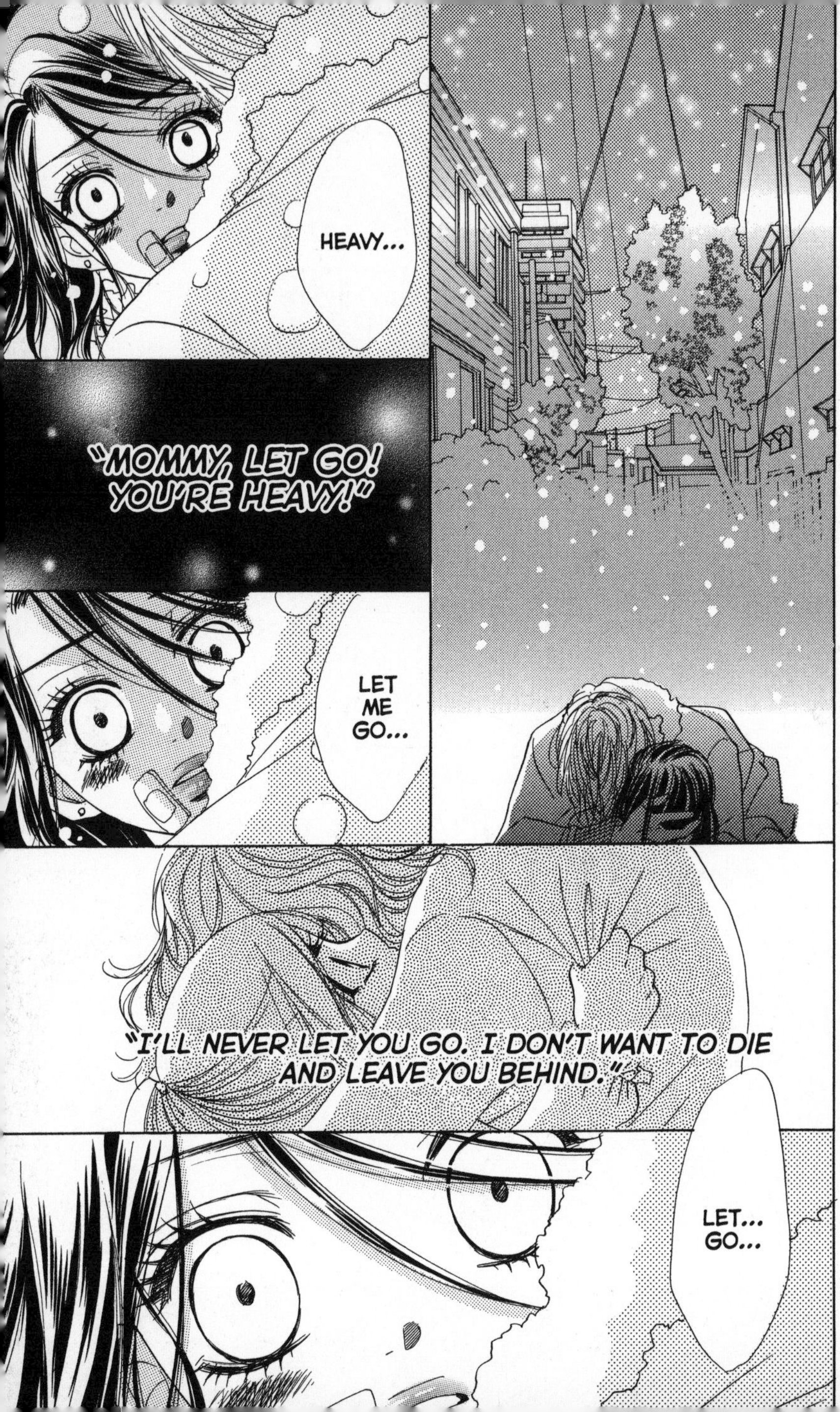
HEAVY...
"MOMMY, LET GO! YOU'RE HEAVY!"
LET ME GO...
"I'LL NEVER LET YOU GO. I DON'T WANT TO DIE AND LEAVE YOU BEHIND."
LET... GO...

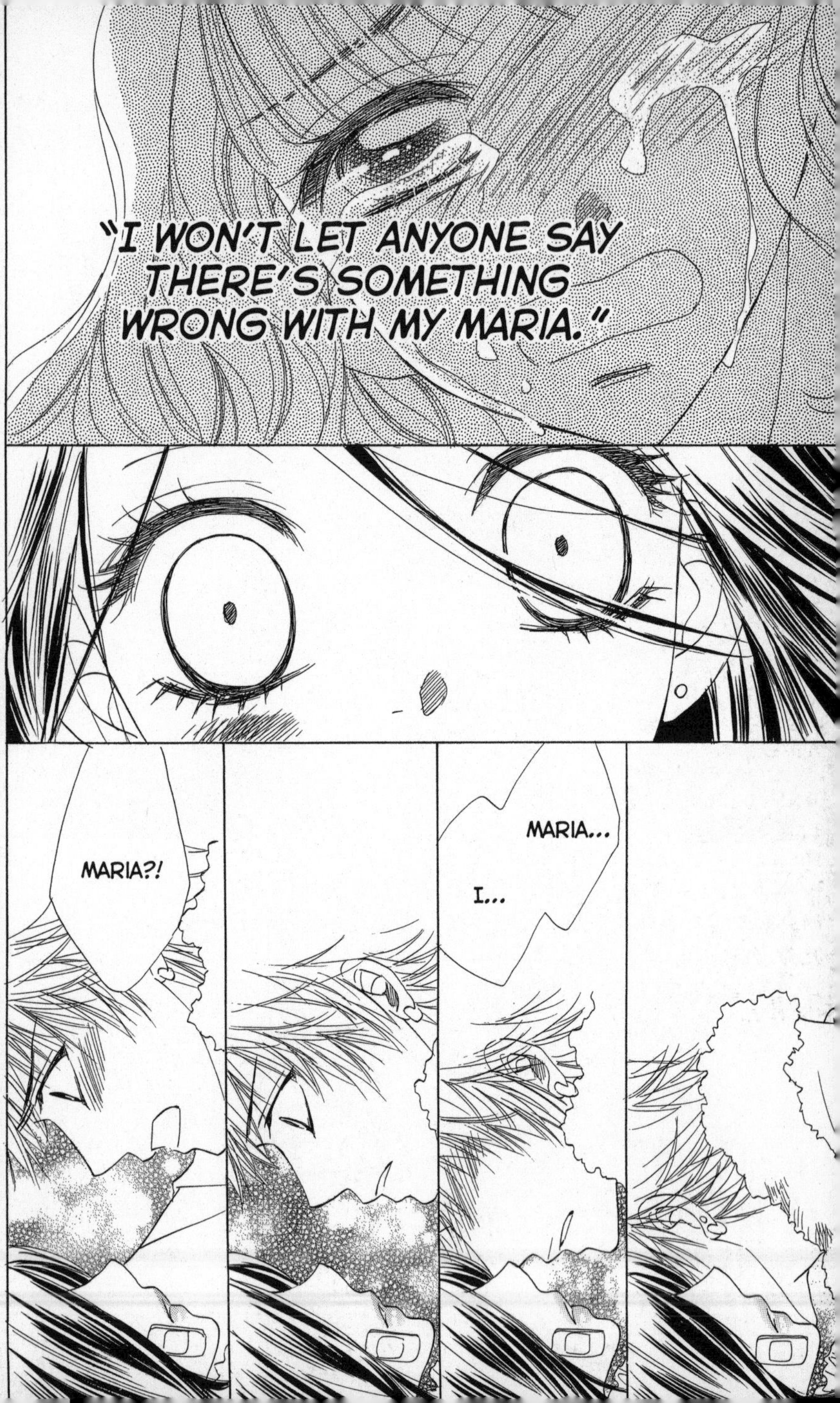
"I WON'T LET ANYONE SAY THERE'S SOMETHING WRONG WITH MY MARIA."
MARIA...
I...
MARIA?!

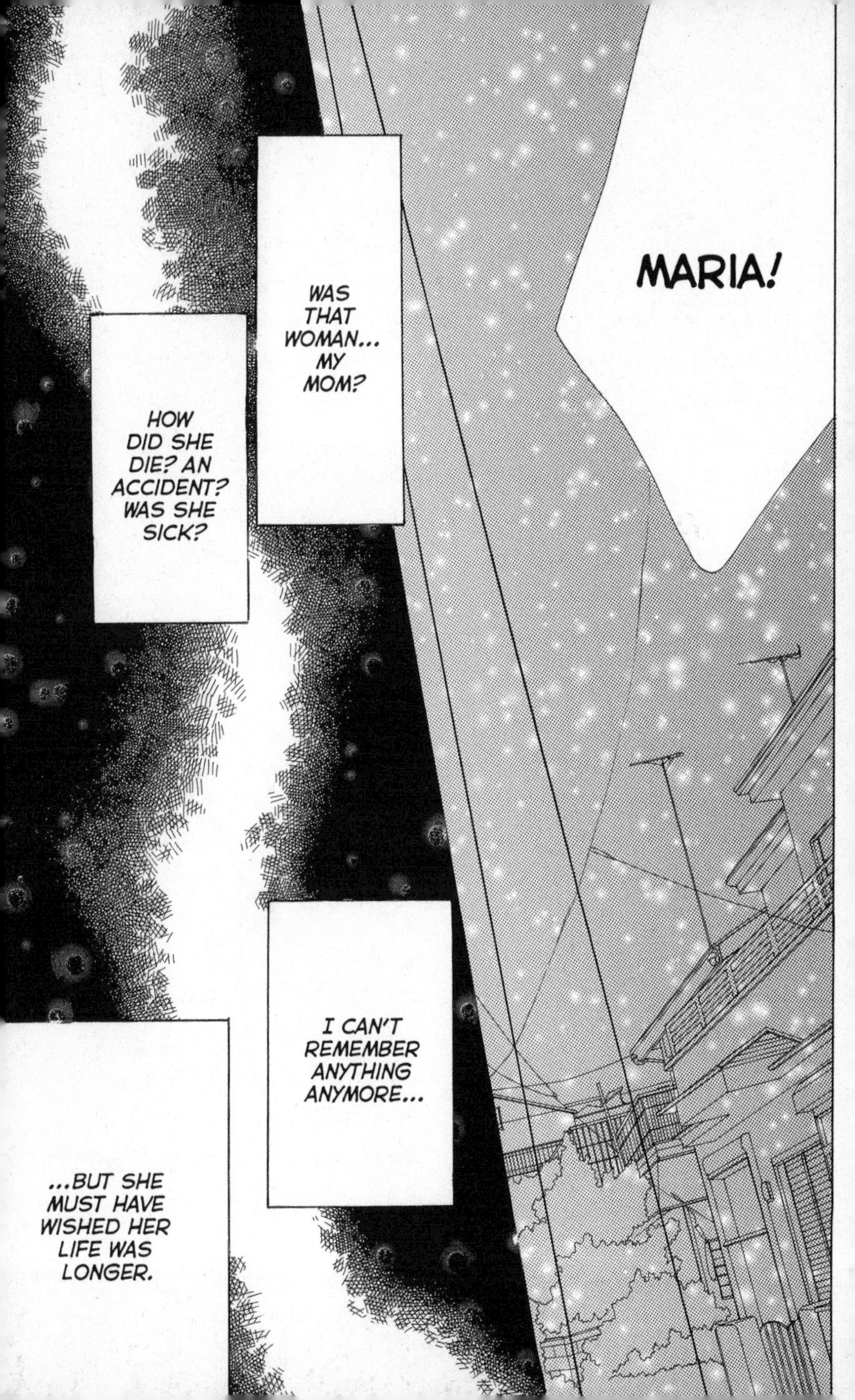
MARIA!
WAS THAT WOMAN... MY MOM?
HOW DID SHE DIE? AN ACCIDENT? WAS SHE SICK?
I CAN'T REMEMBER ANYTHING ANYMORE...
...BUT SHE MUST HAVE WISHED HER LIFE WAS LONGER.

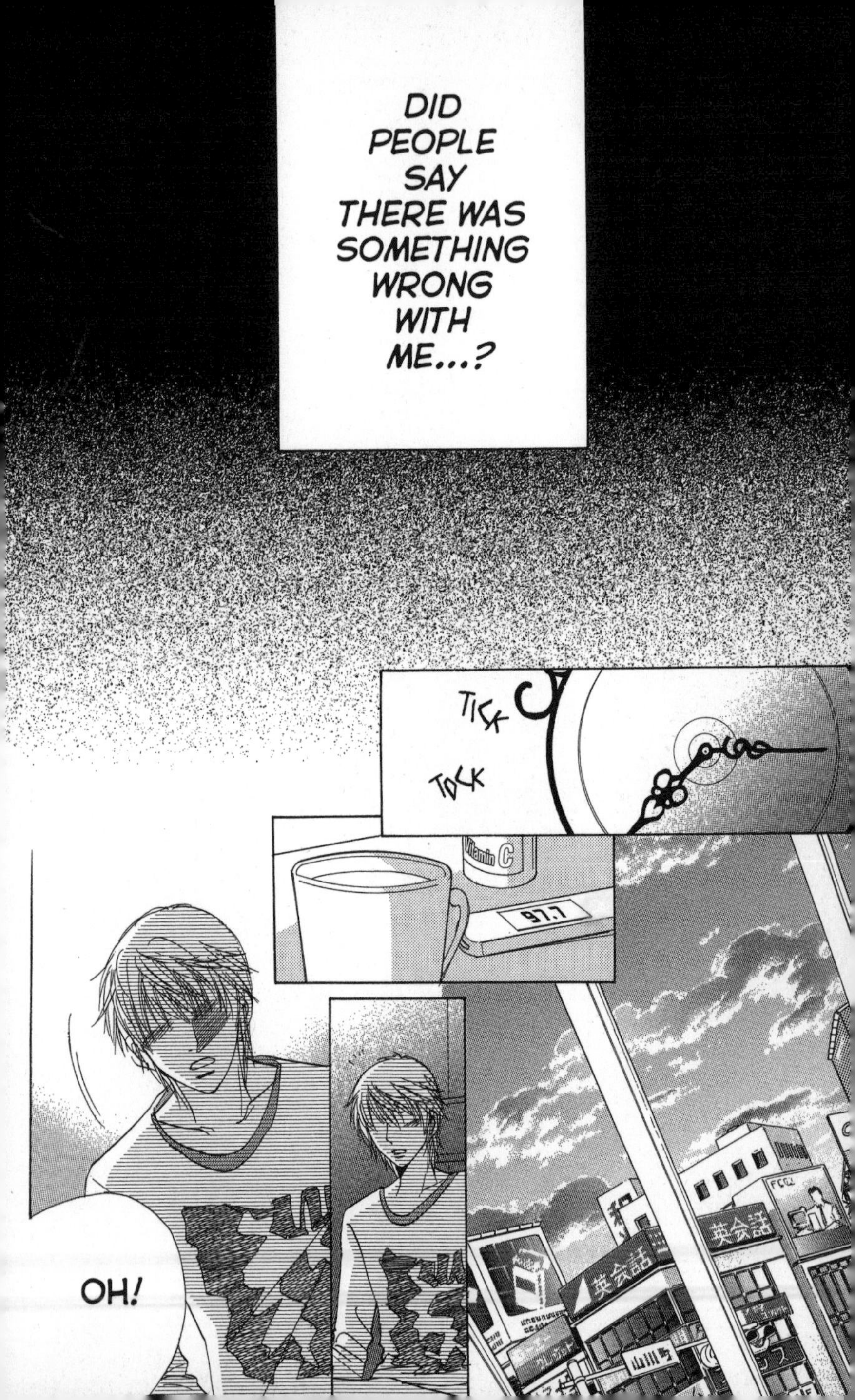
DID PEOPLE SAY THERE WAS SOMETHING WRONG WITH ME...?
TICK
TOCK
Vitamin C
97.7
英会話
英会話
英会話
OH!

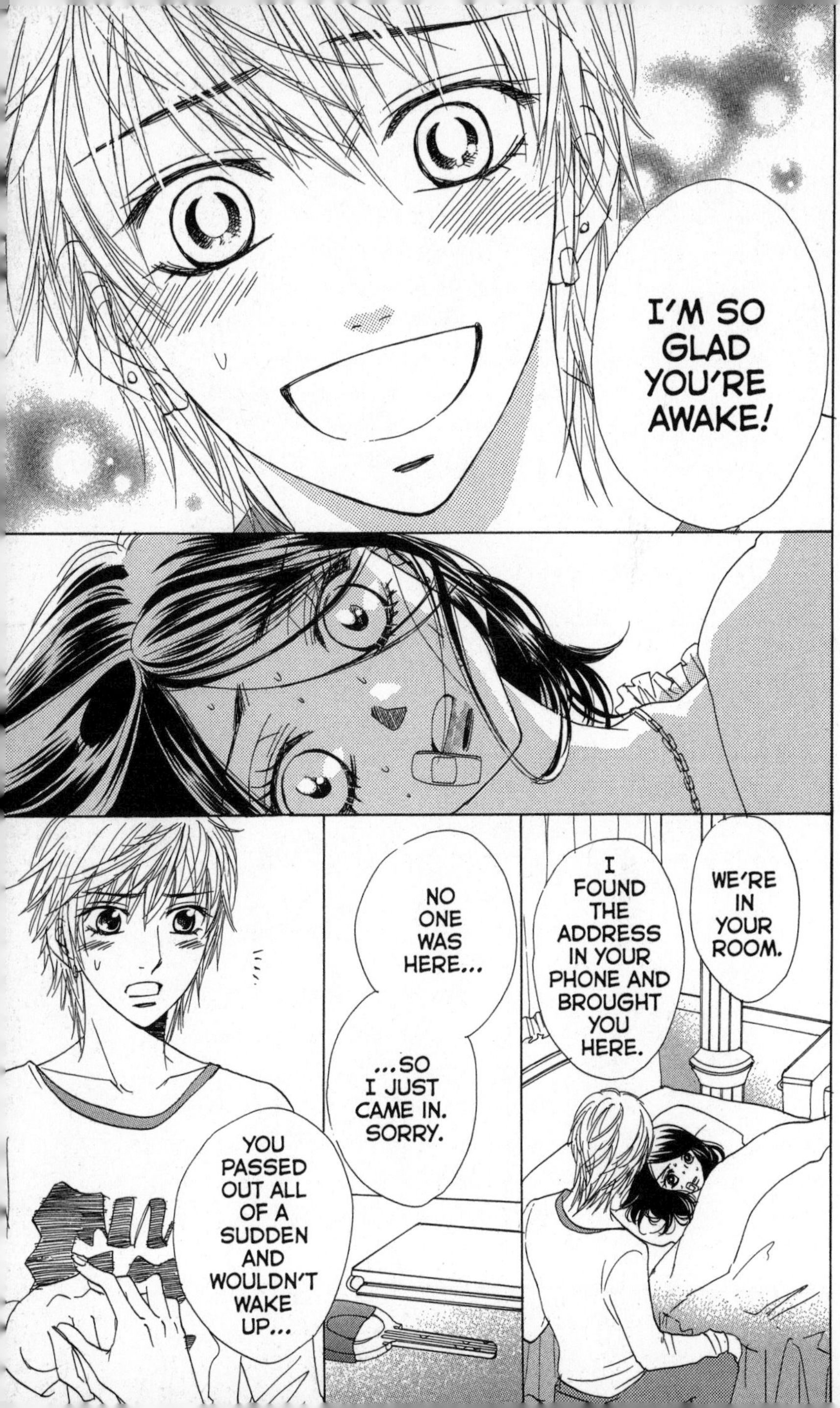
I'M SO GLAD YOU'RE AWAKE!
WE'RE IN YOUR ROOM.
I FOUND THE ADDRESS IN YOUR PHONE AND BROUGHT YOU HERE.
NO ONE WAS HERE...
...SO I JUST CAME IN. SORRY.
YOU PASSED OUT ALL OF A SUDDEN AND WOULDN'T WAKE UP...

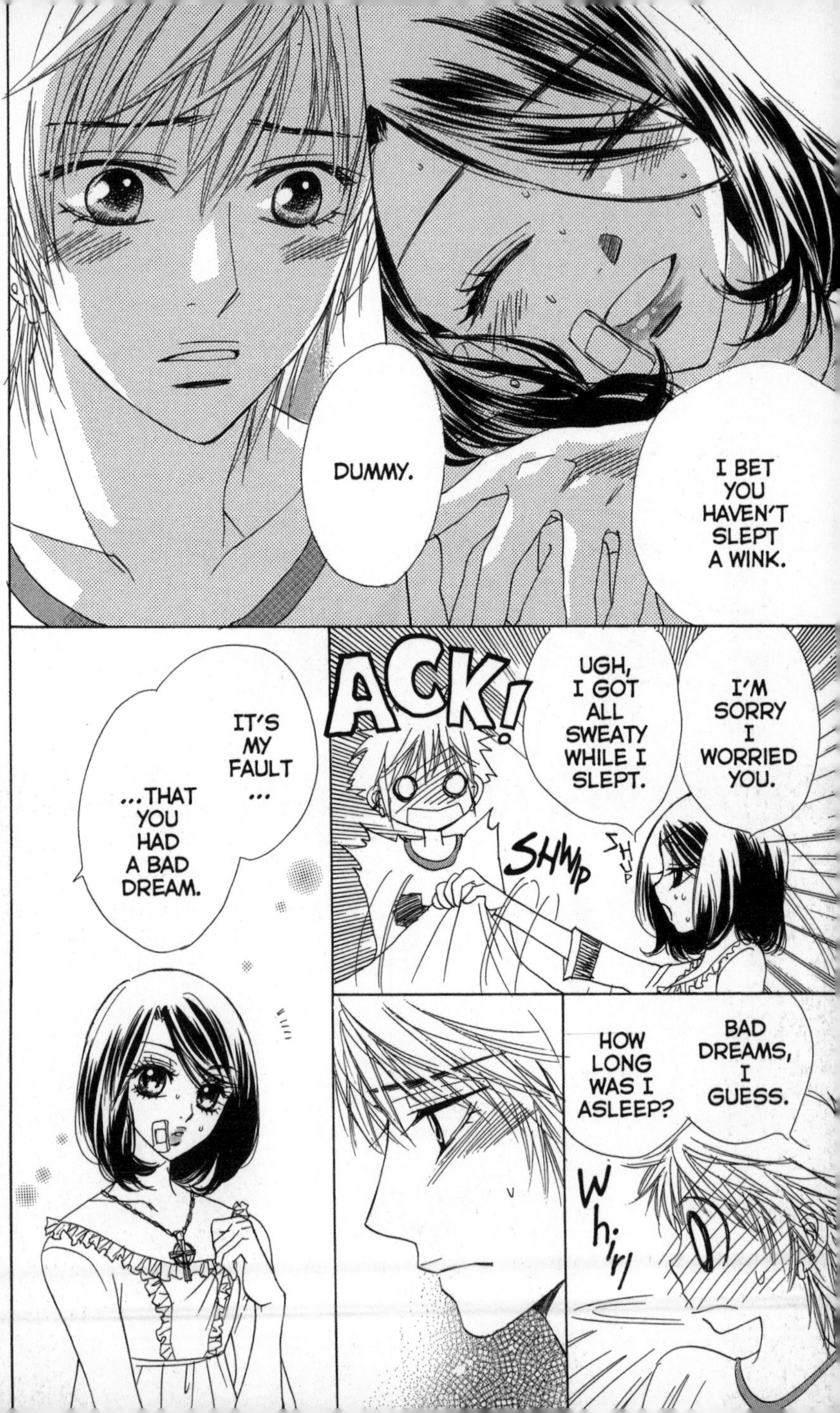
I BET YOU HAVEN'T SLEPT A WINK.
DUMMY.
I'M SORRY I WORRIED YOU.
UGH, I GOT ALL SWEATY WHILE I SLEPT.
SHUP
SHWIP
ACK!
BAD DREAMS, I GUESS.
Whirl
HOW LONG WAS I ASLEEP?
IT'S MY FAULT...
...THAT YOU HAD A BAD DREAM.

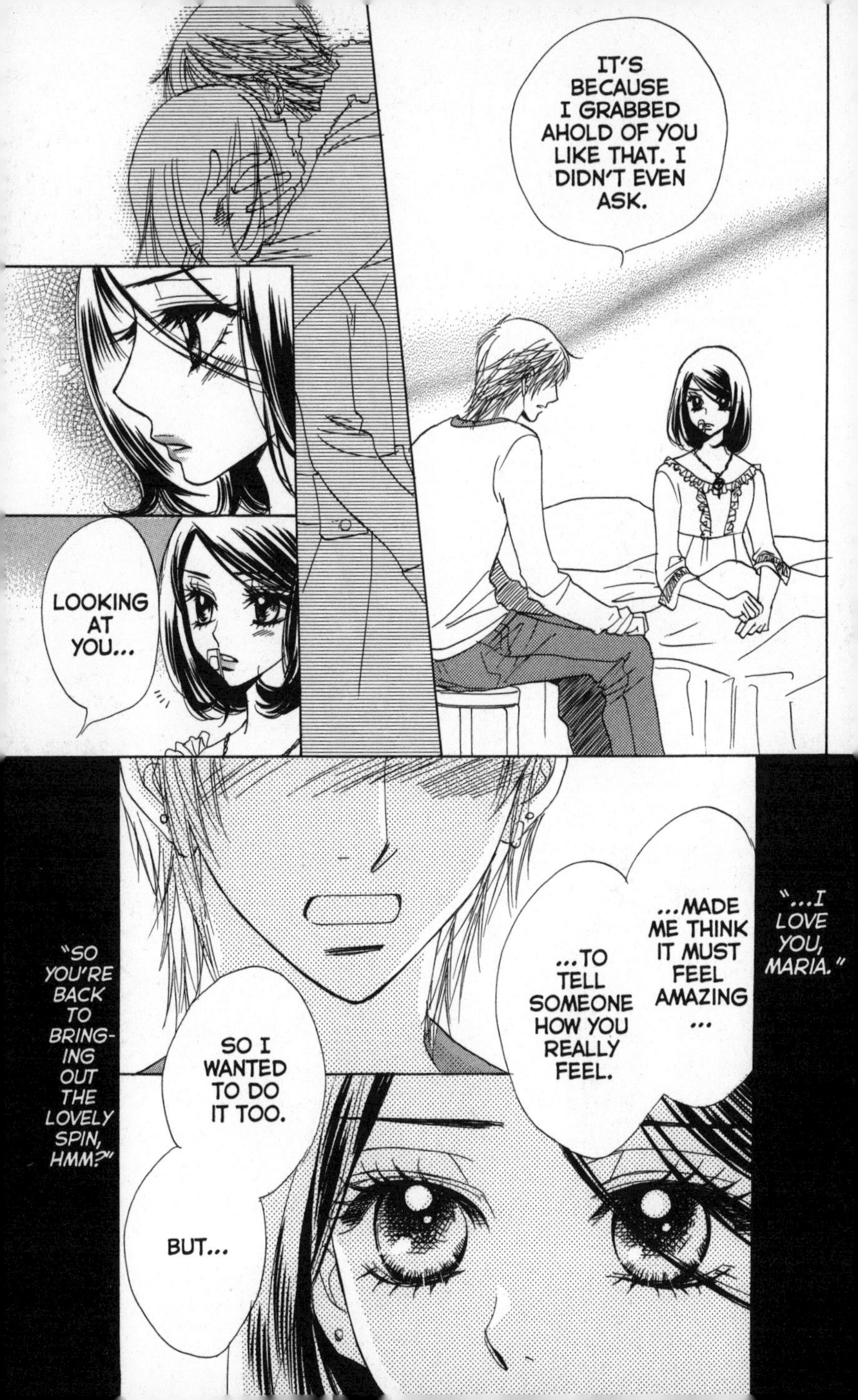
IT'S BECAUSE I GRABBED AHOLD OF YOU LIKE THAT. I DIDN'T EVEN ASK.
LOOKING AT YOU...
"...I LOVE YOU, MARIA."
...MADE ME THINK IT MUST FEEL AMAZING...
...TO TELL SOMEONE HOW YOU REALLY FEEL.
SO I WANTED TO DO IT TOO.
BUT...
"SO YOU'RE BACK TO BRINGING OUT THE LOVELY SPIN, HMM?"

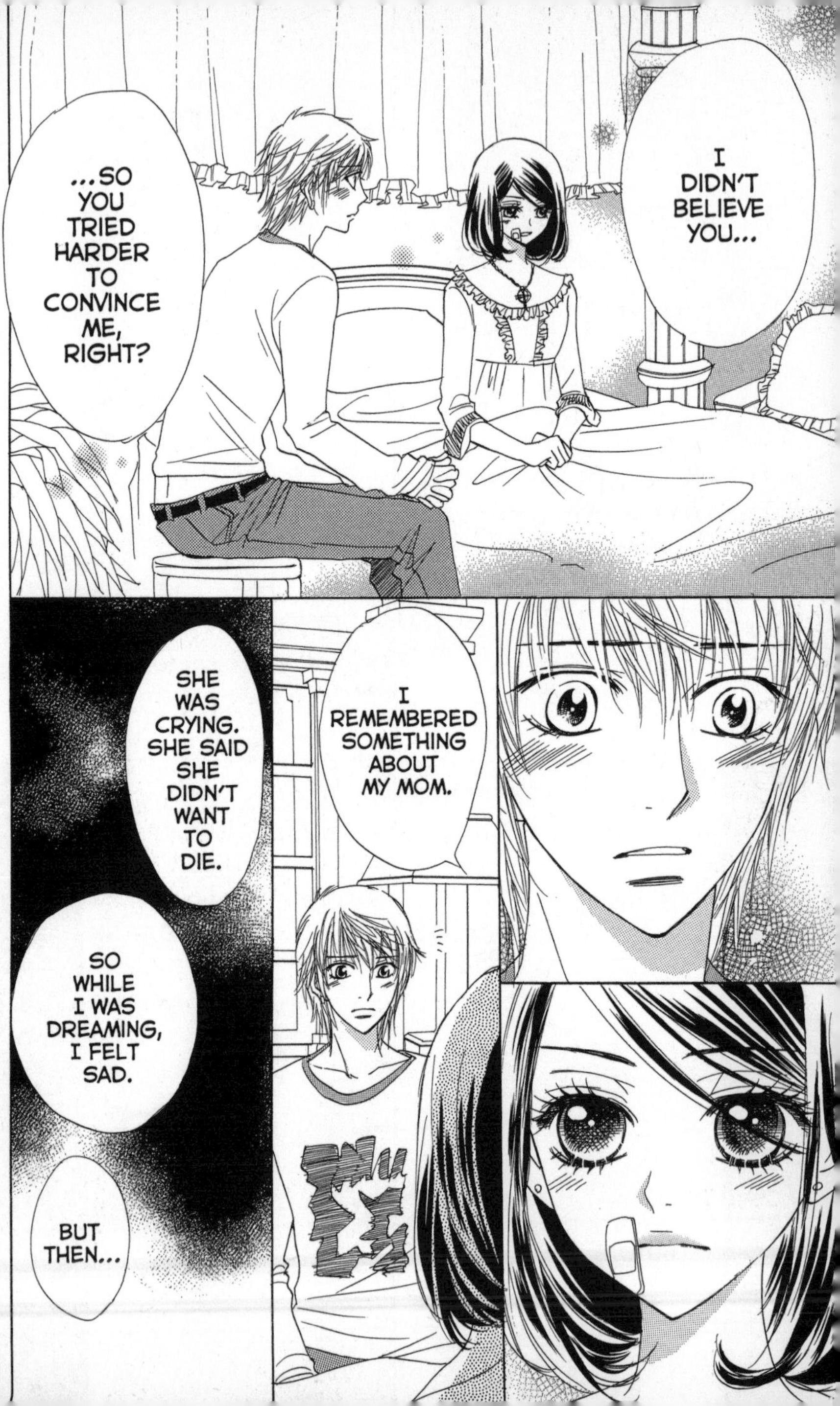
I DIDN'T BELIEVE YOU...
...SO YOU TRIED HARDER TO CONVINCE ME, RIGHT?
I REMEMBERED SOMETHING ABOUT MY MOM.
SHE WAS CRYING. SHE SAID SHE DIDN'T WANT TO DIE.
SO WHILE I WAS DREAMING, I FELT SAD.
BUT THEN...

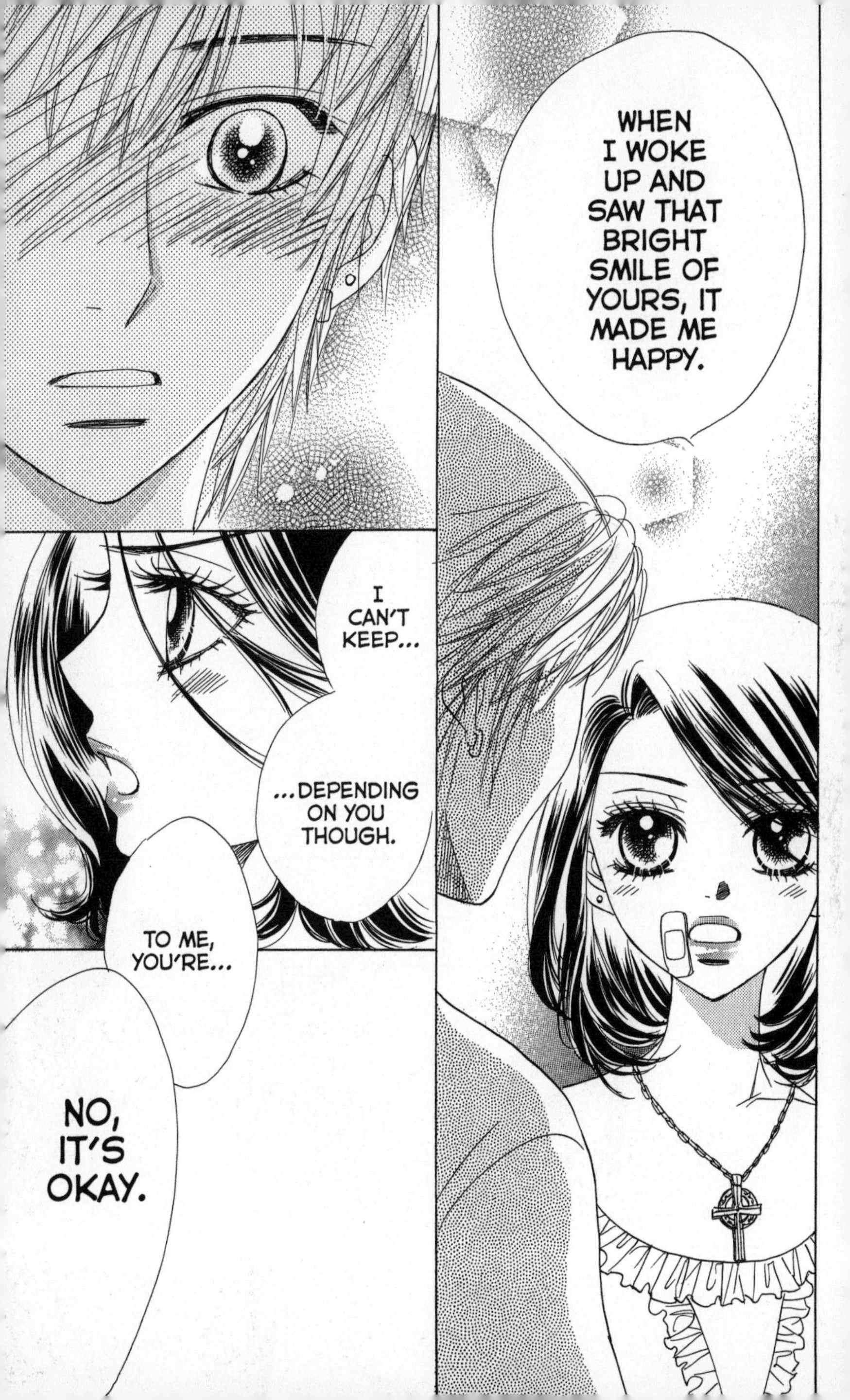
WHEN I WOKE UP AND SAW THAT BRIGHT SMILE OF YOURS, IT MADE ME HAPPY.
I CAN'T KEEP...
...DEPENDING ON YOU THOUGH.
TO ME, YOU'RE...
NO, IT'S OKAY.

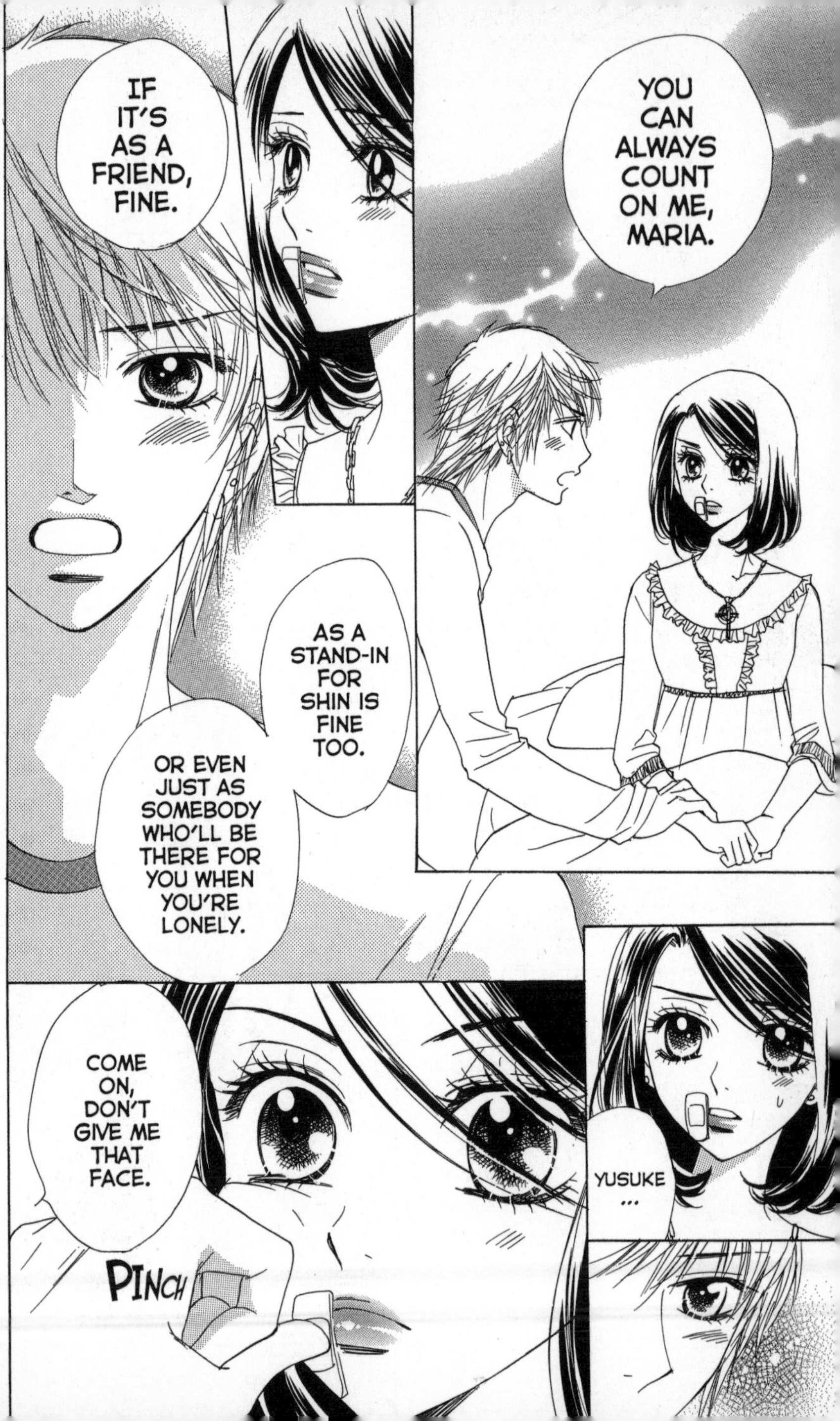
YOU CAN ALWAYS COUNT ON ME, MARIA.
IF IT'S AS A FRIEND, FINE.
AS A STAND-IN FOR SHIN IS FINE TOO.
OR EVEN JUST AS SOMEBODY WHO'LL BE THERE FOR YOU WHEN YOU'RE LONELY.
YUSUKE ...
COME ON, DON'T GIVE ME THAT FACE.
PINCH

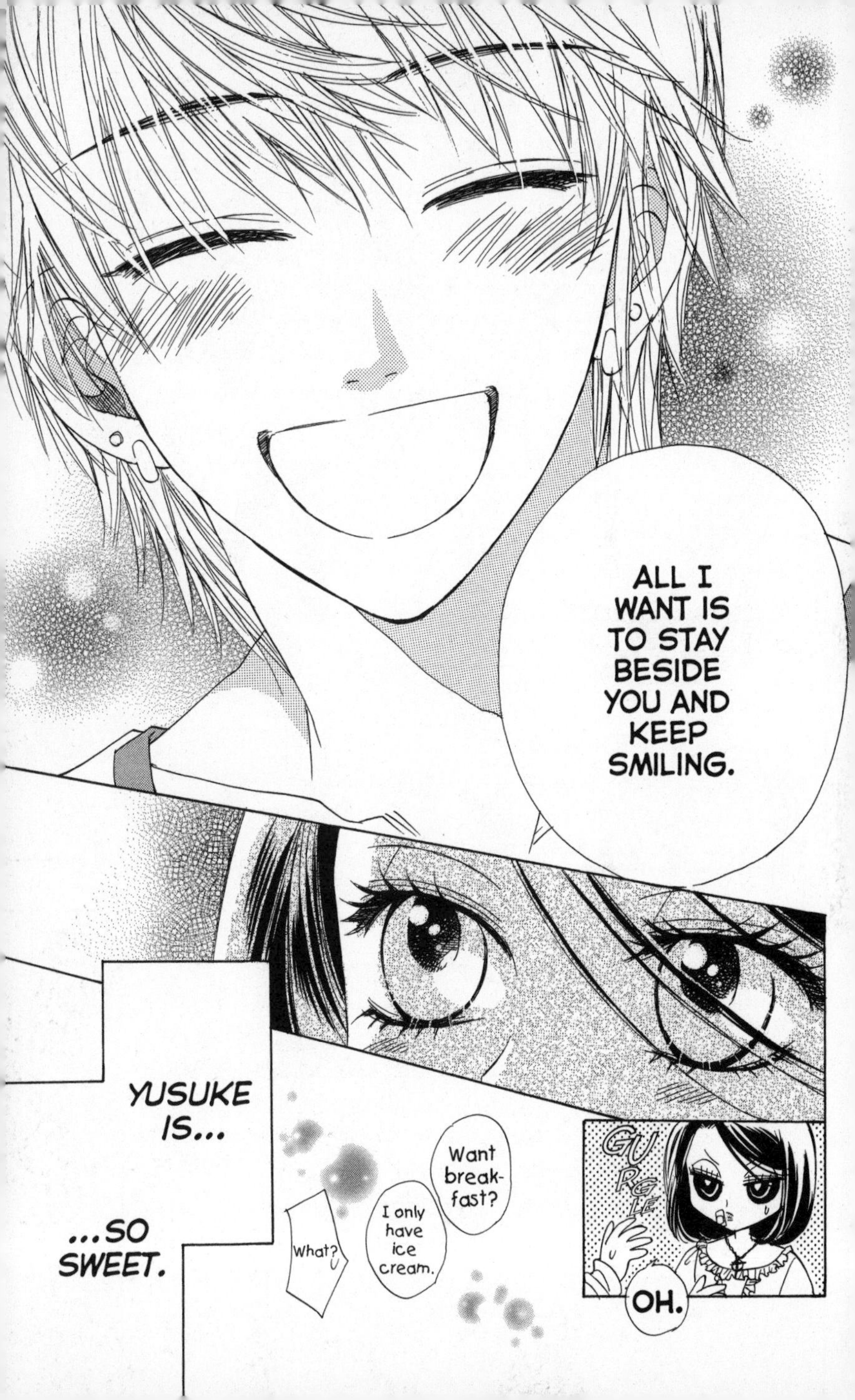
ALL I WANT IS TO STAY BESIDE YOU AND KEEP SMILING.
YUSUKE IS...
...SO SWEET.
GURGLE
OH.
Want breakfast?
I only have ice cream.
What?

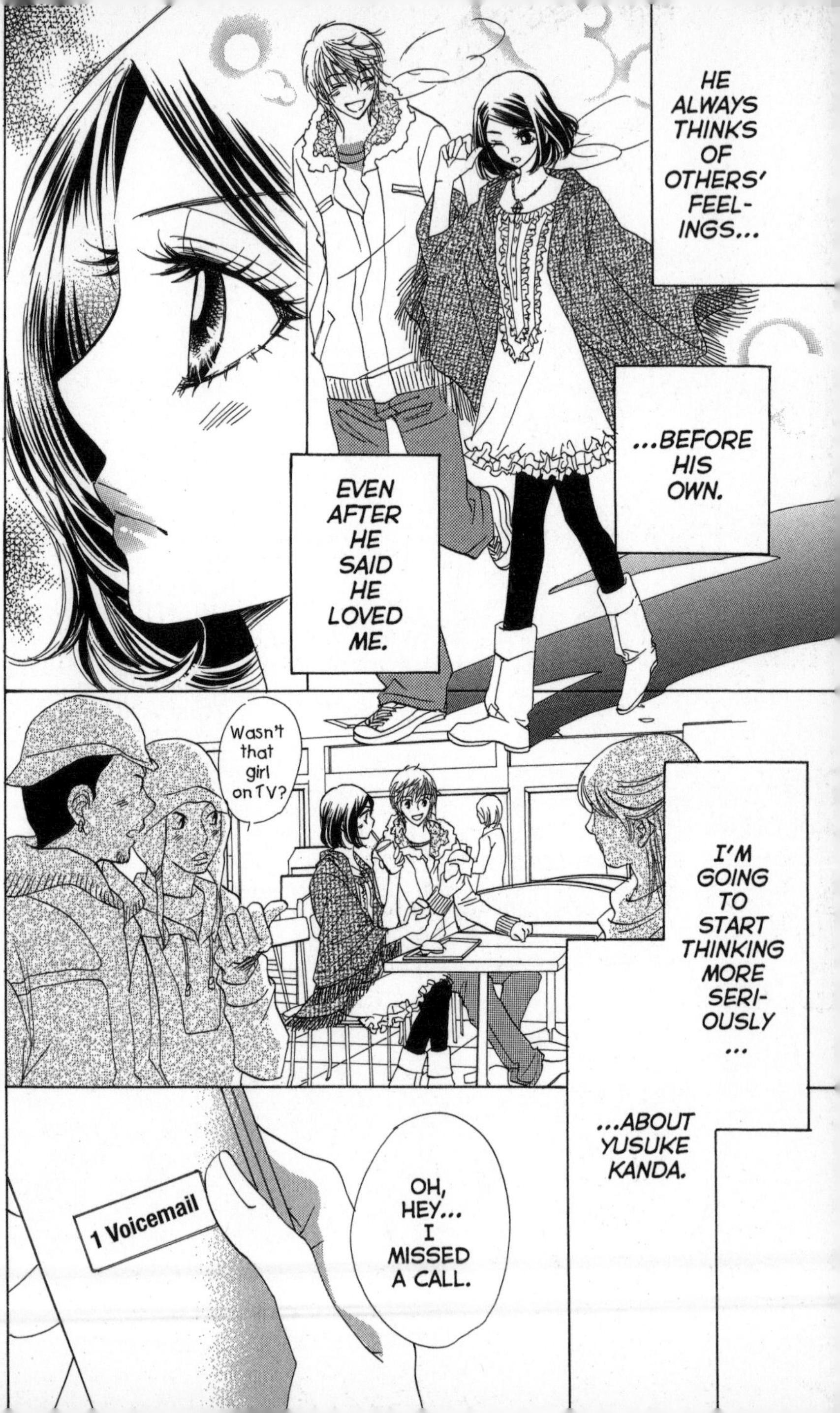
HE ALWAYS THINKS OF OTHERS' FEEL- INGS...
...BEFORE HIS OWN.
EVEN AFTER HE SAID HE LOVED ME.
I'M GOING TO START THINKING MORE SERI- OUSLY ...
Wasn't that girl on TV?
...ABOUT YUSUKE KANDA.
OH, HEY... I MISSED A CALL.
1 Voicemail

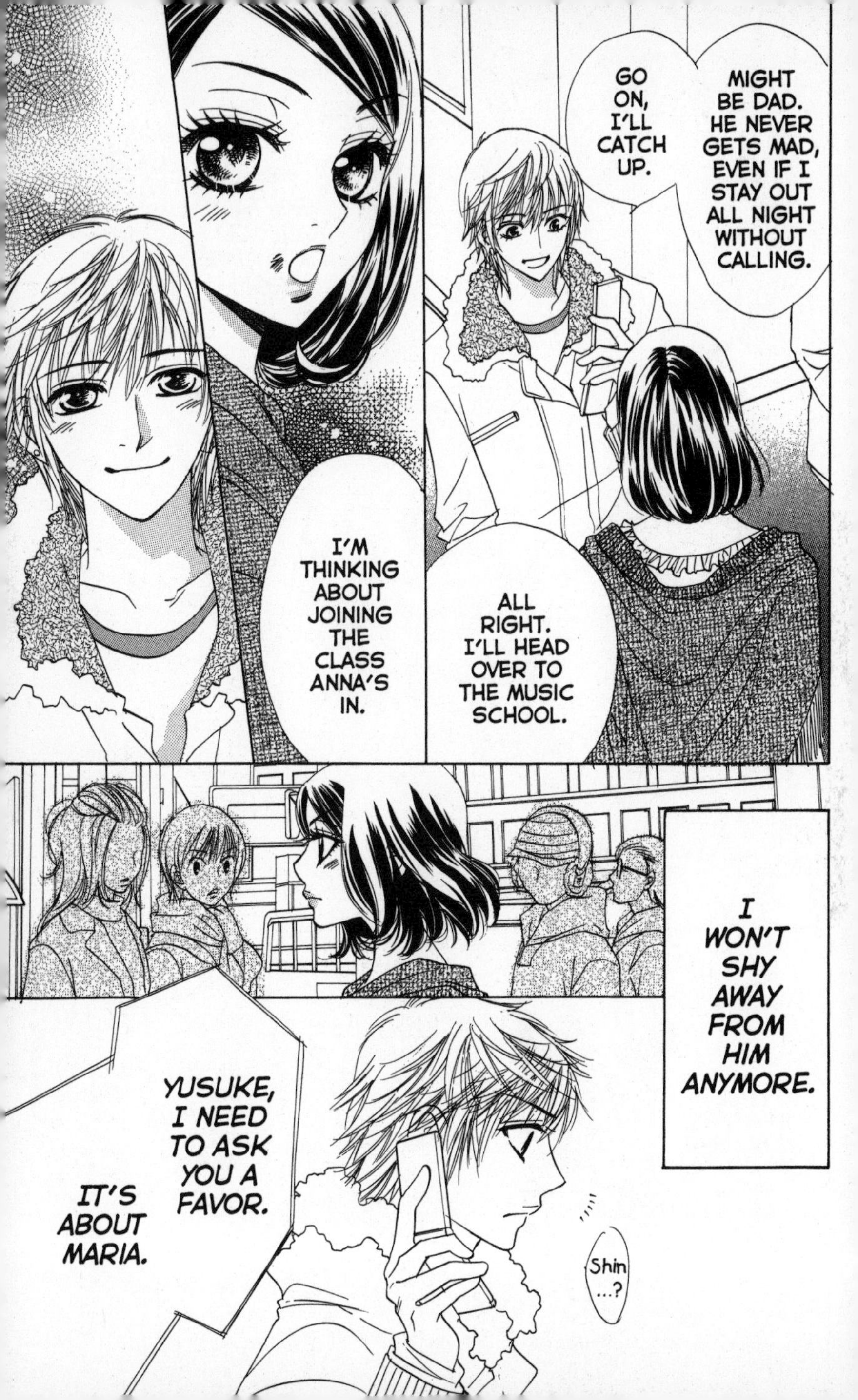
MIGHT BE DAD. HE NEVER GETS MAD, EVEN IF I STAY OUT ALL NIGHT WITHOUT CALLING.
GO ON, I'LL CATCH UP.
ALL RIGHT. I'LL HEAD OVER TO THE MUSIC SCHOOL.
I'M THINKING ABOUT JOINING THE CLASS ANNA'S IN.
I WON'T SHY AWAY FROM HIM ANYMORE.
Shin ...?
YUSUKE, I NEED TO ASK YOU A FAVOR.
IT'S ABOUT MARIA.

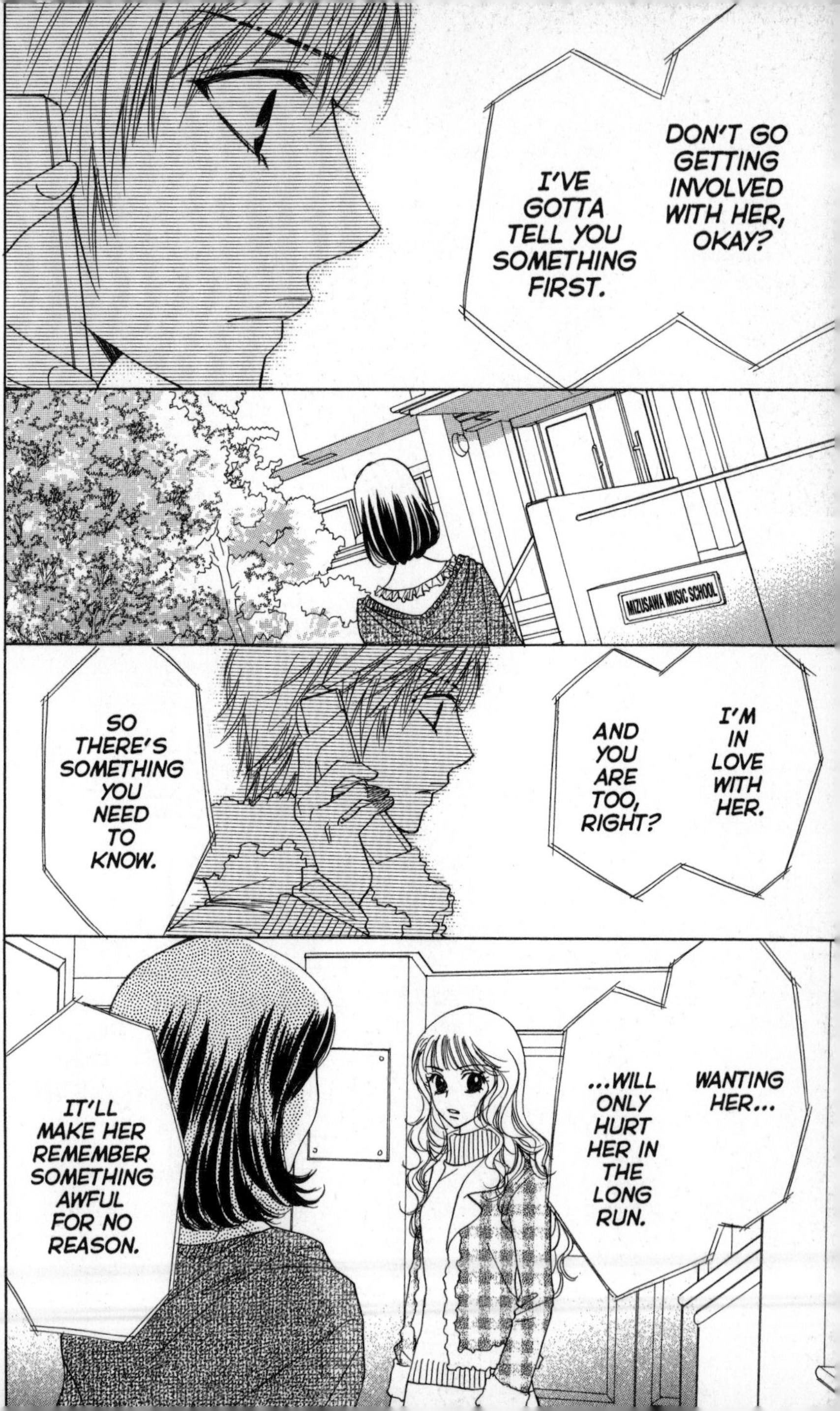
DON'T GO GETTING INVOLVED WITH HER, OKAY?
I'VE GOTTA TELL YOU SOMETHING FIRST.
MIZUSAWA MUSIC SCHOOL
I'M IN LOVE WITH HER.
AND YOU ARE TOO, RIGHT?
SO THERE'S SOMETHING YOU NEED TO KNOW.
WANTING HER...
...WILL ONLY HURT HER IN THE LONG RUN.
IT'LL MAKE HER REMEMBER SOMETHING AWFUL FOR NO REASON.

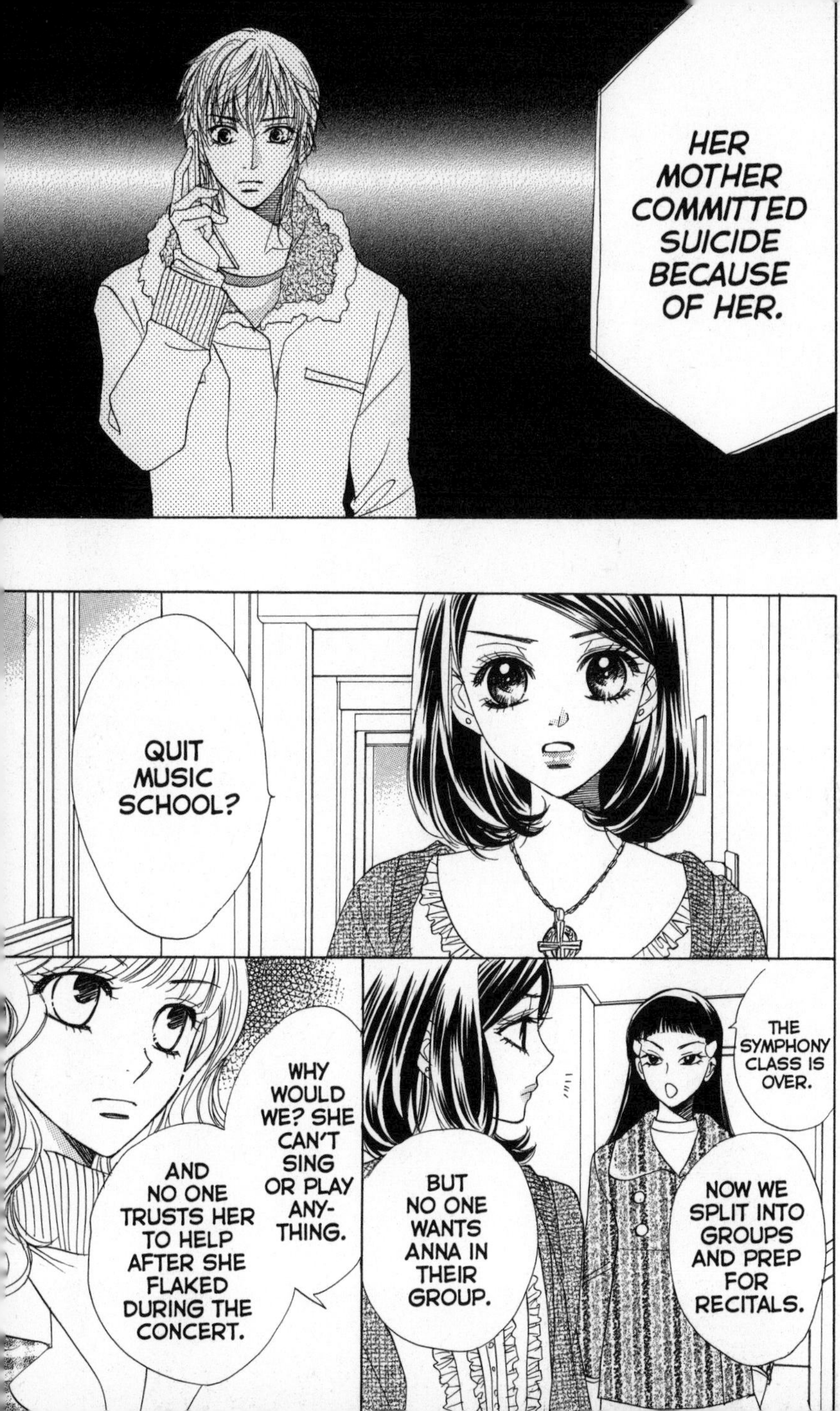
HER MOTHER COMMITTED SUICIDE BECAUSE OF HER.
QUIT MUSIC SCHOOL?
THE SYMPHONY CLASS IS OVER.
NOW WE SPLIT INTO GROUPS AND PREP FOR RECITALS.
BUT NO ONE WANTS ANNA IN THEIR GROUP.
WHY WOULD WE? SHE CAN'T SING OR PLAY ANYTHING.
AND NO ONE TRUSTS HER TO HELP AFTER SHE FLAKED DURING THE CONCERT.

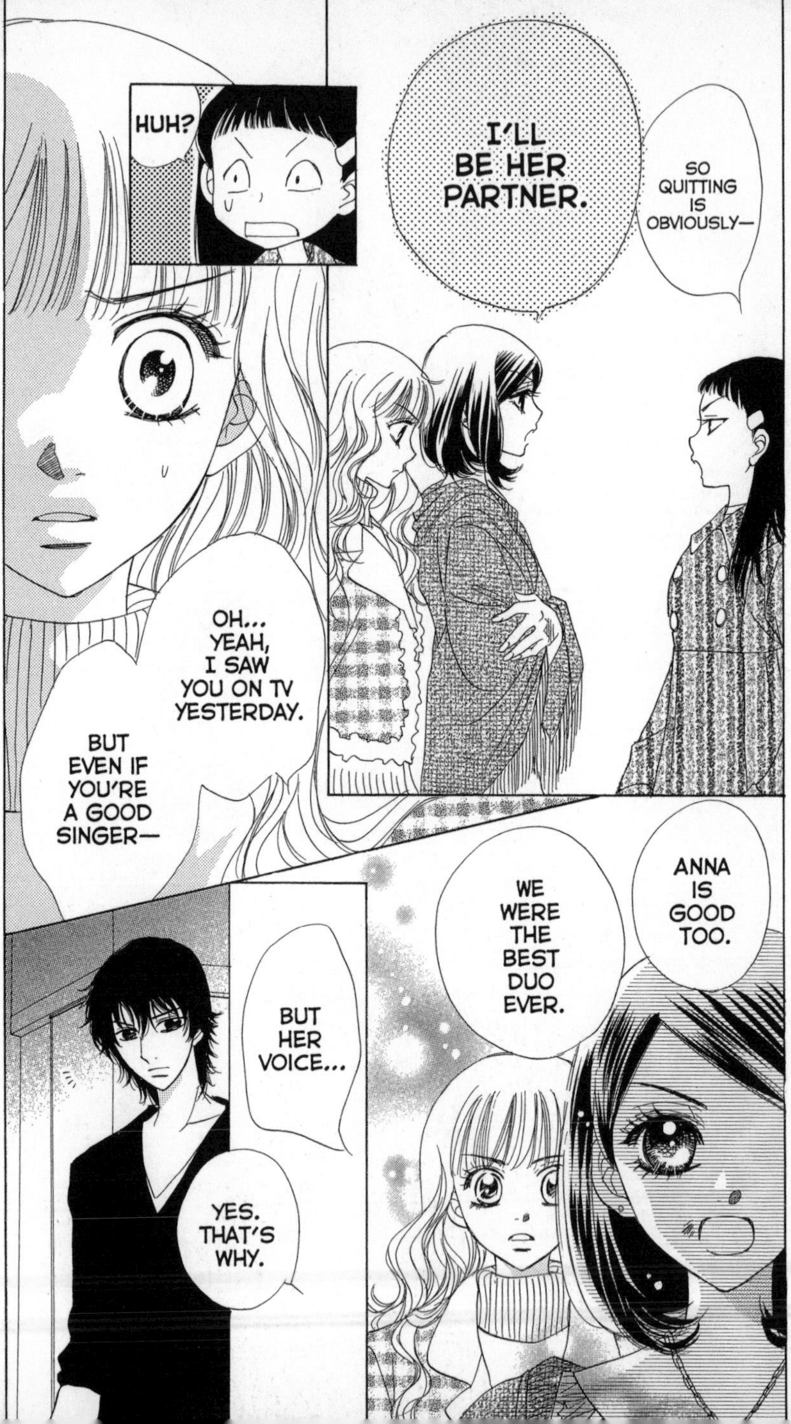
SO QUITTING IS OBVIOUSLY—
I'LL BE HER PARTNER.
HUH?
OH... YEAH, I SAW YOU ON TV YESTERDAY.
BUT EVEN IF YOU'RE A GOOD SINGER—
ANNA IS GOOD TOO.
WE WERE THE BEST DUO EVER.
BUT HER VOICE...
YES. THAT'S WHY.

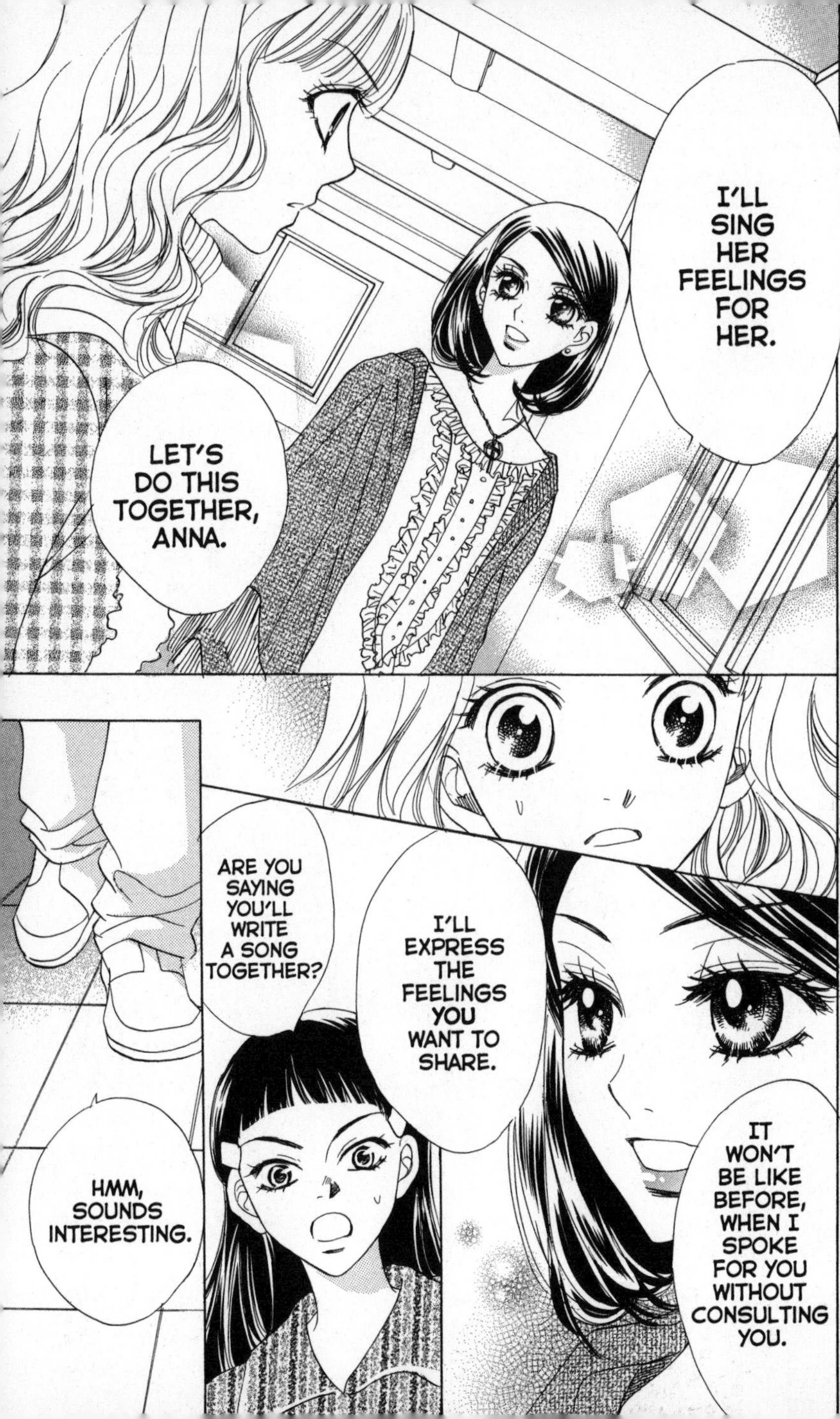
I'LL SING HER FEELINGS FOR HER.
LET'S DO THIS TOGETHER, ANNA.
I'LL EXPRESS THE FEELINGS YOU WANT TO SHARE.
IT WON'T BE LIKE BEFORE, WHEN I SPOKE FOR YOU WITHOUT CONSULTING YOU.
ARE YOU SAYING YOU'LL WRITE A SONG TOGETHER?
HMM, SOUNDS INTERESTING.

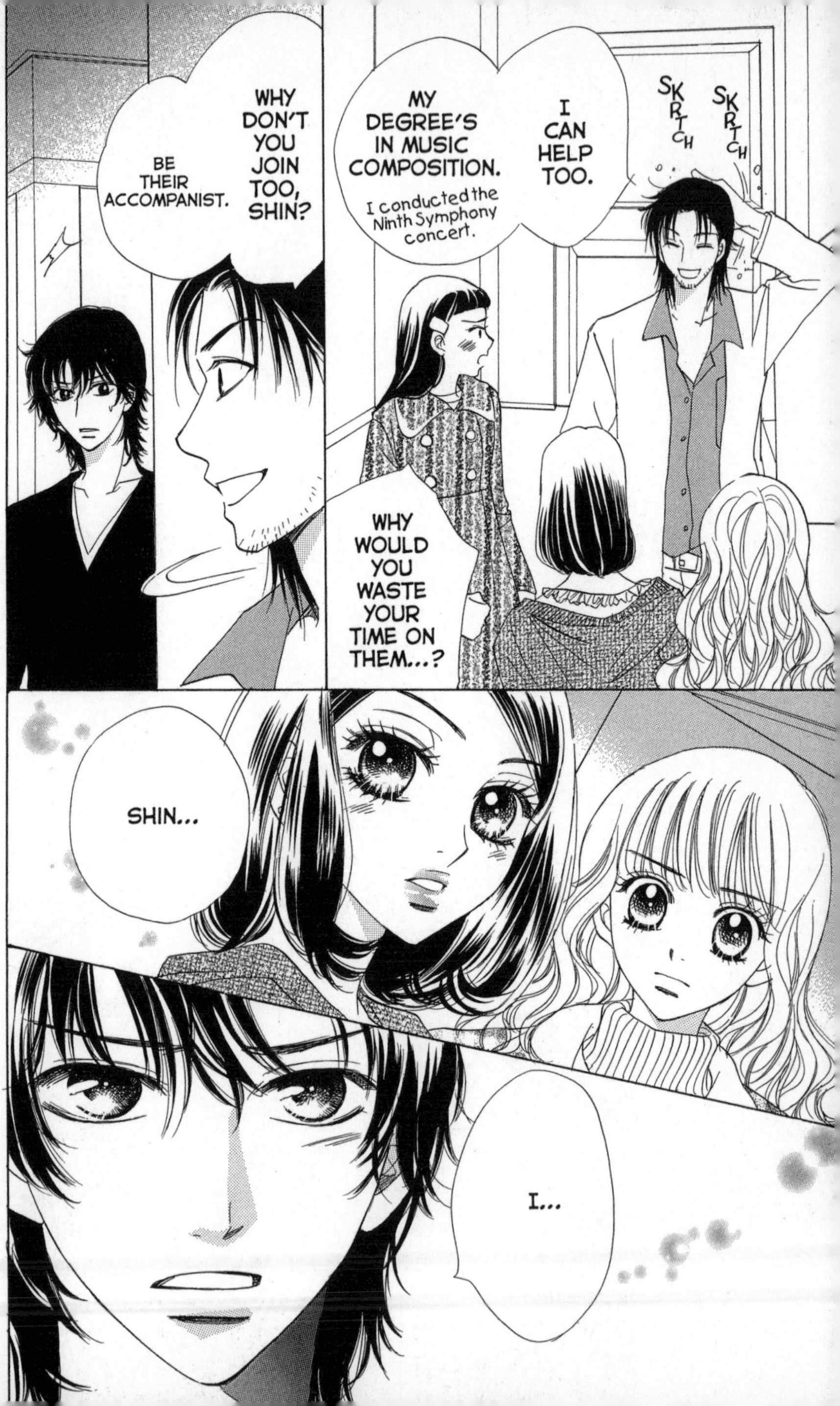
SKRTCH SKRTCH
I CAN HELP TOO.
MY DEGREE'S IN MUSIC COMPOSITION.
I conducted the Ninth Symphony concert.
WHY WOULD YOU WASTE YOUR TIME ON THEM...?
WHY DON'T YOU JOIN TOO, SHIN?
BE THEIR ACCOMPANIST.
SHIN...
I...

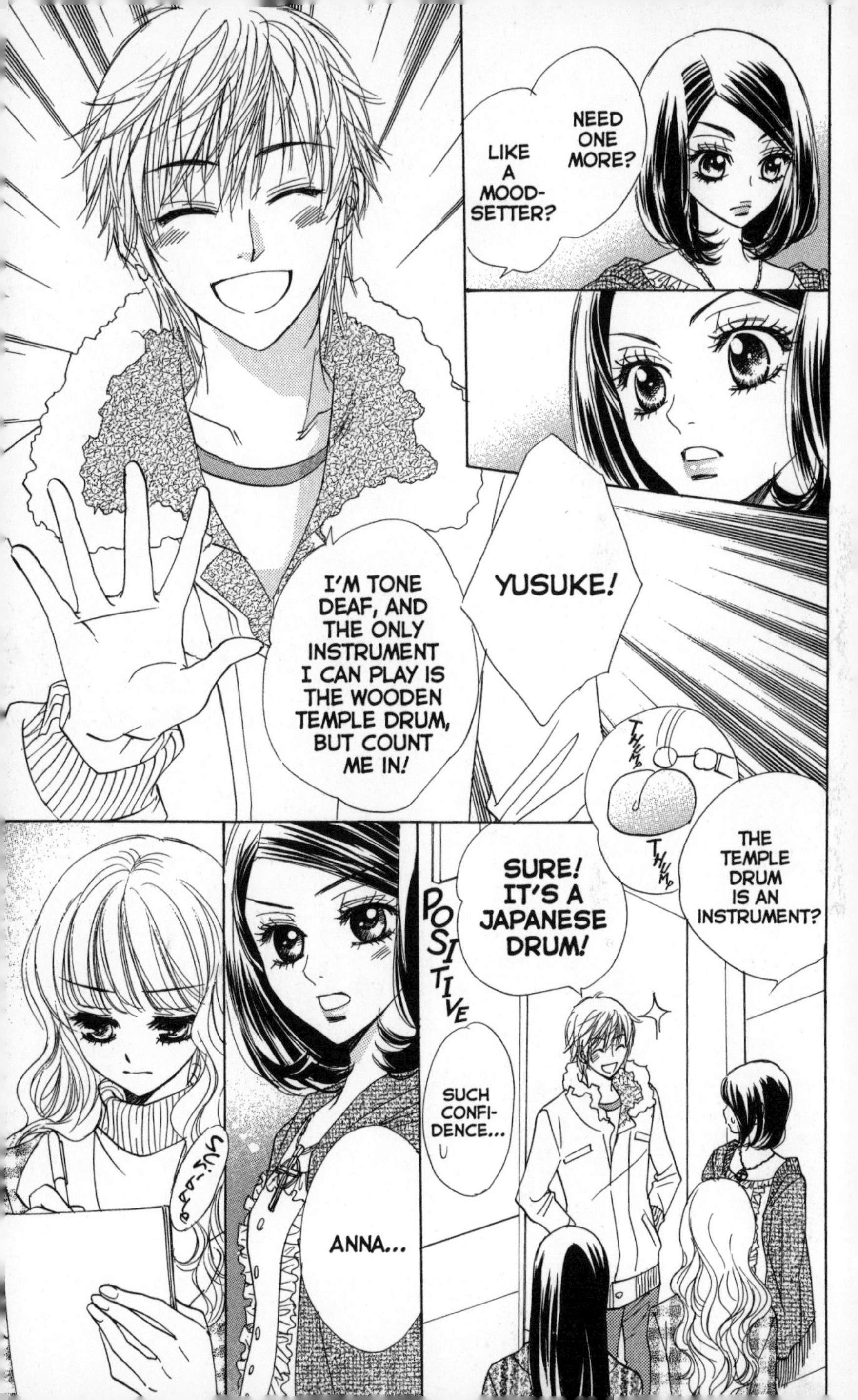
NEED ONE MORE?
LIKE A MOOD-SETTER?
YUSUKE!
I'M TONE DEAF, AND THE ONLY INSTRUMENT I CAN PLAY IS THE WOODEN TEMPLE DRUM, BUT COUNT ME IN!
THE TEMPLE DRUM IS AN INSTRUMENT?
THUMP
THUMP
SURE! IT'S A JAPANESE DRUM!
SUCH CONFIDENCE...
POSITIVE
ANNA...

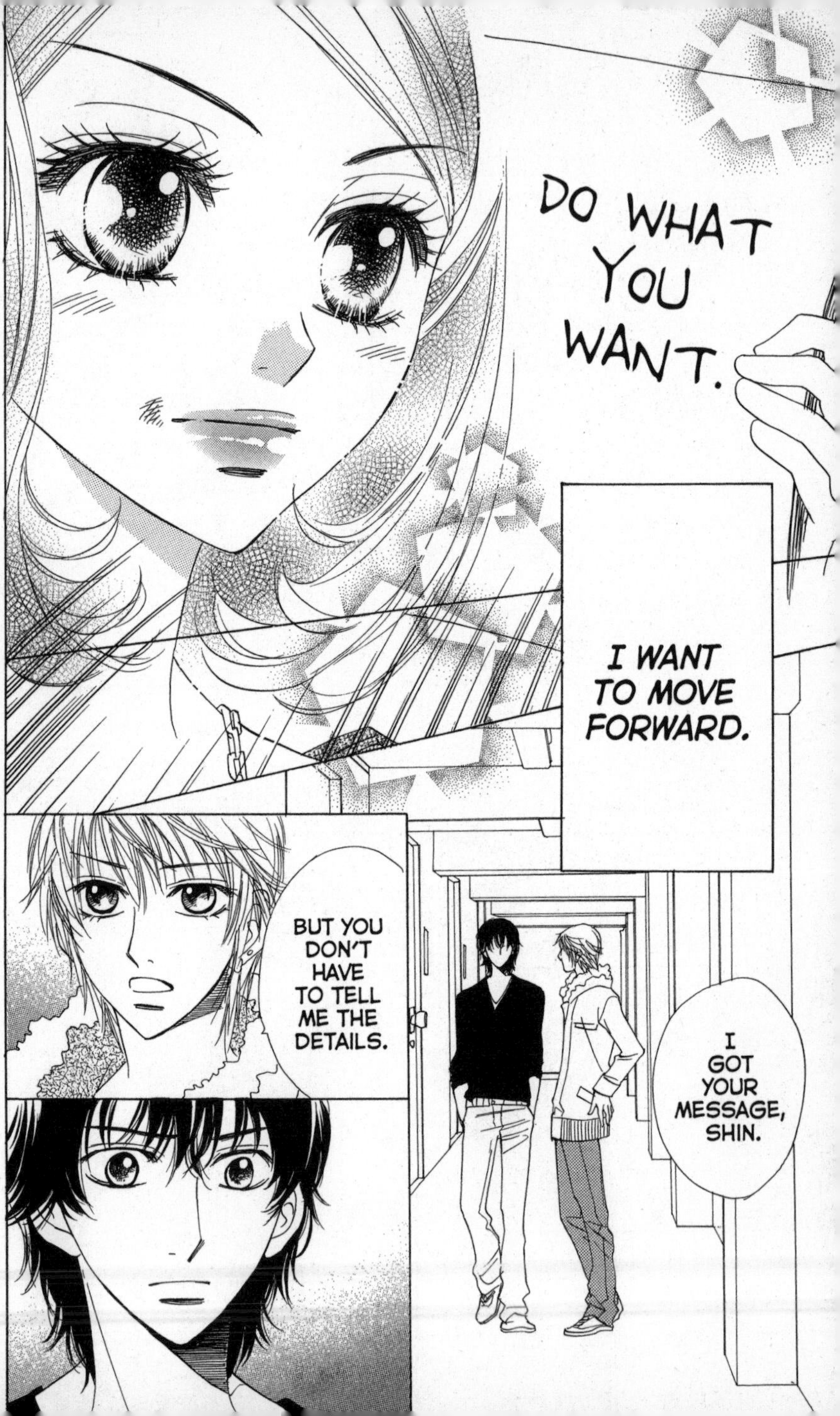
DO WHAT YOU WANT.
I WANT TO MOVE FORWARD.
I GOT YOUR MESSAGE, SHIN.
BUT YOU DON'T HAVE TO TELL ME THE DETAILS.

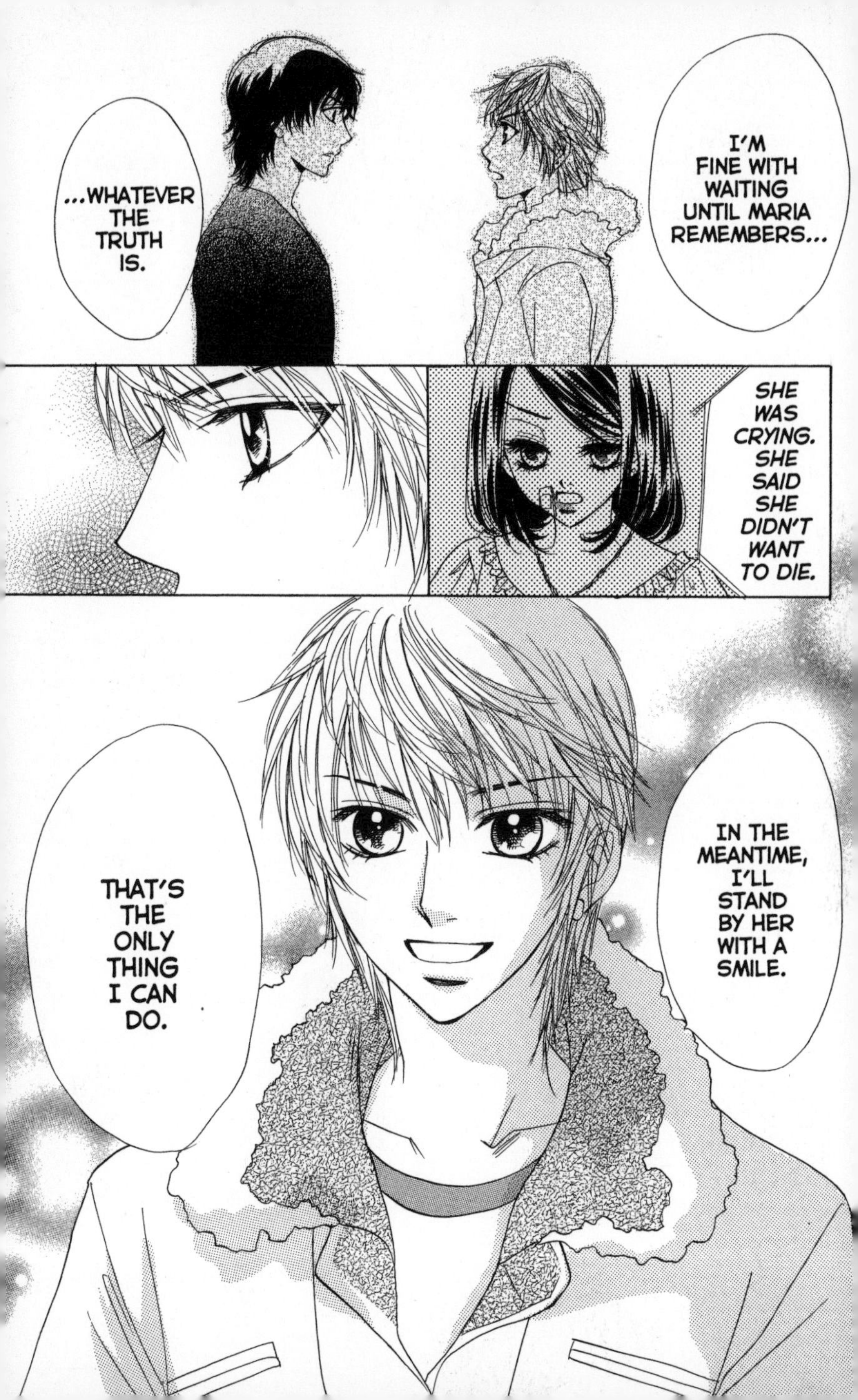
I'M FINE WITH WAITING UNTIL MARIA REMEMBERS...
...WHATEVER THE TRUTH IS.
SHE WAS CRYING. SHE SAID SHE DIDN'T WANT TO DIE.
IN THE MEANTIME, I'LL STAND BY HER WITH A SMILE.
THAT'S THE ONLY THING I CAN DO.

A Devil and
Her Love Song

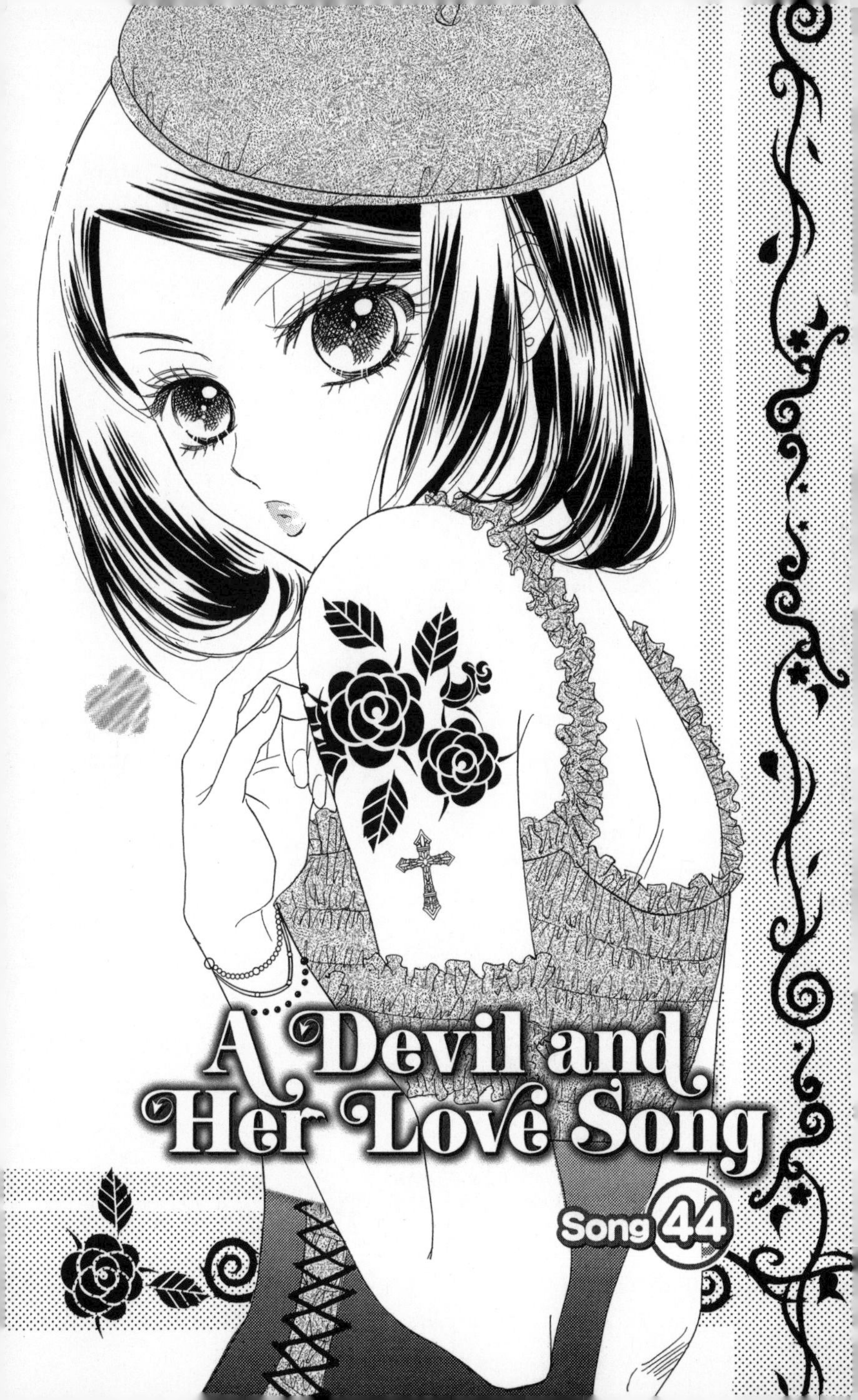
A Devil and Her Love Song
Song 44

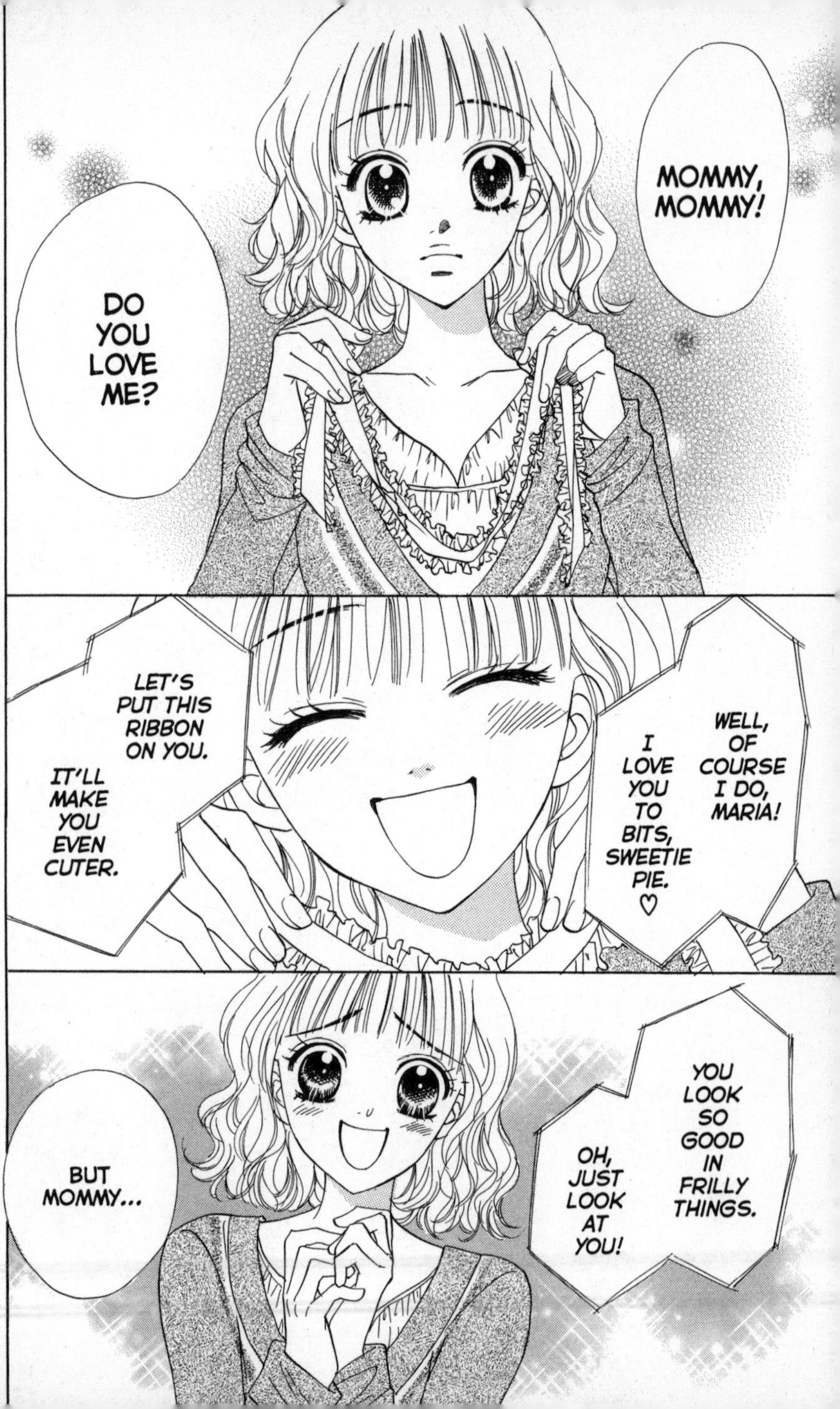
MOMMY, MOMMY!
DO YOU LOVE ME?
WELL, OF COURSE I DO, MARIA!
I LOVE YOU TO BITS, SWEETIE PIE. ♡
LET'S PUT THIS RIBBON ON YOU.
IT'LL MAKE YOU EVEN CUTER.
YOU LOOK SO GOOD IN FRILLY THINGS.
OH, JUST LOOK AT YOU!
BUT MOMMY...

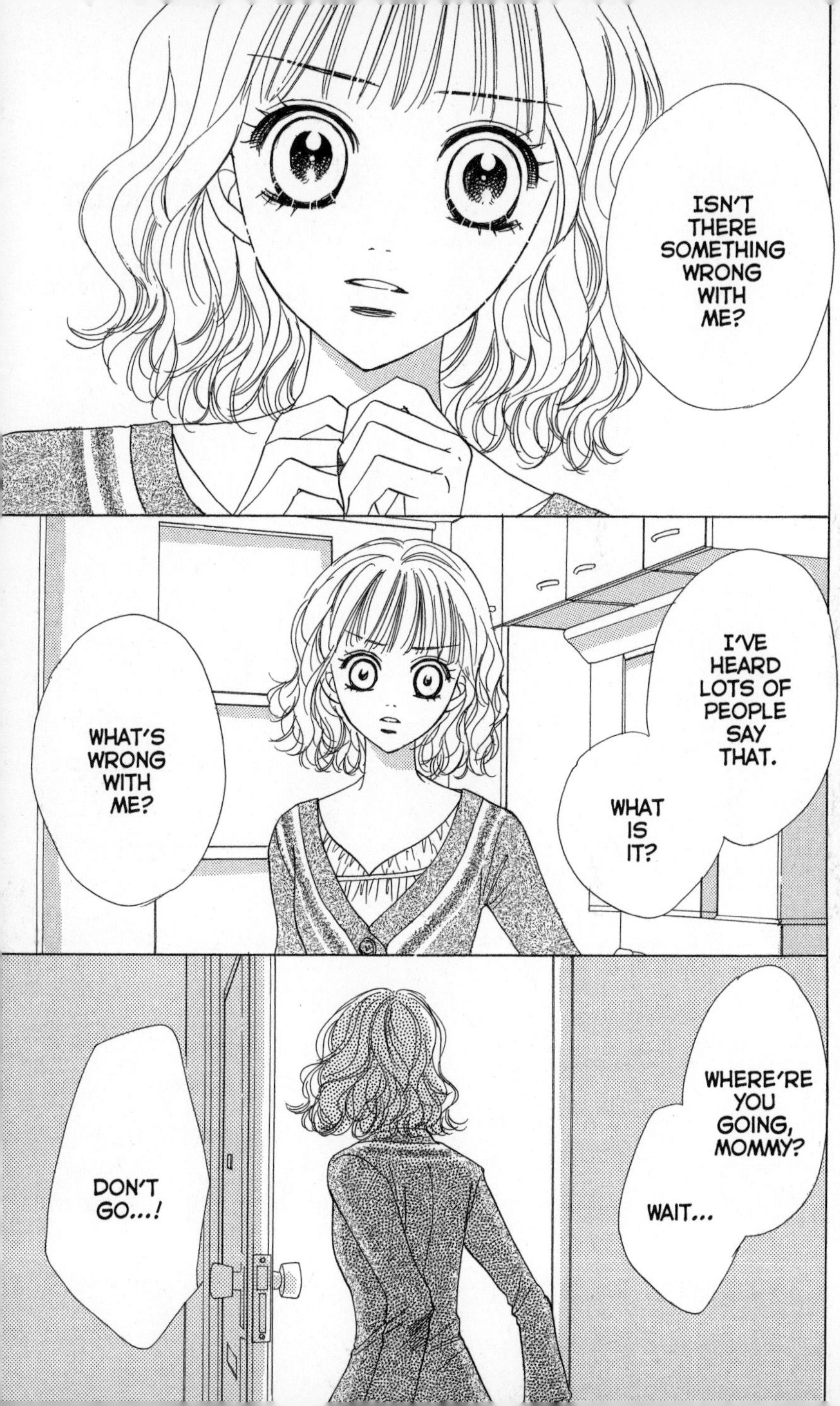
ISN'T THERE SOMETHING WRONG WITH ME?
I'VE HEARD LOTS OF PEOPLE SAY THAT.
WHAT IS IT?
WHAT'S WRONG WITH ME?
WHERE'RE YOU GOING, MOMMY?
WAIT...
DON'T GO...!

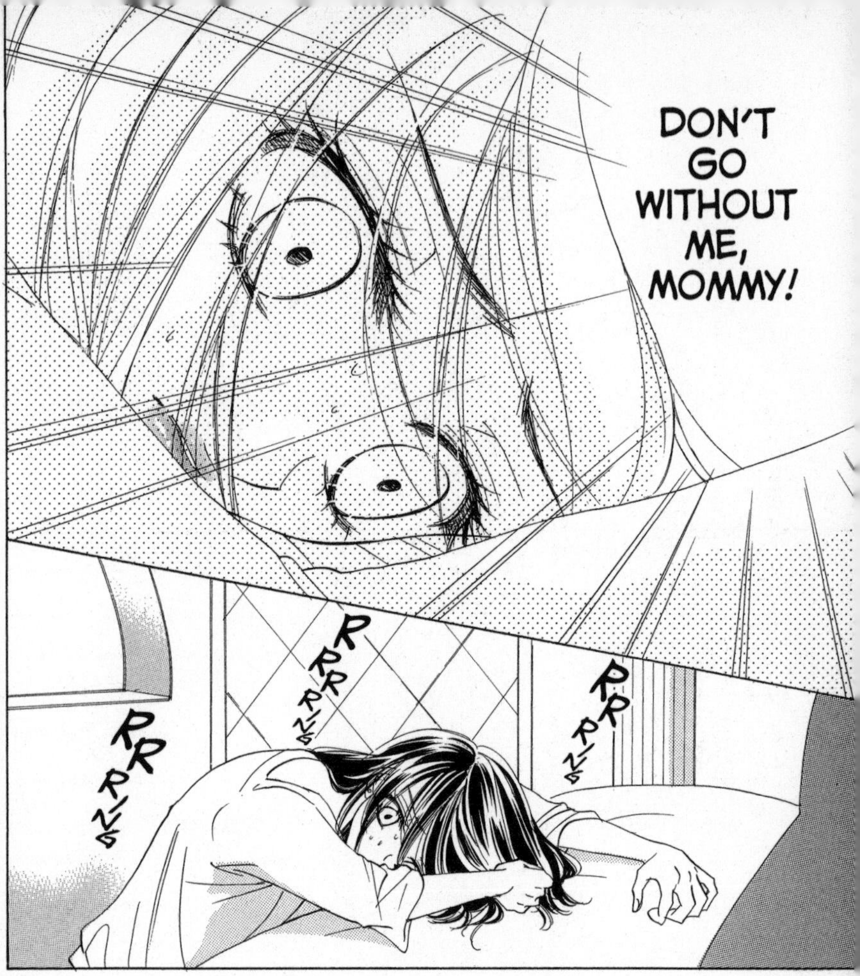
DON'T GO WITHOUT ME, MOMMY!
RRRING
RRRING
RRRING

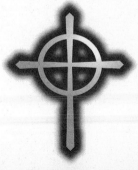

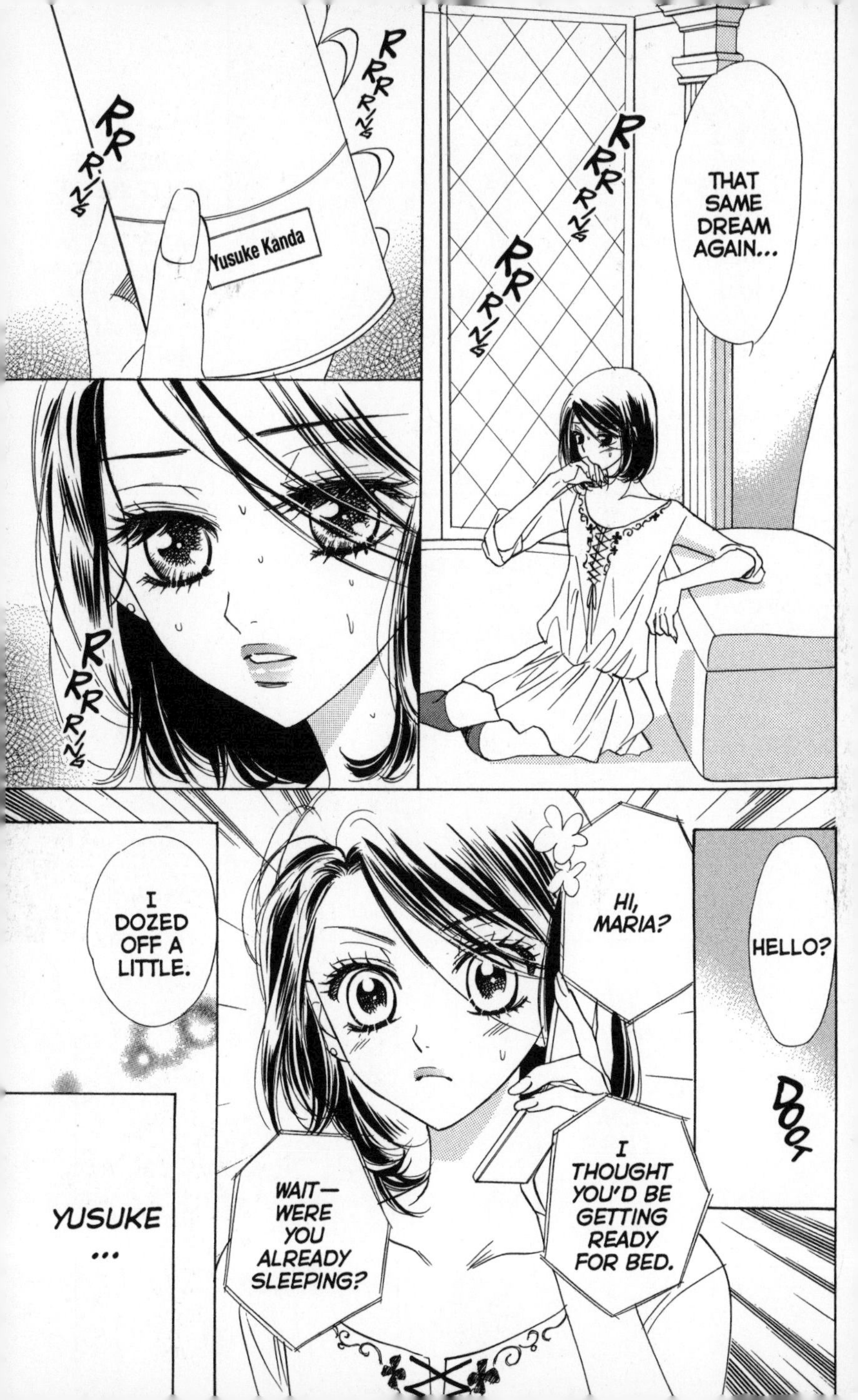
THAT SAME DREAM AGAIN...
RRRRING
RRRING
RRRRING
RRRING
Yusuke Kanda
RRRRING
HELLO?
DOOT
HI, MARIA?
I THOUGHT YOU'D BE GETTING READY FOR BED.
WAIT—WERE YOU ALREADY SLEEPING?
I DOZED OFF A LITTLE.
YUSUKE...

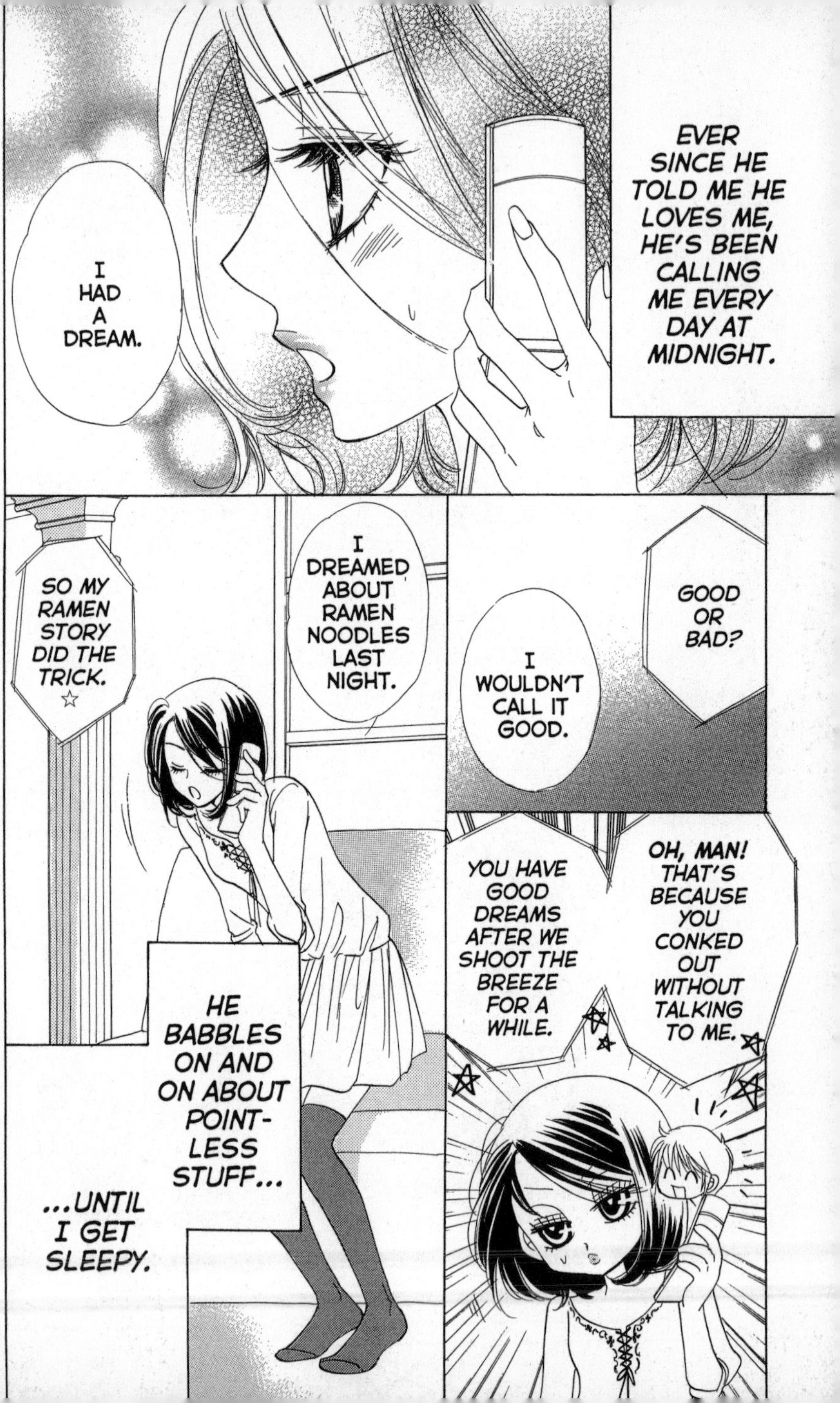
EVER SINCE HE TOLD ME HE LOVES ME, HE'S BEEN CALLING ME EVERY DAY AT MIDNIGHT.
I HAD A DREAM.
GOOD OR BAD?
I WOULDN'T CALL IT GOOD.
OH, MAN! THAT'S BECAUSE YOU CONKED OUT WITHOUT TALKING TO ME.
YOU HAVE GOOD DREAMS AFTER WE SHOOT THE BREEZE FOR A WHILE.
I DREAMED ABOUT RAMEN NOODLES LAST NIGHT.
SO MY RAMEN STORY DID THE TRICK. ☆
HE BABBLES ON AND ON ABOUT POINT-LESS STUFF...
...UNTIL I GET SLEEPY.

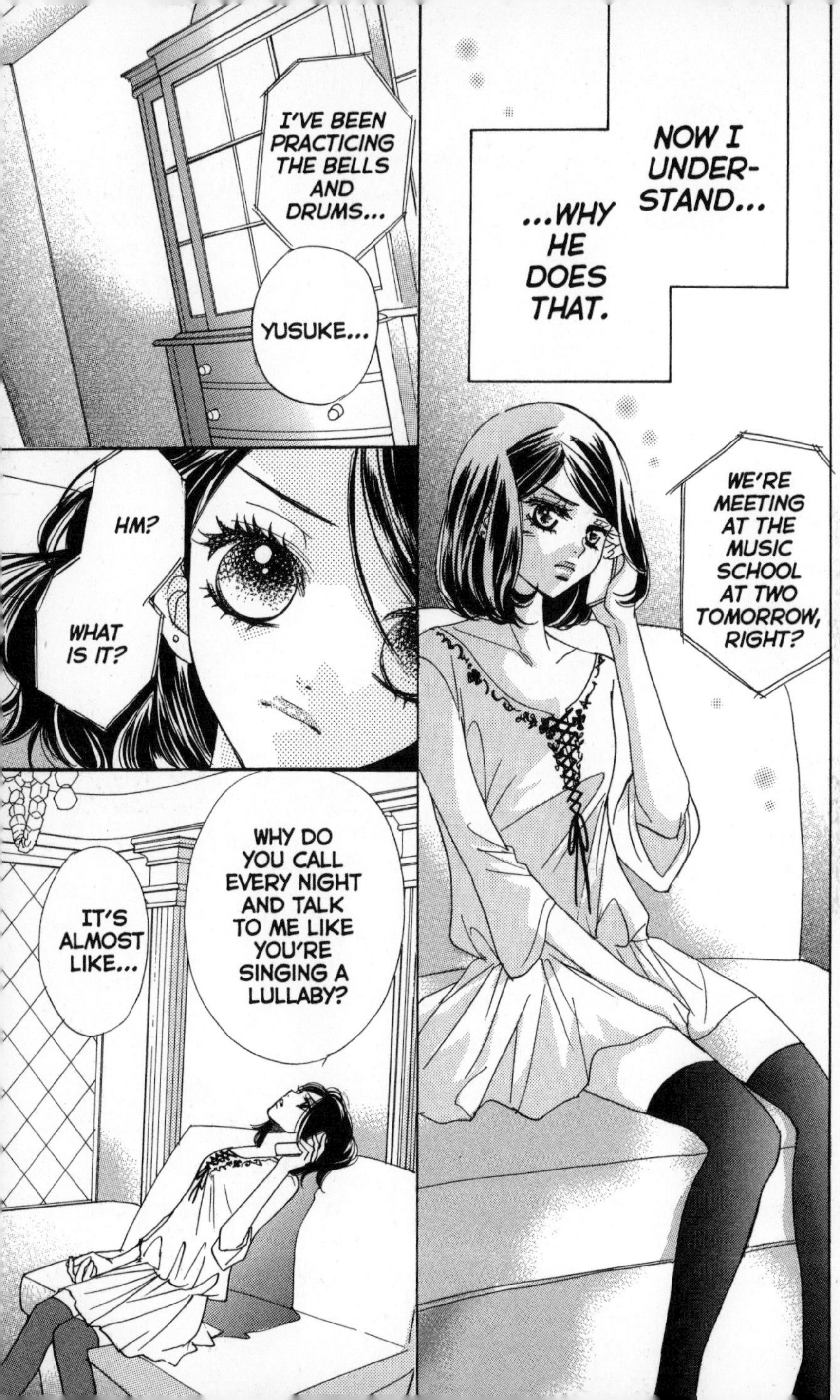
NOW I UNDER-STAND...
...WHY HE DOES THAT.
WE'RE MEETING AT THE MUSIC SCHOOL AT TWO TOMORROW, RIGHT?
I'VE BEEN PRACTICING THE BELLS AND DRUMS...
YUSUKE...
HM?
WHAT IS IT?
WHY DO YOU CALL EVERY NIGHT AND TALK TO ME LIKE YOU'RE SINGING A LULLABY?
IT'S ALMOST LIKE...

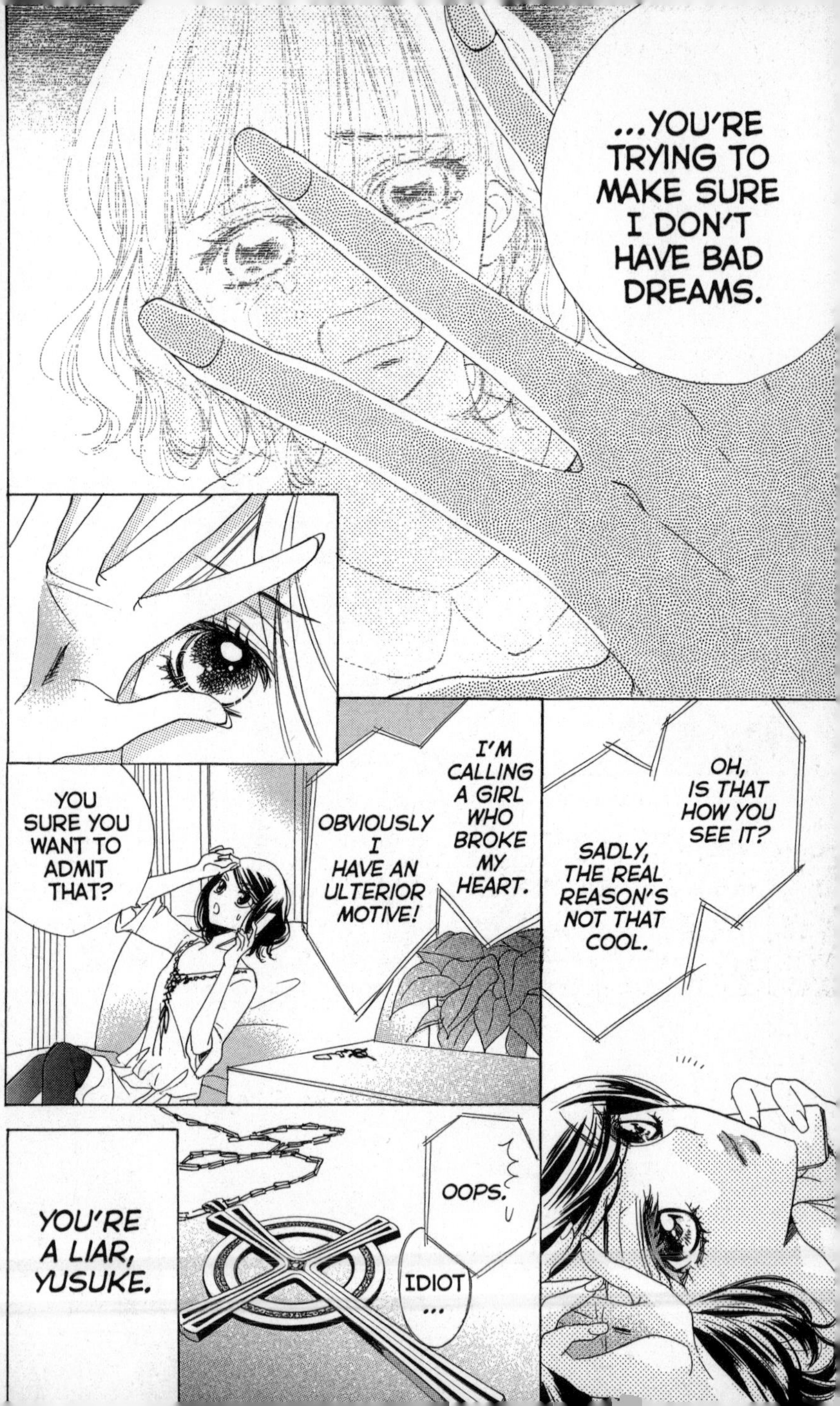
...YOU'RE TRYING TO MAKE SURE I DON'T HAVE BAD DREAMS.
OH, IS THAT HOW YOU SEE IT?
SADLY, THE REAL REASON'S NOT THAT COOL.
I'M CALLING A GIRL WHO BROKE MY HEART.
OBVIOUSLY I HAVE AN ULTERIOR MOTIVE!
YOU SURE YOU WANT TO ADMIT THAT?
OOPS.
IDIOT...
YOU'RE A LIAR, YUSUKE.

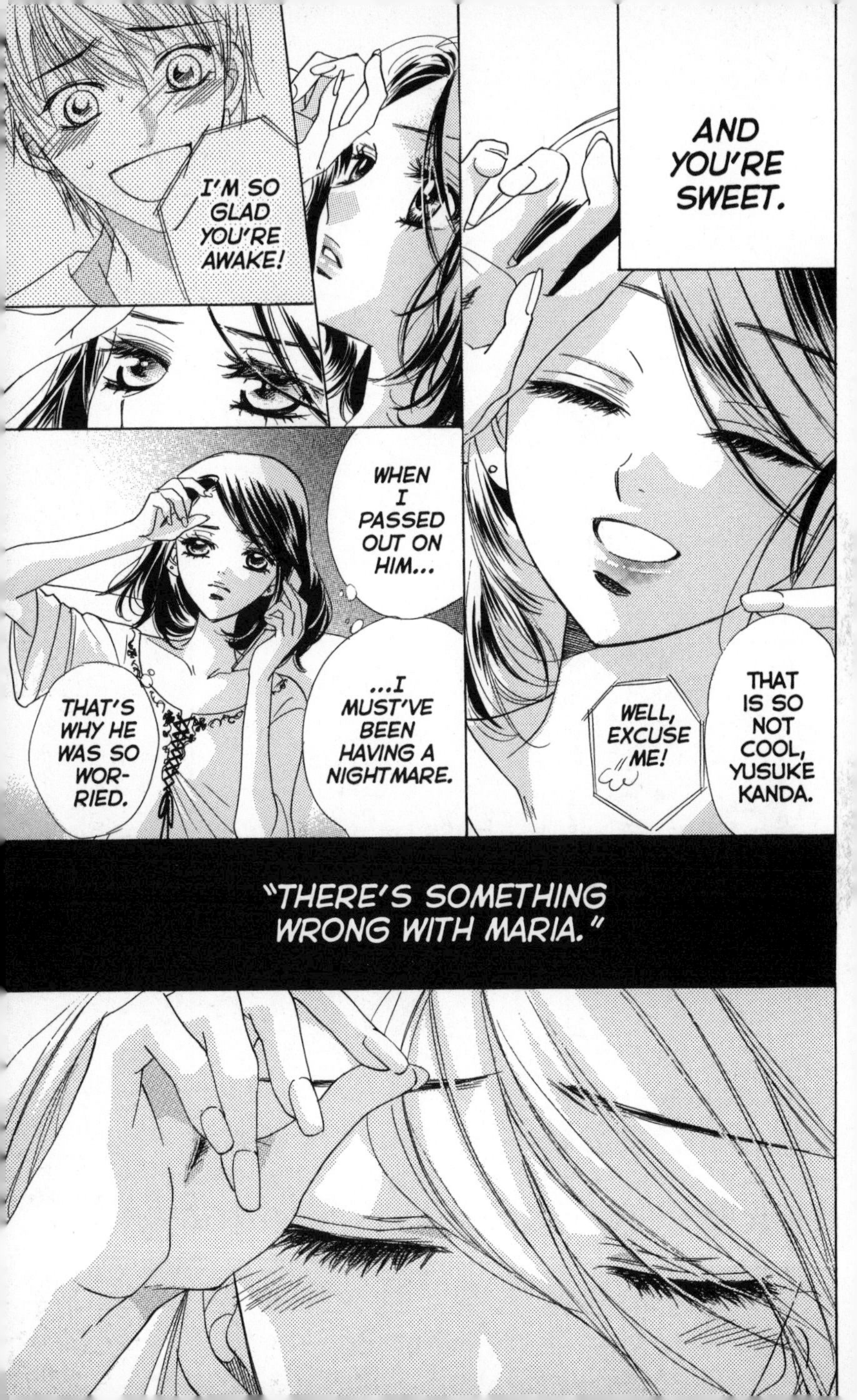
AND YOU'RE SWEET.
THAT IS SO NOT COOL, YUSUKE KANDA.
WELL, EXCUSE ME!
I'M SO GLAD YOU'RE AWAKE!
WHEN I PASSED OUT ON HIM...
...I MUST'VE BEEN HAVING A NIGHTMARE.
THAT'S WHY HE WAS SO WOR-RIED.
"THERE'S SOMETHING WRONG WITH MARIA."

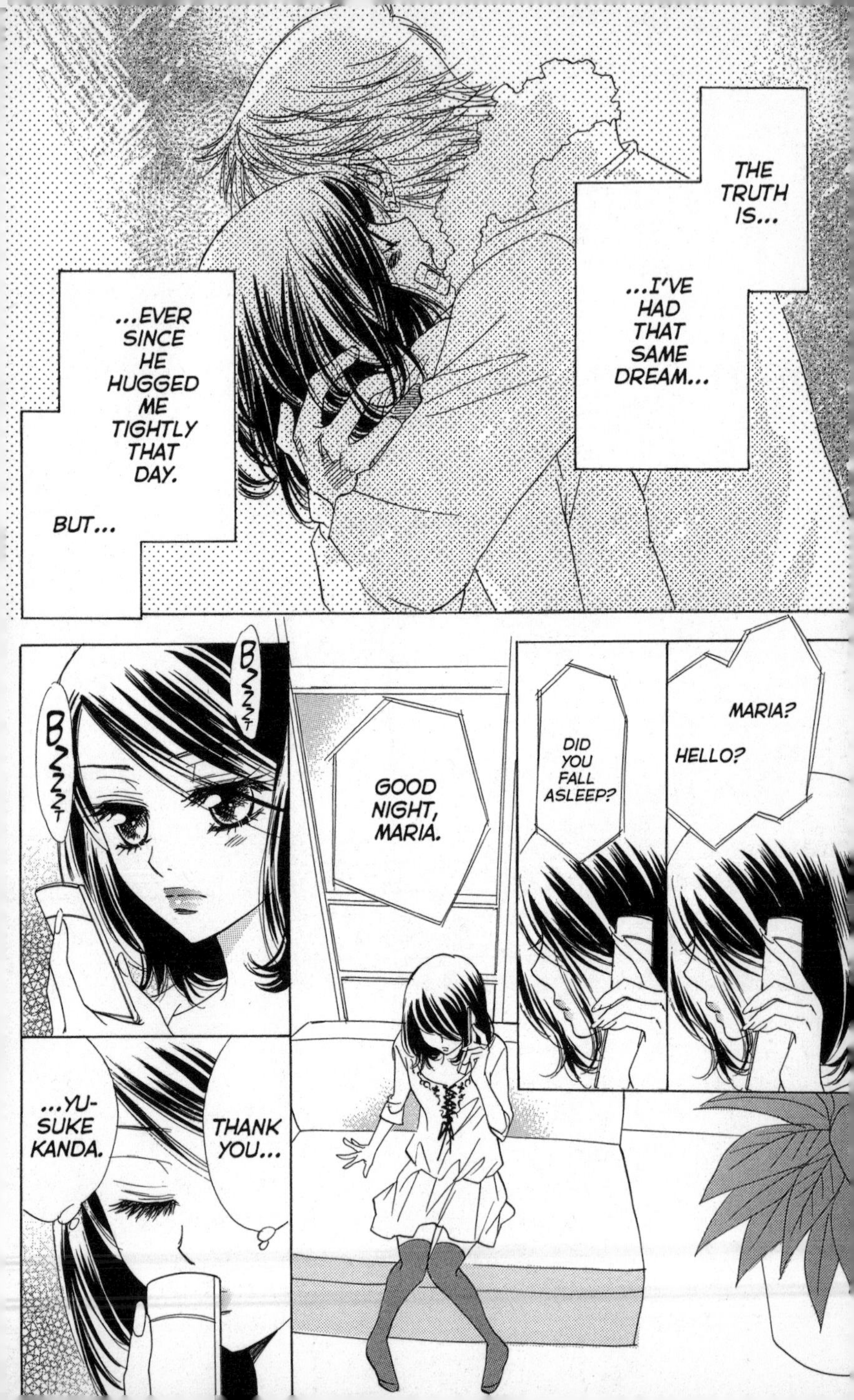
THE TRUTH IS...
...I'VE HAD THAT SAME DREAM...
...EVER SINCE HE HUGGED ME TIGHTLY THAT DAY.
BUT...
MARIA?
HELLO?
DID YOU FALL ASLEEP?
GOOD NIGHT, MARIA.
BZZZT
BZZZT
THANK YOU...
...YUSUKE KANDA.

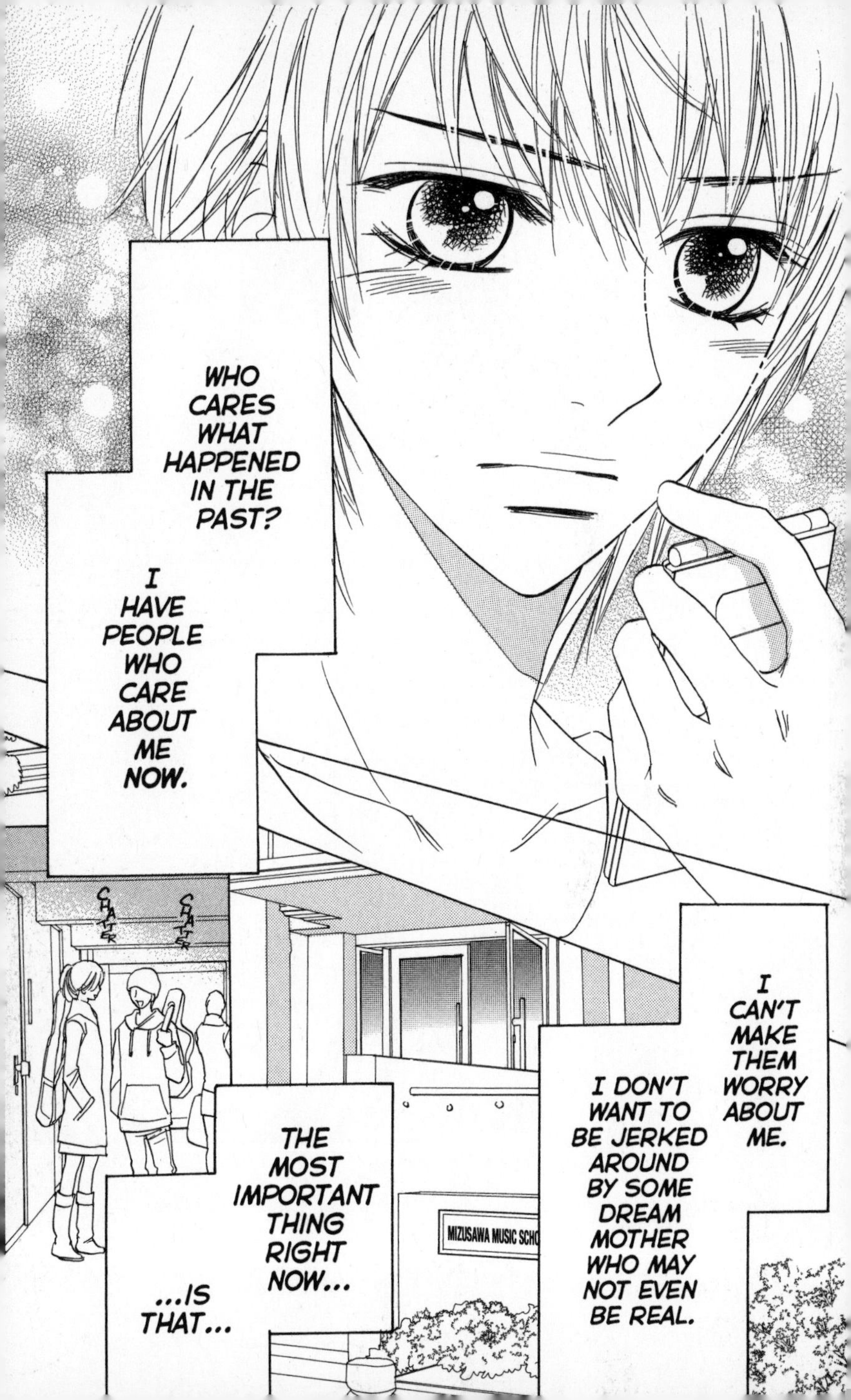
WHO CARES WHAT HAPPENED IN THE PAST?
I HAVE PEOPLE WHO CARE ABOUT ME NOW.
I CAN'T MAKE THEM WORRY ABOUT ME.
I DON'T WANT TO BE JERKED AROUND BY SOME DREAM MOTHER WHO MAY NOT EVEN BE REAL.
MIZUSAWA MUSIC SCHO
CHATTER
CHATTER
THE MOST IMPORTANT THING RIGHT NOW...
...IS THAT...

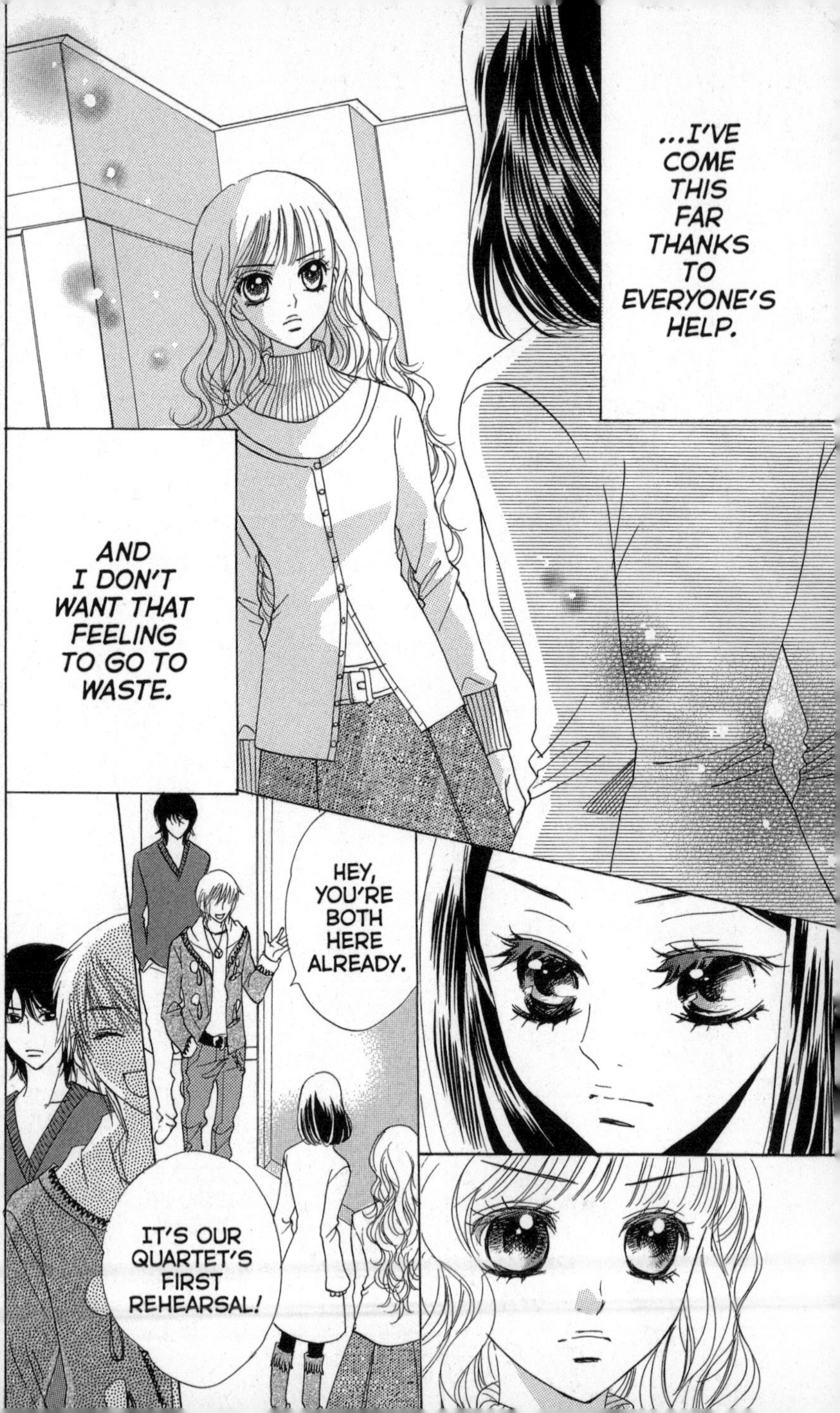
...I'VE COME THIS FAR THANKS TO EVERYONE'S HELP.
AND I DON'T WANT THAT FEELING TO GO TO WASTE.
HEY, YOU'RE BOTH HERE ALREADY.
IT'S OUR QUARTET'S FIRST REHEARSAL!

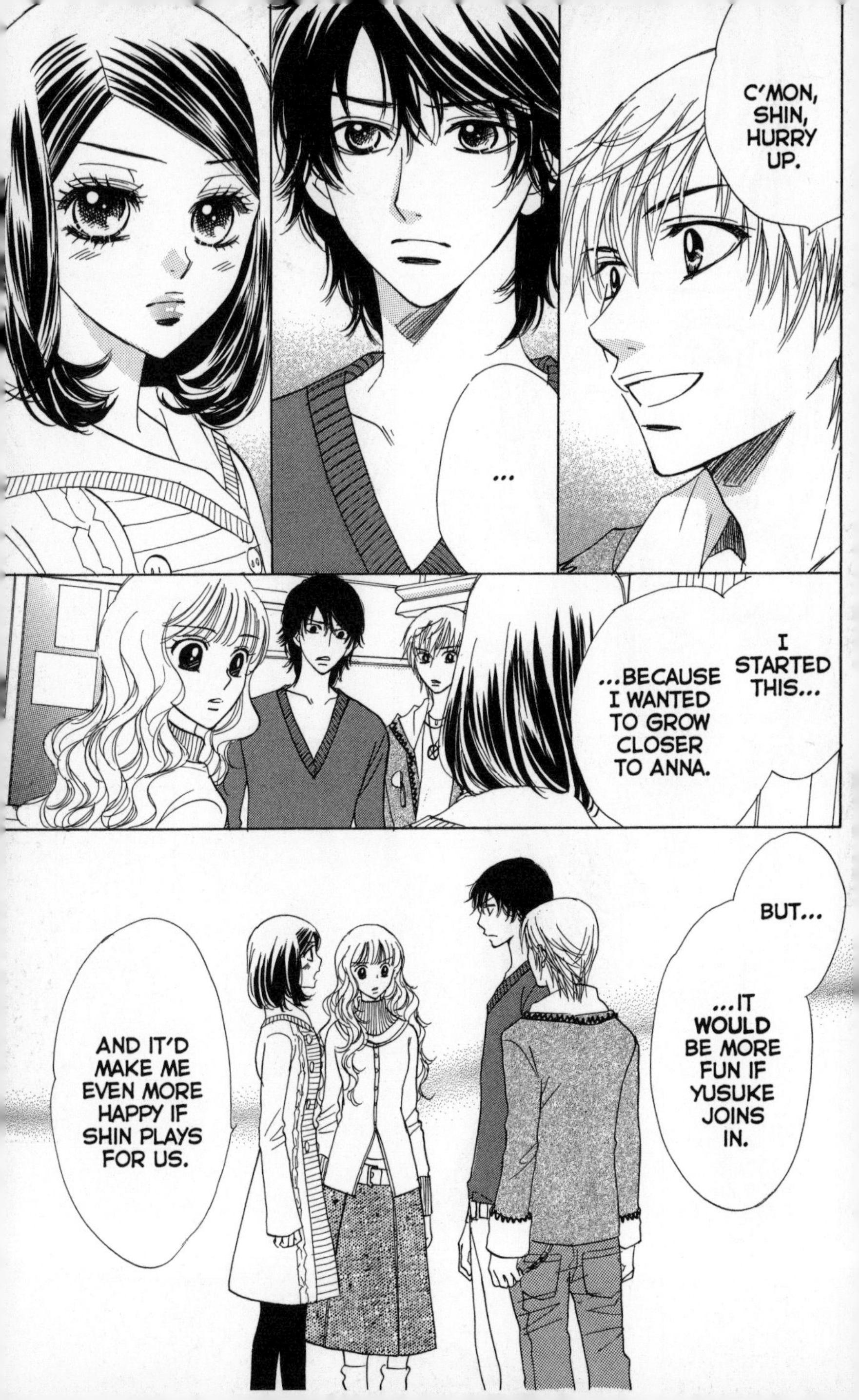
C'MON, SHIN, HURRY UP.
...
I STARTED THIS...
...BECAUSE I WANTED TO GROW CLOSER TO ANNA.
BUT...
...IT WOULD BE MORE FUN IF YUSUKE JOINS IN.
AND IT'D MAKE ME EVEN MORE HAPPY IF SHIN PLAYS FOR US.

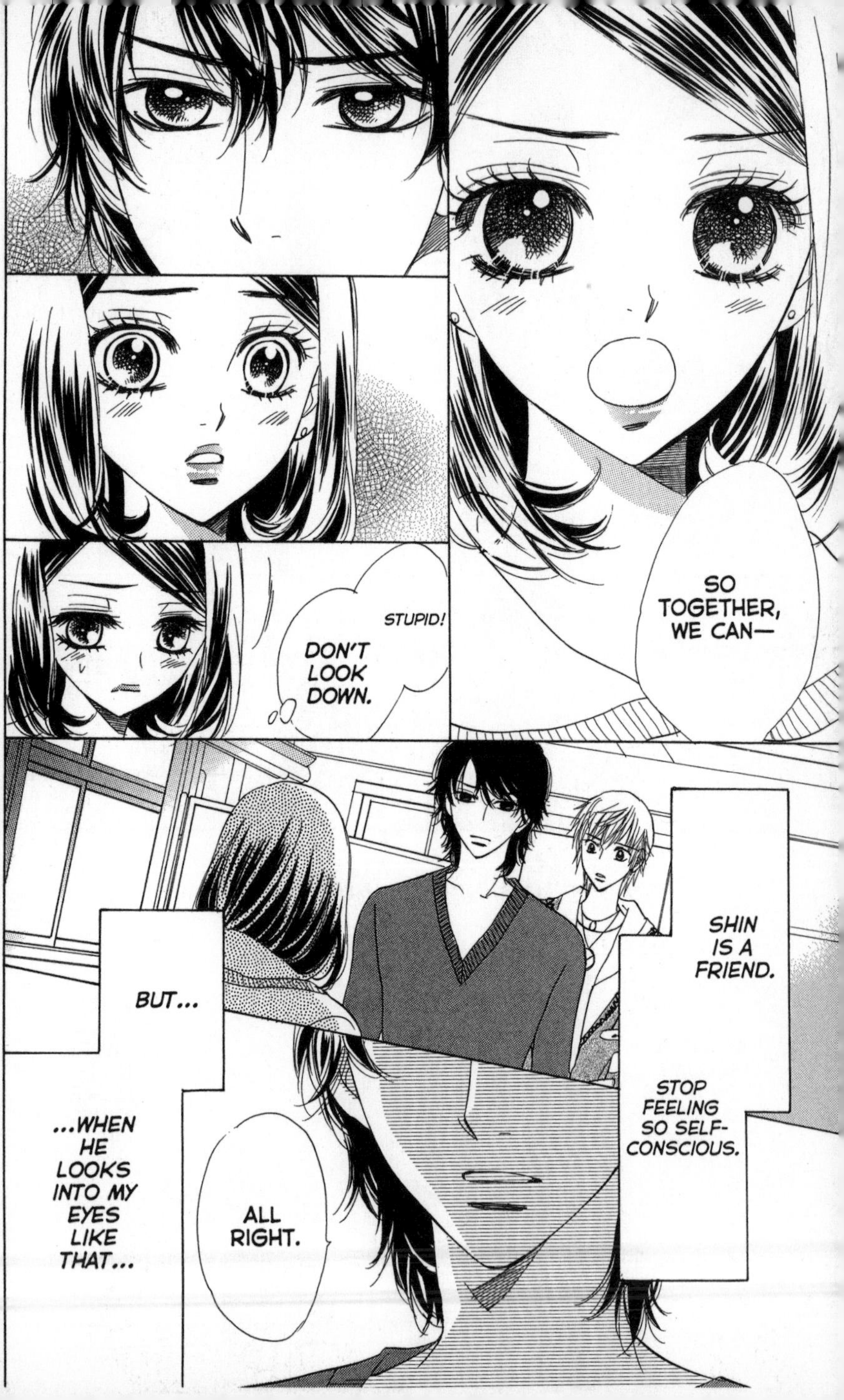
SO TOGETHER, WE CAN—
STUPID!
DON'T LOOK DOWN.
SHIN IS A FRIEND.
STOP FEELING SO SELF-CONSCIOUS.
BUT...
ALL RIGHT.
...WHEN HE LOOKS INTO MY EYES LIKE THAT...

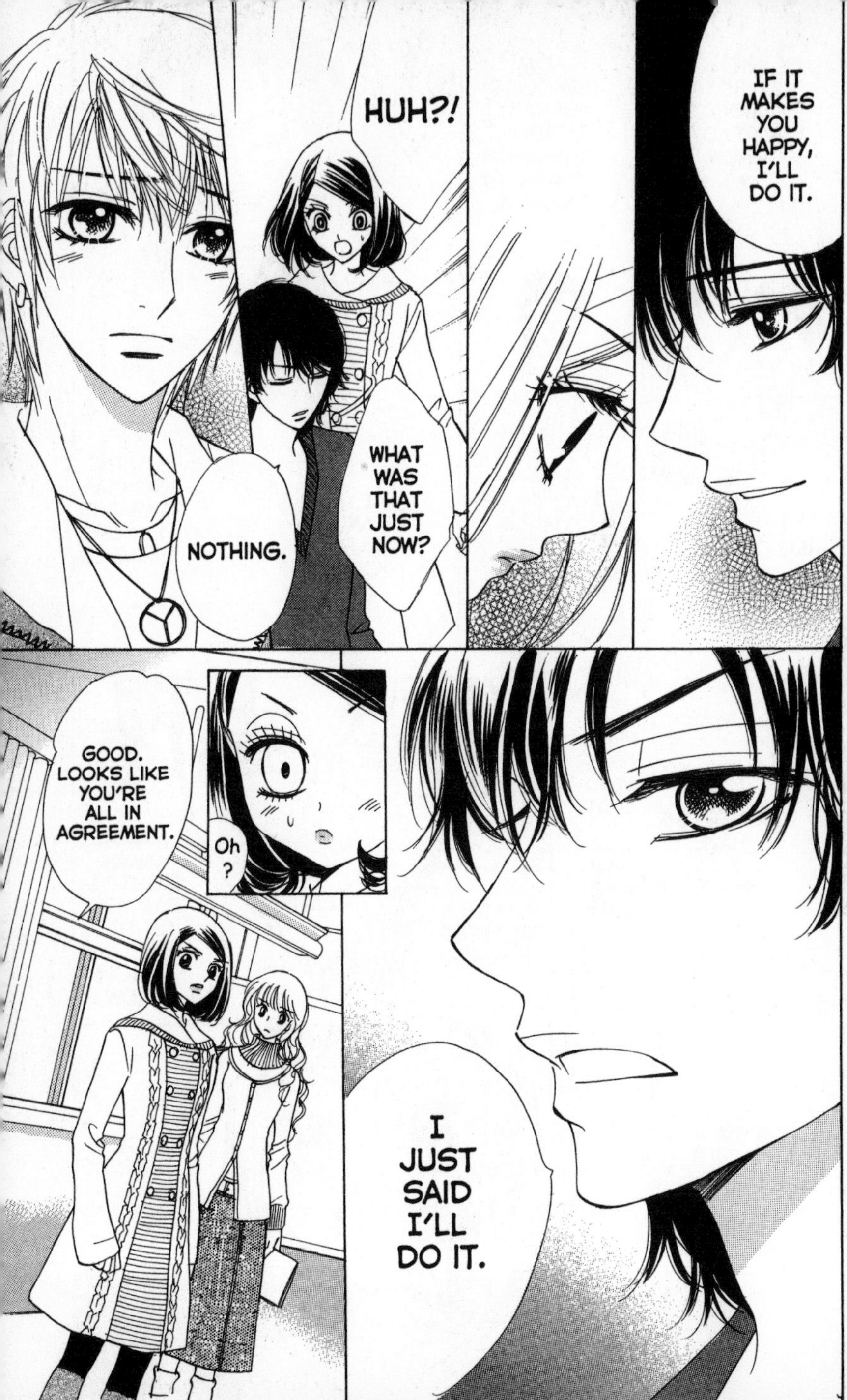
IF IT MAKES YOU HAPPY, I'LL DO IT.
HUH?!
WHAT WAS THAT JUST NOW?
NOTHING.
I JUST SAID I'LL DO IT.
Oh ?
GOOD. LOOKS LIKE YOU'RE ALL IN AGREEMENT.

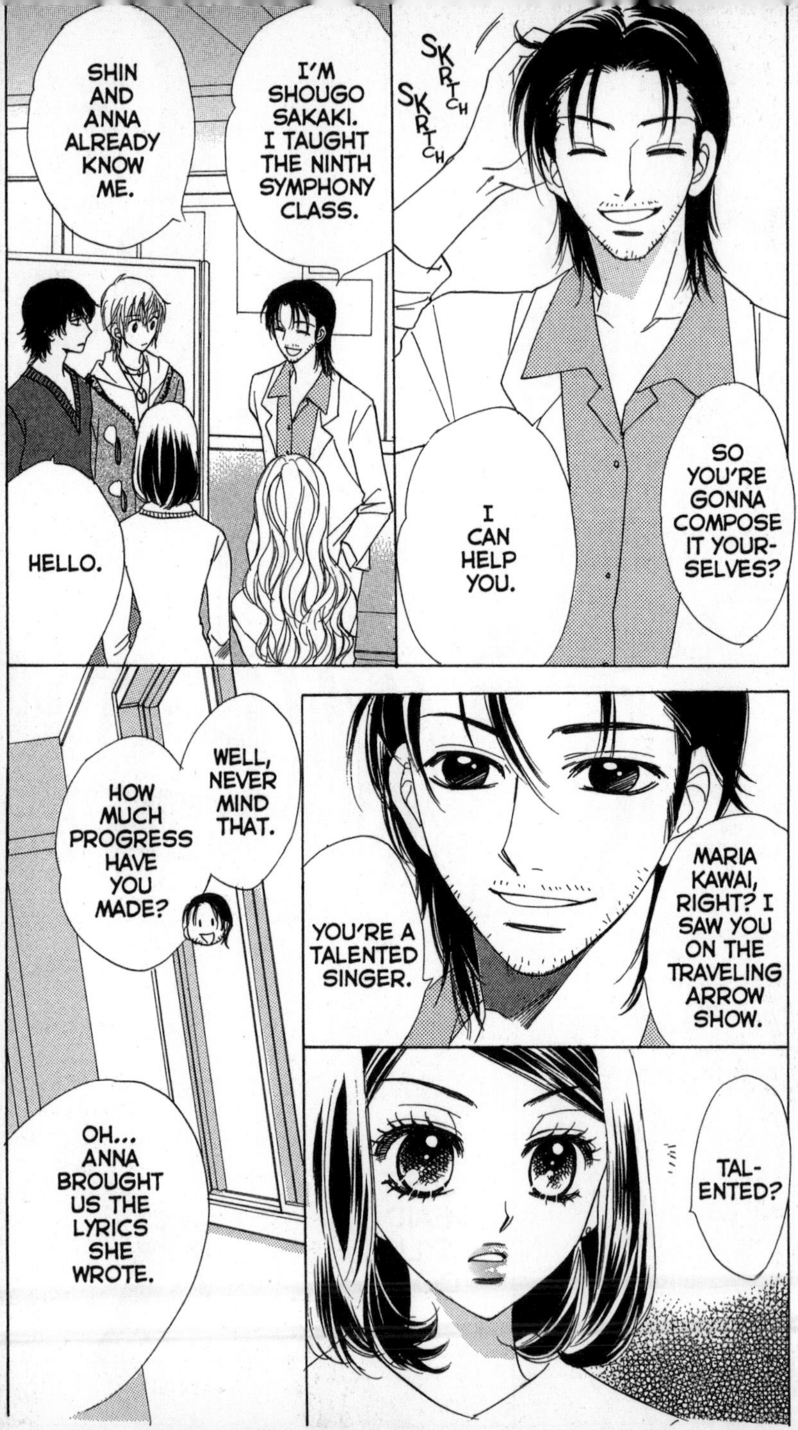
SKRTCH
SKRTCH
SO YOU'RE GONNA COMPOSE IT YOUR-SELVES?
I CAN HELP YOU.
I'M SHOUGO SAKAKI. I TAUGHT THE NINTH SYMPHONY CLASS.
SHIN AND ANNA ALREADY KNOW ME.
HELLO.
MARIA KAWAI, RIGHT? I SAW YOU ON THE TRAVELING ARROW SHOW.
YOU'RE A TALENTED SINGER.
TAL-ENTED?
WELL, NEVER MIND THAT.
HOW MUCH PROGRESS HAVE YOU MADE?
OH... ANNA BROUGHT US THE LYRICS SHE WROTE.

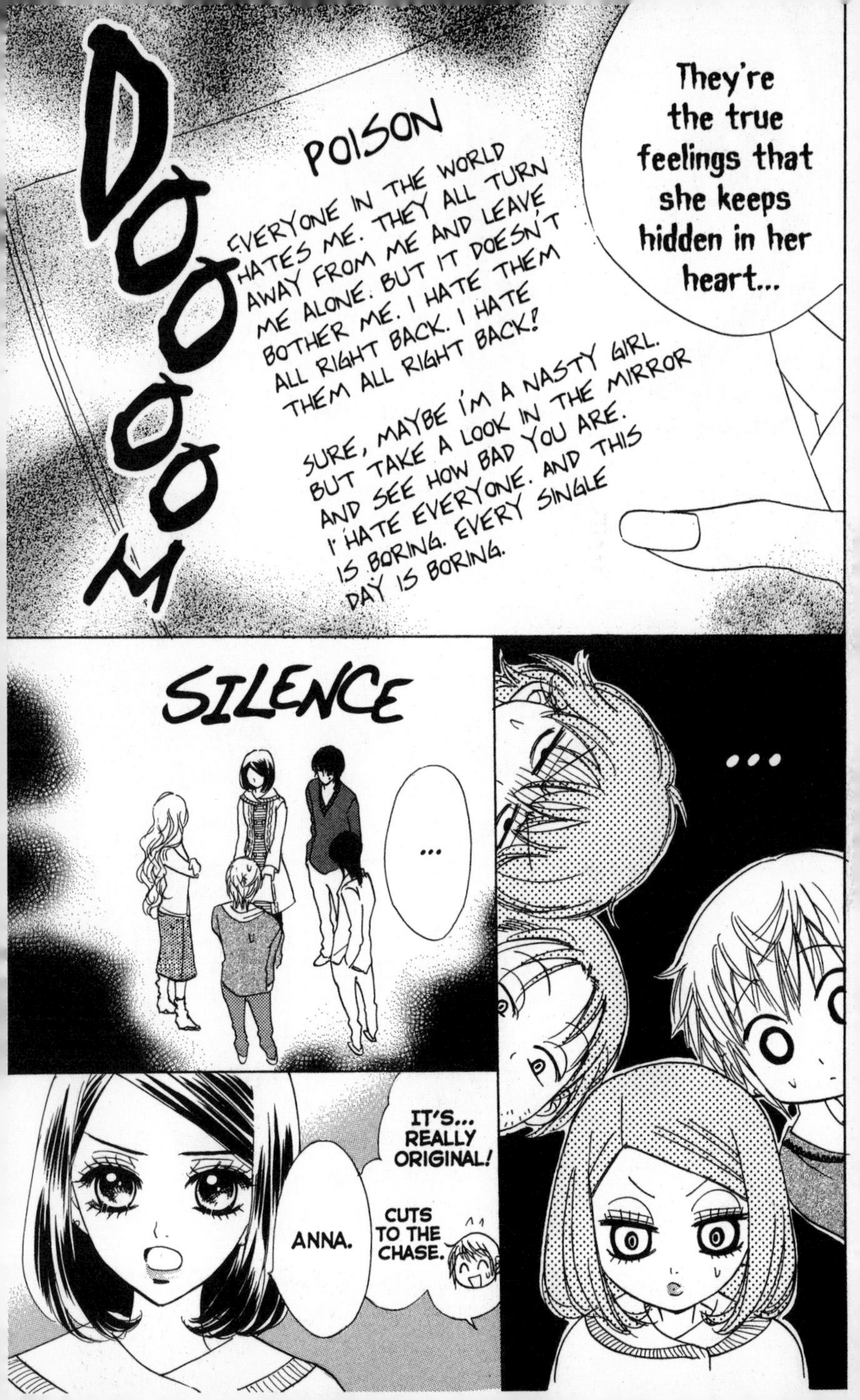

They're the true feelings that she keeps hidden in her heart...
POISON
EVERYONE IN THE WORLD HATES ME. THEY ALL TURN AWAY FROM ME AND LEAVE ME ALONE. BUT IT DOESN'T BOTHER ME. I HATE THEM ALL RIGHT BACK. I HATE THEM ALL RIGHT BACK!
SURE, MAYBE I'M A NASTY GIRL. BUT TAKE A LOOK IN THE MIRROR AND SEE HOW BAD YOU ARE. I HATE EVERYONE. AND THIS IS BORING. EVERY SINGLE DAY IS BORING.
DOOOOOM
...
SILENCE
...
IT'S... REALLY ORIGINAL!
ANNA.
CUTS TO THE CHASE.

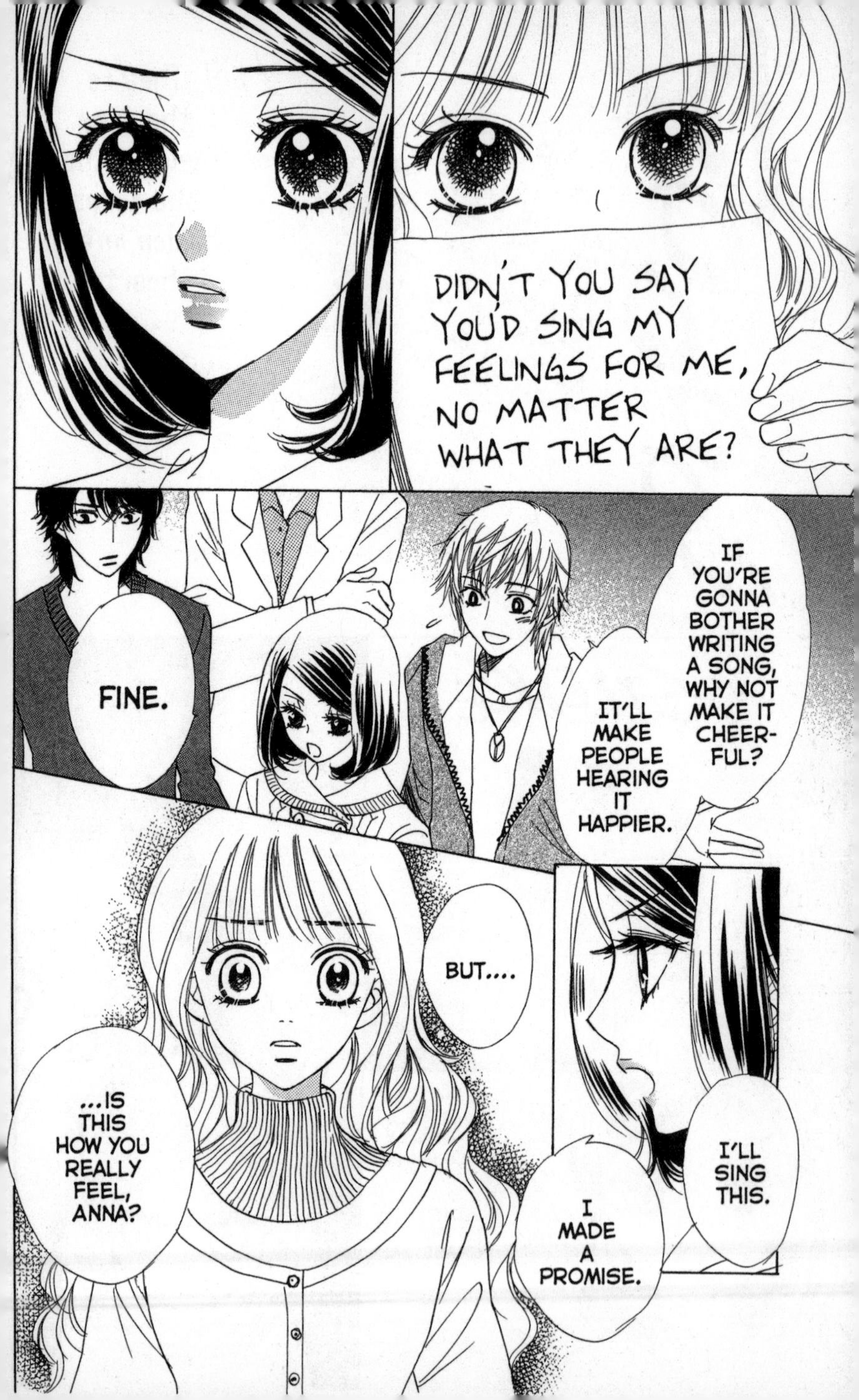
DIDN'T YOU SAY YOU'D SING MY FEELINGS FOR ME, NO MATTER WHAT THEY ARE?
IF YOU'RE GONNA BOTHER WRITING A SONG, WHY NOT MAKE IT CHEER-FUL?
IT'LL MAKE PEOPLE HEARING IT HAPPIER.
FINE.
I'LL SING THIS.
I MADE A PROMISE.
BUT....
...IS THIS HOW YOU REALLY FEEL, ANNA?

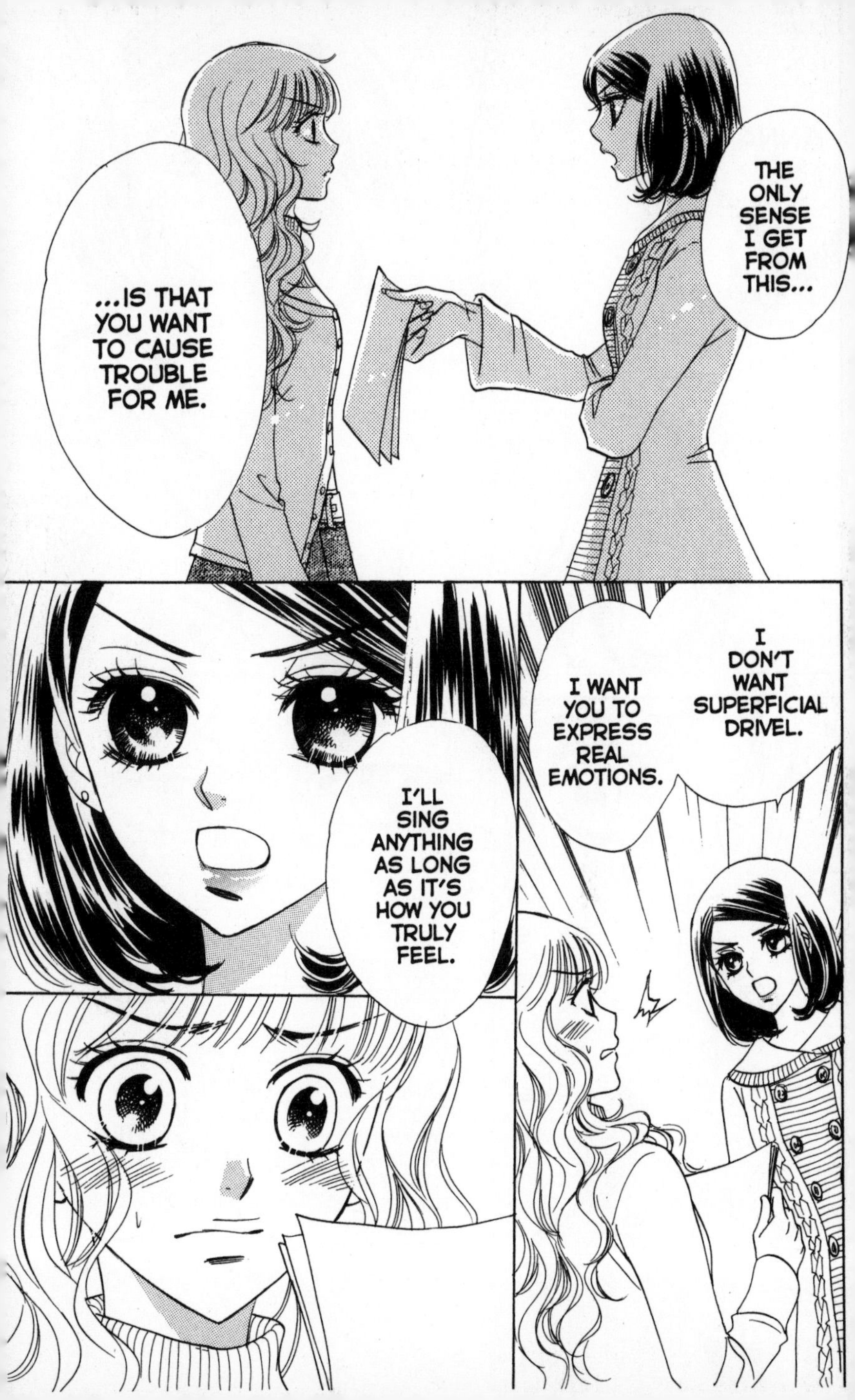
THE ONLY SENSE I GET FROM THIS...
...IS THAT YOU WANT TO CAUSE TROUBLE FOR ME.
I DON'T WANT SUPERFICIAL DRIVEL.
I WANT YOU TO EXPRESS REAL EMOTIONS.
I'LL SING ANYTHING AS LONG AS IT'S HOW YOU TRULY FEEL.

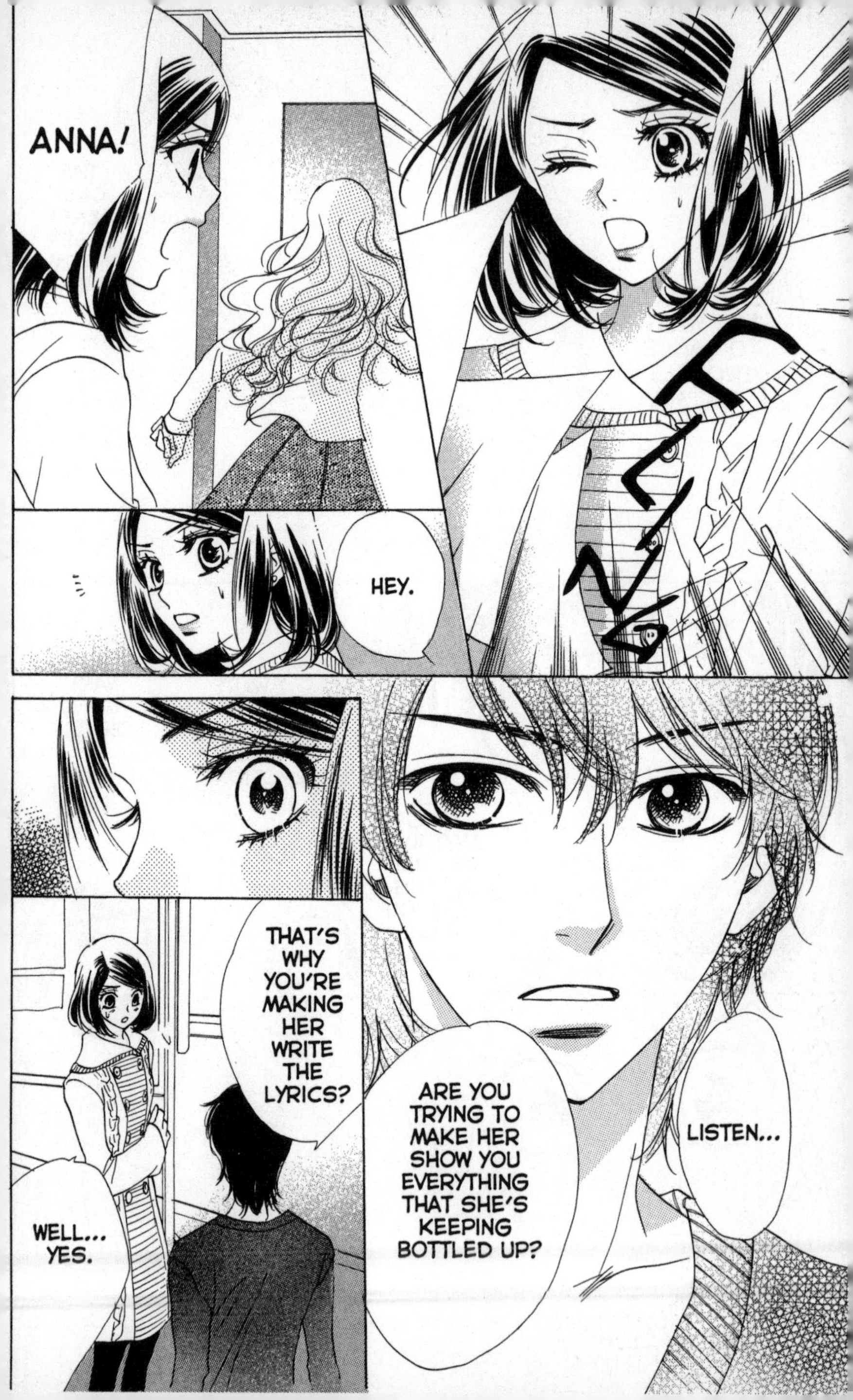
ANNA!
HEY.
LISTEN...
ARE YOU TRYING TO MAKE HER SHOW YOU EVERYTHING THAT SHE'S KEEPING BOTTLED UP?
THAT'S WHY YOU'RE MAKING HER WRITE THE LYRICS?
WELL... YES.

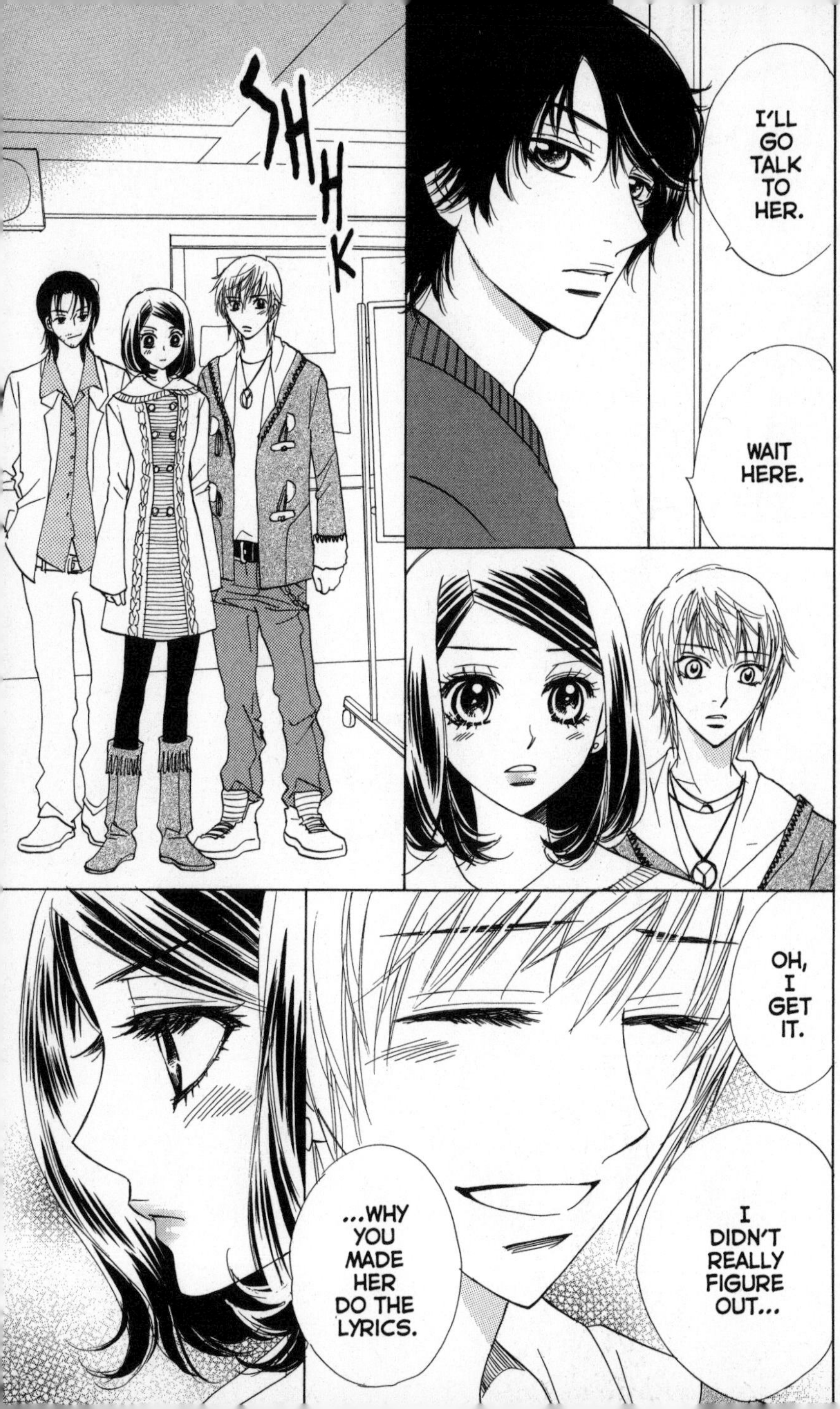
I'LL GO TALK TO HER.
WAIT HERE.
SHHK
OH, I GET IT.
I DIDN'T REALLY FIGURE OUT...
...WHY YOU MADE HER DO THE LYRICS.

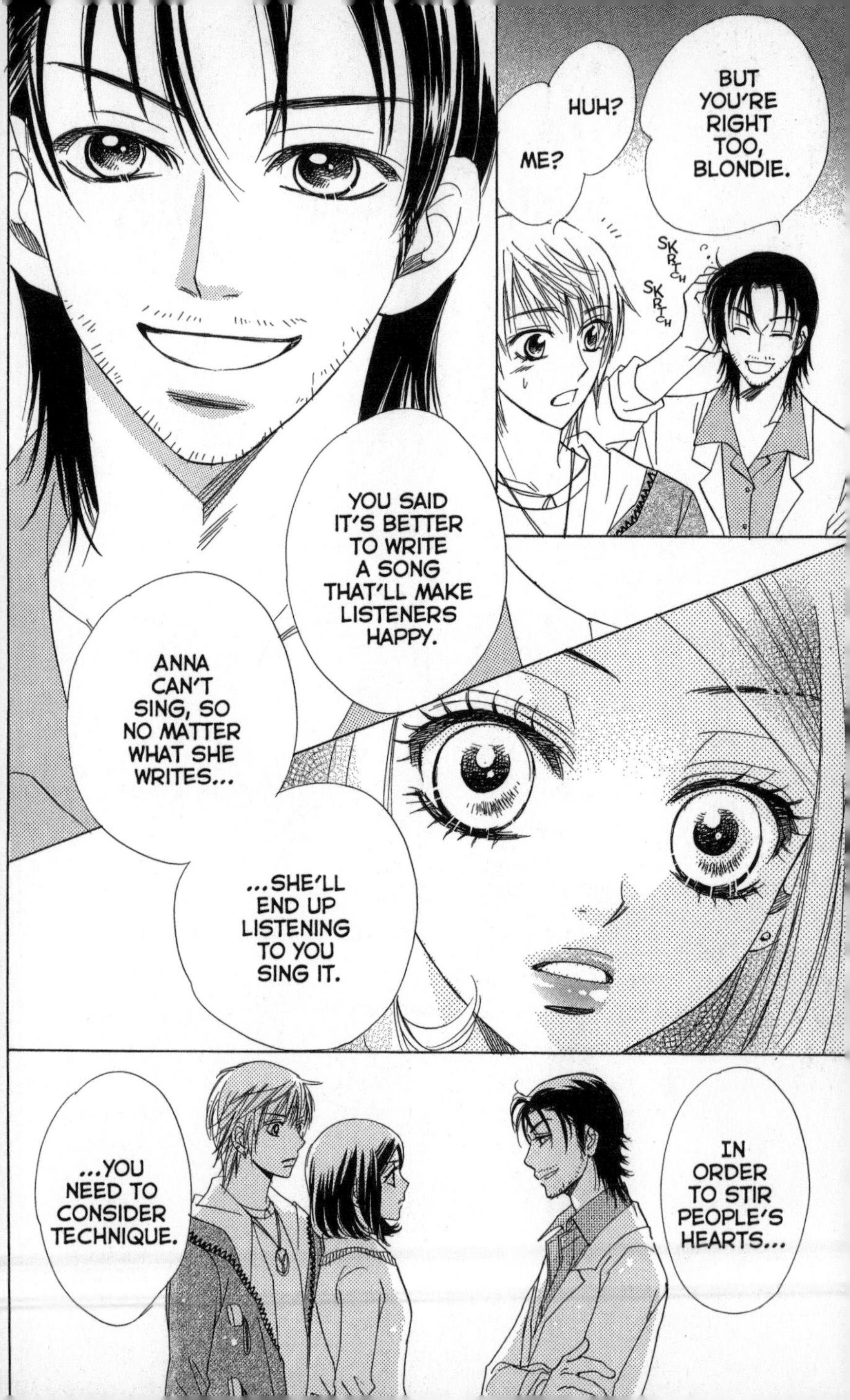
BUT YOU'RE RIGHT TOO, BLONDIE.
HUH? ME?
SKRTCH SKRTCH
YOU SAID IT'S BETTER TO WRITE A SONG THAT'LL MAKE LISTENERS HAPPY.
ANNA CAN'T SING, SO NO MATTER WHAT SHE WRITES...
...SHE'LL END UP LISTENING TO YOU SING IT.
IN ORDER TO STIR PEOPLE'S HEARTS...
...YOU NEED TO CONSIDER TECHNIQUE.

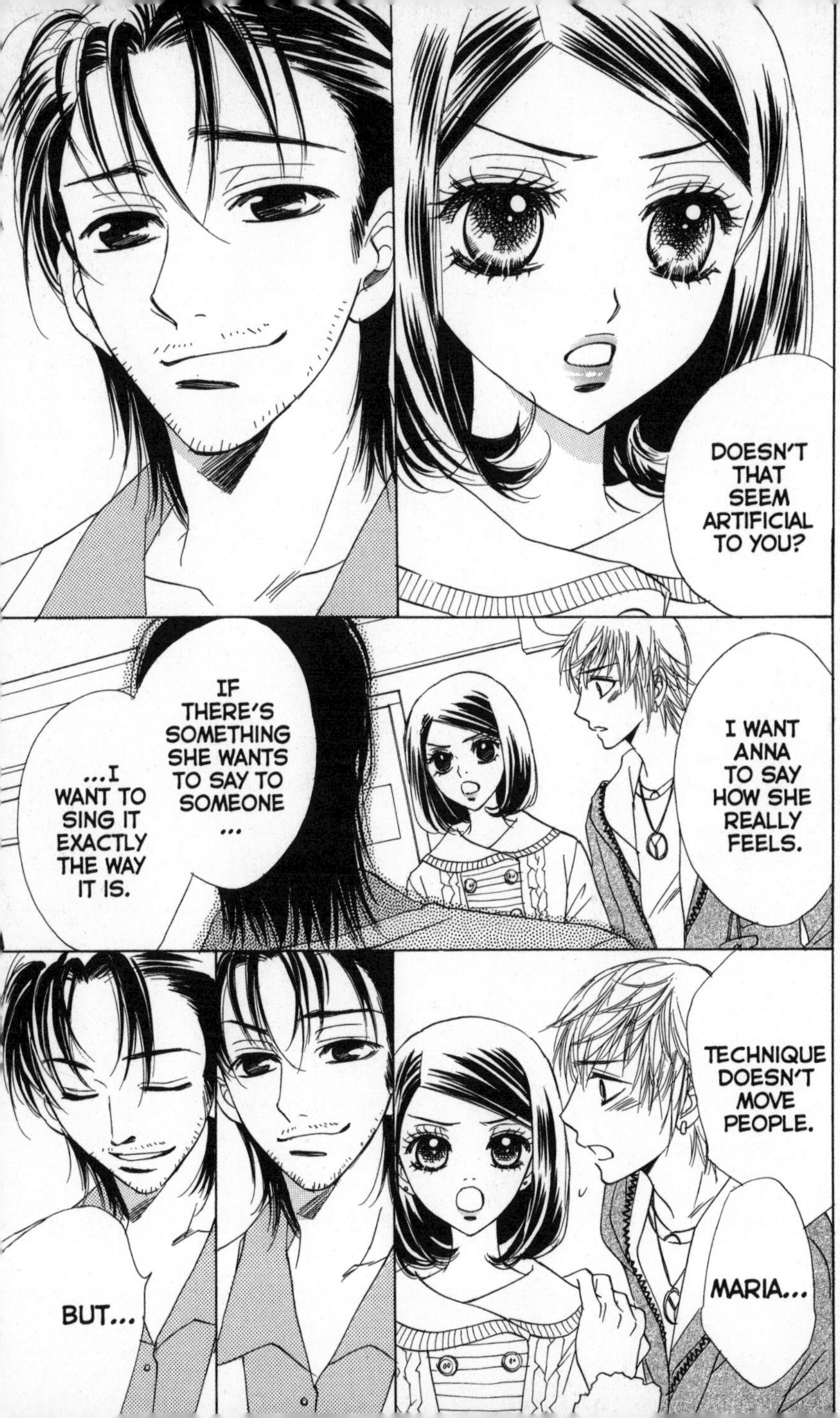
DOESN'T THAT SEEM ARTIFICIAL TO YOU?
I WANT ANNA TO SAY HOW SHE REALLY FEELS.
IF THERE'S SOMETHING SHE WANTS TO SAY TO SOMEONE...
...I WANT TO SING IT EXACTLY THE WAY IT IS.
TECHNIQUE DOESN'T MOVE PEOPLE.
MARIA...
BUT...

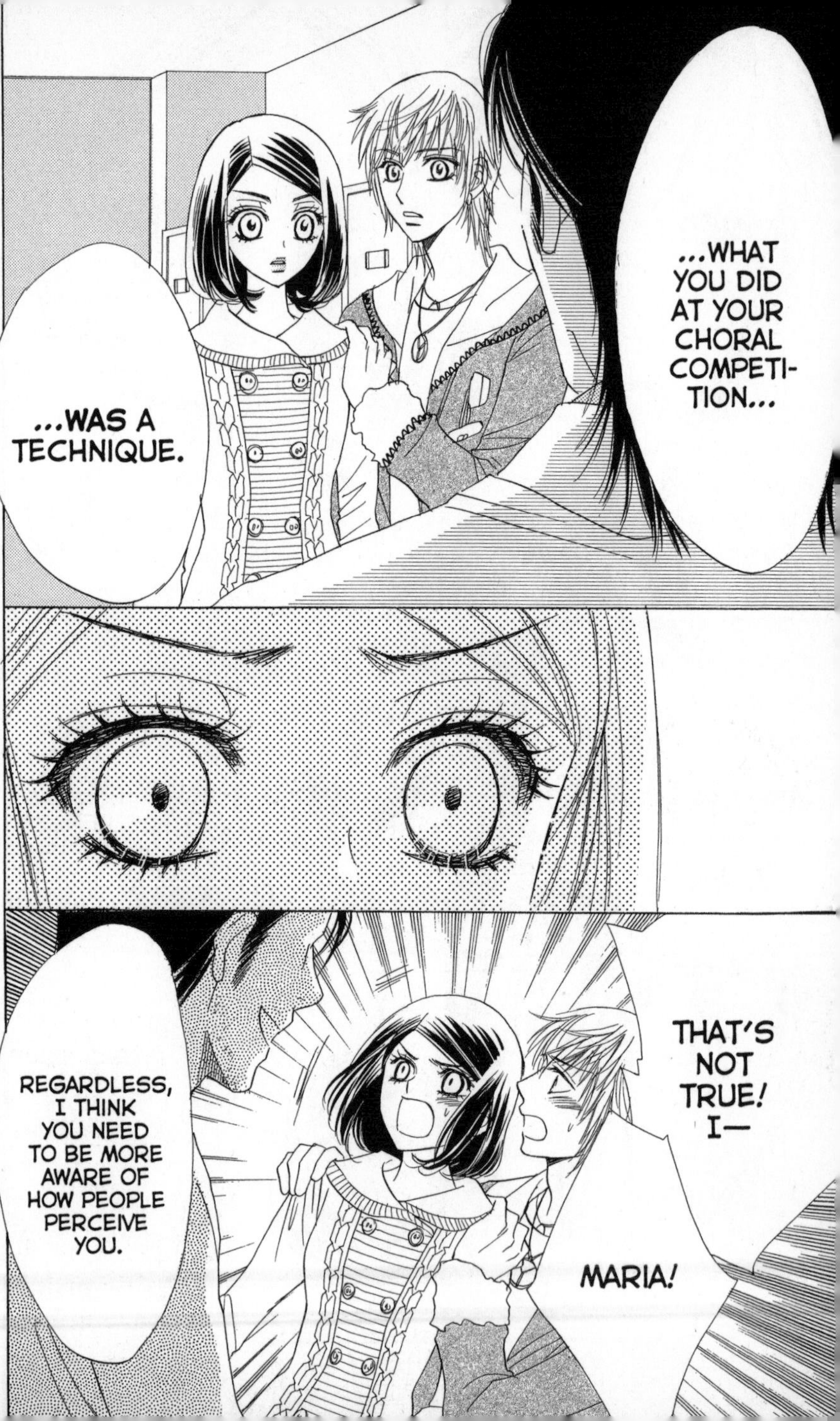

...WHAT YOU DID AT YOUR CHORAL COMPETITION...
...WAS A TECHNIQUE.
THAT'S NOT TRUE! I—
REGARDLESS, I THINK YOU NEED TO BE MORE AWARE OF HOW PEOPLE PERCEIVE YOU.
MARIA!

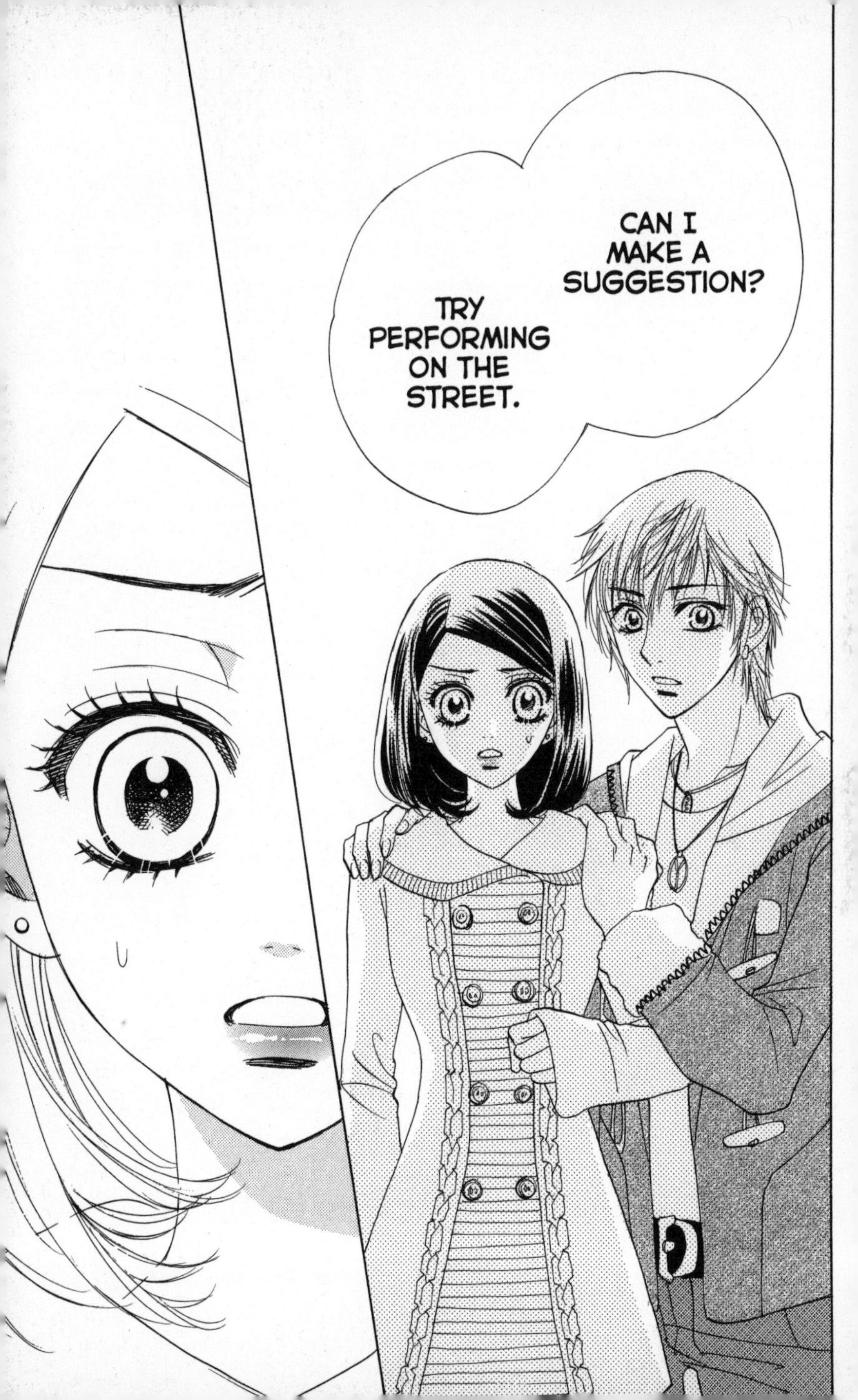
CAN I MAKE A SUGGESTION?
TRY PERFORMING ON THE STREET.

A Devil and
Her Love Song

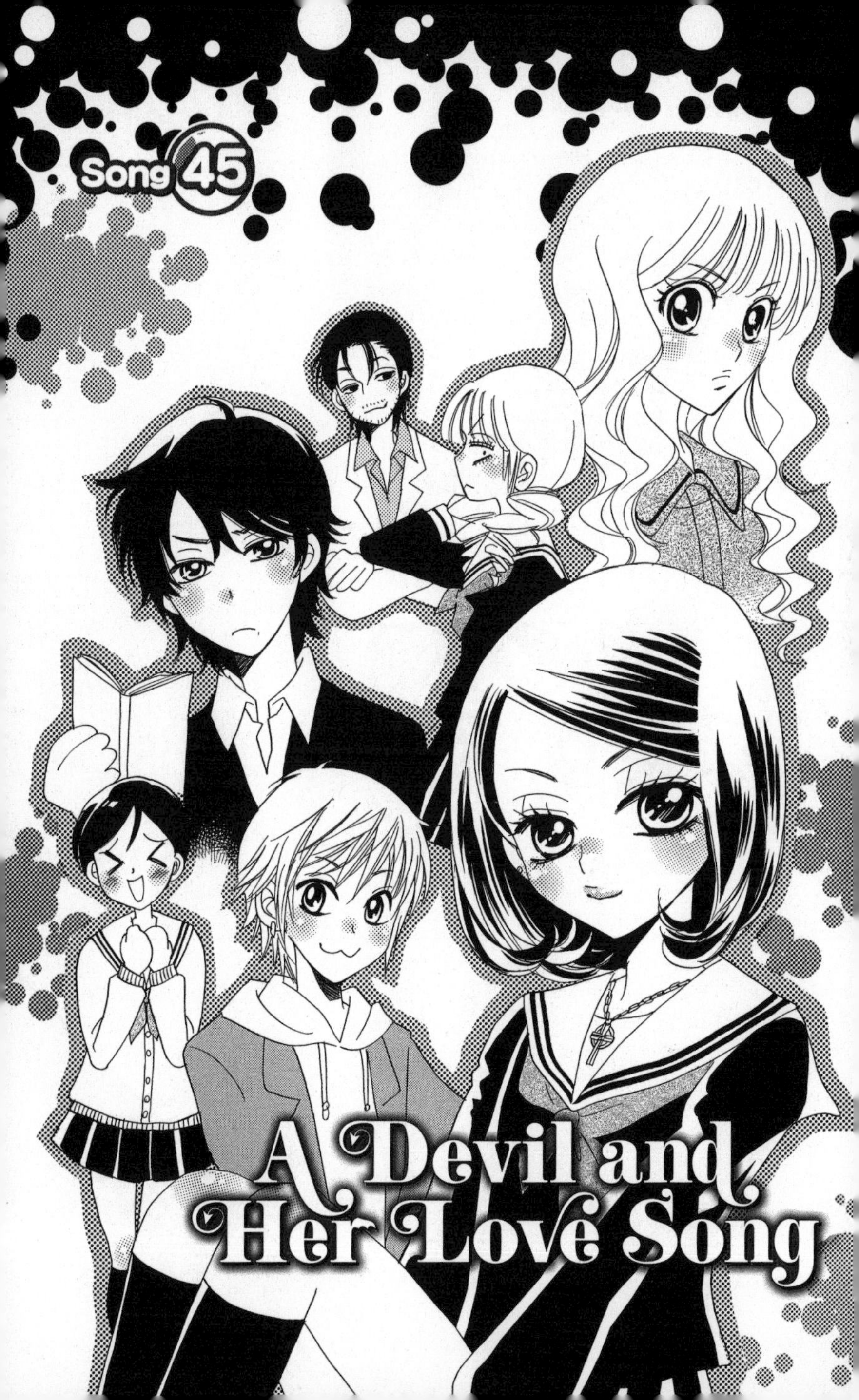
Song 45
A Devil and Her Love Song

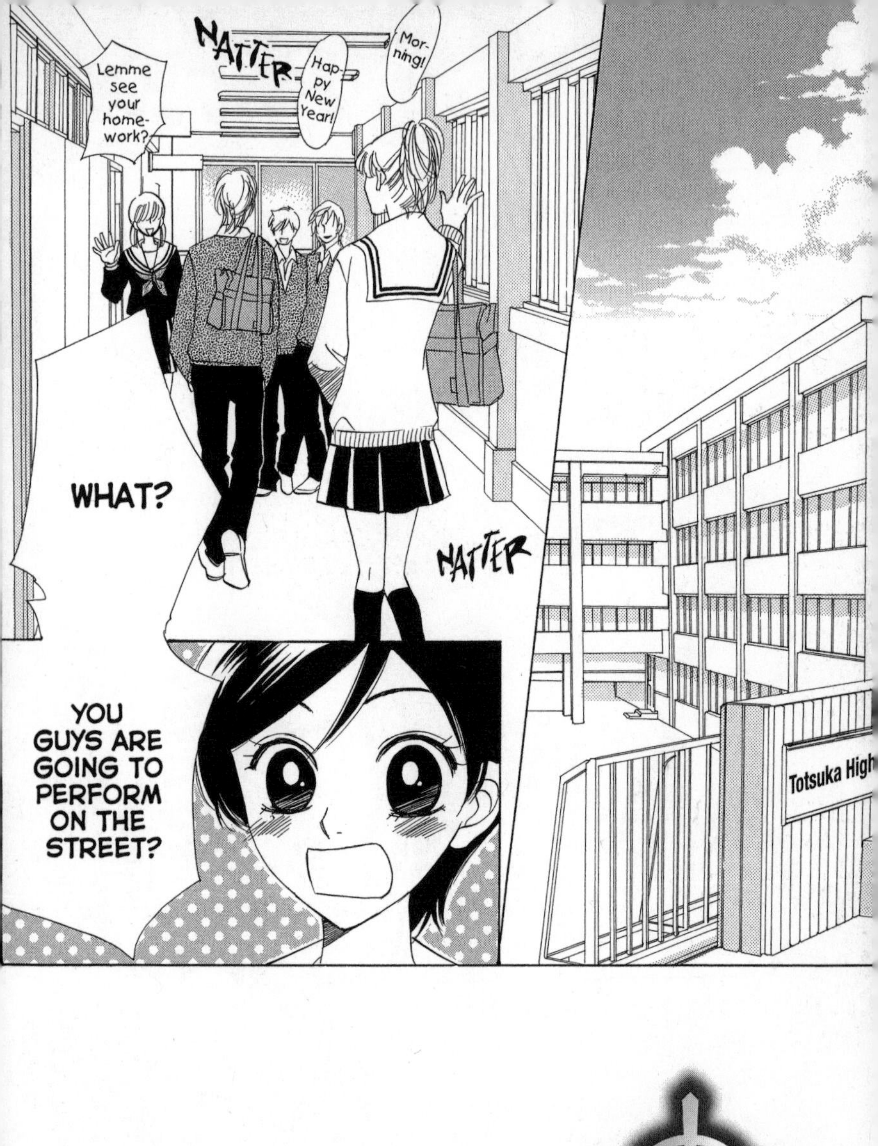
Totsuka High
Morning!
Happy New Year!
NATTER
Lemme see your homework?
NATTER
WHAT?
YOU GUYS ARE GOING TO PERFORM ON THE STREET?

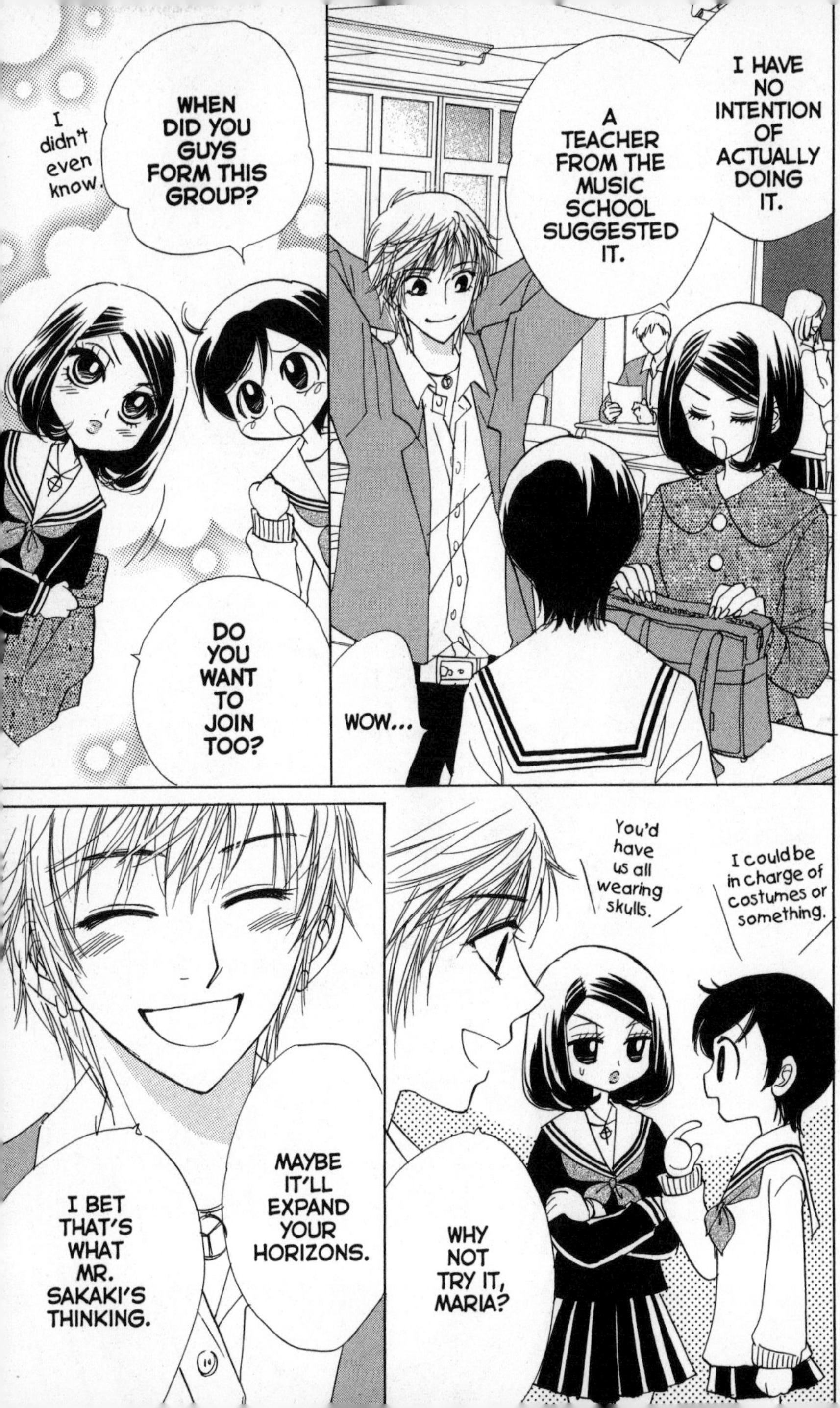
I HAVE NO INTENTION OF ACTUALLY DOING IT.
A TEACHER FROM THE MUSIC SCHOOL SUGGESTED IT.
WOW...
WHEN DID YOU GUYS FORM THIS GROUP?
I didn't even know.
DO YOU WANT TO JOIN TOO?
I could be in charge of costumes or something.
You'd have us all wearing skulls.
WHY NOT TRY IT, MARIA?
MAYBE IT'LL EXPAND YOUR HORIZONS.
I BET THAT'S WHAT MR. SAKAKI'S THINKING.

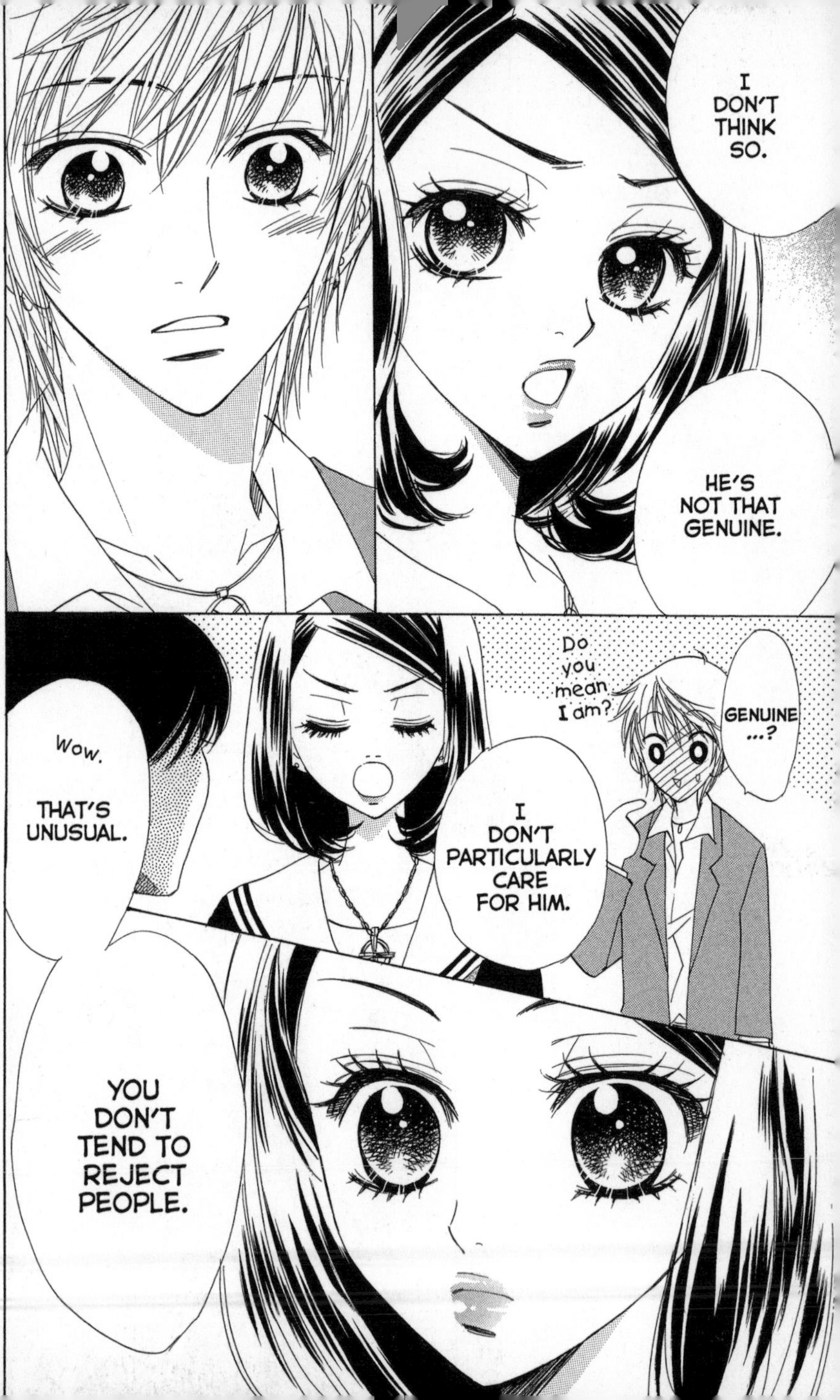
I DON'T THINK SO.
HE'S NOT THAT GENUINE.
GENUINE ...?
Do you mean I am?
I DON'T PARTICULARLY CARE FOR HIM.
Wow.
THAT'S UNUSUAL.
YOU DON'T TEND TO REJECT PEOPLE.

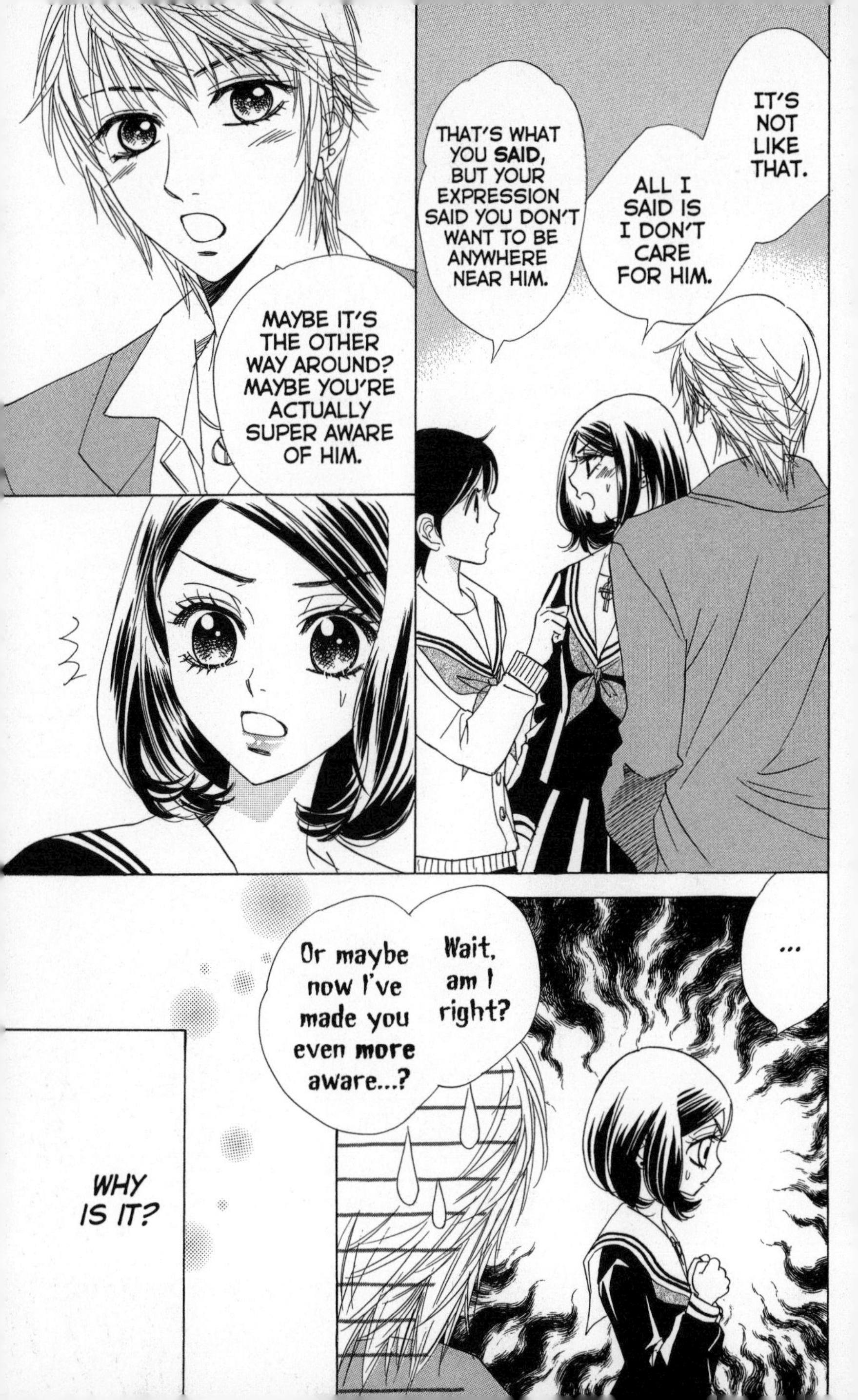
IT'S NOT LIKE THAT.
ALL I SAID IS I DON'T CARE FOR HIM.
THAT'S WHAT YOU SAID, BUT YOUR EXPRESSION SAID YOU DON'T WANT TO BE ANYWHERE NEAR HIM.
MAYBE IT'S THE OTHER WAY AROUND? MAYBE YOU'RE ACTUALLY SUPER AWARE OF HIM.
...
Wait, am I right?
Or maybe now I've made you even more aware...?
WHY IS IT?

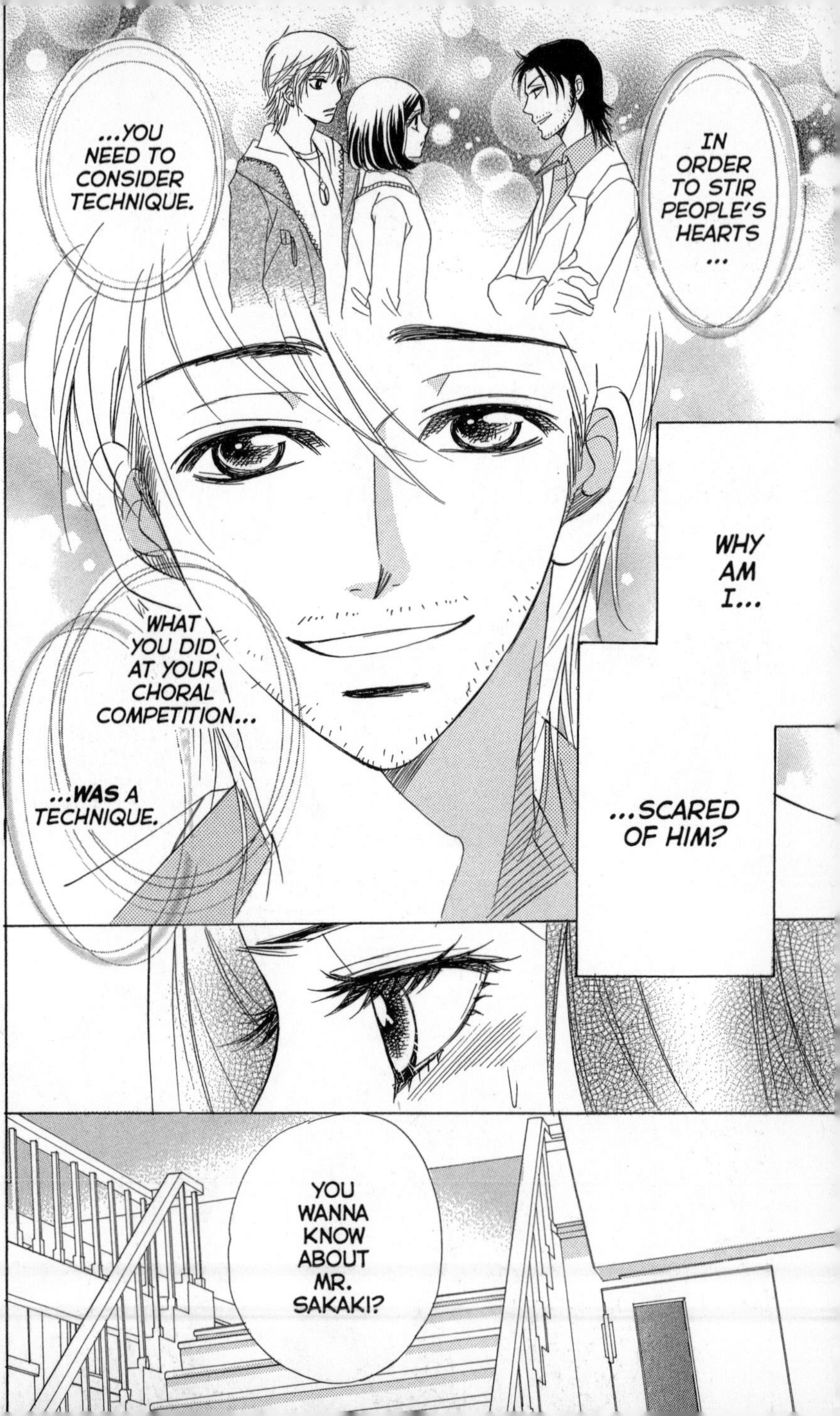
IN ORDER TO STIR PEOPLE'S HEARTS...
...YOU NEED TO CONSIDER TECHNIQUE.
WHAT YOU DID AT YOUR CHORAL COMPETITION...
...WAS A TECHNIQUE.
WHY AM I...
...SCARED OF HIM?
YOU WANNA KNOW ABOUT MR. SAKAKI?

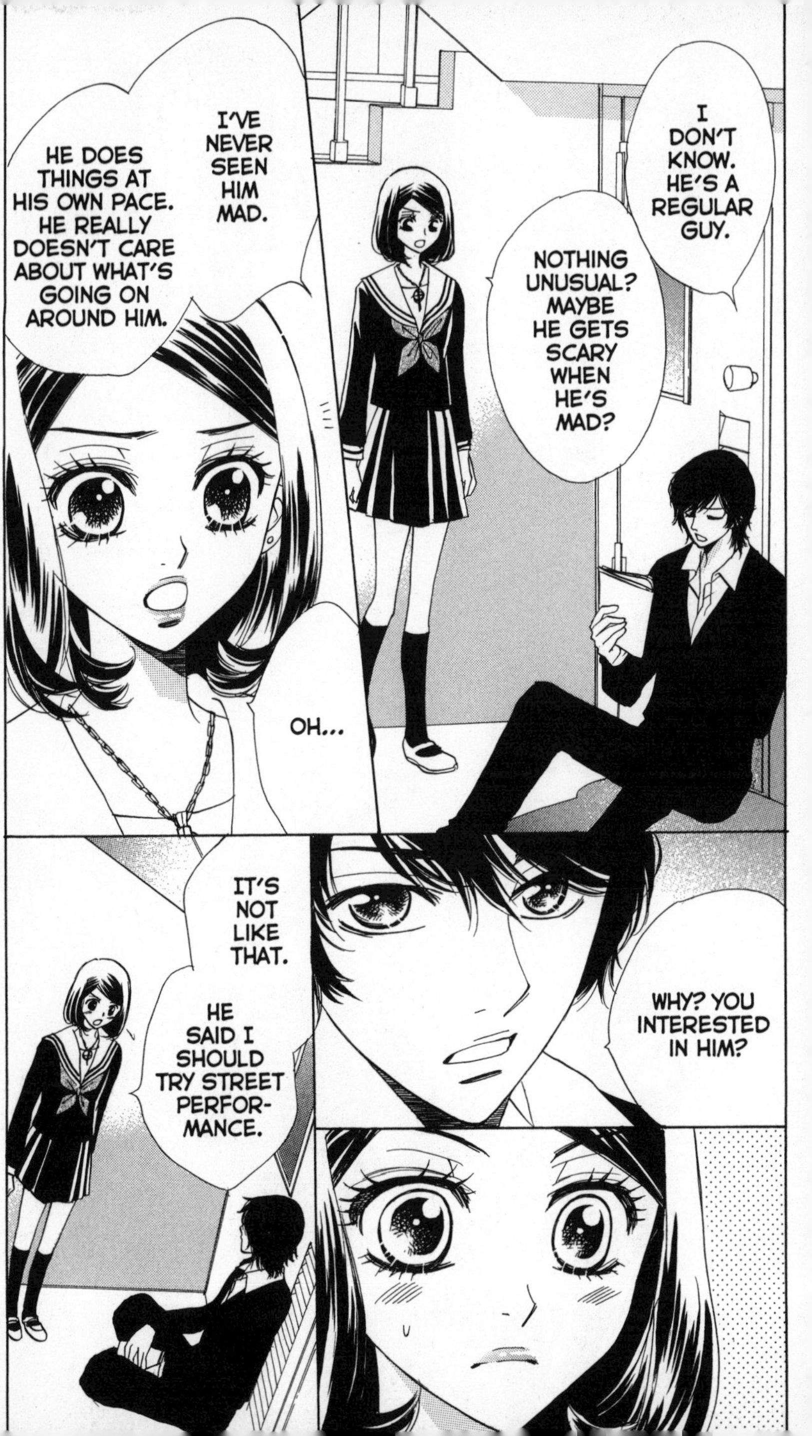
I DON'T KNOW. HE'S A REGULAR GUY.
NOTHING UNUSUAL? MAYBE HE GETS SCARY WHEN HE'S MAD?
I'VE NEVER SEEN HIM MAD.
HE DOES THINGS AT HIS OWN PACE. HE REALLY DOESN'T CARE ABOUT WHAT'S GOING ON AROUND HIM.
OH...
WHY? YOU INTERESTED IN HIM?
IT'S NOT LIKE THAT.
HE SAID I SHOULD TRY STREET PERFORMANCE.

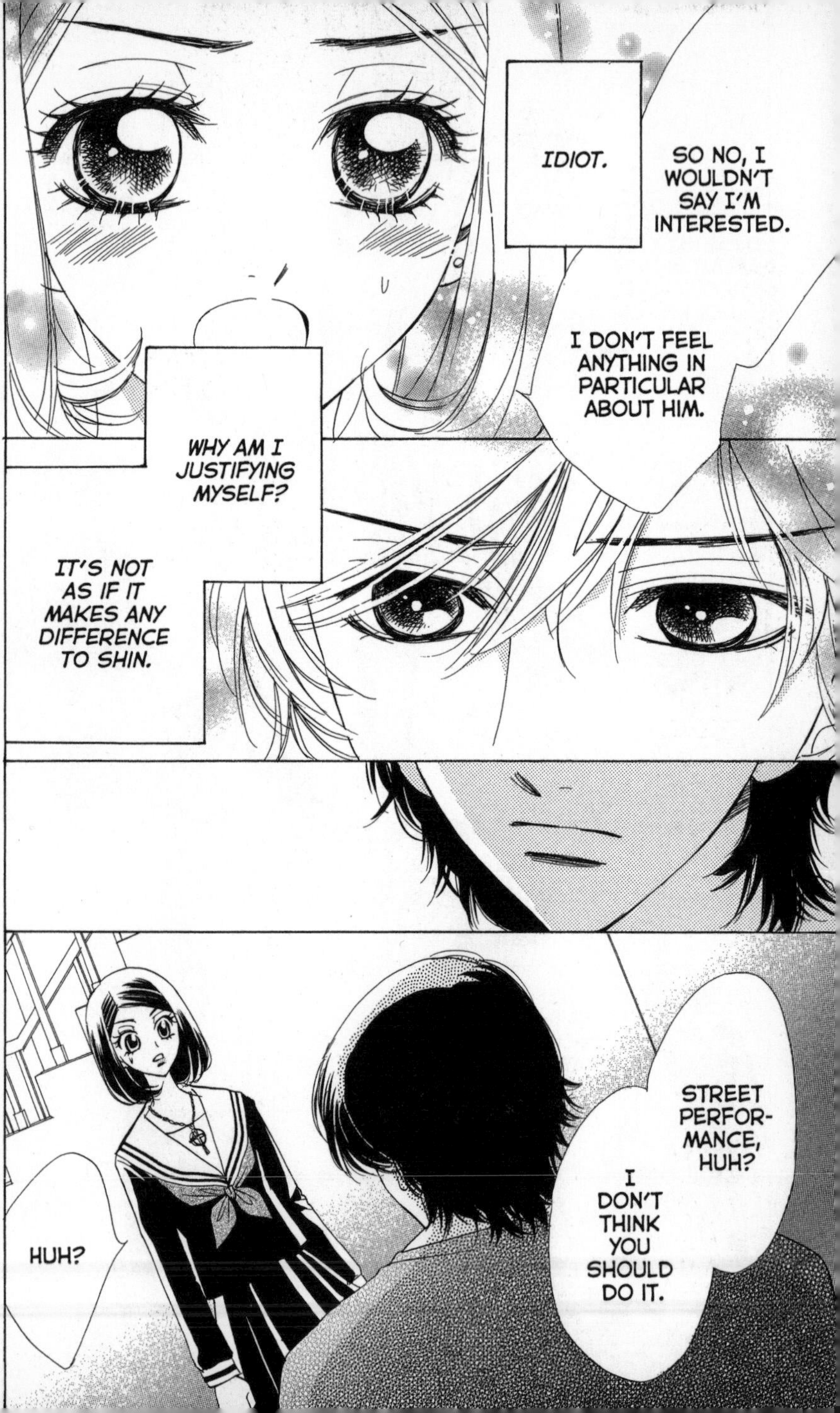
SO NO, I WOULDN'T SAY I'M INTERESTED.
I DON'T FEEL ANYTHING IN PARTICULAR ABOUT HIM.
IDIOT.
WHY AM I JUSTIFYING MYSELF?
IT'S NOT AS IF IT MAKES ANY DIFFERENCE TO SHIN.
STREET PERFORMANCE, HUH?
I DON'T THINK YOU SHOULD DO IT.
HUH?

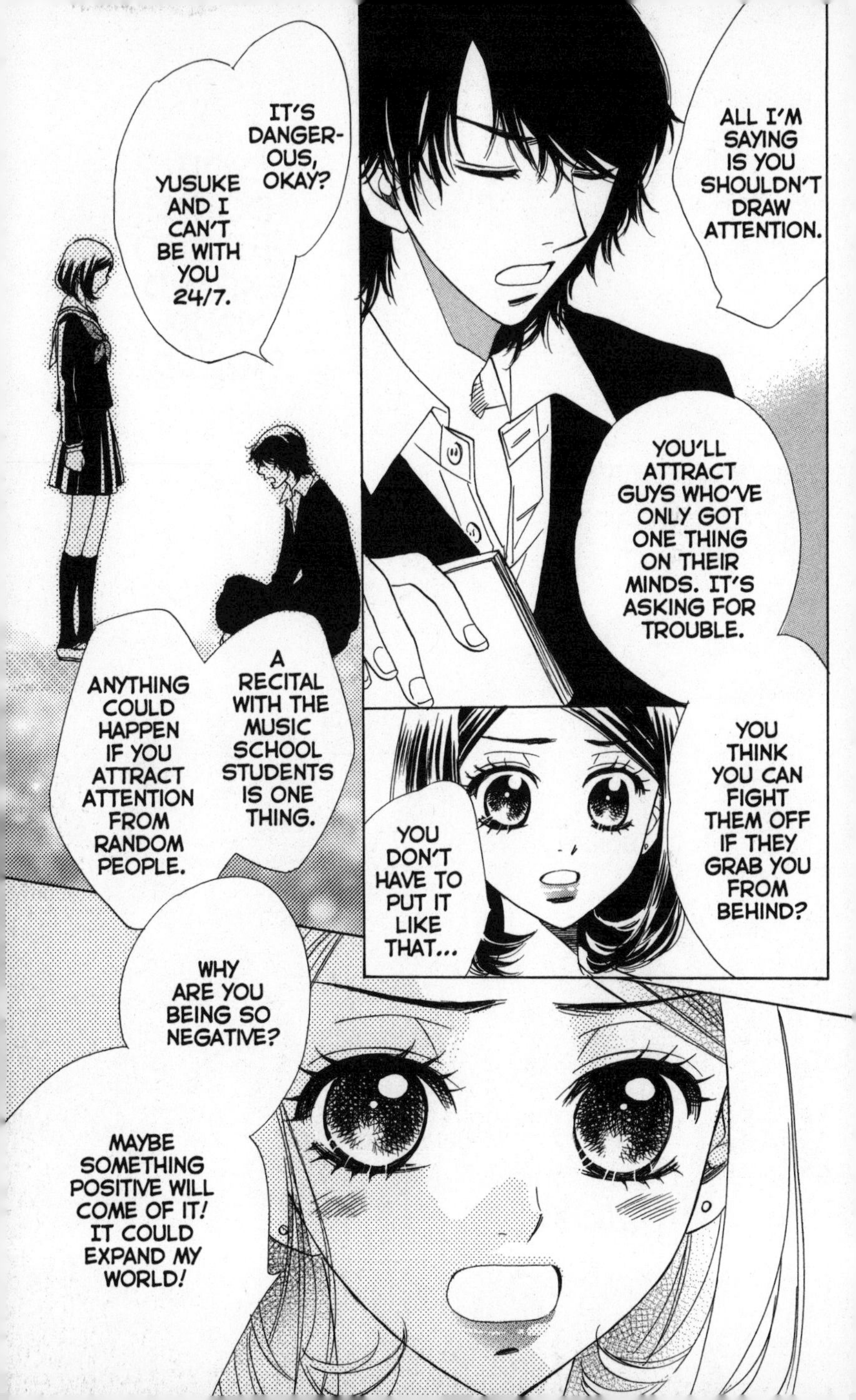
ALL I'M SAYING IS YOU SHOULDN'T DRAW ATTENTION.
YOU'LL ATTRACT GUYS WHO'VE ONLY GOT ONE THING ON THEIR MINDS. IT'S ASKING FOR TROUBLE.
YOU THINK YOU CAN FIGHT THEM OFF IF THEY GRAB YOU FROM BEHIND?
YOU DON'T HAVE TO PUT IT LIKE THAT...
IT'S DANGER-OUS, OKAY?
YUSUKE AND I CAN'T BE WITH YOU 24/7.
A RECITAL WITH THE MUSIC SCHOOL STUDENTS IS ONE THING.
ANYTHING COULD HAPPEN IF YOU ATTRACT ATTENTION FROM RANDOM PEOPLE.
WHY ARE YOU BEING SO NEGATIVE?
MAYBE SOMETHING POSITIVE WILL COME OF IT! IT COULD EXPAND MY WORLD!

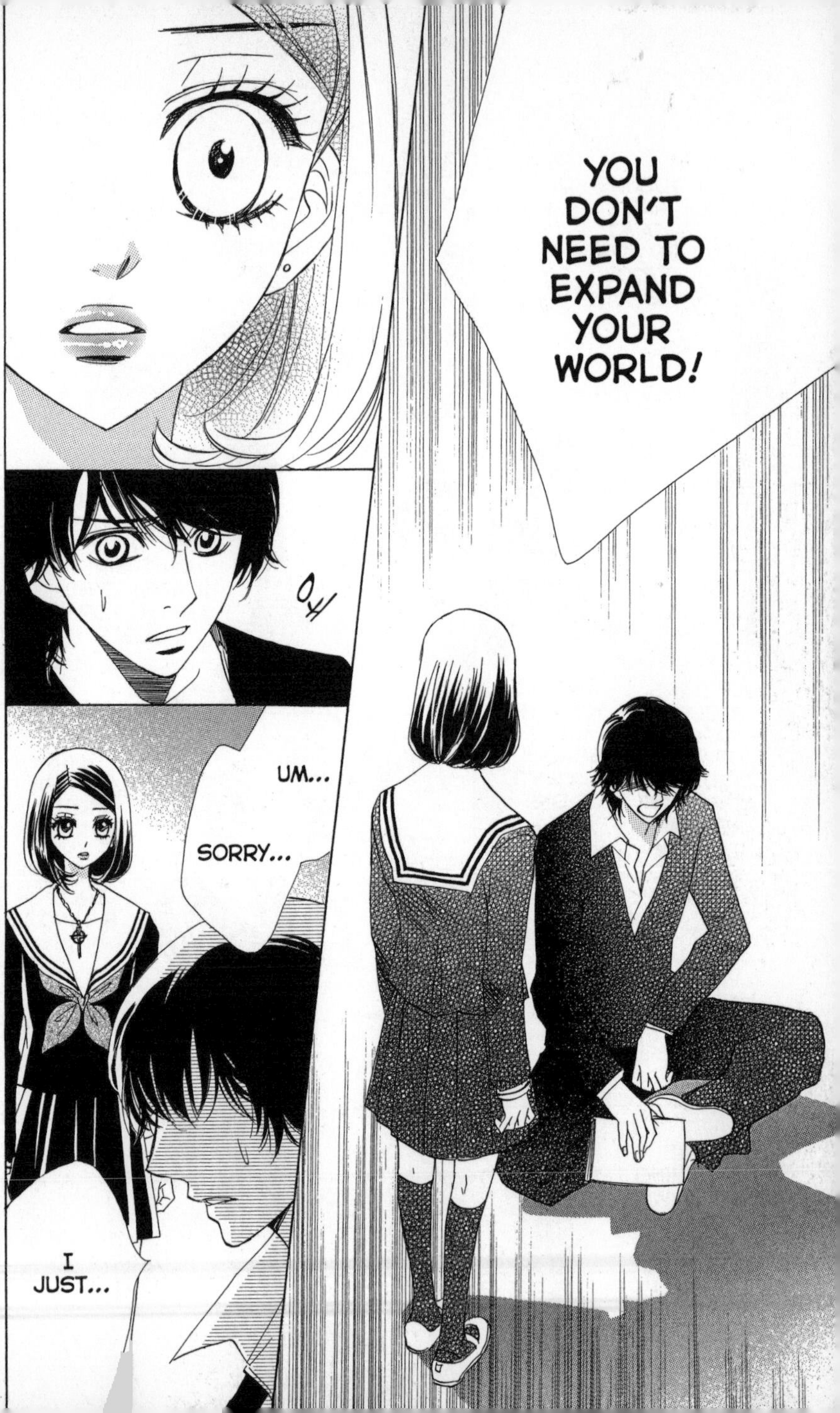
YOU DON'T NEED TO EXPAND YOUR WORLD!
OH
UM...
SORRY...
I JUST...

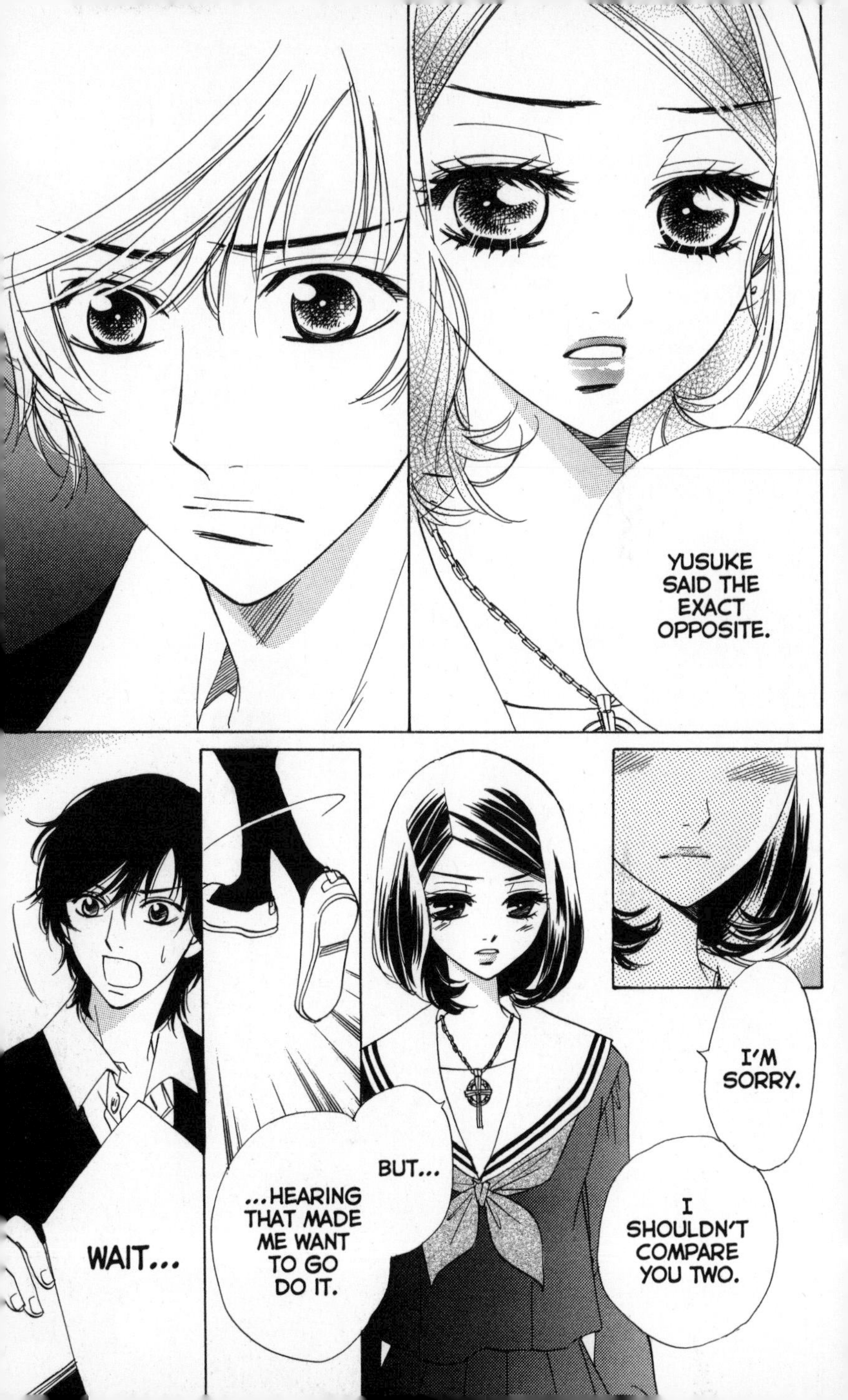
YUSUKE SAID THE EXACT OPPOSITE.
I'M SORRY.
I SHOULDN'T COMPARE YOU TWO.
BUT...
...HEARING THAT MADE ME WANT TO GO DO IT.
WAIT...

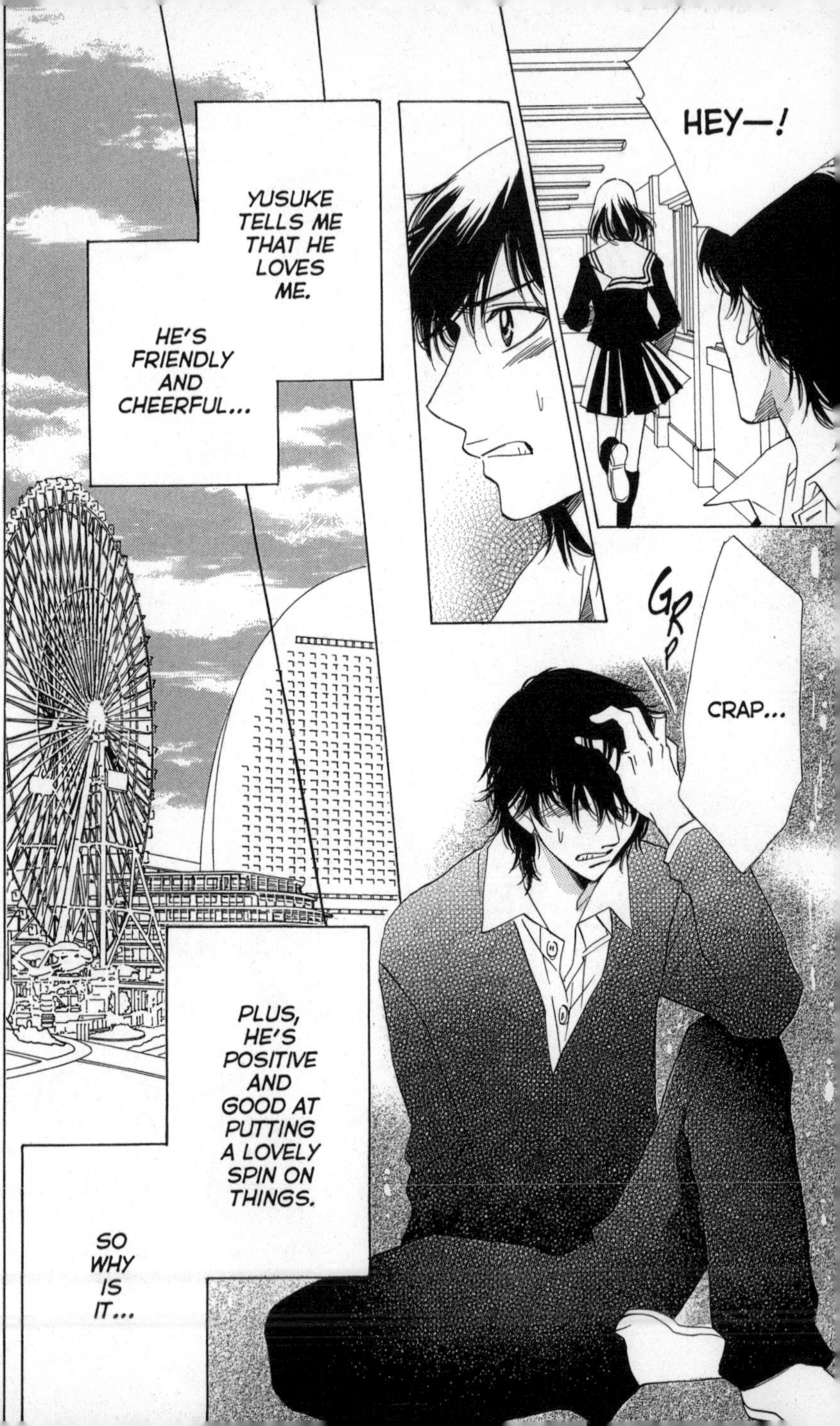
HEY—!
GRP
CRAP...
YUSUKE TELLS ME THAT HE LOVES ME.
HE'S FRIENDLY AND CHEERFUL...
PLUS, HE'S POSITIVE AND GOOD AT PUTTING A LOVELY SPIN ON THINGS.
SO WHY IS IT...

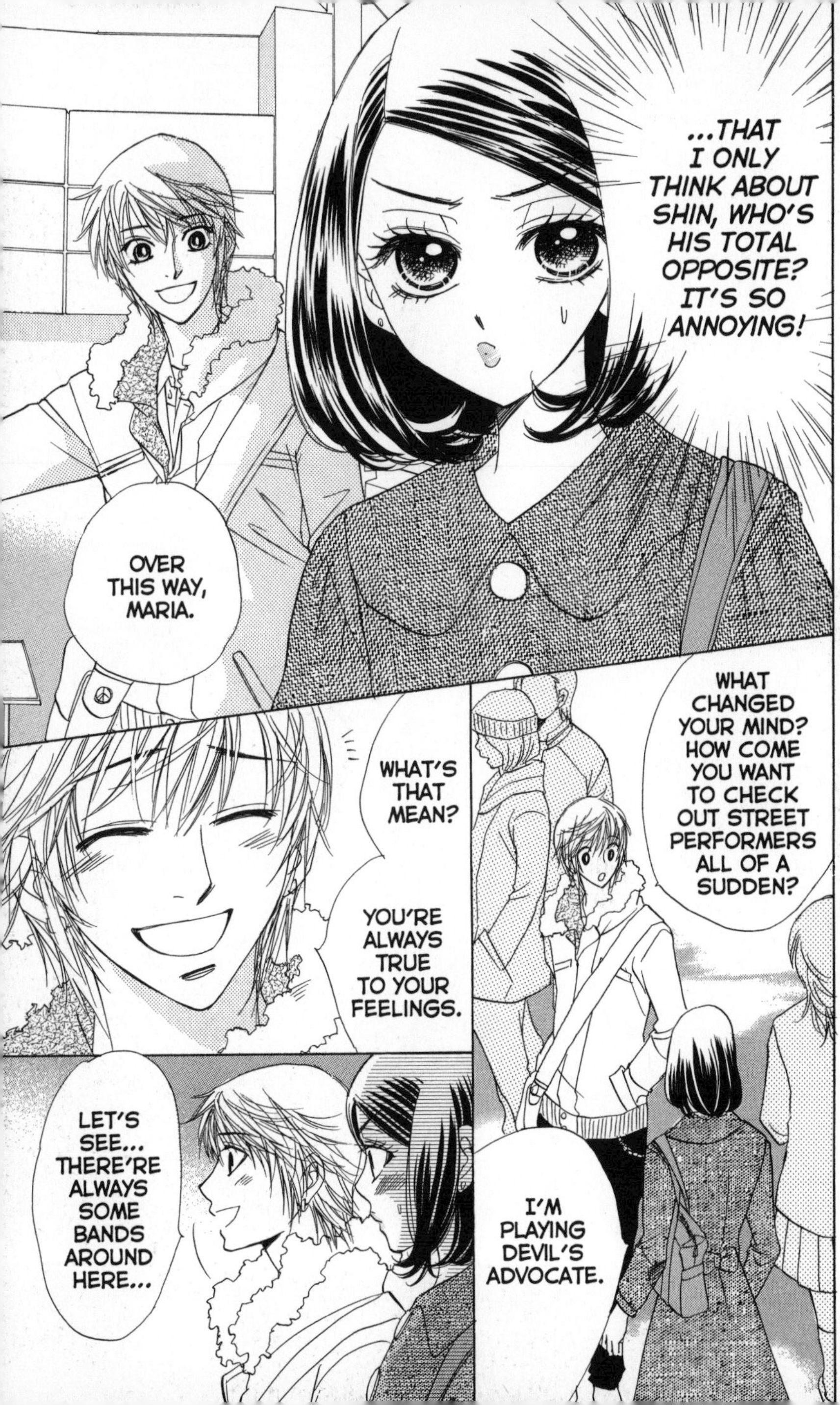
...THAT I ONLY THINK ABOUT SHIN, WHO'S HIS TOTAL OPPOSITE? IT'S SO ANNOYING!
OVER THIS WAY, MARIA.
WHAT CHANGED YOUR MIND? HOW COME YOU WANT TO CHECK OUT STREET PERFORMERS ALL OF A SUDDEN?
I'M PLAYING DEVIL'S ADVOCATE.
WHAT'S THAT MEAN?
YOU'RE ALWAYS TRUE TO YOUR FEELINGS.
LET'S SEE... THERE'RE ALWAYS SOME BANDS AROUND HERE...

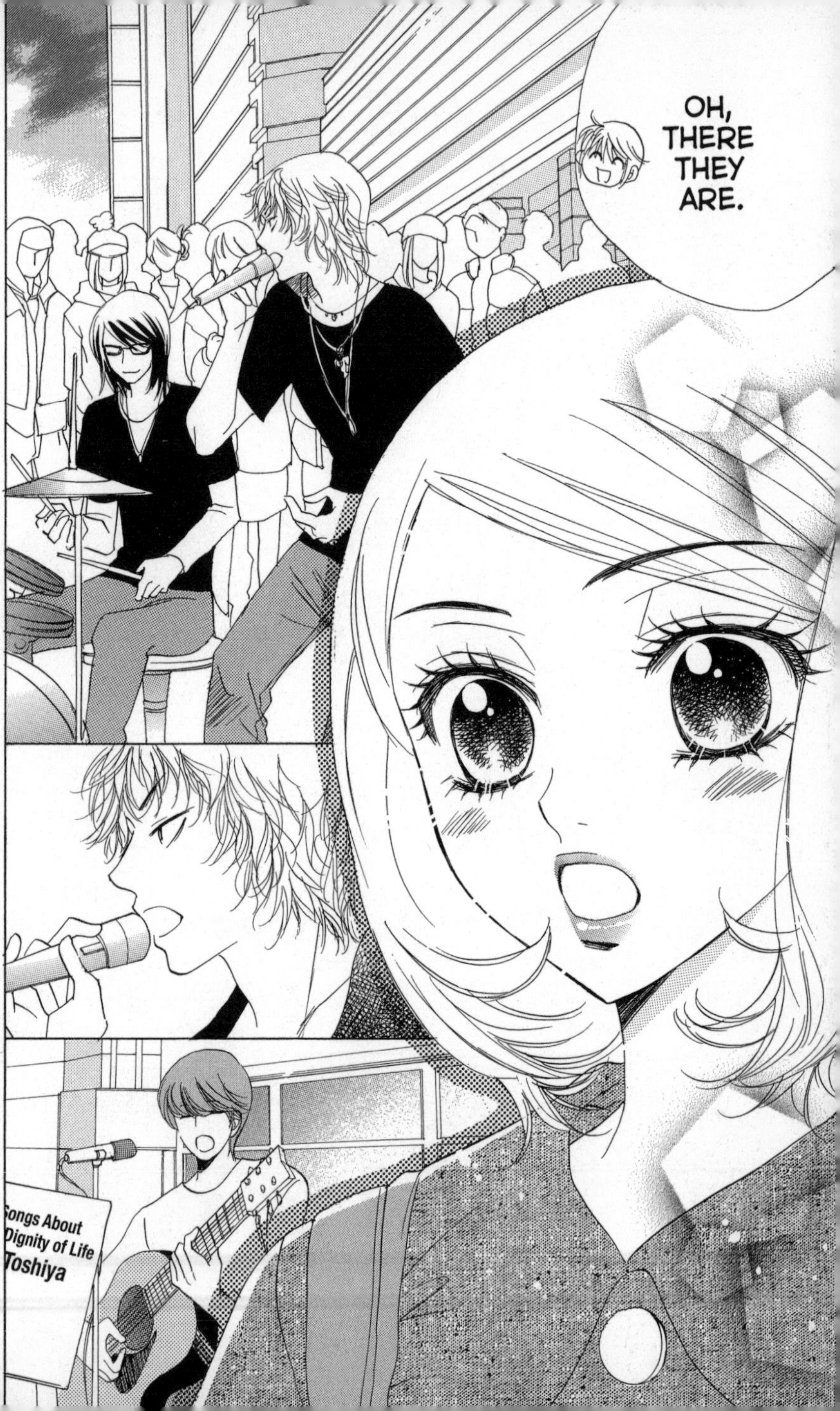
OH, THERE THEY ARE.
Songs About Dignity of Life Toshiya

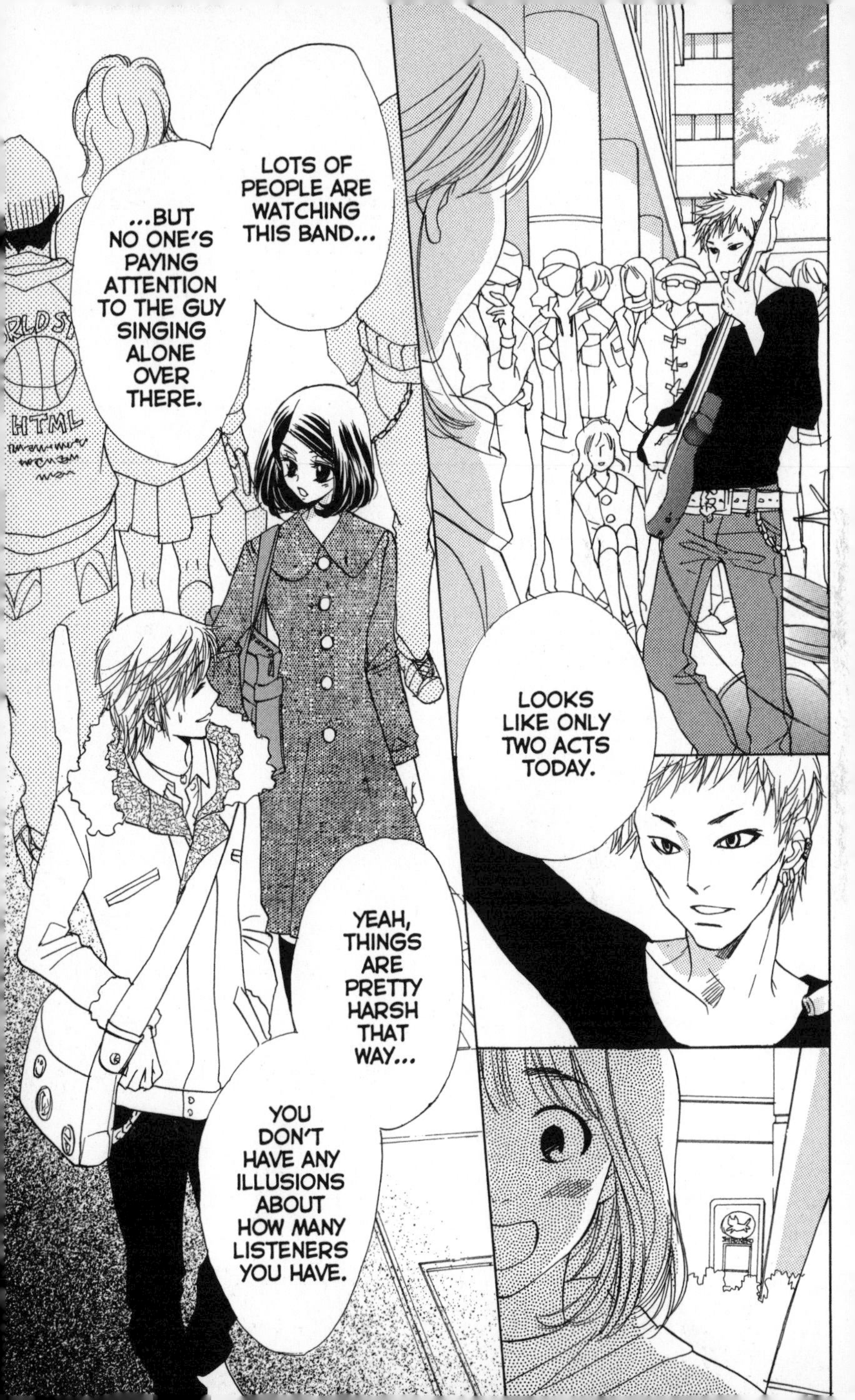
LOOKS LIKE ONLY TWO ACTS TODAY.
YEAH, THINGS ARE PRETTY HARSH THAT WAY...
YOU DON'T HAVE ANY ILLUSIONS ABOUT HOW MANY LISTENERS YOU HAVE.
LOTS OF PEOPLE ARE WATCHING THIS BAND...
...BUT NO ONE'S PAYING ATTENTION TO THE GUY SINGING ALONE OVER THERE.

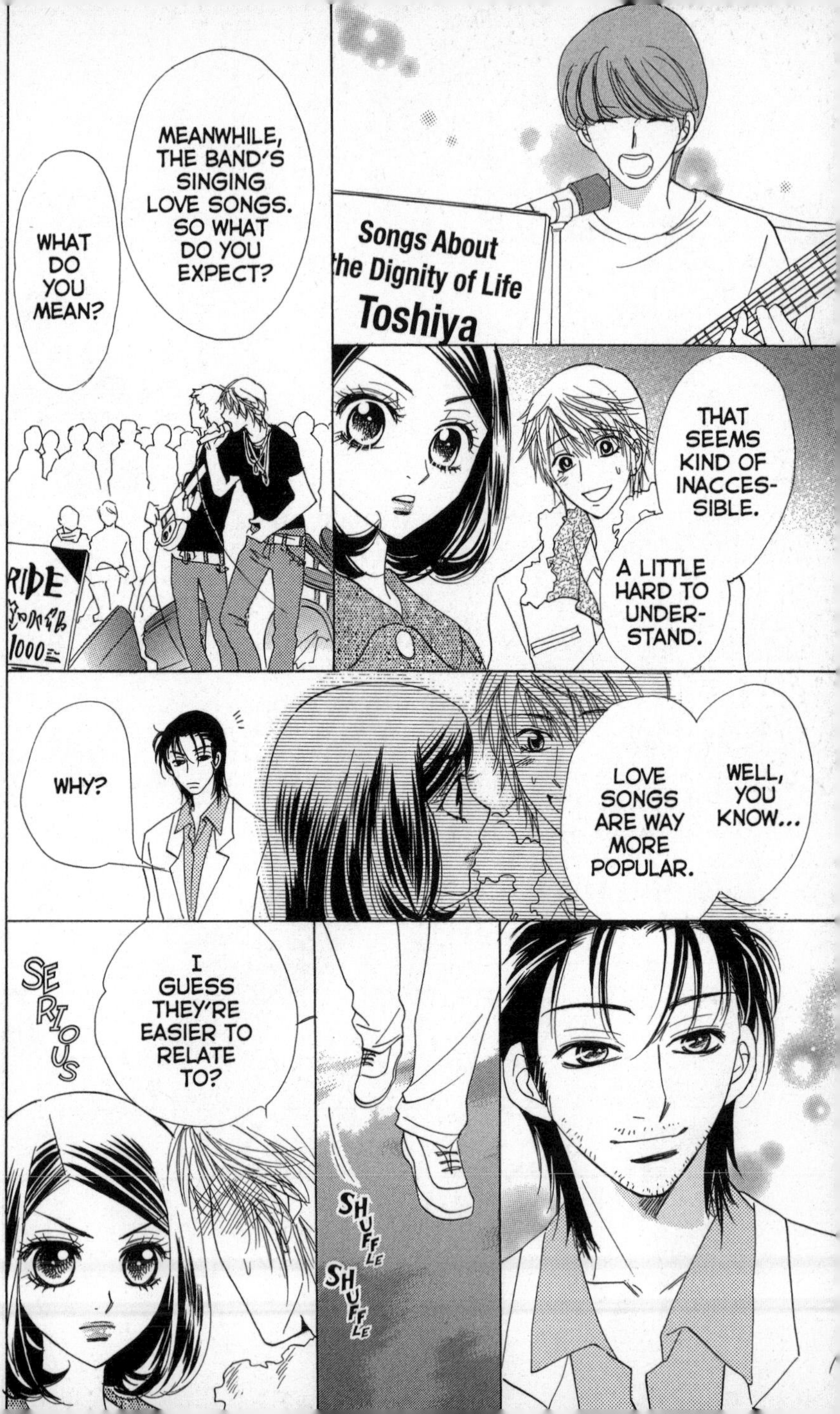
Songs About the Dignity of Life
Toshiya
THAT SEEMS KIND OF INACCES-SIBLE.
A LITTLE HARD TO UNDER-STAND.
MEANWHILE, THE BAND'S SINGING LOVE SONGS. SO WHAT DO YOU EXPECT?
WHAT DO YOU MEAN?
WELL, YOU KNOW...
LOVE SONGS ARE WAY MORE POPULAR.
WHY?
SHUFFLE
SHUFFLE
I GUESS THEY'RE EASIER TO RELATE TO?
SERIOUS

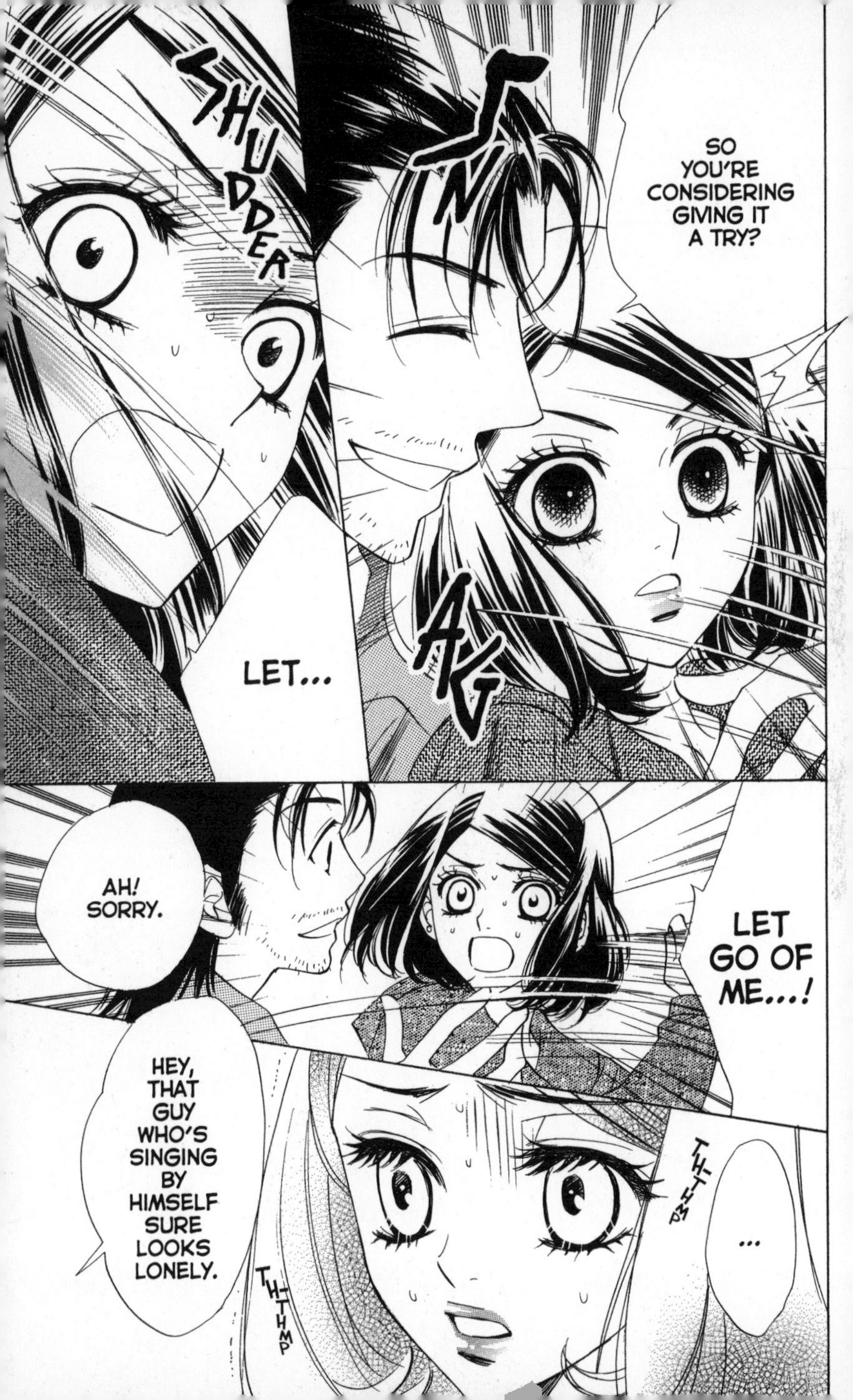
SO YOU'RE CONSIDERING GIVING IT A TRY?
AG
SHUDDER
LET...
LET GO OF ME...!
AH! SORRY.
...
HEY, THAT GUY WHO'S SINGING BY HIMSELF SURE LOOKS LONELY.

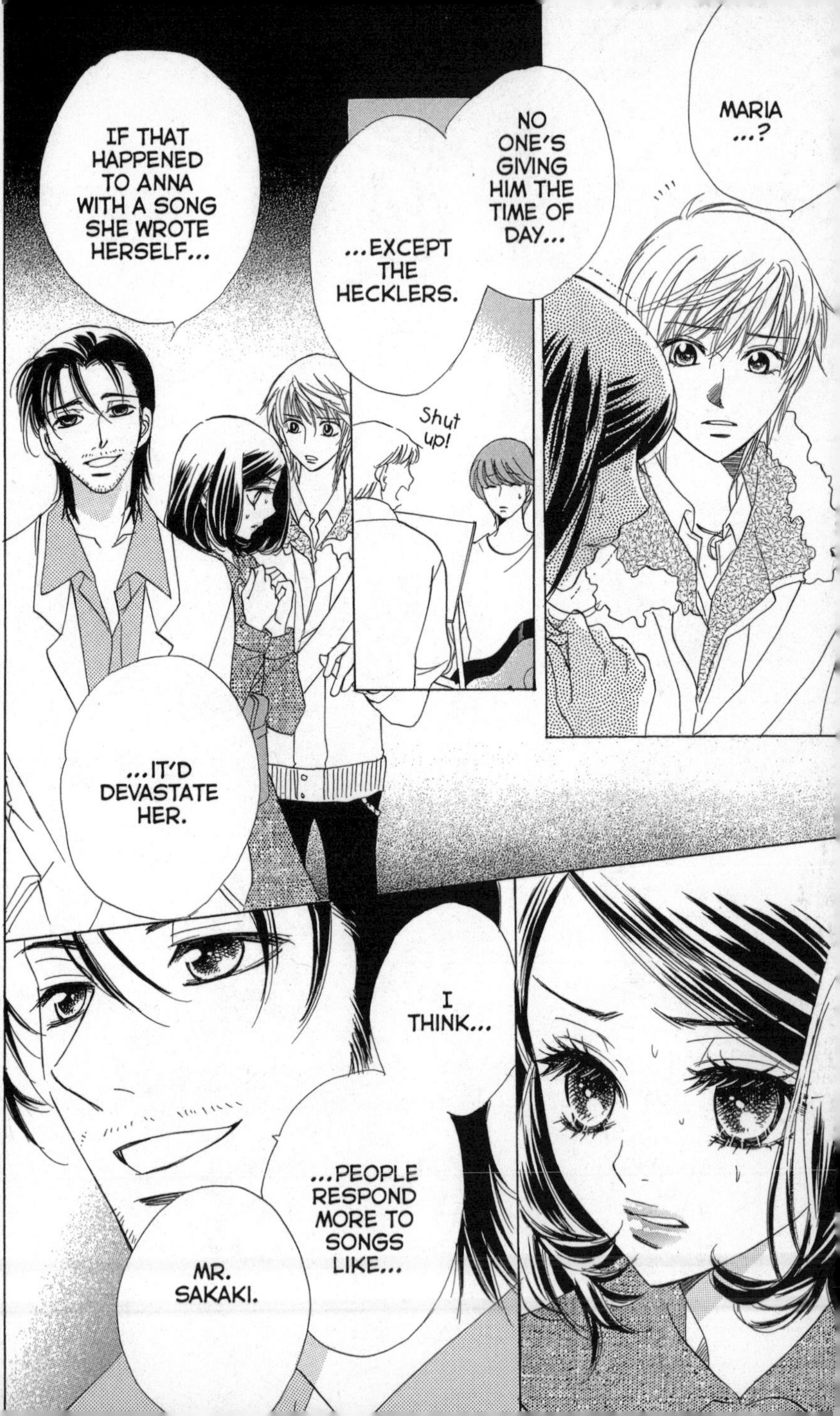
MARIA ...?
NO ONE'S GIVING HIM THE TIME OF DAY...
...EXCEPT THE HECKLERS.
Shut up!
IF THAT HAPPENED TO ANNA WITH A SONG SHE WROTE HERSELF...
...IT'D DEVASTATE HER.
I THINK...
...PEOPLE RESPOND MORE TO SONGS LIKE...
MR. SAKAKI.

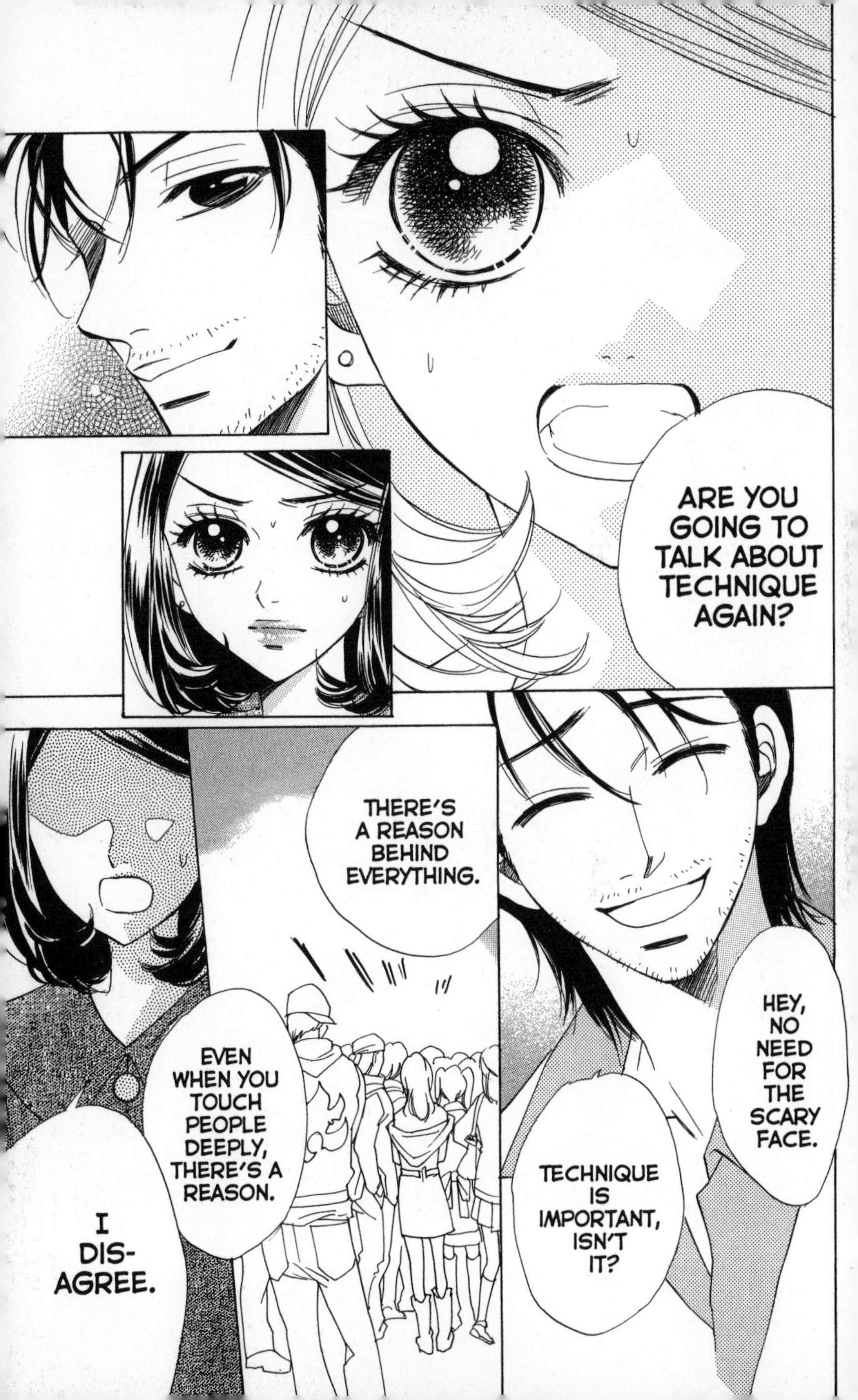
ARE YOU GOING TO TALK ABOUT TECHNIQUE AGAIN?
HEY, NO NEED FOR THE SCARY FACE.
TECHNIQUE IS IMPORTANT, ISN'T IT?
THERE'S A REASON BEHIND EVERYTHING.
EVEN WHEN YOU TOUCH PEOPLE DEEPLY, THERE'S A REASON.
I DIS-AGREE.

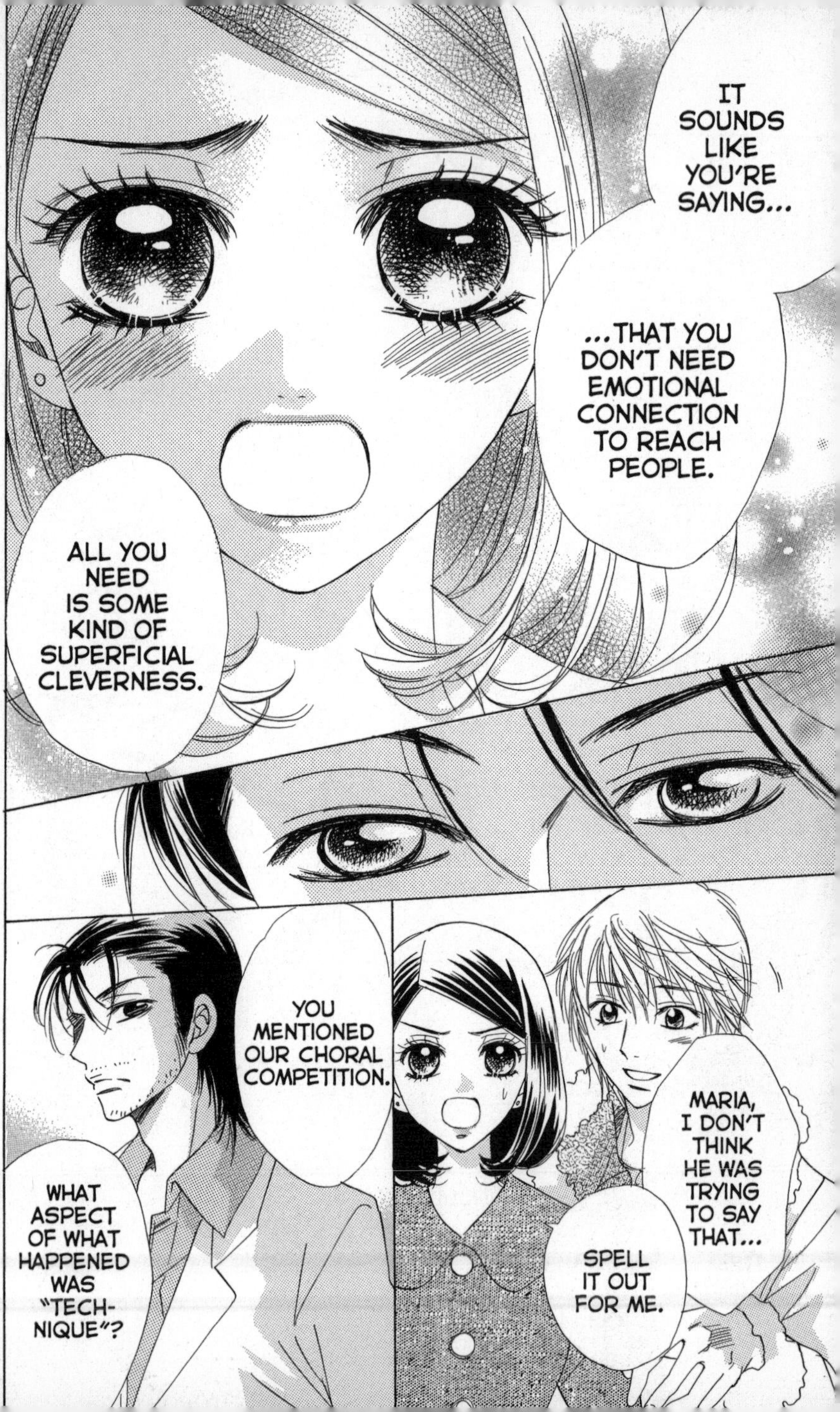
IT SOUNDS LIKE YOU'RE SAYING...
...THAT YOU DON'T NEED EMOTIONAL CONNECTION TO REACH PEOPLE.
ALL YOU NEED IS SOME KIND OF SUPERFICIAL CLEVERNESS.
MARIA, I DON'T THINK HE WAS TRYING TO SAY THAT...
SPELL IT OUT FOR ME.
YOU MENTIONED OUR CHORAL COMPETITION.
WHAT ASPECT OF WHAT HAPPENED WAS "TECH-NIQUE"?

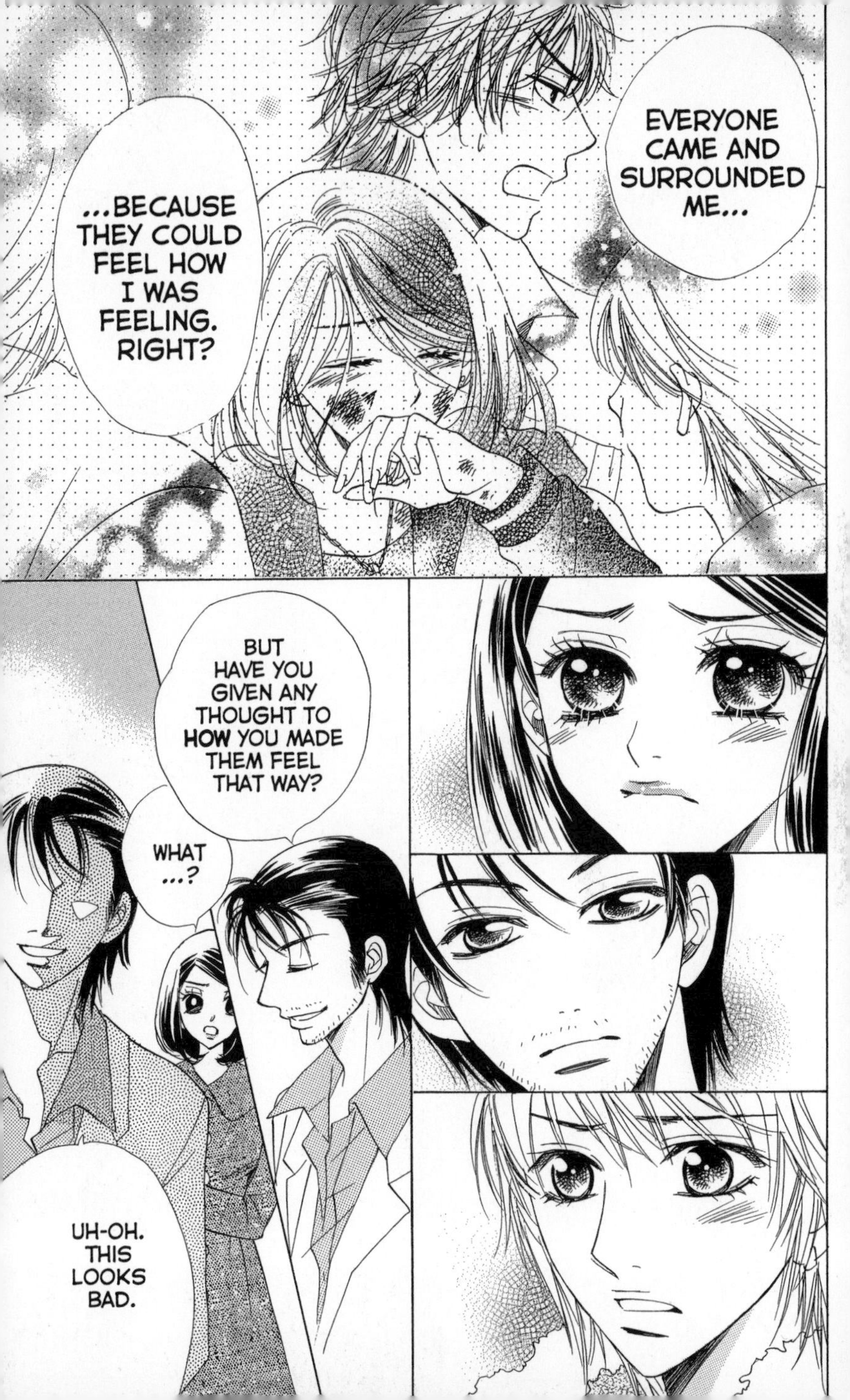
EVERYONE CAME AND SURROUNDED ME...
...BECAUSE THEY COULD FEEL HOW I WAS FEELING. RIGHT?
BUT HAVE YOU GIVEN ANY THOUGHT TO HOW YOU MADE THEM FEEL THAT WAY?
WHAT ...?
UH-OH. THIS LOOKS BAD.

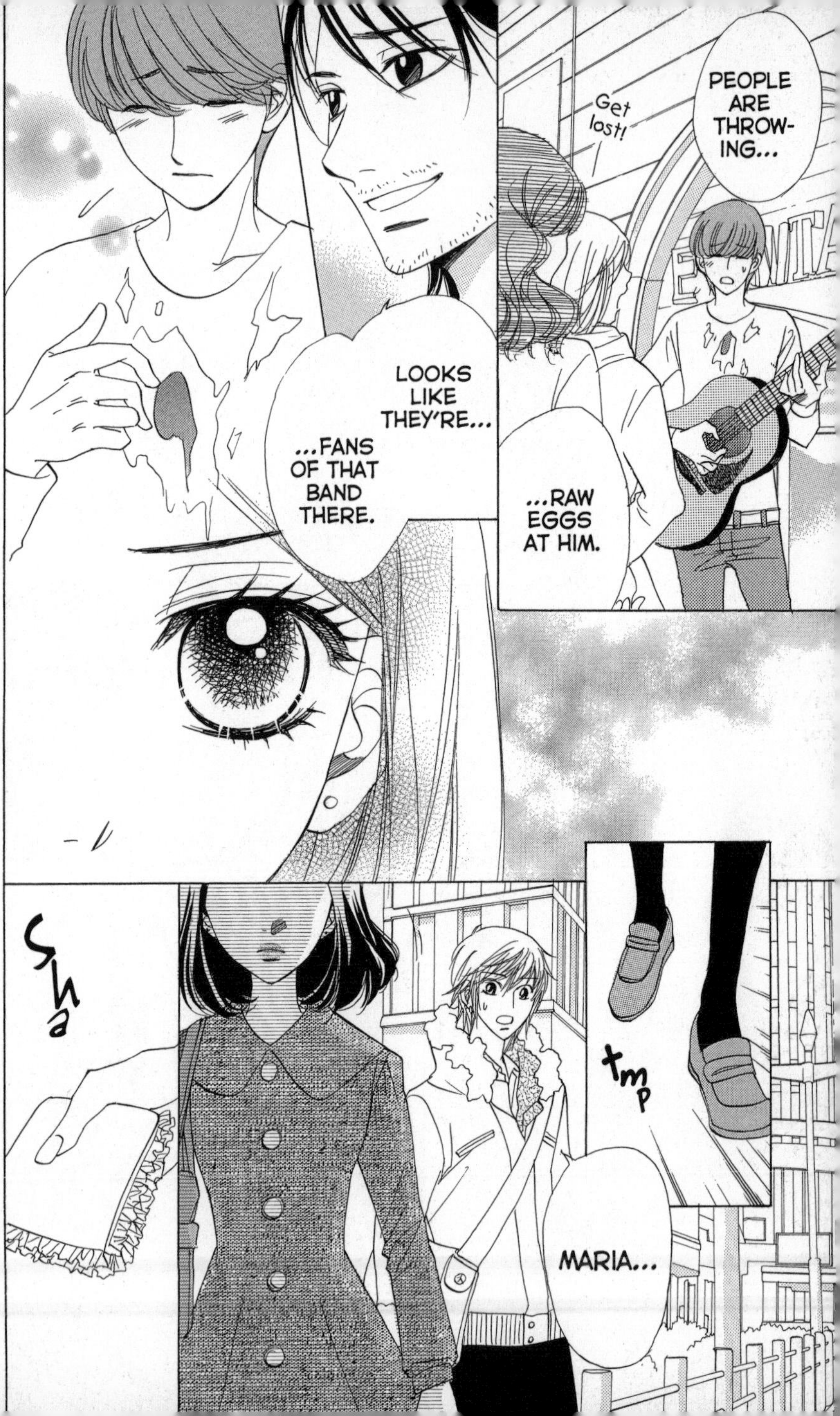
PEOPLE ARE THROWING...
Get lost!
...RAW EGGS AT HIM.
LOOKS LIKE THEY'RE...
...FANS OF THAT BAND THERE.
tmp
MARIA...
Sha

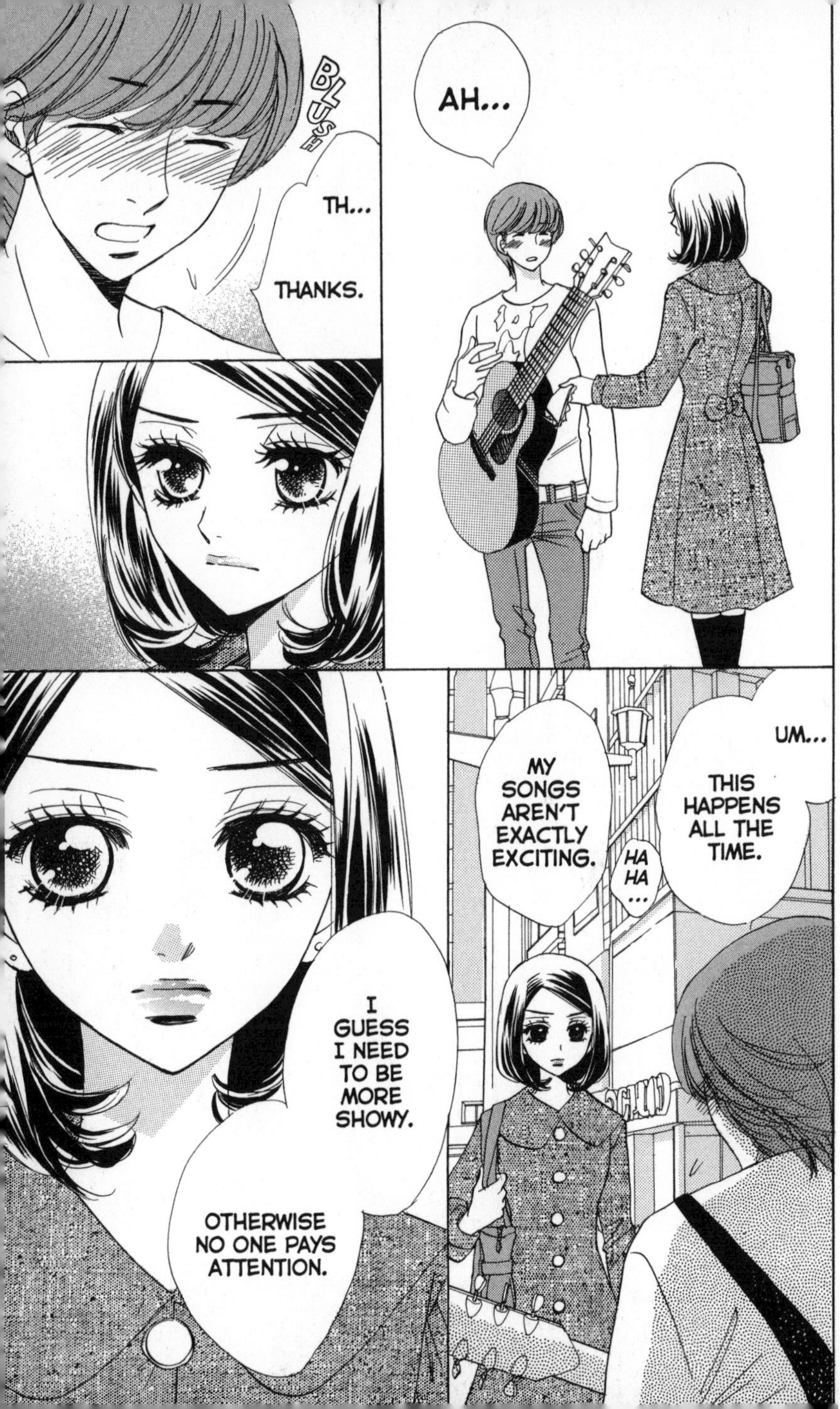
AH...
BLUSH
TH...
THANKS.
UM...
THIS HAPPENS ALL THE TIME.
HA HA ...
MY SONGS AREN'T EXACTLY EXCITING.
I GUESS I NEED TO BE MORE SHOWY.
OTHERWISE NO ONE PAYS ATTENTION.

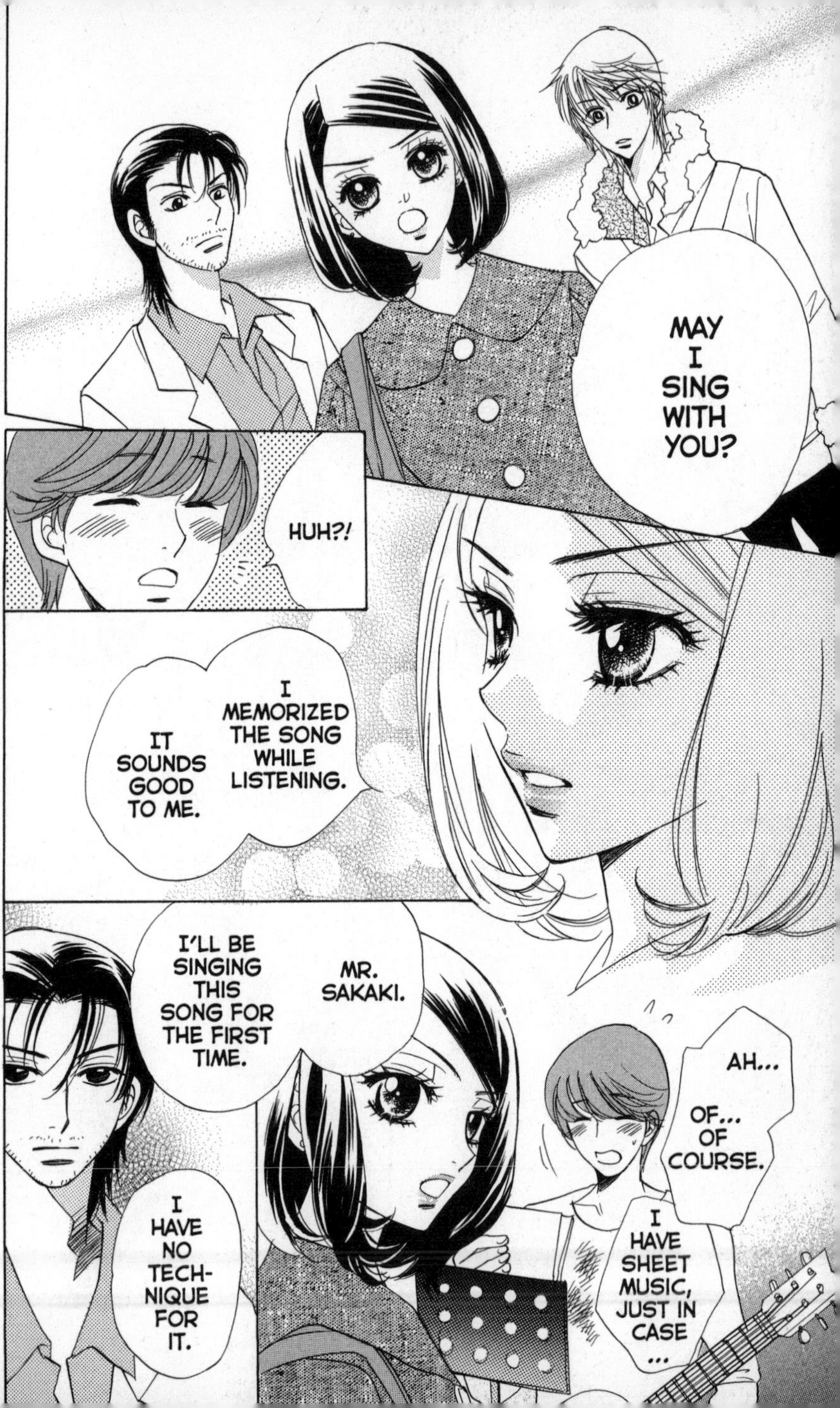
MAY I SING WITH YOU?
HUH?!
I MEMORIZED THE SONG WHILE LISTENING.
IT SOUNDS GOOD TO ME.
AH...
OF... OF COURSE.
I HAVE SHEET MUSIC, JUST IN CASE...
MR. SAKAKI.
I'LL BE SINGING THIS SONG FOR THE FIRST TIME.
I HAVE NO TECH-NIQUE FOR IT.

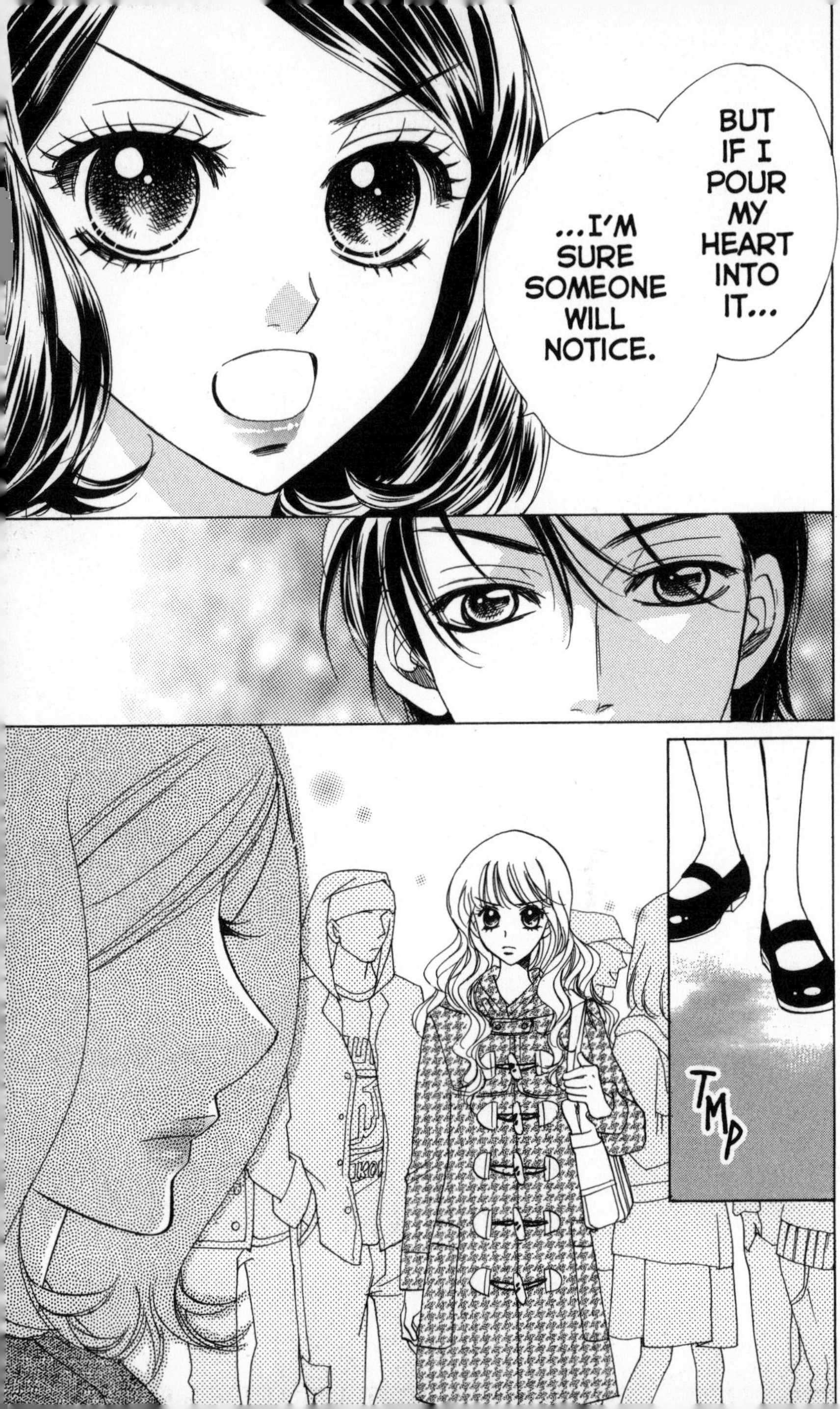
BUT IF I POUR MY HEART INTO IT...
...I'M SURE SOMEONE WILL NOTICE.
TMP

A Devil and
Her Love Song

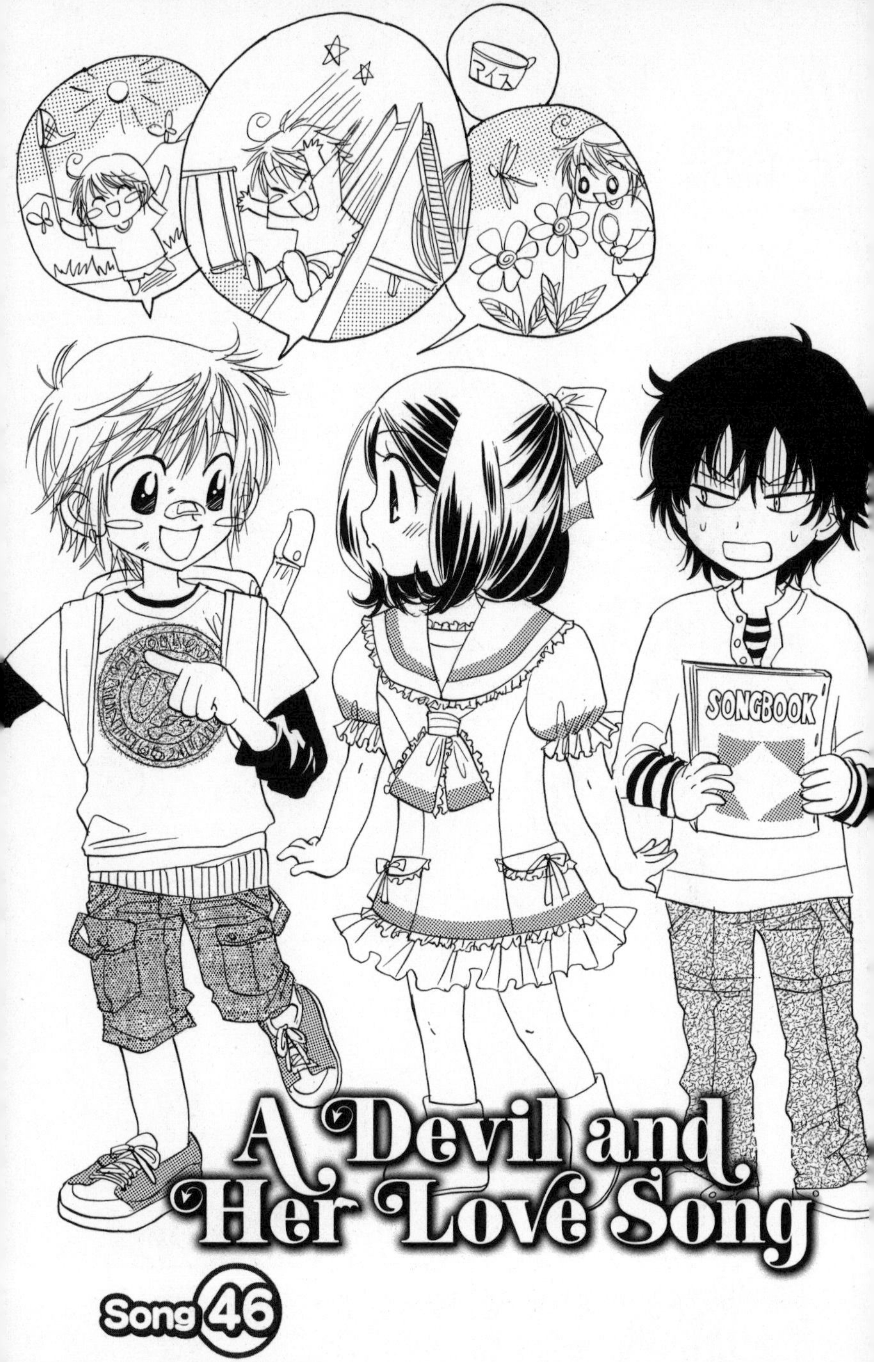
アイス
SONGBOOK

A Devil and Her Love Song

Song 46

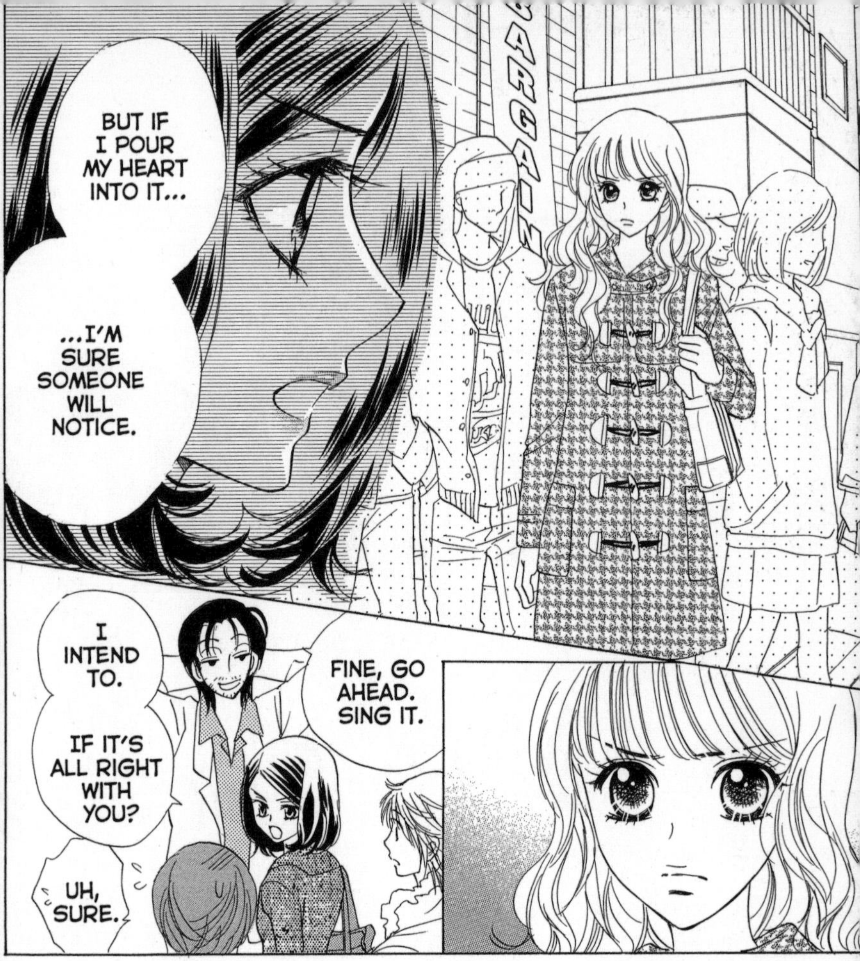
BUT IF I POUR MY HEART INTO IT...
...I'M SURE SOMEONE WILL NOTICE.
ARGAIN
FINE, GO AHEAD. SING IT.
I INTEND TO.
IF IT'S ALL RIGHT WITH YOU?
UH, SURE.

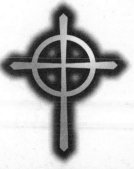

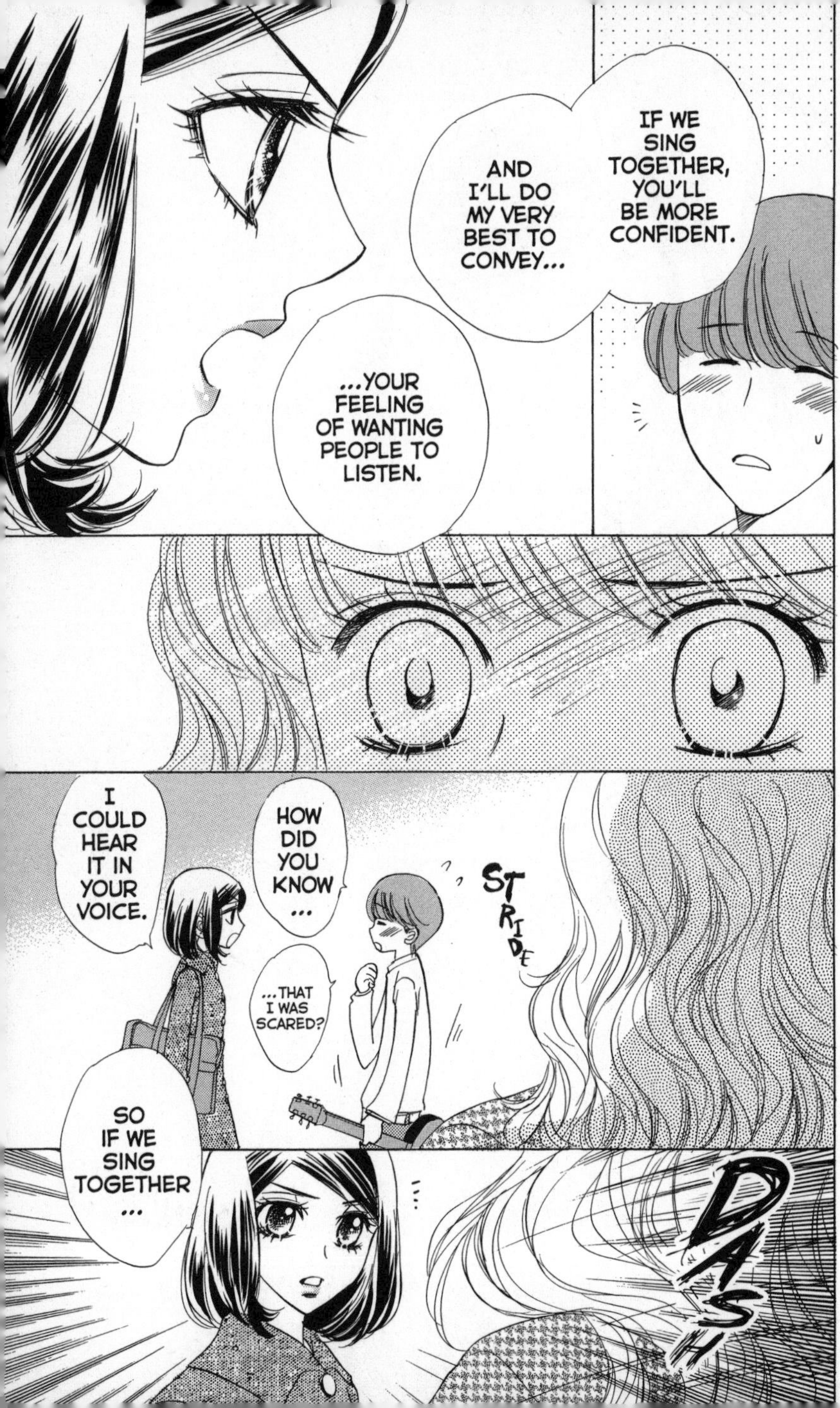
IF WE SING TOGETHER, YOU'LL BE MORE CONFIDENT.
AND I'LL DO MY VERY BEST TO CONVEY...
...YOUR FEELING OF WANTING PEOPLE TO LISTEN.
STRIDE
HOW DID YOU KNOW...
...THAT I WAS SCARED?
I COULD HEAR IT IN YOUR VOICE.
SO IF WE SING TOGETHER...
DASH
...

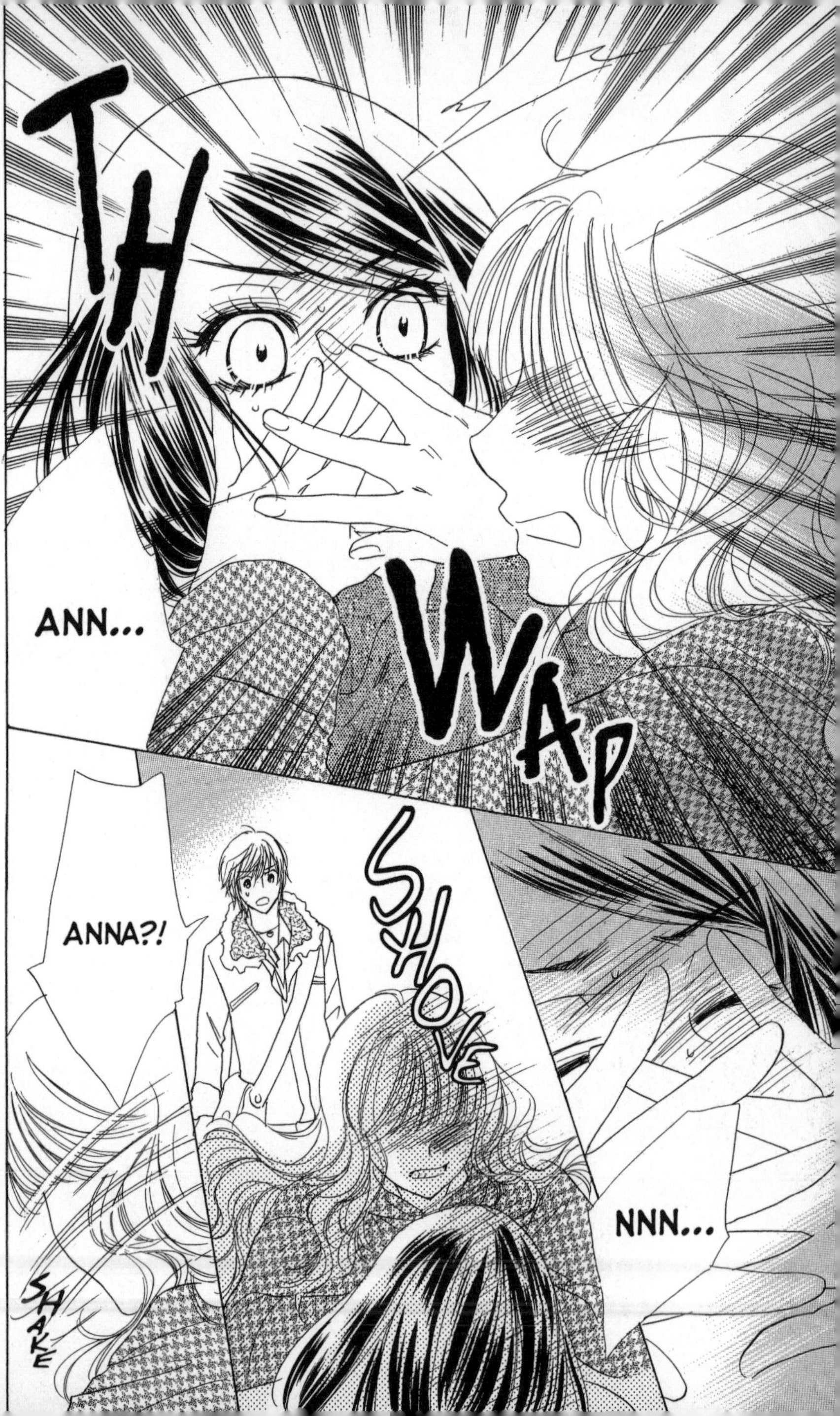
TH
WAP
ANN...
NNN...
SHOVE
ANNA?!
SHAKE

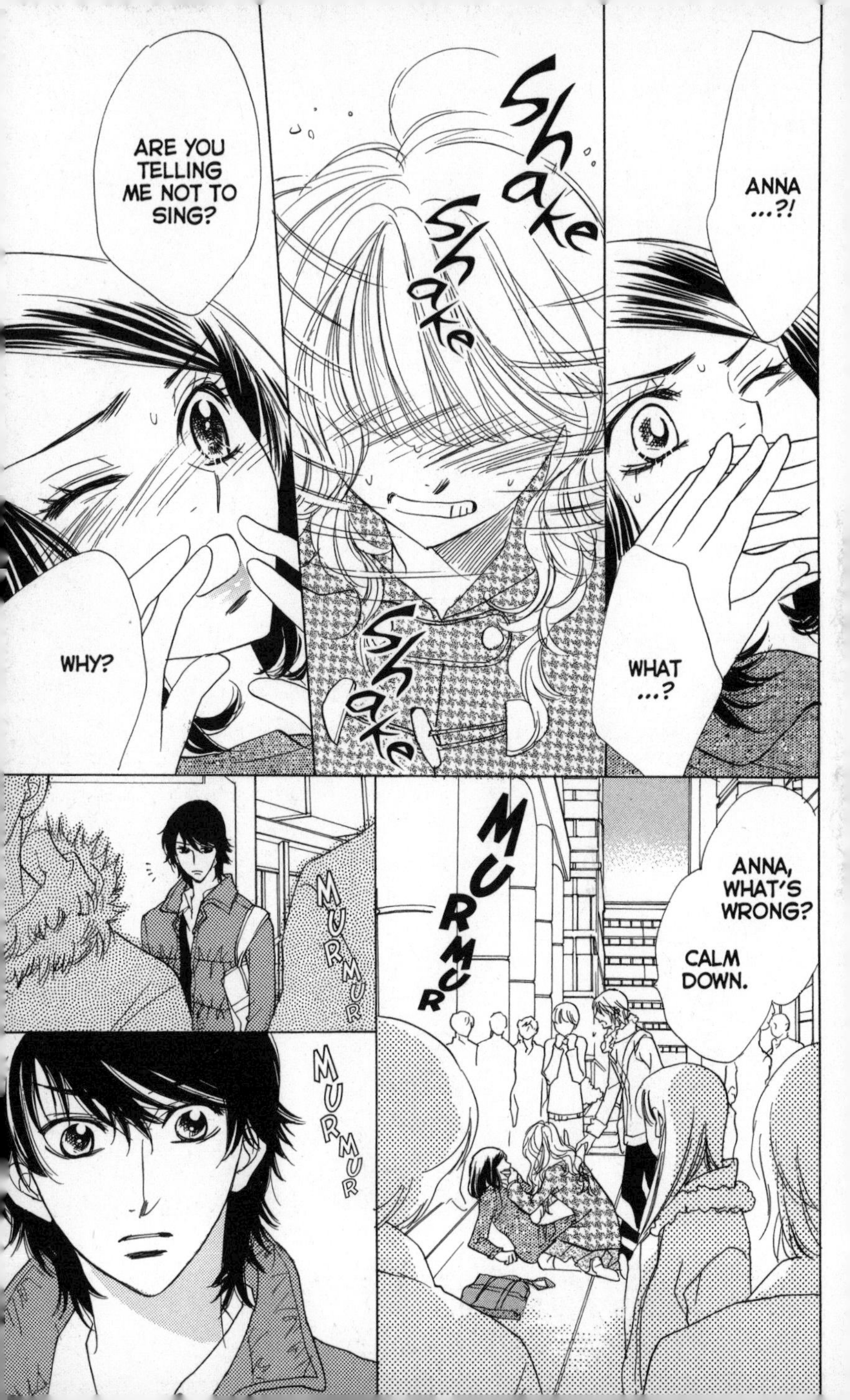
ANNA ...?!
WHAT ...?
Shake
Shake
Shake
ARE YOU TELLING ME NOT TO SING?
WHY?
ANNA, WHAT'S WRONG?
CALM DOWN.
MURMUR
MURMUR
MURMUR
MURMUR
MURMUR

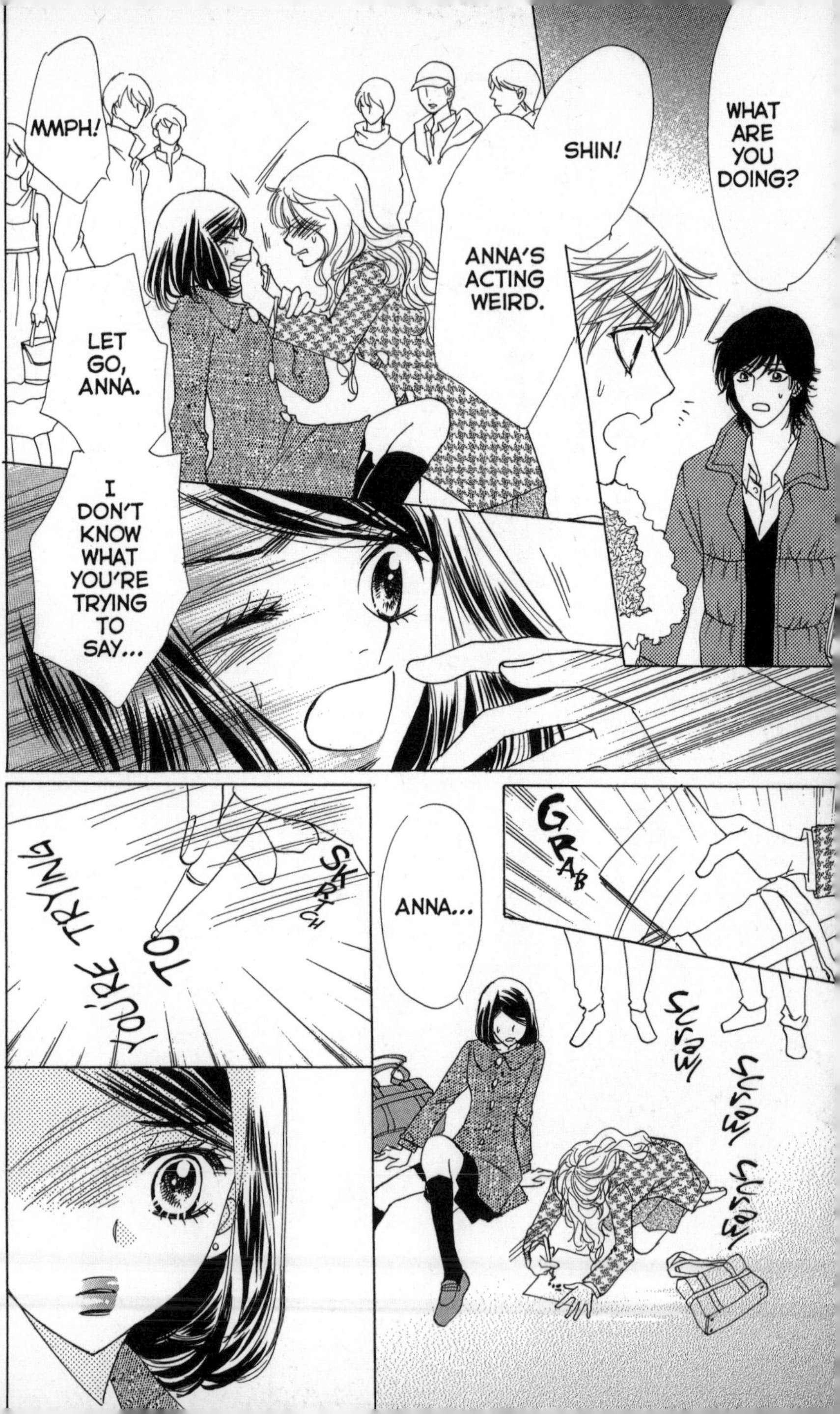
WHAT ARE YOU DOING?
SHIN!
ANNA'S ACTING WEIRD.
MMPH!
LET GO, ANNA.
I DON'T KNOW WHAT YOU'RE TRYING TO SAY...
GRAB
ANNA...
SCRAWL
SCRAWL
SCRAWL
SKRTCH
YOU'RE TRYING TO

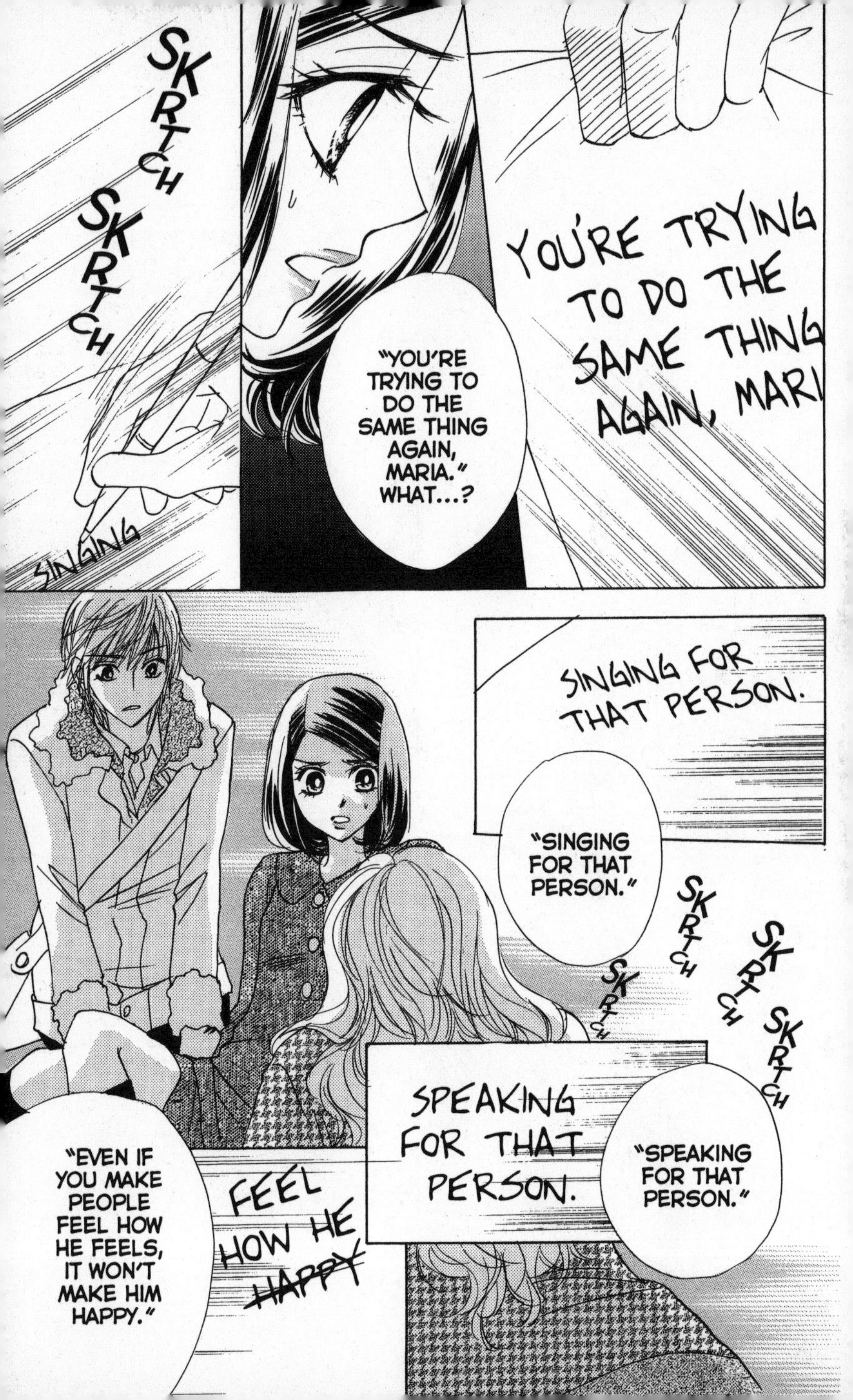
YOU'RE TRYING TO DO THE SAME THING AGAIN, MARI
"YOU'RE TRYING TO DO THE SAME THING AGAIN, MARIA." WHAT...?
SKRTCH SKRTCH
SINGING
SINGING FOR THAT PERSON.
"SINGING FOR THAT PERSON."
SKRTCH SKRTCH SKRTCH SKRTCH
SPEAKING FOR THAT PERSON.
"SPEAKING FOR THAT PERSON."
FEEL HOW HE HAPPY
"EVEN IF YOU MAKE PEOPLE FEEL HOW HE FEELS, IT WON'T MAKE HIM HAPPY."

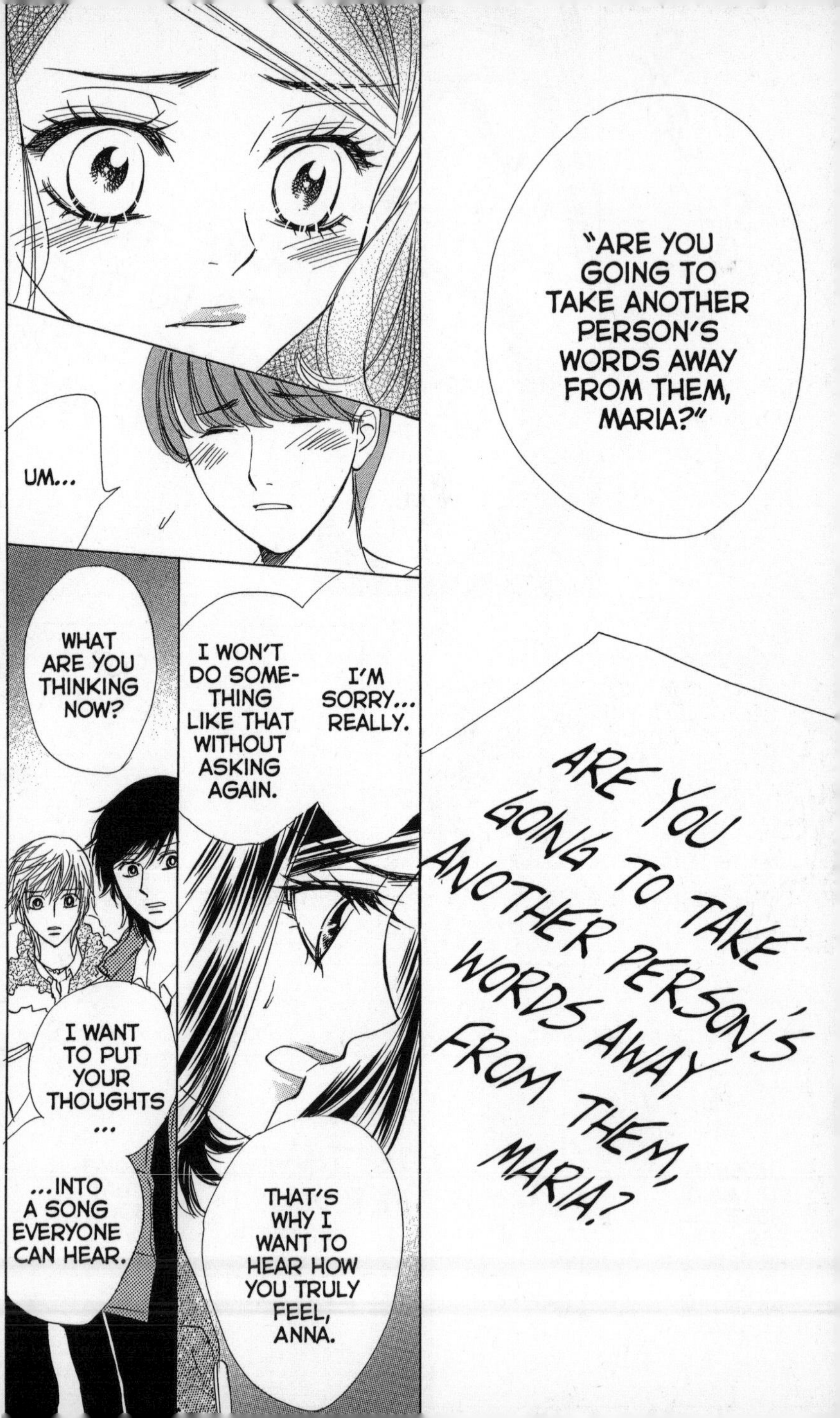
"ARE YOU GOING TO TAKE ANOTHER PERSON'S WORDS AWAY FROM THEM, MARIA?"
ARE YOU GOING TO TAKE ANOTHER PERSON'S WORDS AWAY FROM THEM, MARIA?
UM...
I'M SORRY... REALLY.
I WON'T DO SOME-THING LIKE THAT WITHOUT ASKING AGAIN.
THAT'S WHY I WANT TO HEAR HOW YOU TRULY FEEL, ANNA.
WHAT ARE YOU THINKING NOW?
I WANT TO PUT YOUR THOUGHTS...
...INTO A SONG EVERYONE CAN HEAR.

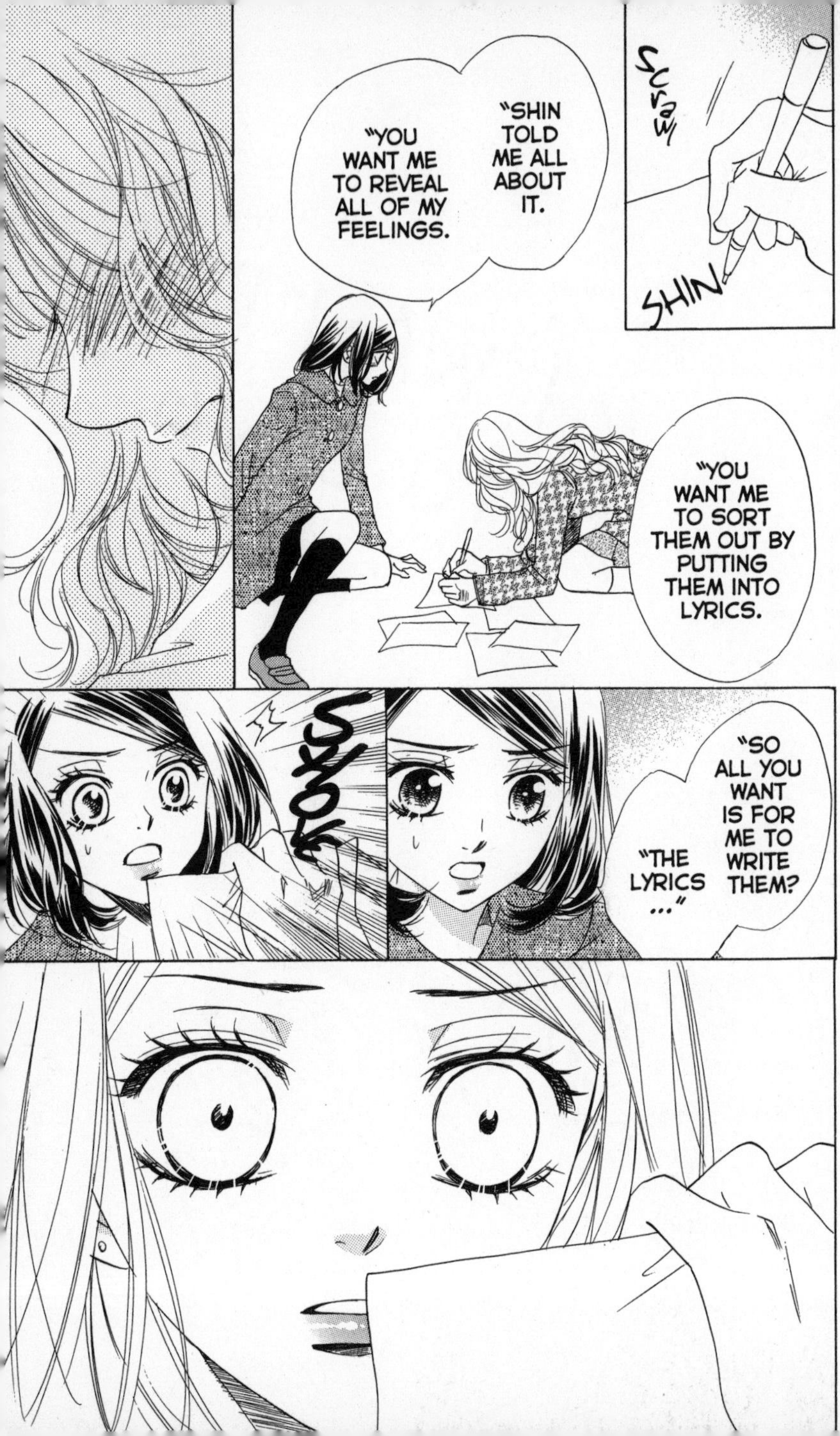
SCRAWL
SHIN
"SHIN TOLD ME ALL ABOUT IT.
"YOU WANT ME TO REVEAL ALL OF MY FEELINGS.
"YOU WANT ME TO SORT THEM OUT BY PUTTING THEM INTO LYRICS.
"SO ALL YOU WANT IS FOR ME TO WRITE THEM?
"THE LYRICS ..."
STOK

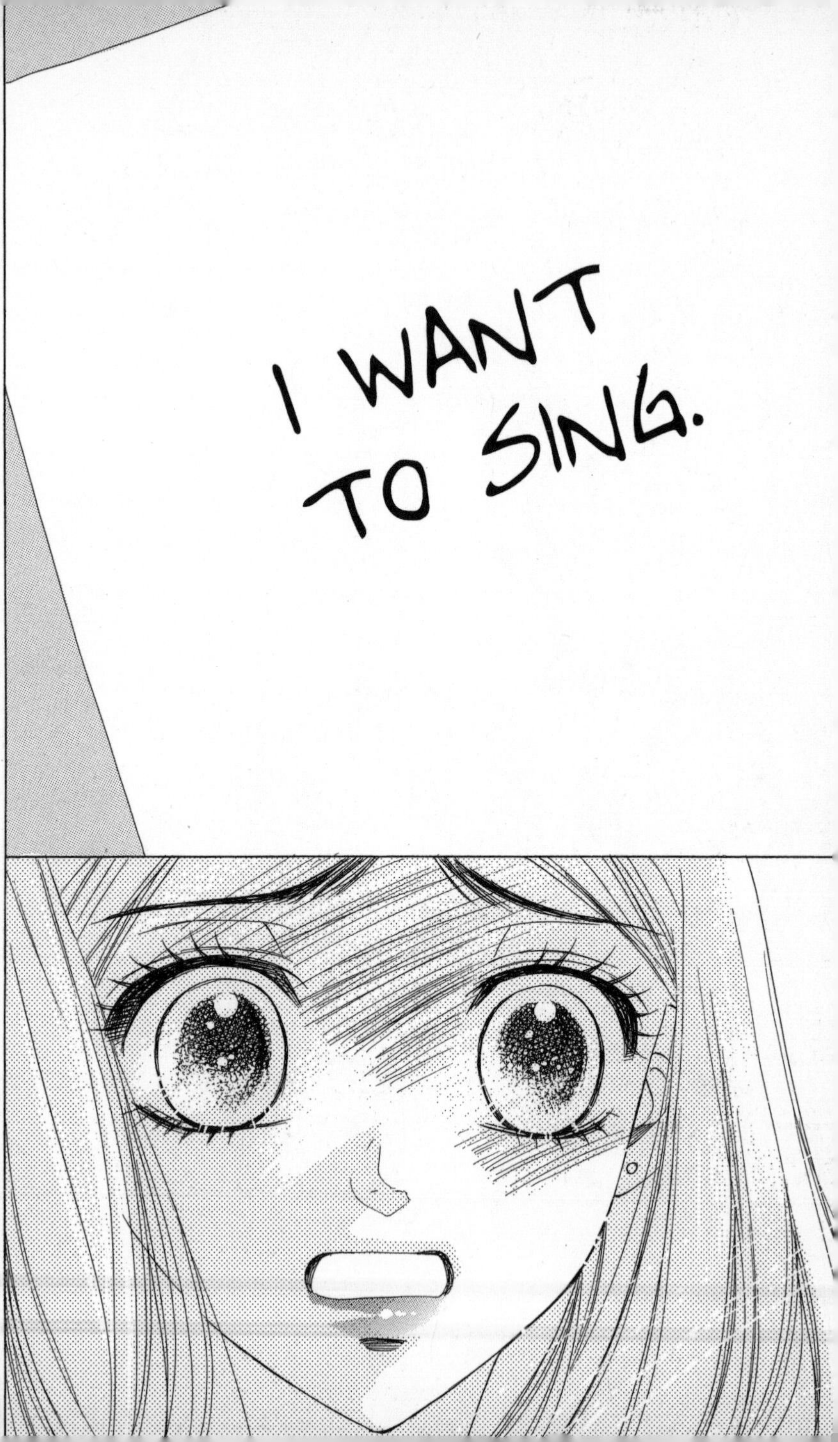
I WANT TO SING.

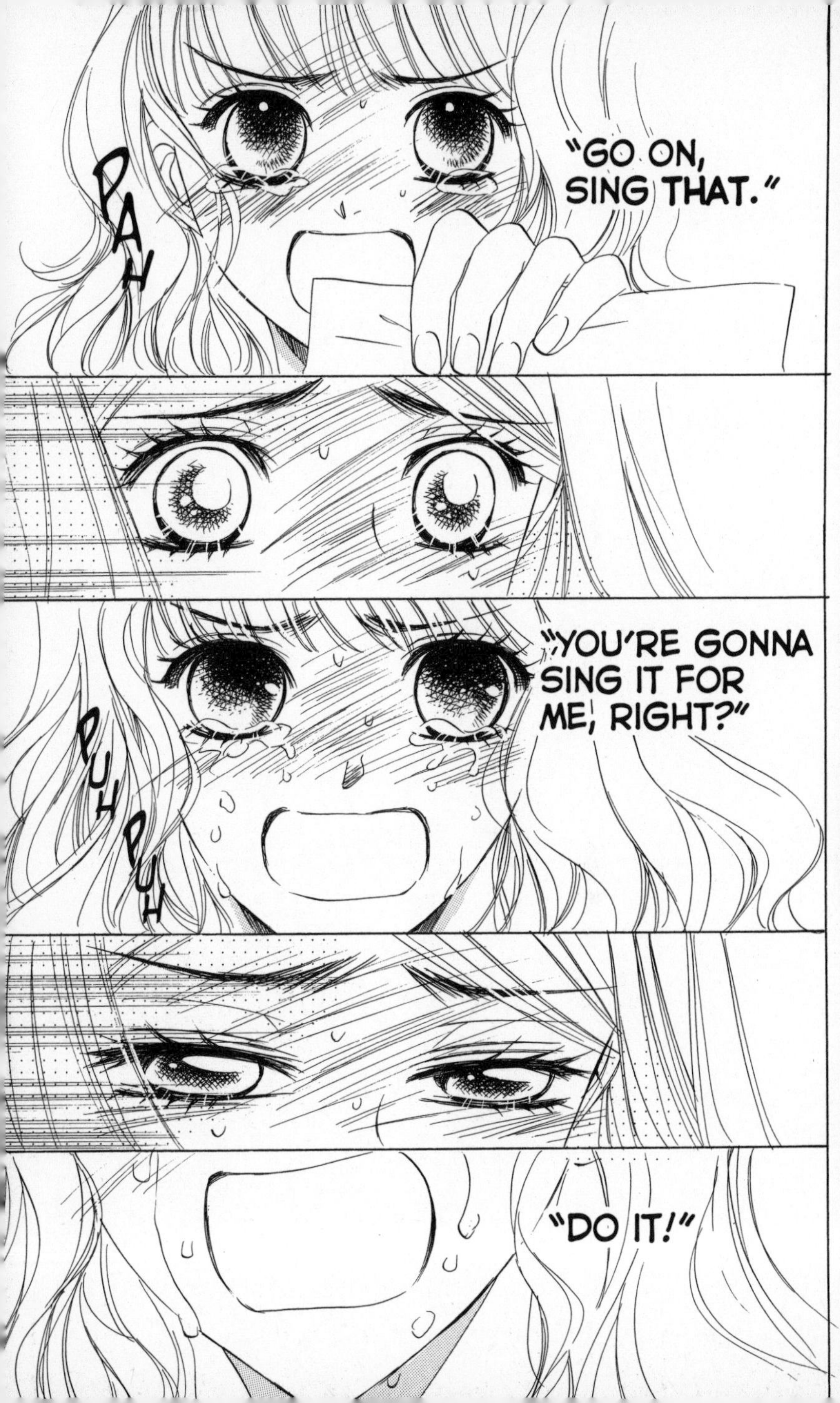
"GO ON, SING THAT."
PAH
"YOU'RE GONNA SING IT FOR ME, RIGHT?"
PUH PUH PUH
"DO IT!"

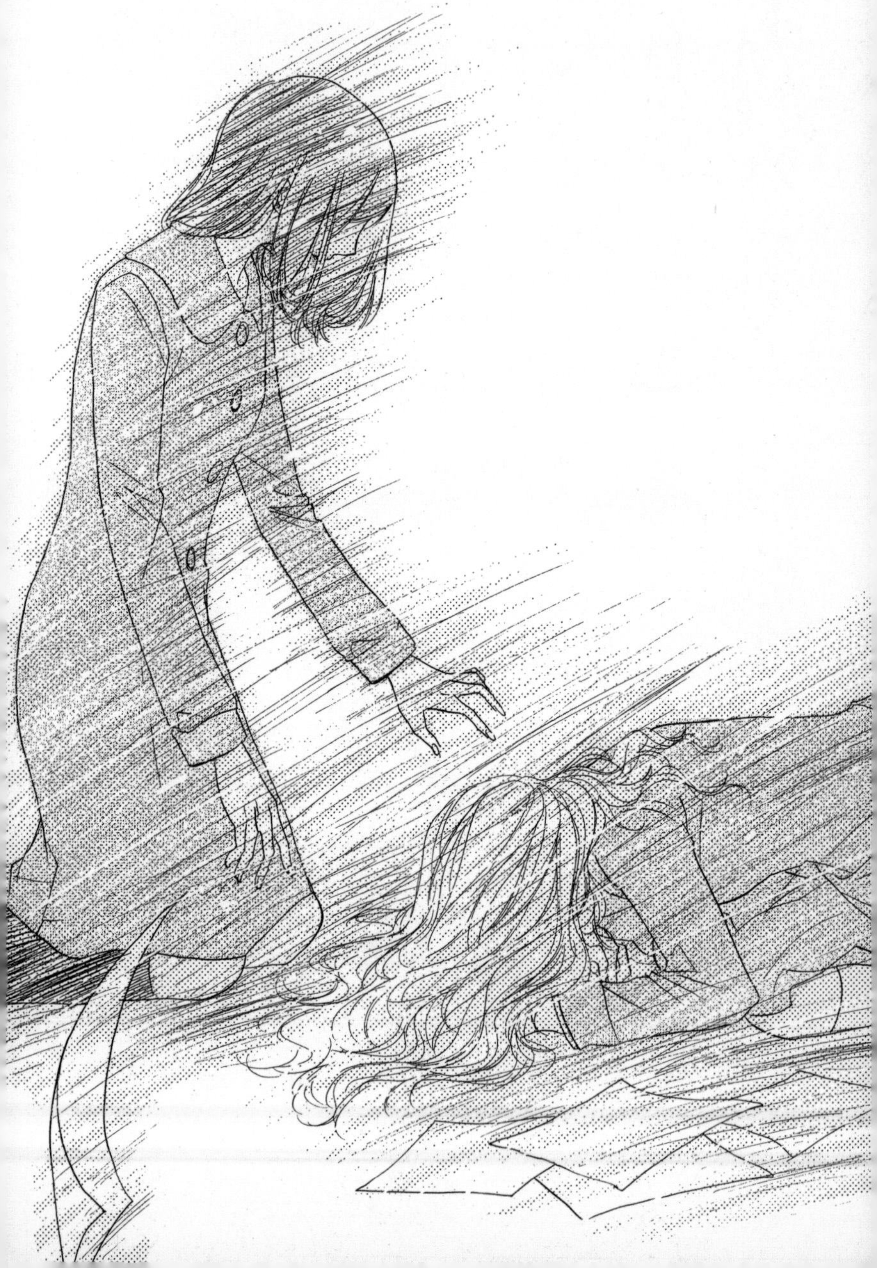

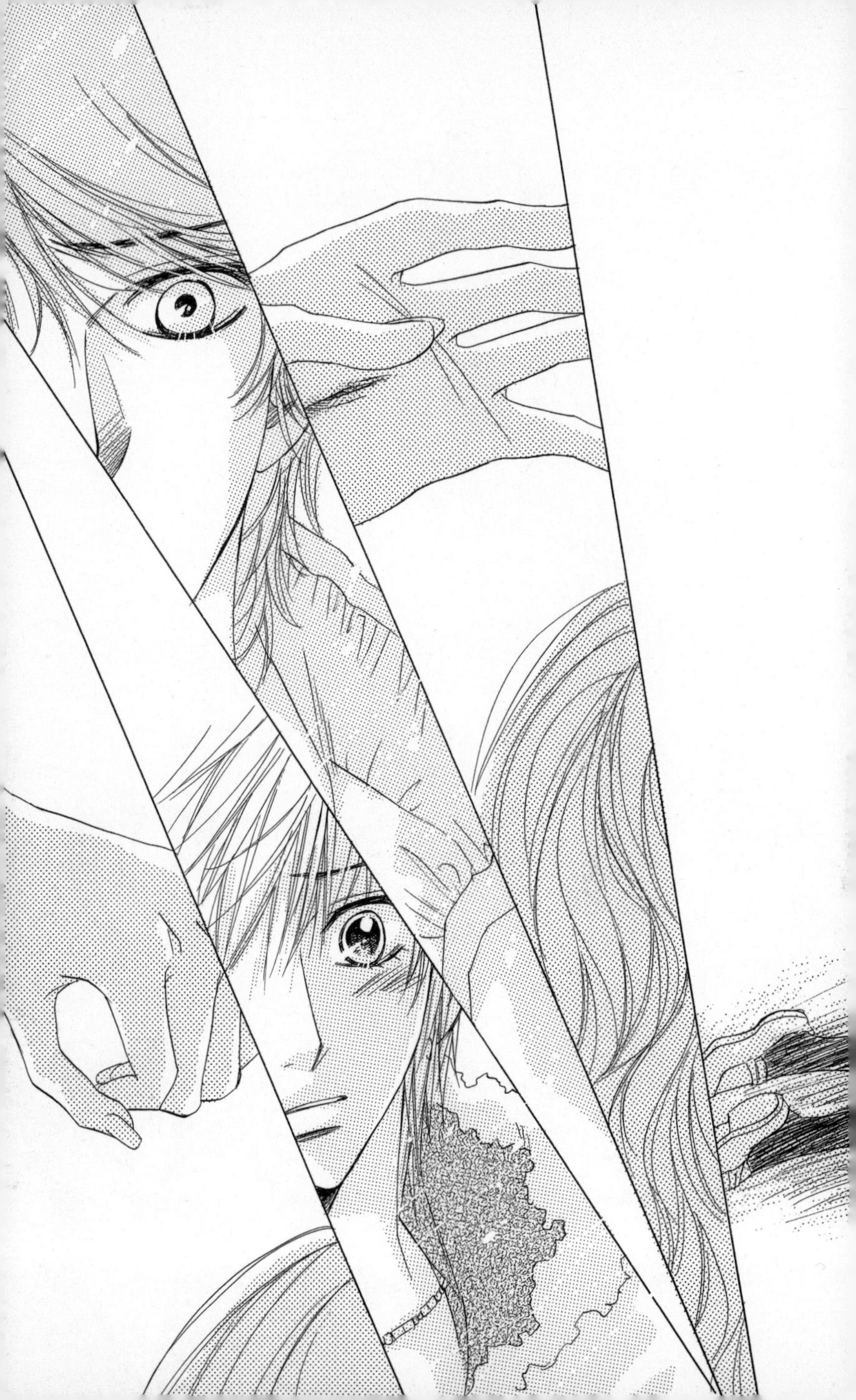

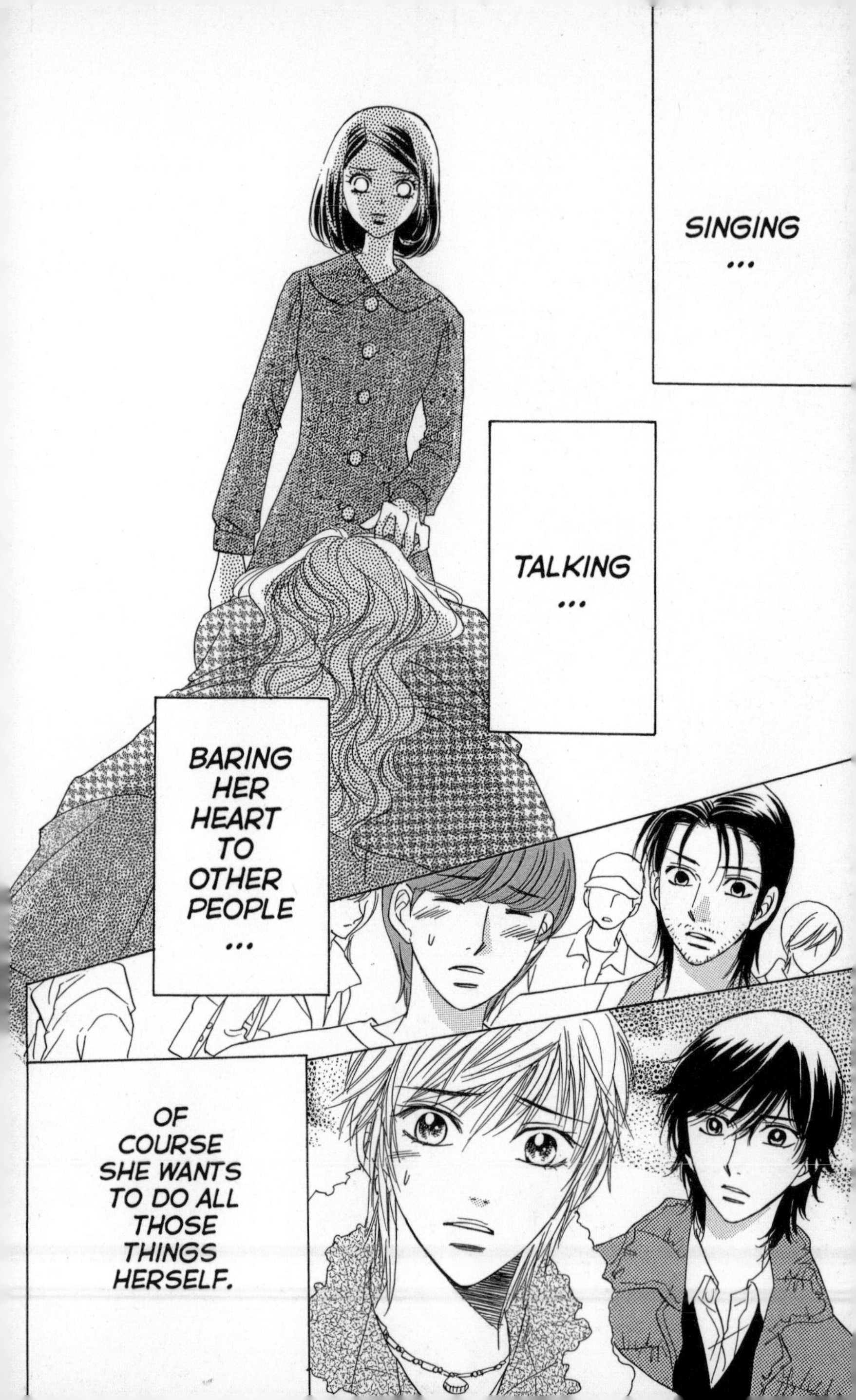
SINGING ...
TALKING ...
BARING HER HEART TO OTHER PEOPLE ...
OF COURSE SHE WANTS TO DO ALL THOSE THINGS HERSELF.

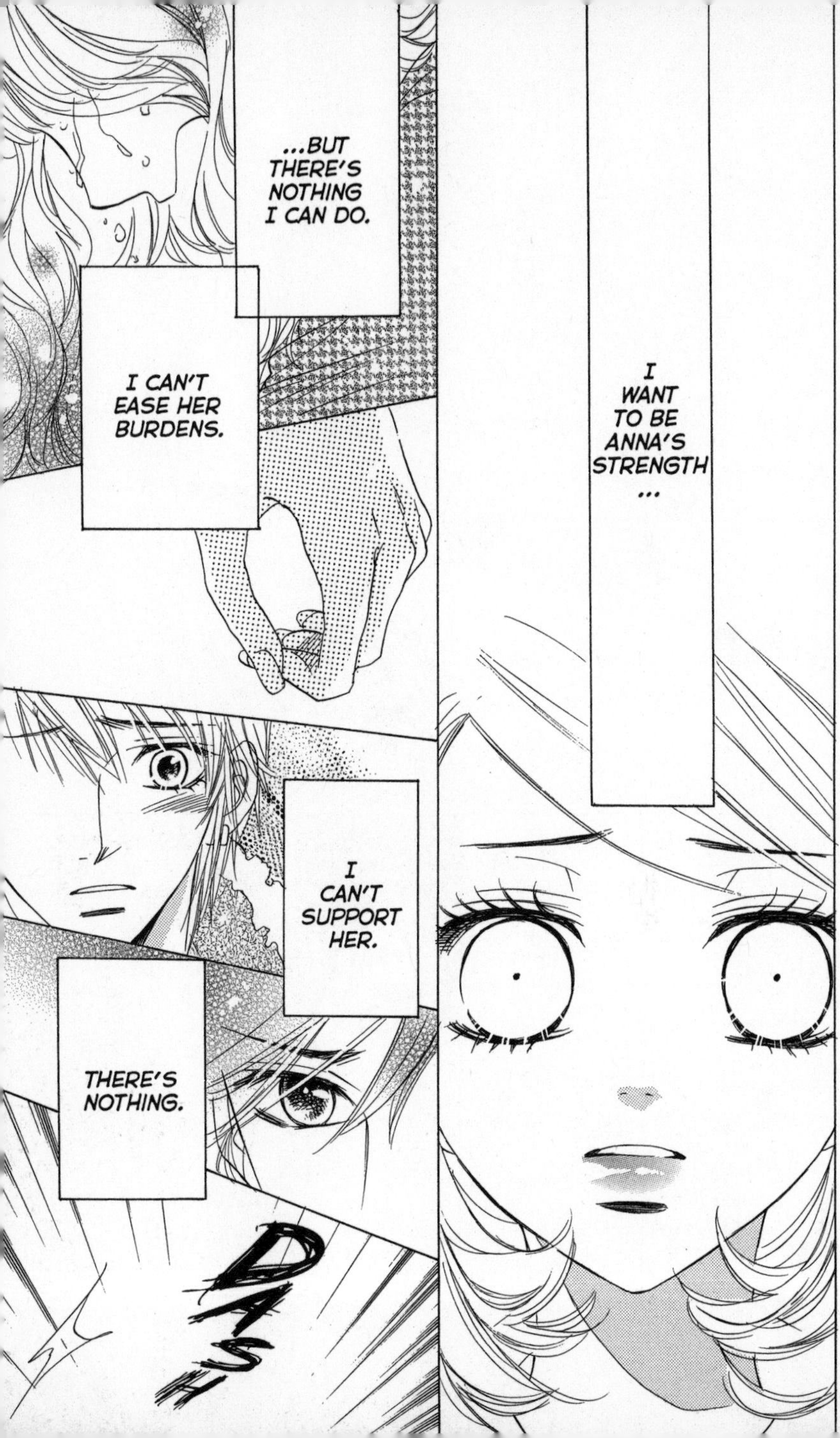
I WANT TO BE ANNA'S STRENGTH ...
...BUT THERE'S NOTHING I CAN DO.
I CAN'T EASE HER BURDENS.
I CAN'T SUPPORT HER.
THERE'S NOTHING.
DASH

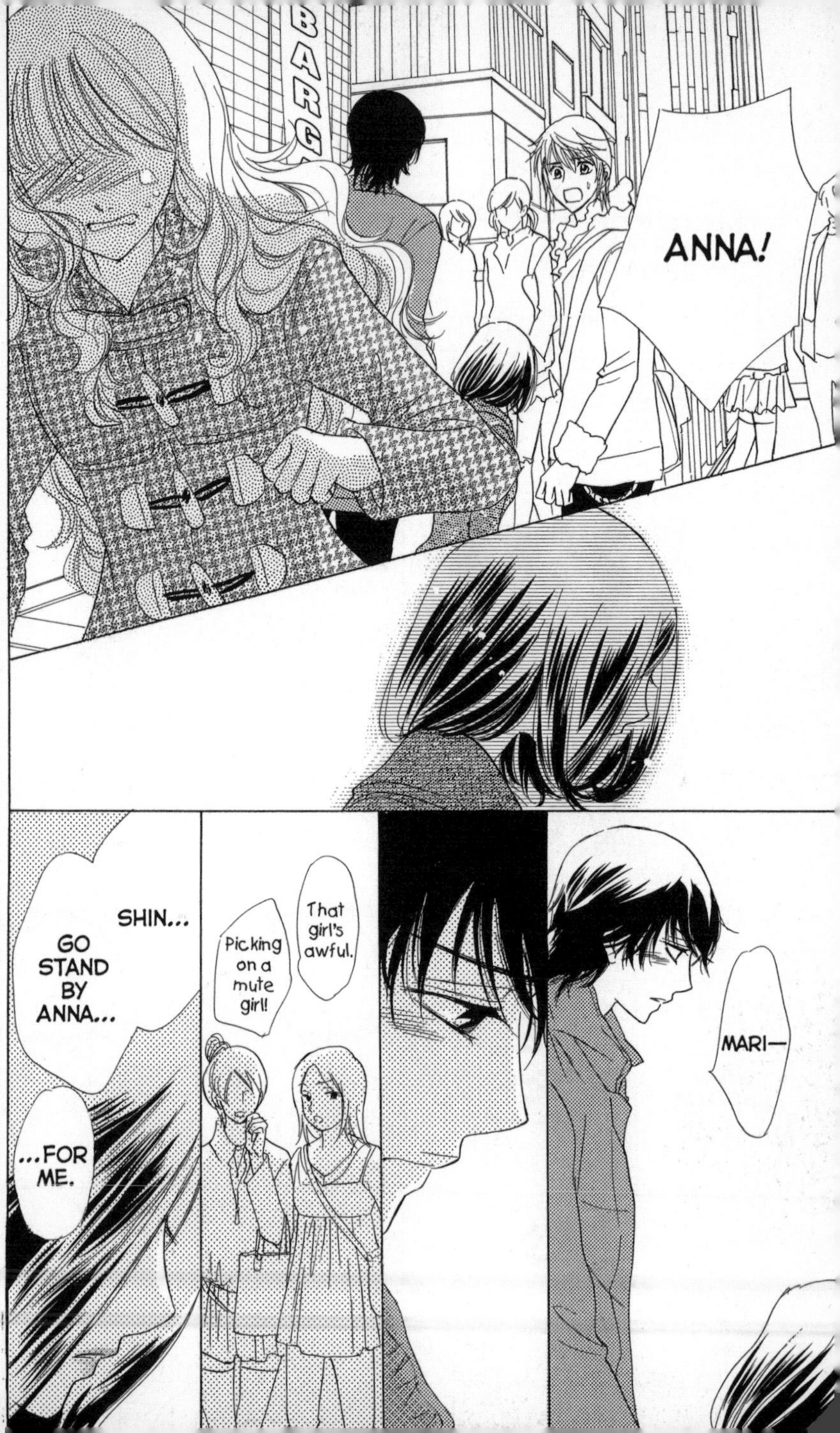
ANNA!
MARI—
That girl's awful.
Picking on a mute girl!
SHIN...
GO STAND BY ANNA...
...FOR ME.

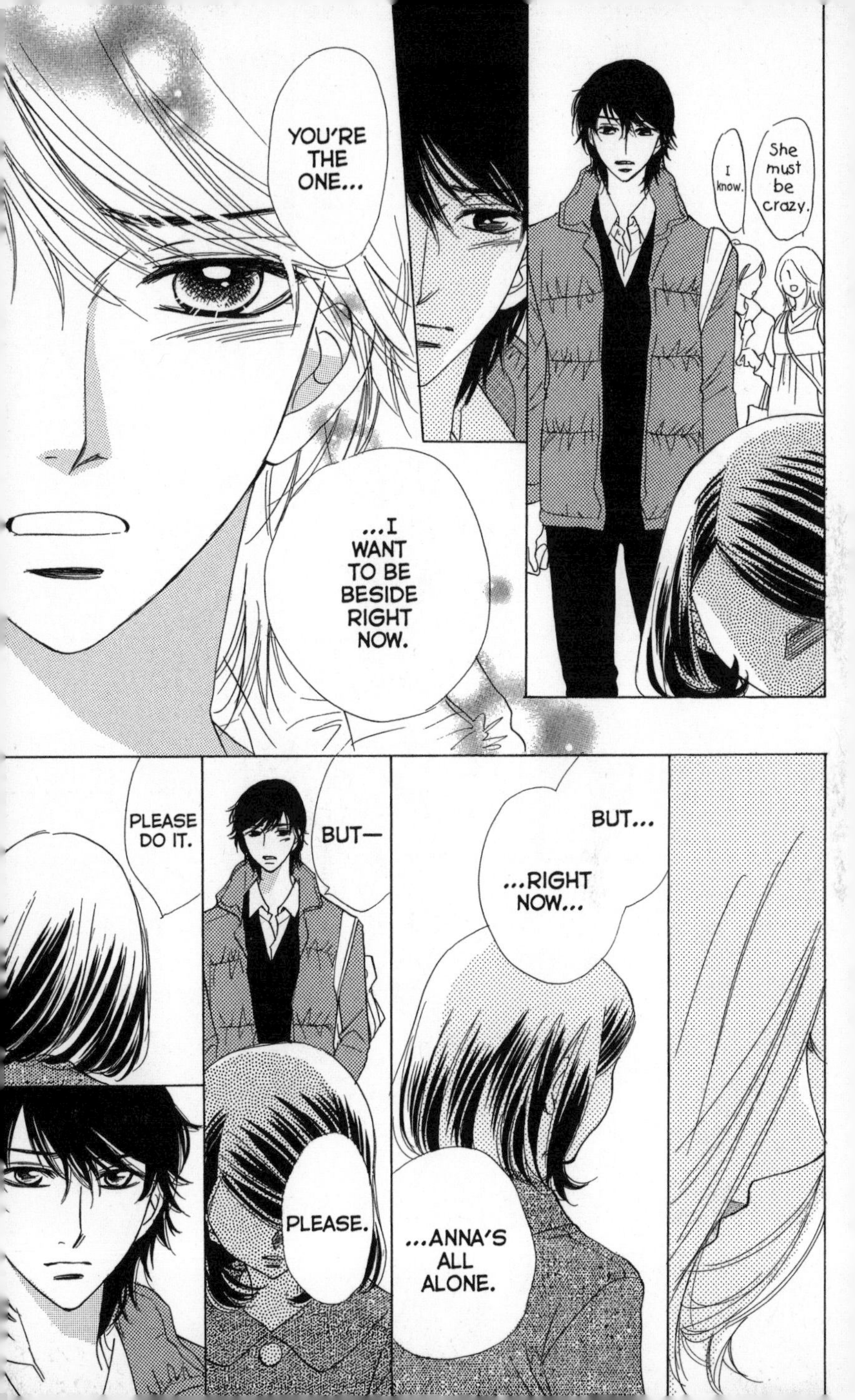
She must be crazy.
I know.
YOU'RE THE ONE...
...I WANT TO BE BESIDE RIGHT NOW.
BUT...
...RIGHT NOW...
...ANNA'S ALL ALONE.
BUT—
PLEASE DO IT.
PLEASE.

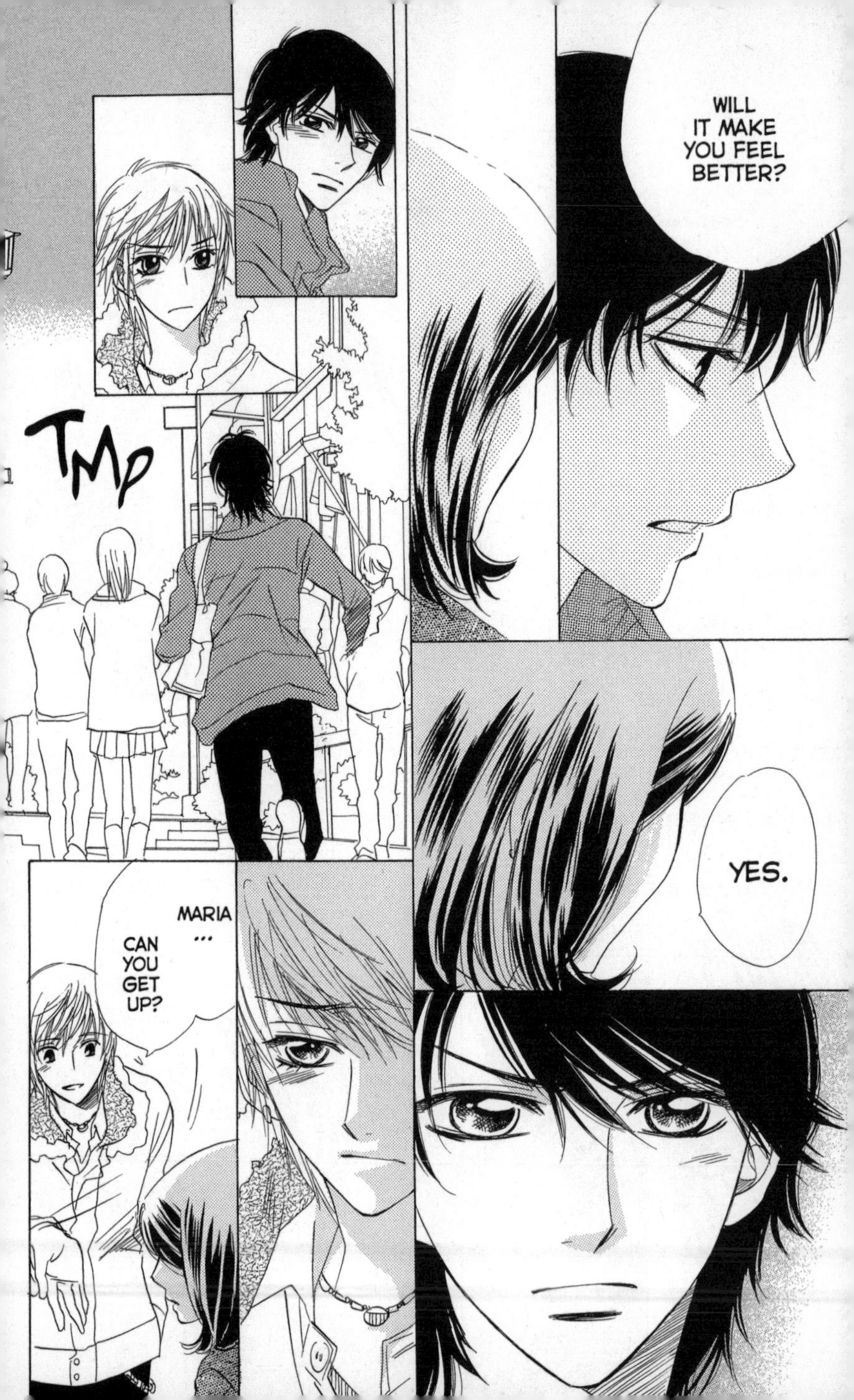
WILL IT MAKE YOU FEEL BETTER?
YES.
TMP
MARIA ...
CAN YOU GET UP?

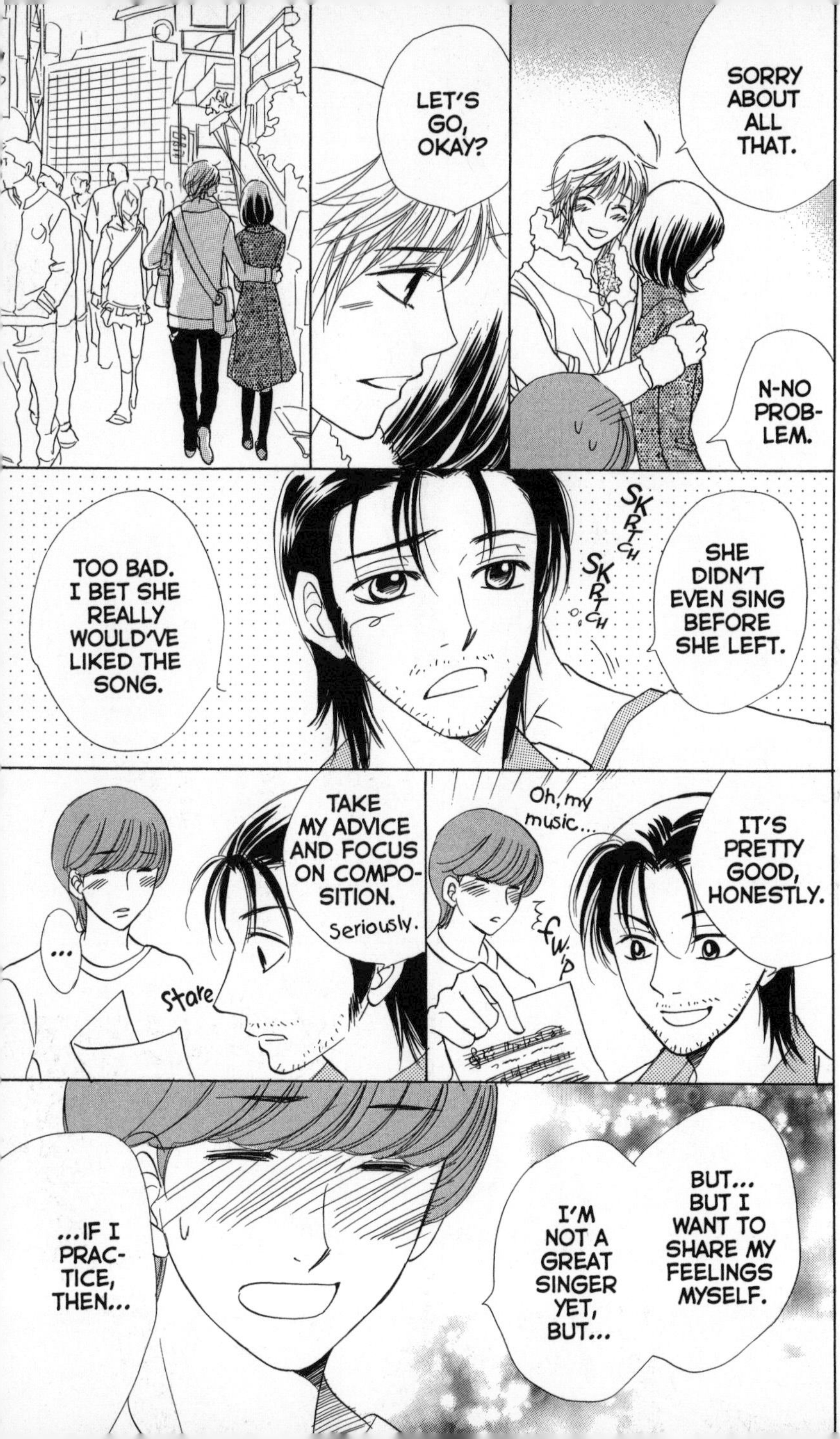
SORRY ABOUT ALL THAT.
N-NO PROBLEM.
LET'S GO, OKAY?
SHE DIDN'T EVEN SING BEFORE SHE LEFT.
SKRTCH SKRTCH
TOO BAD. I BET SHE REALLY WOULD'VE LIKED THE SONG.
IT'S PRETTY GOOD, HONESTLY.
Oh, my music...
FWIP
TAKE MY ADVICE AND FOCUS ON COMPOSITION.
Seriously.
Stare
...
BUT... BUT I WANT TO SHARE MY FEELINGS MYSELF.
I'M NOT A GREAT SINGER YET, BUT...
...IF I PRACTICE, THEN...

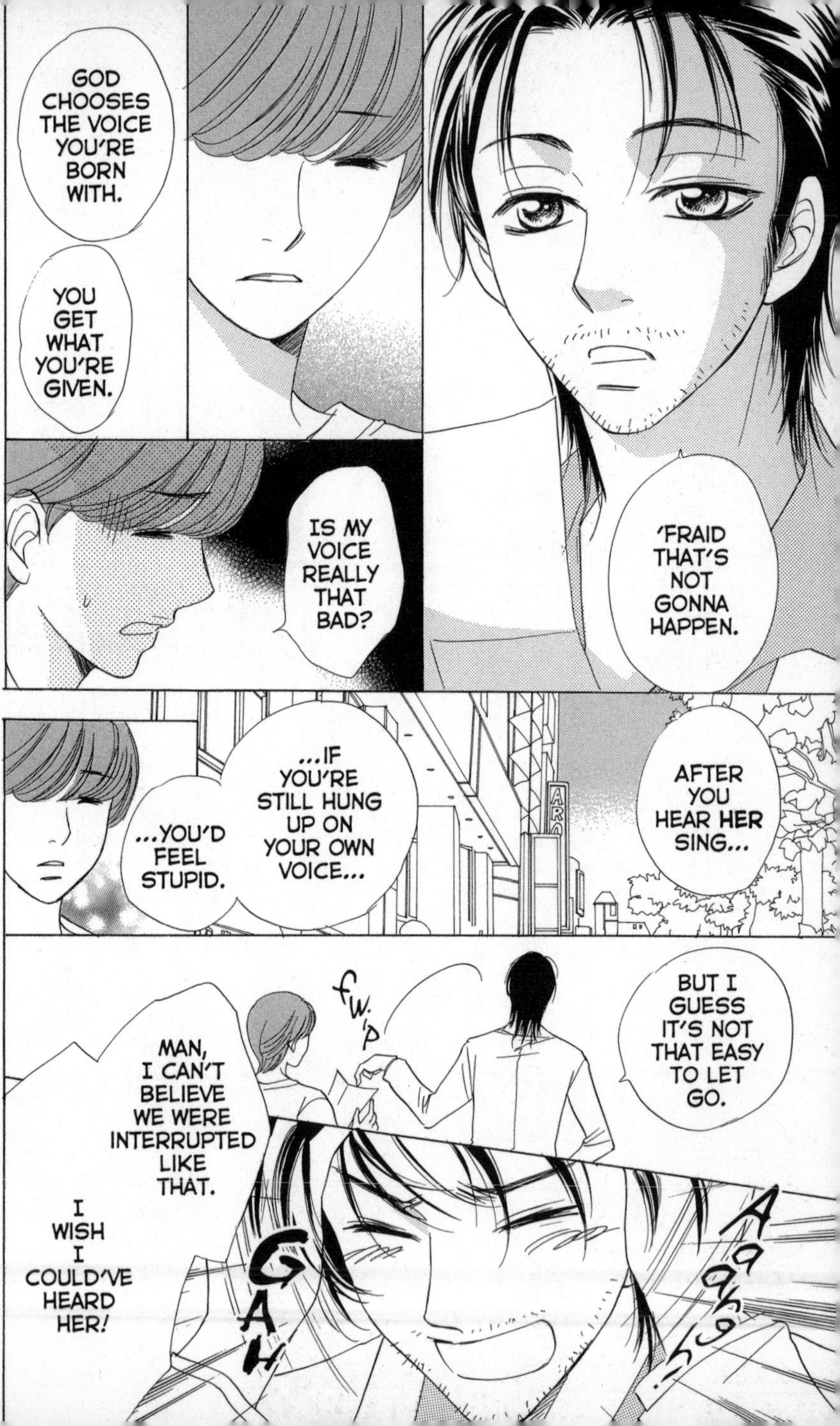

'FRAID THAT'S NOT GONNA HAPPEN.
GOD CHOOSES THE VOICE YOU'RE BORN WITH.
YOU GET WHAT YOU'RE GIVEN.
IS MY VOICE REALLY THAT BAD?
AFTER YOU HEAR HER SING...
...IF YOU'RE STILL HUNG UP ON YOUR OWN VOICE...
...YOU'D FEEL STUPID.
BUT I GUESS IT'S NOT THAT EASY TO LET GO.
FW:P
MAN, I CAN'T BELIEVE WE WERE INTERRUPTED LIKE THAT.
Aaagh!
GAH
I WISH I COULD'VE HEARD HER!

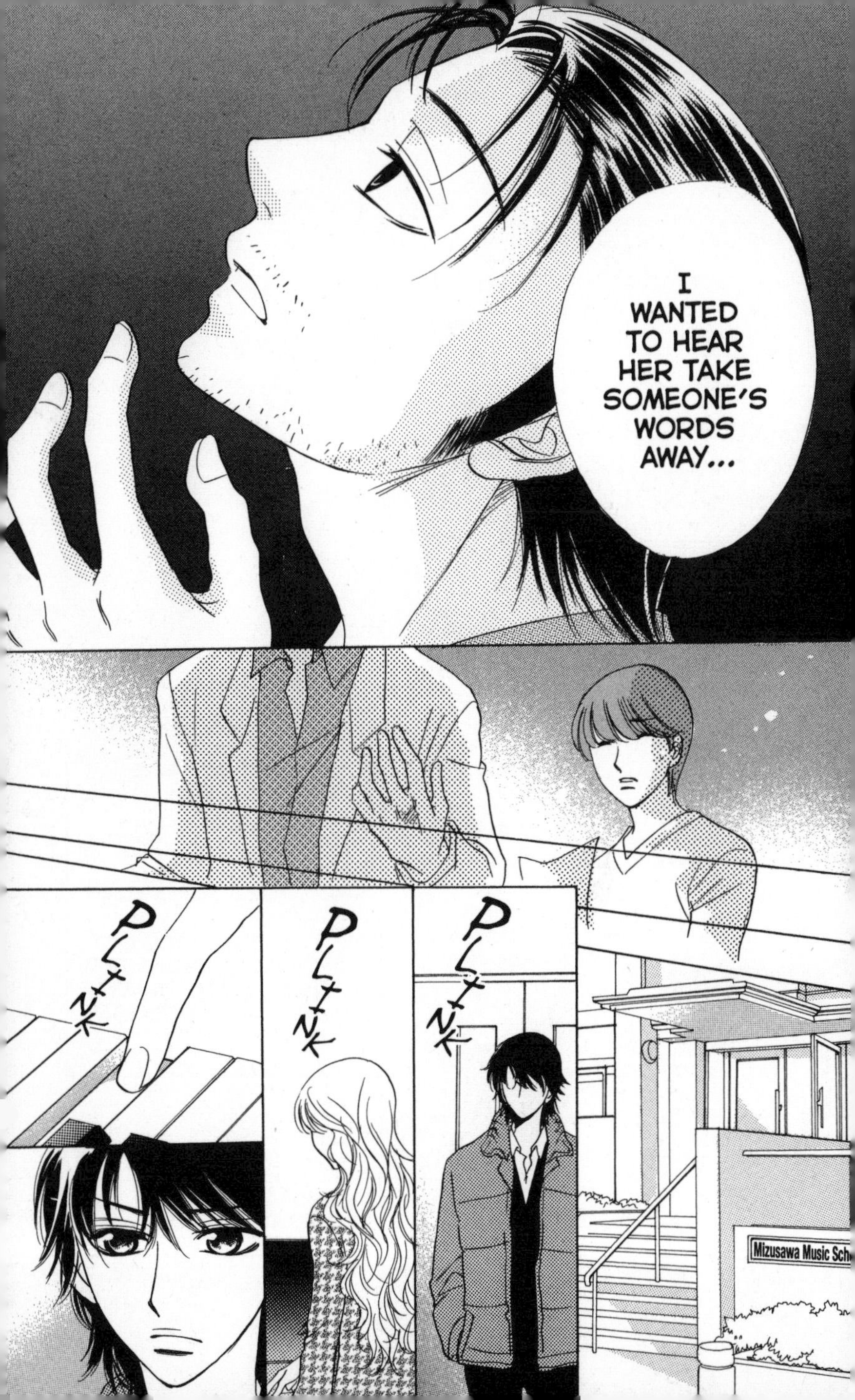
I WANTED TO HEAR HER TAKE SOMEONE'S WORDS AWAY...
PLINK
PLINK
PLINK
Mizusawa Music Sch

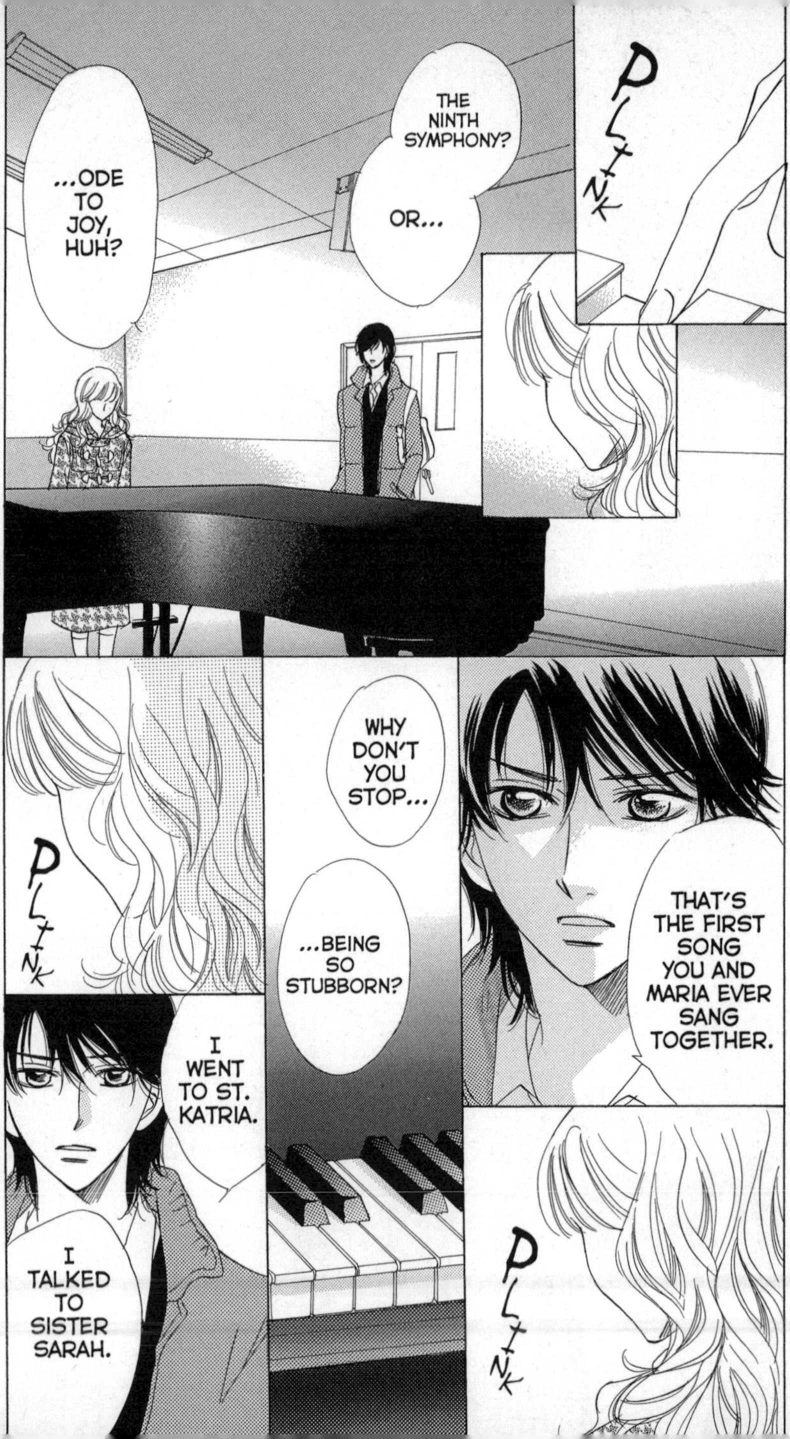
PLINK
THE NINTH SYMPHONY?
OR...
...ODE TO JOY, HUH?
THAT'S THE FIRST SONG YOU AND MARIA EVER SANG TOGETHER.
WHY DON'T YOU STOP...
...BEING SO STUBBORN?
PLINK
PLINK
I WENT TO ST. KATRIA.
I TALKED TO SISTER SARAH.

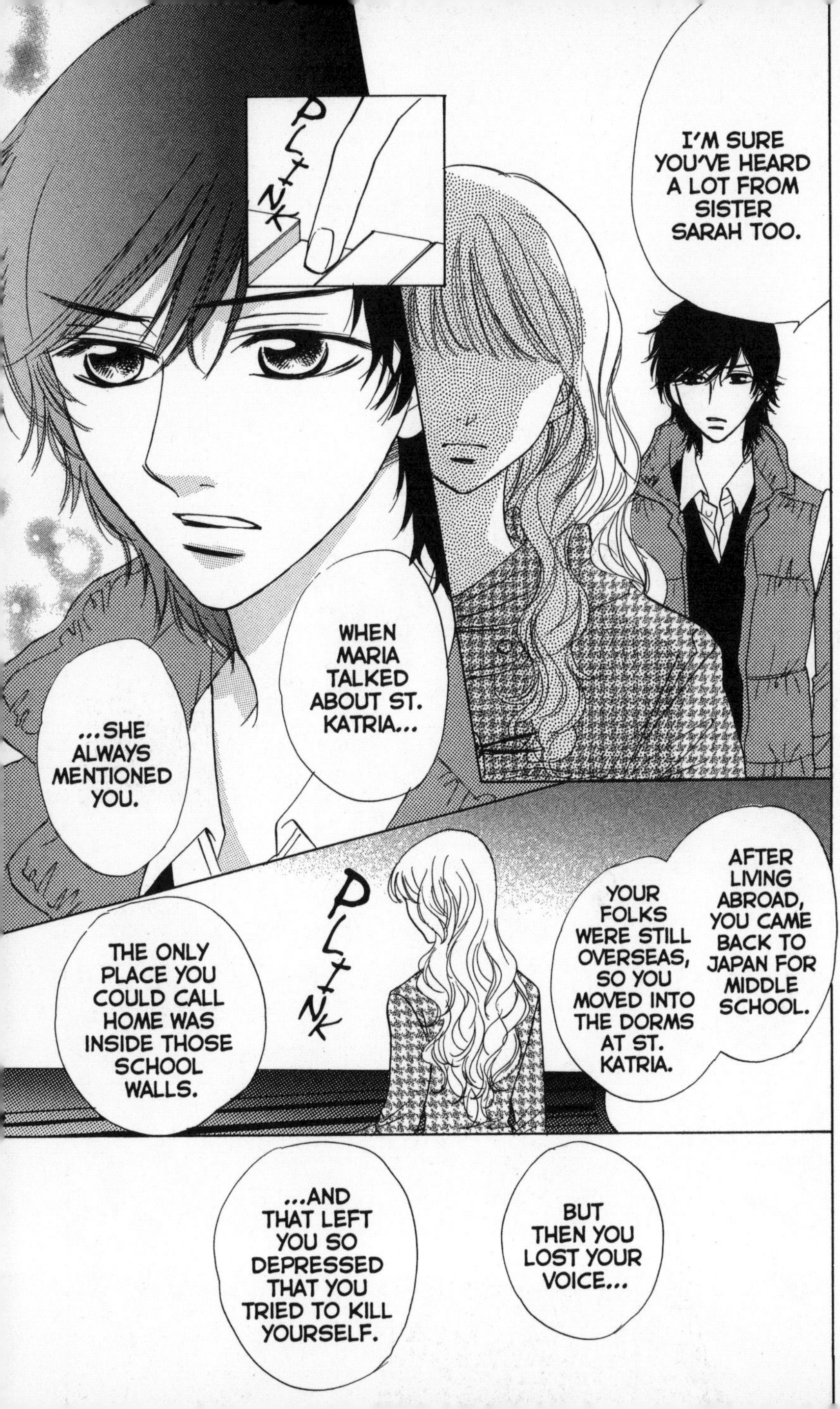
I'M SURE YOU'VE HEARD A LOT FROM SISTER SARAH TOO.
PLTNK
WHEN MARIA TALKED ABOUT ST. KATRIA...
...SHE ALWAYS MENTIONED YOU.
AFTER LIVING ABROAD, YOU CAME BACK TO JAPAN FOR MIDDLE SCHOOL.
YOUR FOLKS WERE STILL OVERSEAS, SO YOU MOVED INTO THE DORMS AT ST. KATRIA.
PLTNK
THE ONLY PLACE YOU COULD CALL HOME WAS INSIDE THOSE SCHOOL WALLS.
BUT THEN YOU LOST YOUR VOICE...
...AND THAT LEFT YOU SO DEPRESSED THAT YOU TRIED TO KILL YOURSELF.

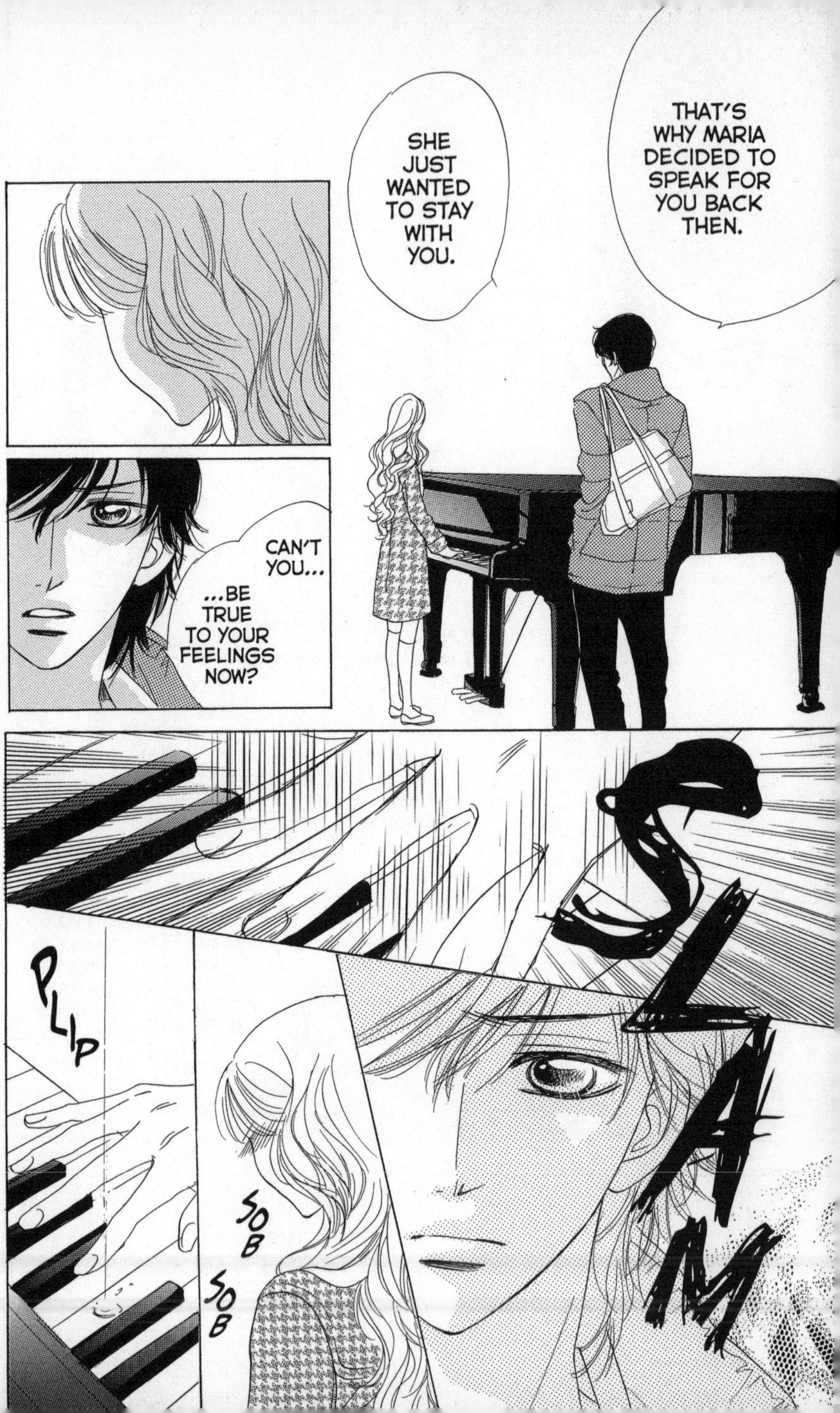
THAT'S WHY MARIA DECIDED TO SPEAK FOR YOU BACK THEN.
SHE JUST WANTED TO STAY WITH YOU.
CAN'T YOU...
...BE TRUE TO YOUR FEELINGS NOW?
SLAM
PLIP
SOB SOB

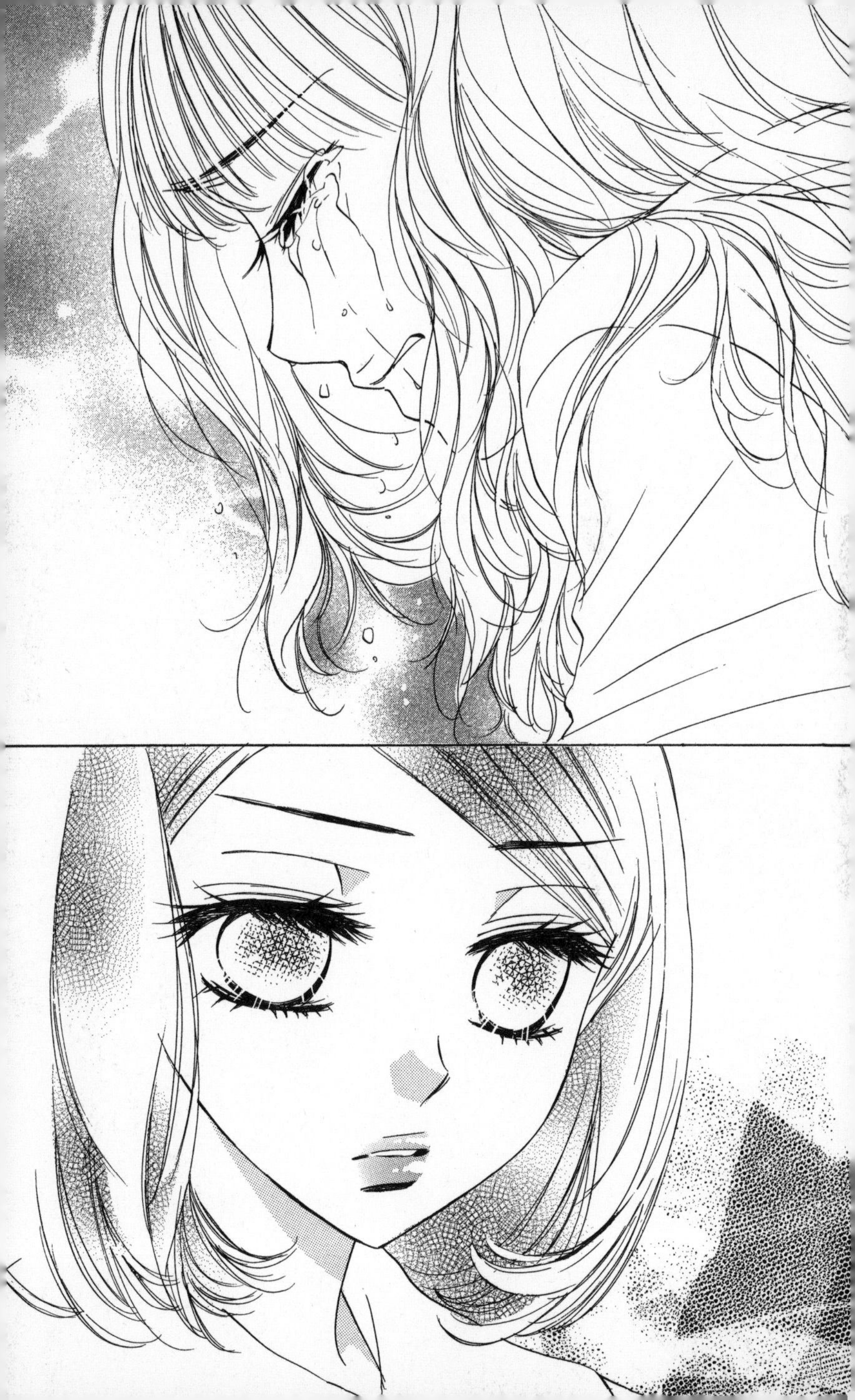

A Devil and
Her Love Song

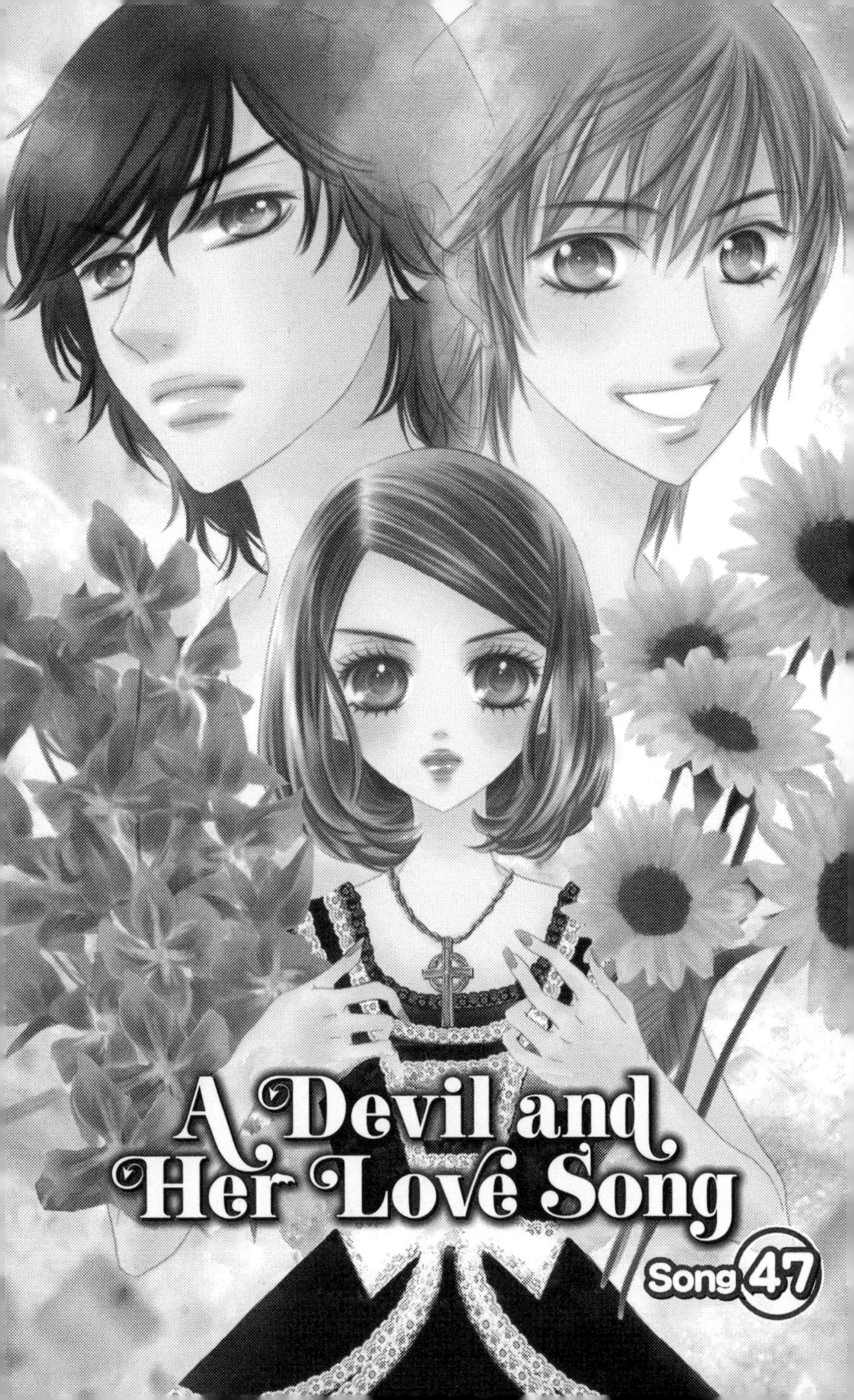
A Devil and Her Love Song
Song 47

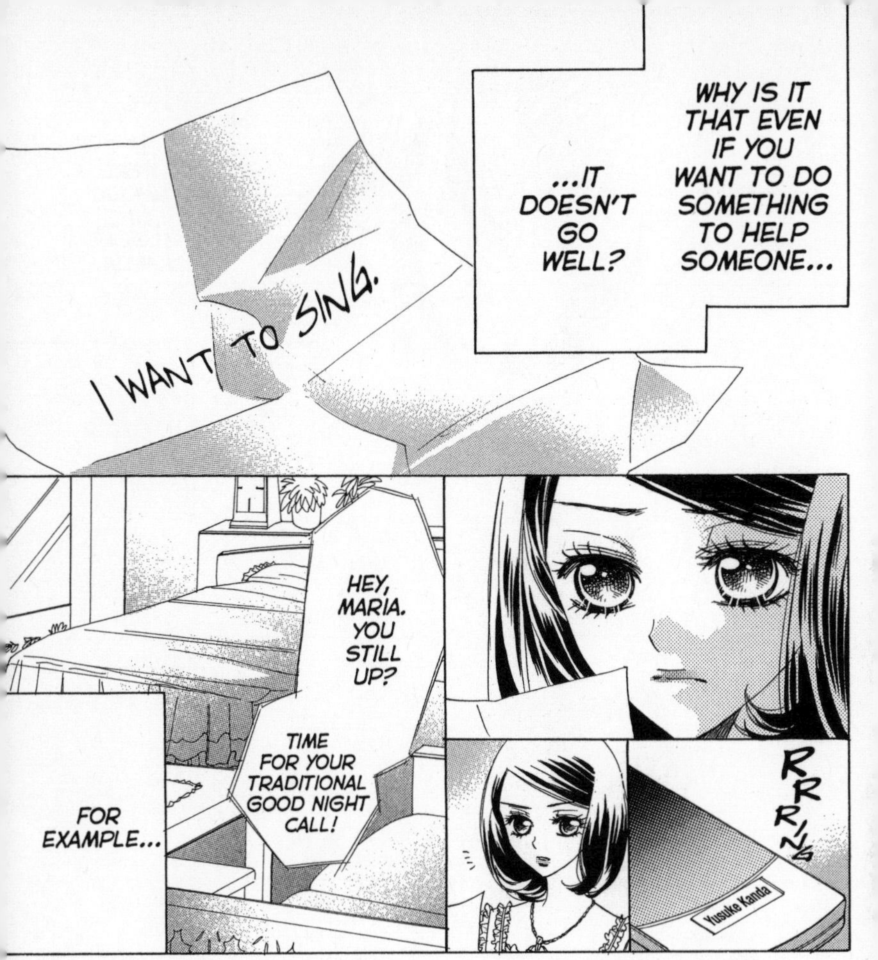
WHY IS IT THAT EVEN IF YOU WANT TO DO SOMETHING TO HELP SOMEONE...
...IT DOESN'T GO WELL?
I WANT TO SING.
RRRING
Yusuke Kanda
HEY, MARIA. YOU STILL UP?
TIME FOR YOUR TRADITIONAL GOOD NIGHT CALL!
FOR EXAMPLE...

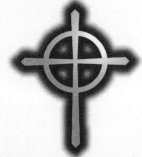

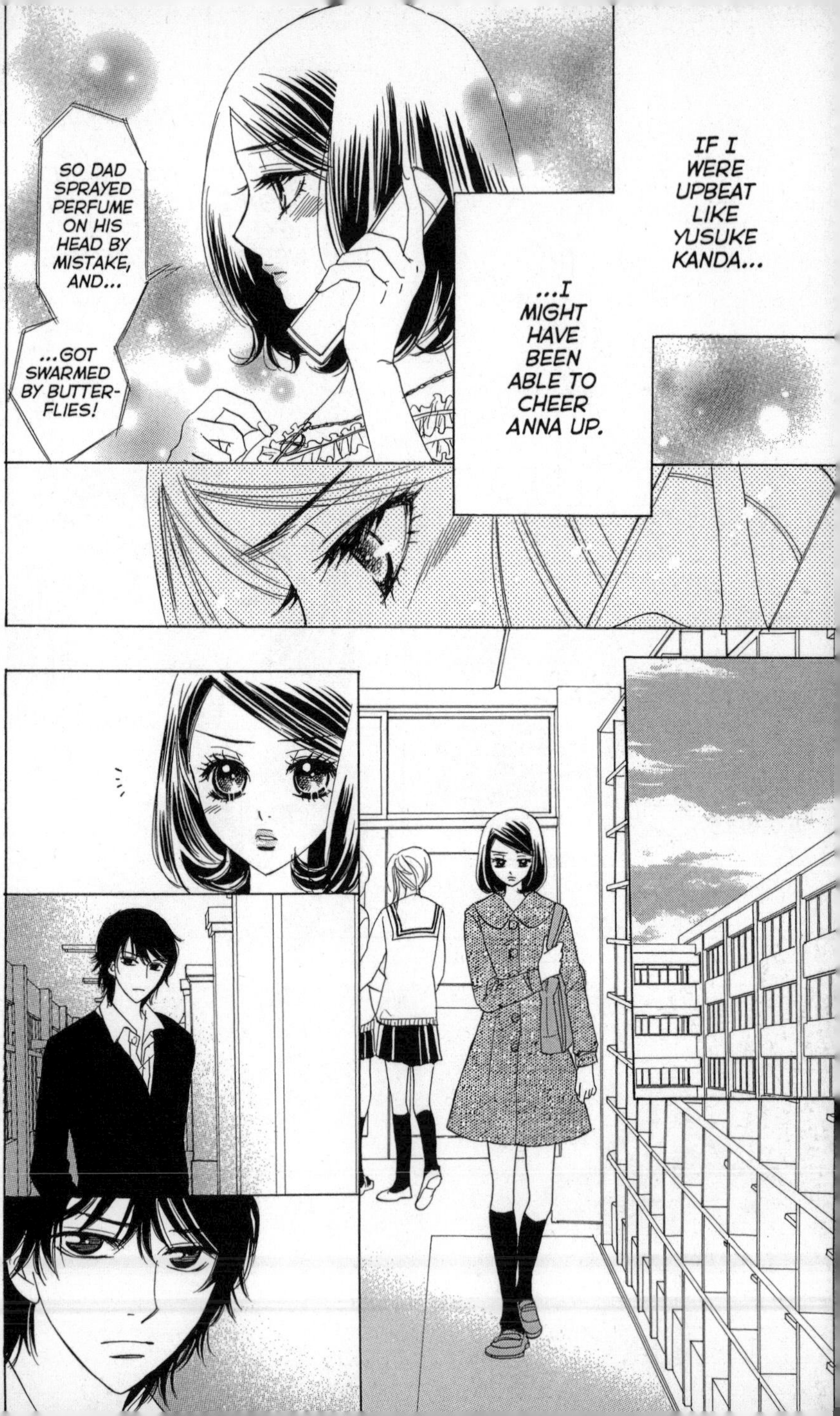
IF I WERE UPBEAT LIKE YUSUKE KANDA...
...I MIGHT HAVE BEEN ABLE TO CHEER ANNA UP.
SO DAD SPRAYED PERFUME ON HIS HEAD BY MISTAKE, AND...
...GOT SWARMED BY BUTTER-FLIES!

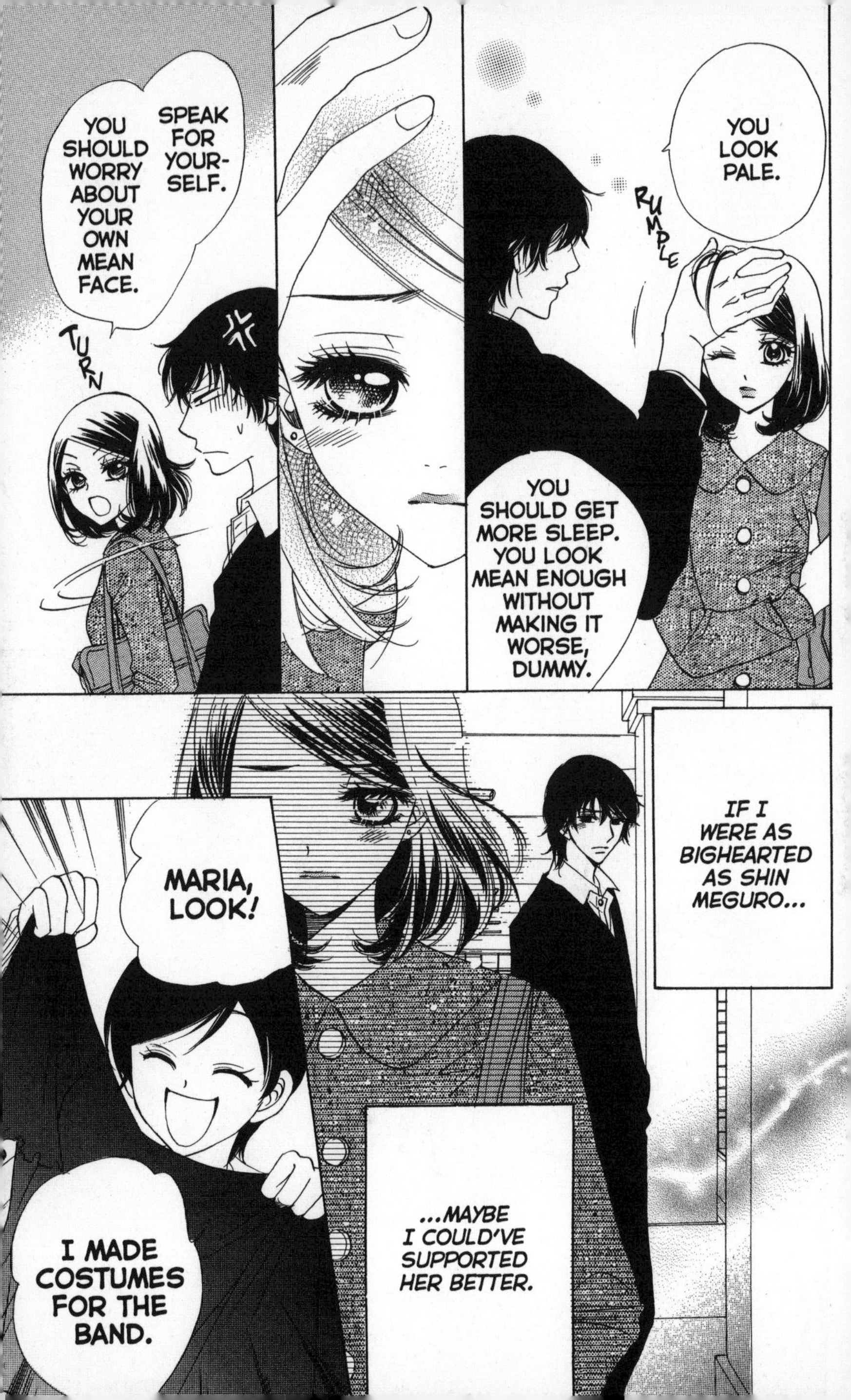
YOU LOOK PALE.
RUMPLE
YOU SHOULD GET MORE SLEEP. YOU LOOK MEAN ENOUGH WITHOUT MAKING IT WORSE, DUMMY.
SPEAK FOR YOURSELF.
YOU SHOULD WORRY ABOUT YOUR OWN MEAN FACE.
TURN
IF I WERE AS BIGHEARTED AS SHIN MEGURO...
...MAYBE I COULD'VE SUPPORTED HER BETTER.
MARIA, LOOK!
I MADE COSTUMES FOR THE BAND.

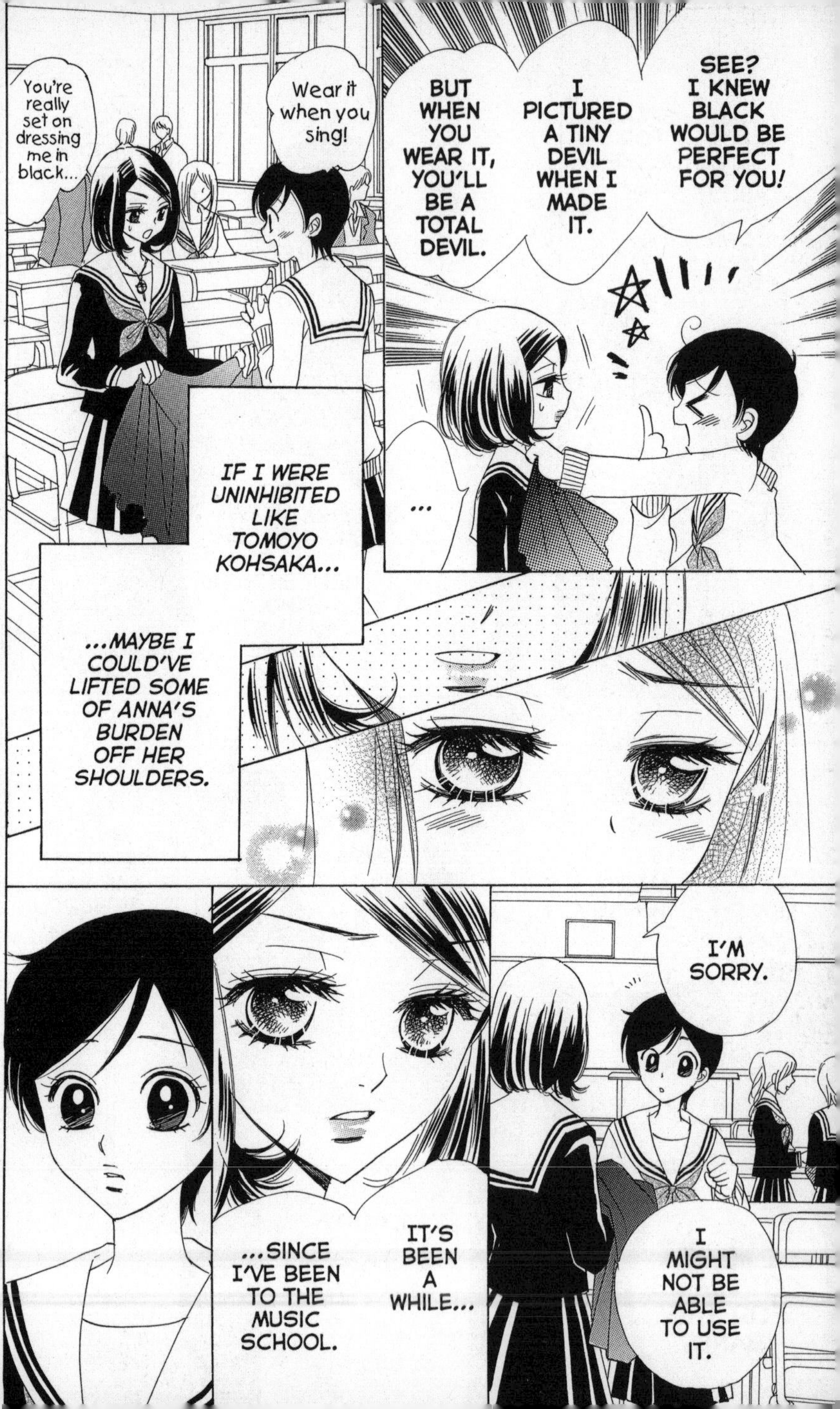
SEE? I KNEW BLACK WOULD BE PERFECT FOR YOU!
I PICTURED A TINY DEVIL WHEN I MADE IT.
BUT WHEN YOU WEAR IT, YOU'LL BE A TOTAL DEVIL.
...
Wear it when you sing!
You're really set on dressing me in black...
IF I WERE UNINHIBITED LIKE TOMOYO KOHSAKA...
...MAYBE I COULD'VE LIFTED SOME OF ANNA'S BURDEN OFF HER SHOULDERS.
I'M SORRY.
I MIGHT NOT BE ABLE TO USE IT.
IT'S BEEN A WHILE...
...SINCE I'VE BEEN TO THE MUSIC SCHOOL.

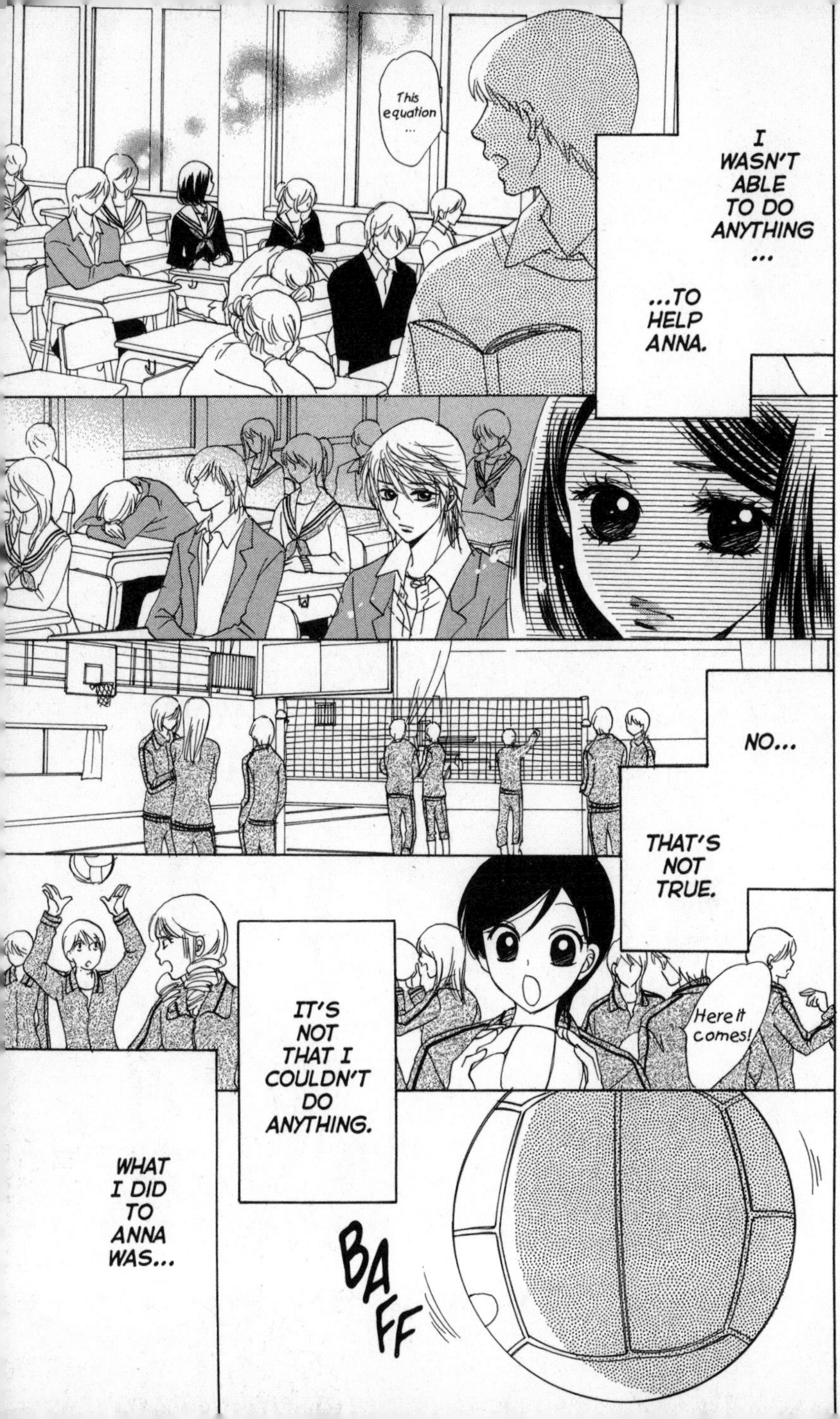

This equation...
I WASN'T ABLE TO DO ANYTHING...
...TO HELP ANNA.
NO...
THAT'S NOT TRUE.
Here it comes!
IT'S NOT THAT I COULDN'T DO ANYTHING.
BAFF
WHAT I DID TO ANNA WAS...

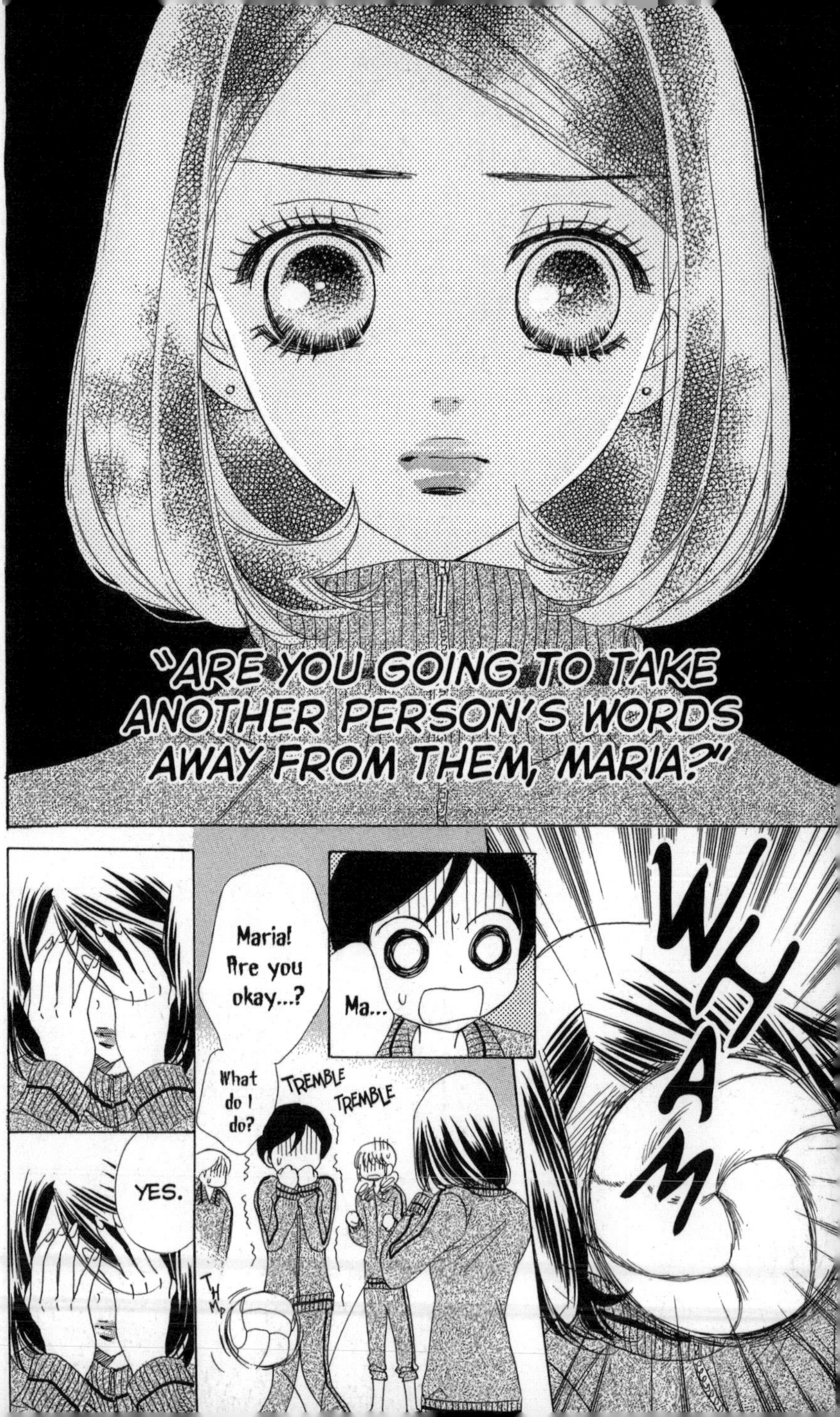
"ARE YOU GOING TO TAKE ANOTHER PERSON'S WORDS AWAY FROM THEM, MARIA?"
WHAM
Ma...
Maria! Are you okay...?
TREMBLE TREMBLE
What do I do?
THMP
YES.

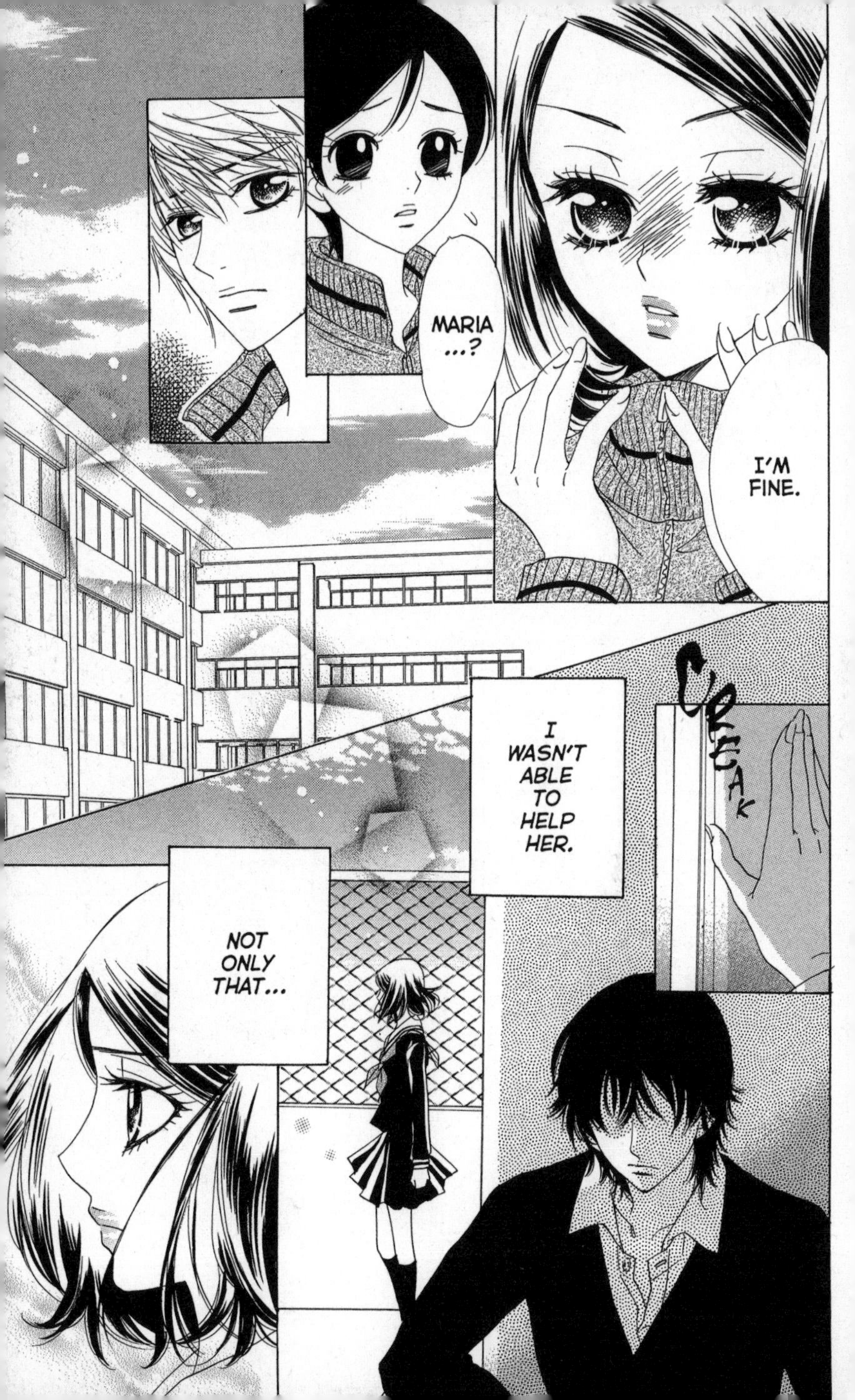
I'M FINE.
MARIA ...?
CREAK
I WASN'T ABLE TO HELP HER.
NOT ONLY THAT...

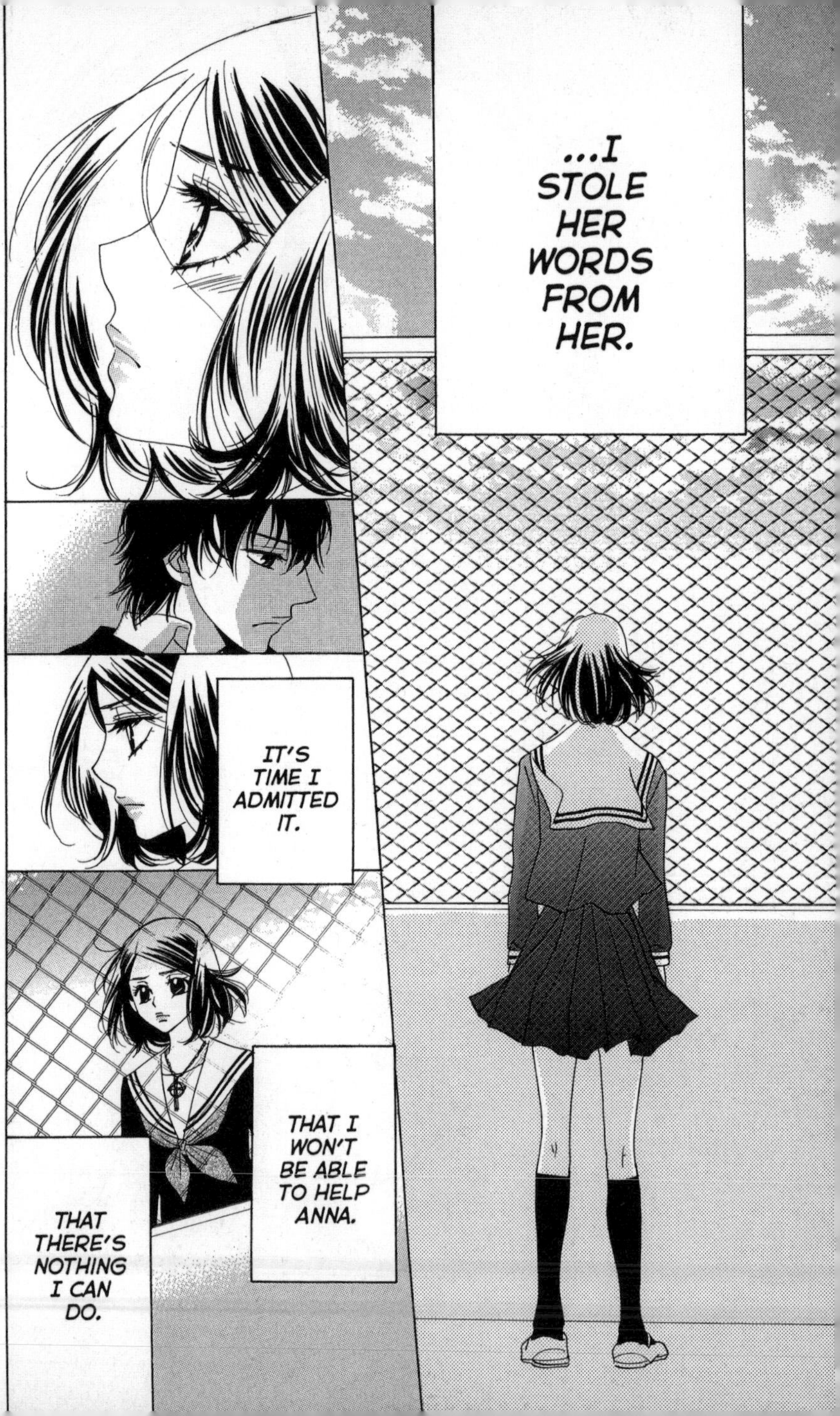
...I STOLE HER WORDS FROM HER.
IT'S TIME I ADMITTED IT.
THAT I WON'T BE ABLE TO HELP ANNA.
THAT THERE'S NOTHING I CAN DO.

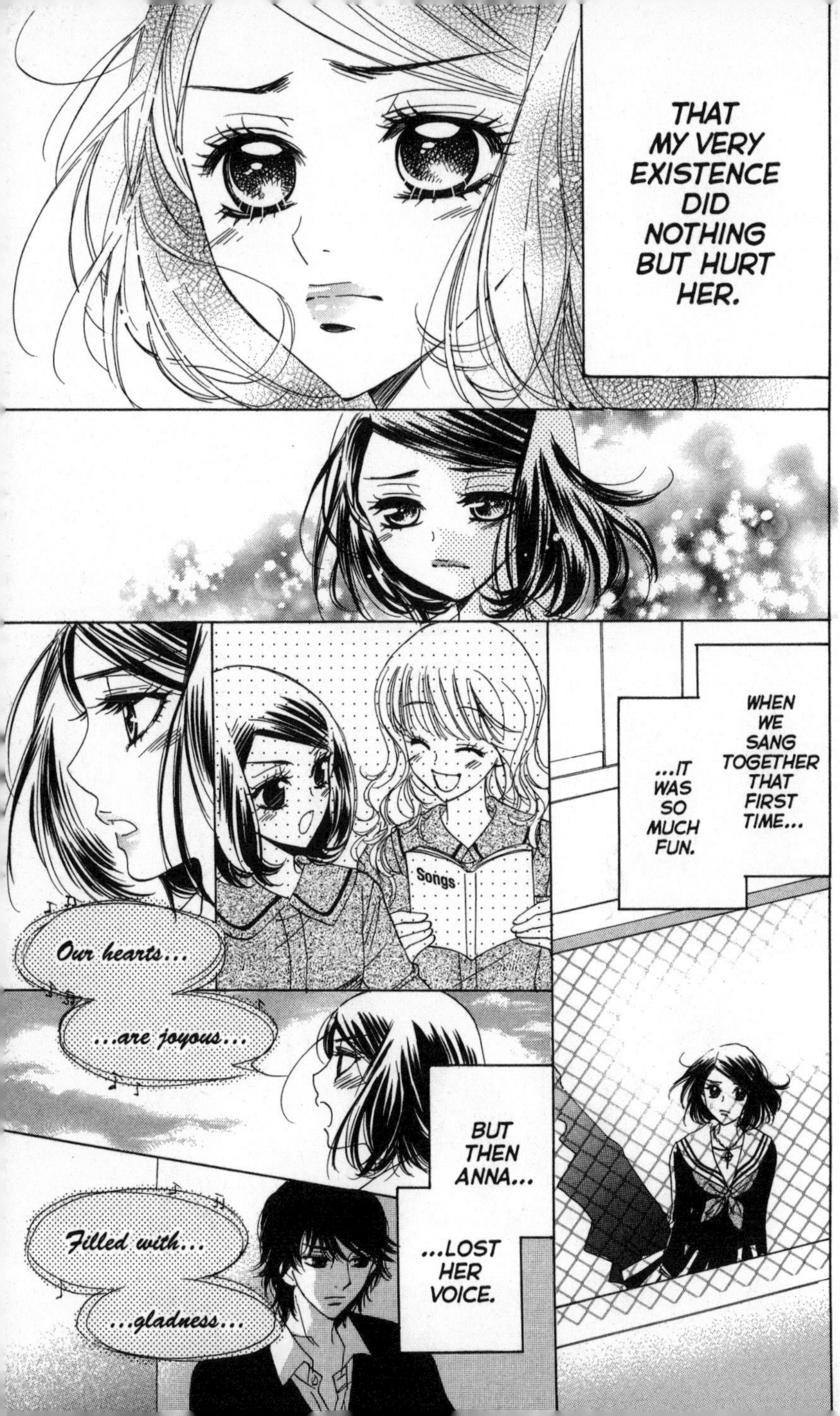
THAT MY VERY EXISTENCE DID NOTHING BUT HURT HER.
WHEN WE SANG TOGETHER THAT FIRST TIME...
...IT WAS SO MUCH FUN.
Songs
Our hearts...
...are joyous...
BUT THEN ANNA...
Filled with...
...LOST HER VOICE.
...gladness...

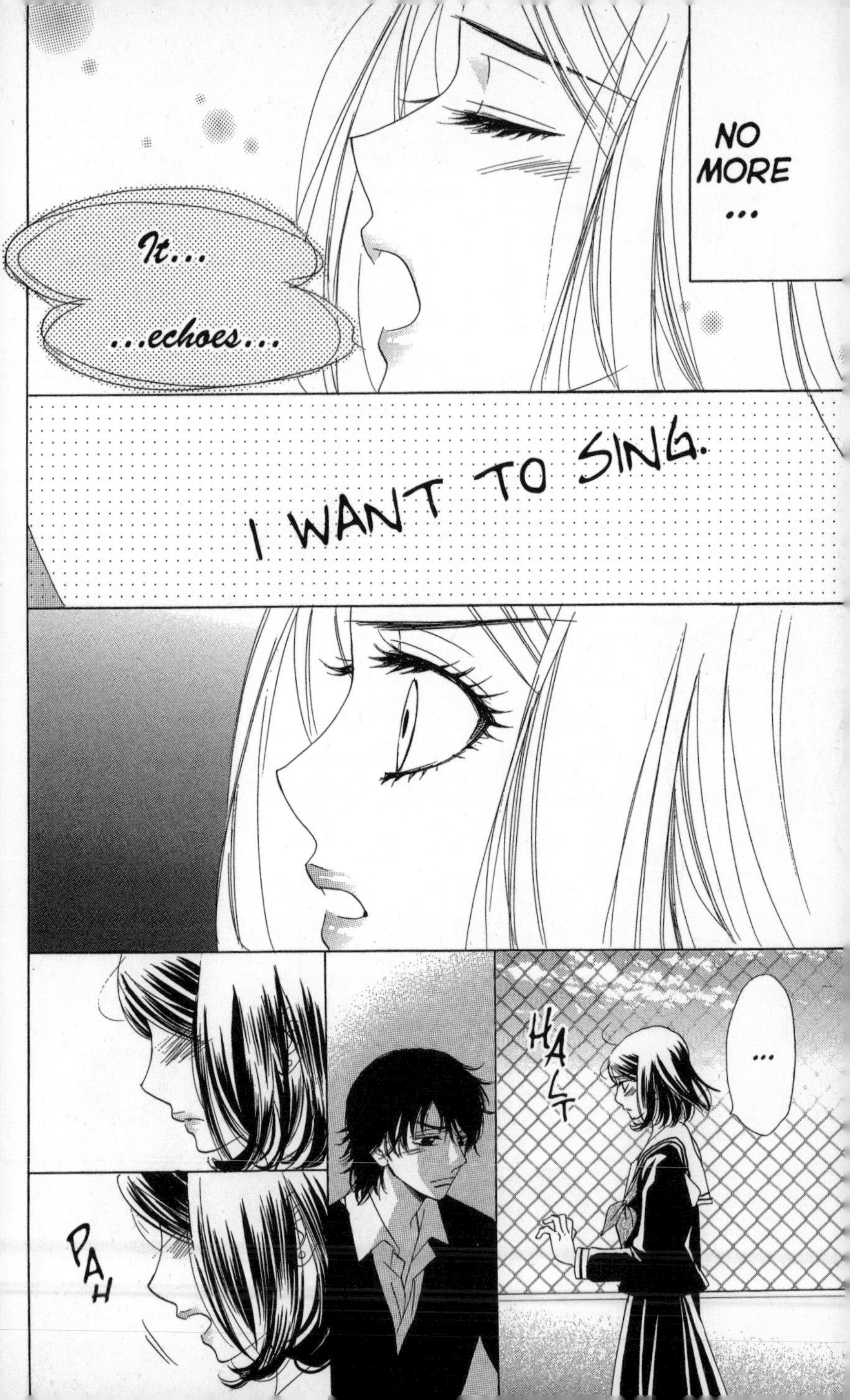
NO MORE ...
It... ...echoes...
I WANT TO SING.
...
HALT
PAH

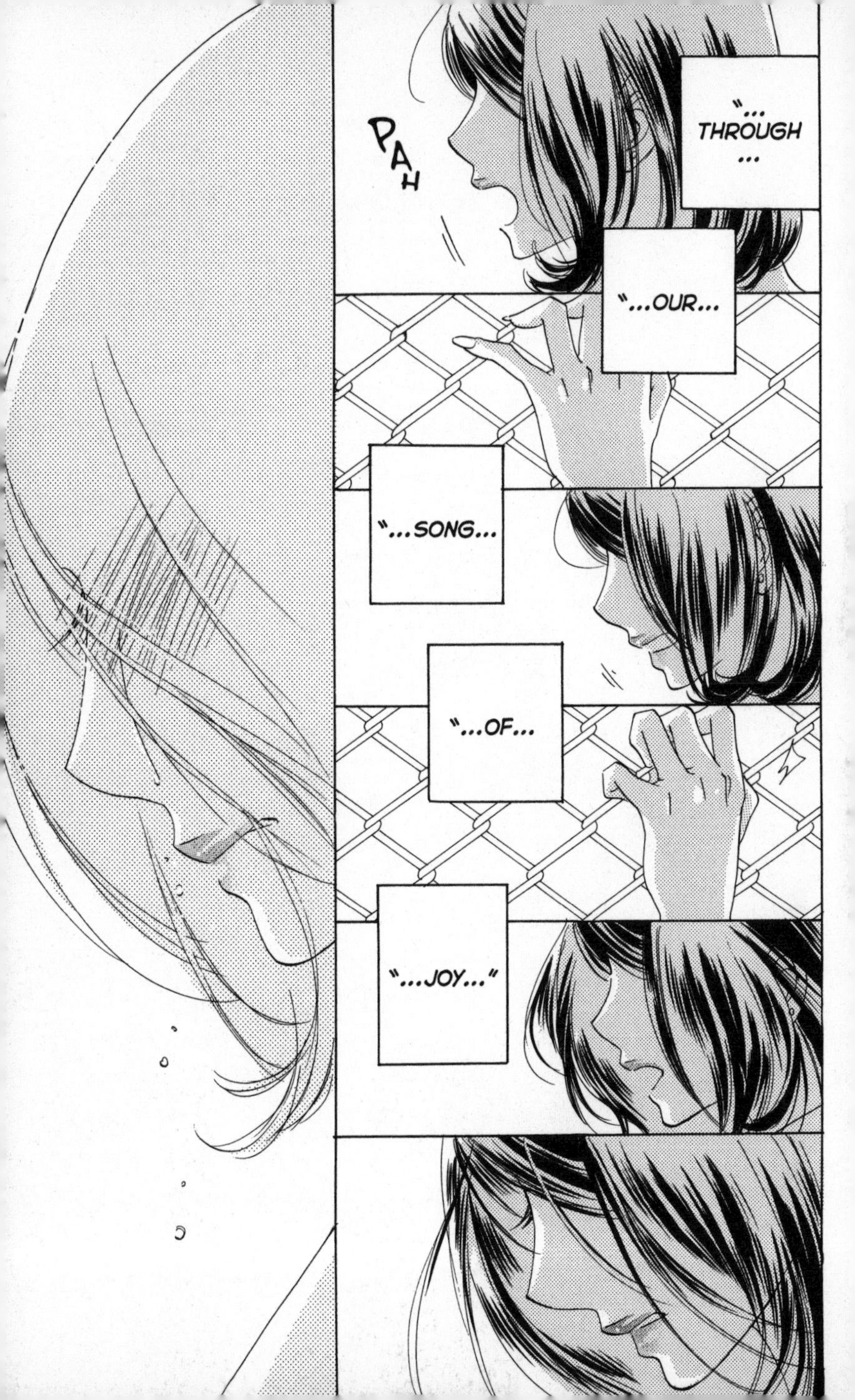
"... THROUGH ...
PAH
"...OUR...
"...SONG...
"...OF...
"...JOY..."

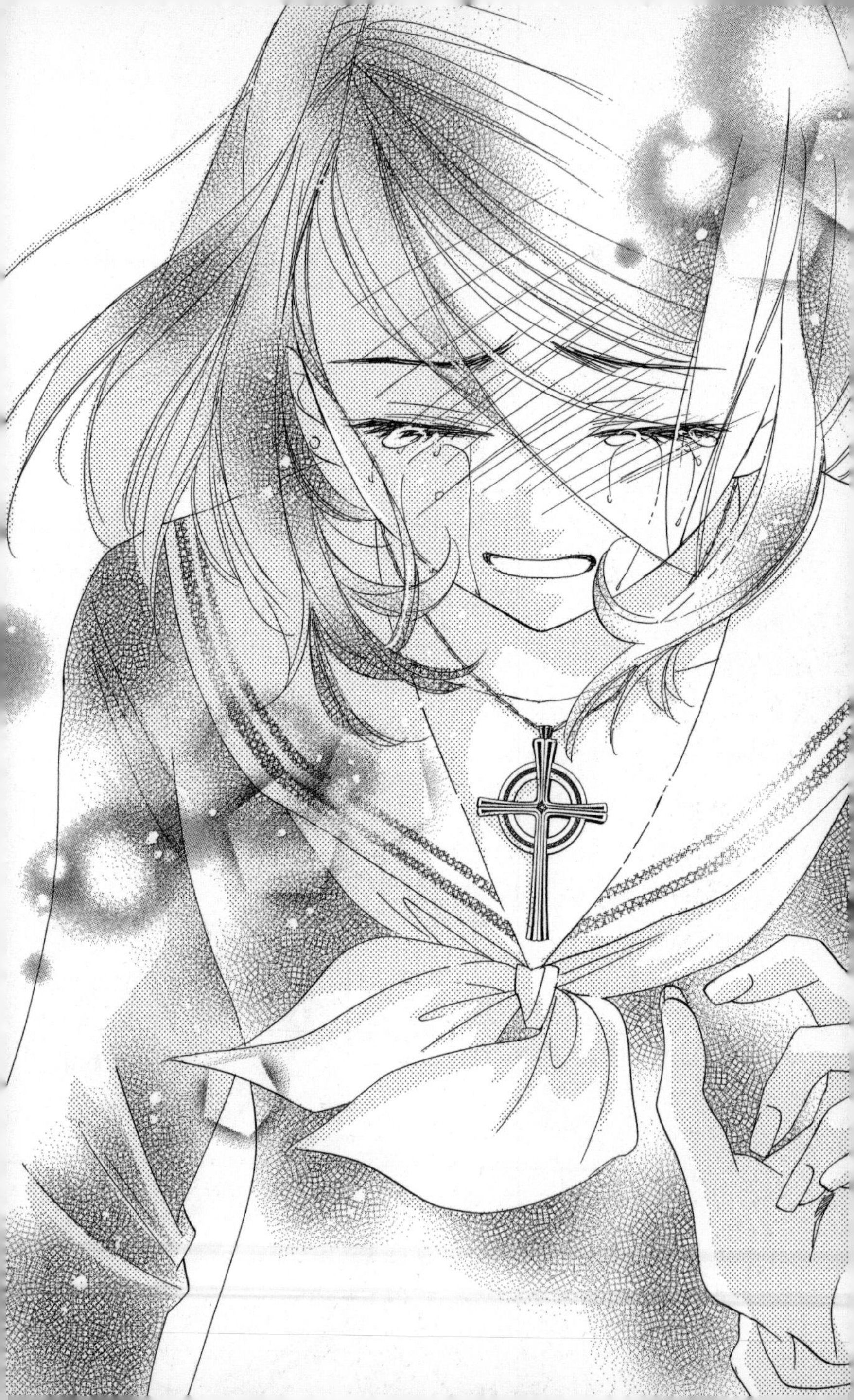

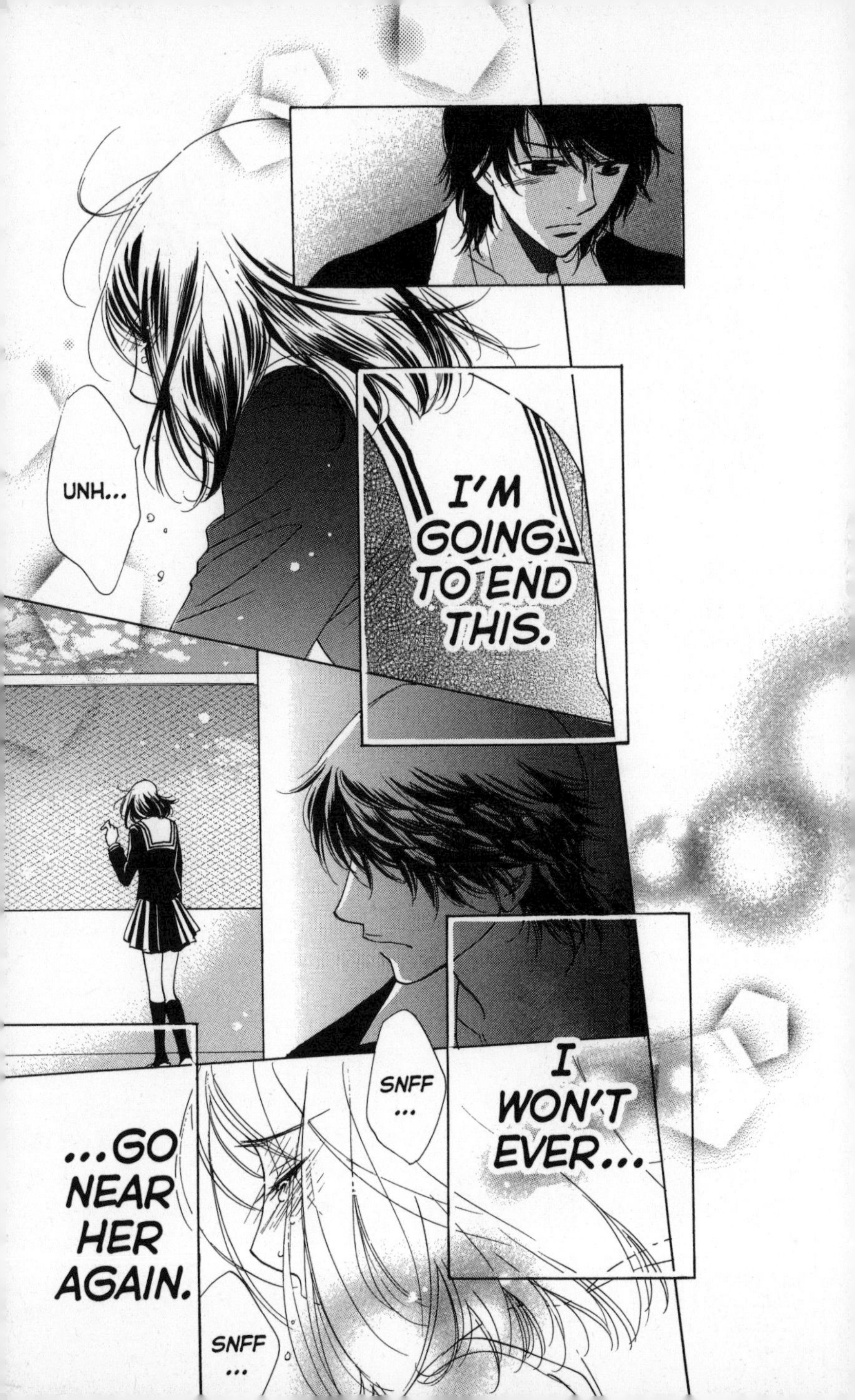
I'M GOING TO END THIS.
UNH...
I WON'T EVER...
SNFF ...
...GO NEAR HER AGAIN.
SNFF ...

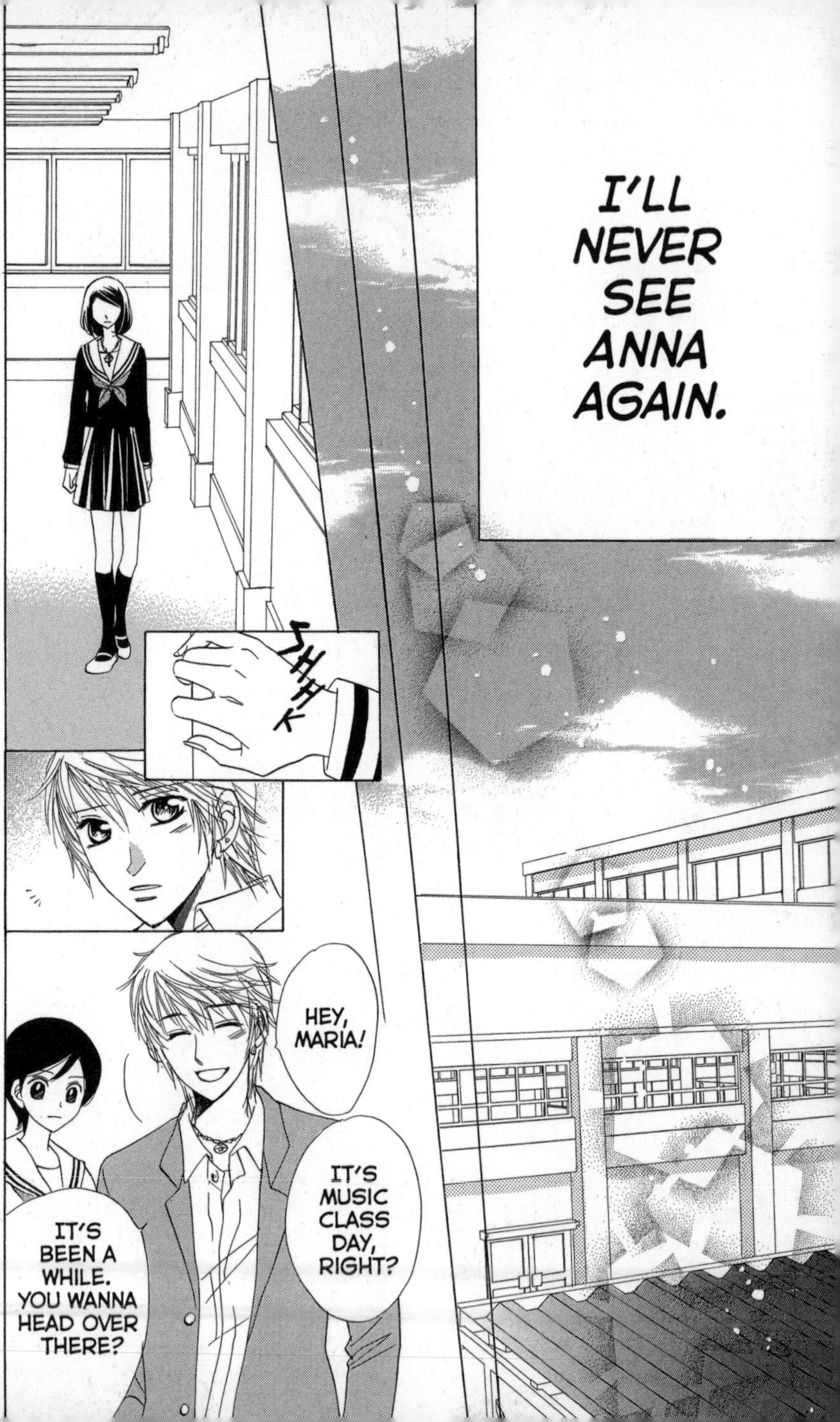
I'LL NEVER SEE ANNA AGAIN.
SHHHK
HEY, MARIA!
IT'S MUSIC CLASS DAY, RIGHT?
IT'S BEEN A WHILE. YOU WANNA HEAD OVER THERE?

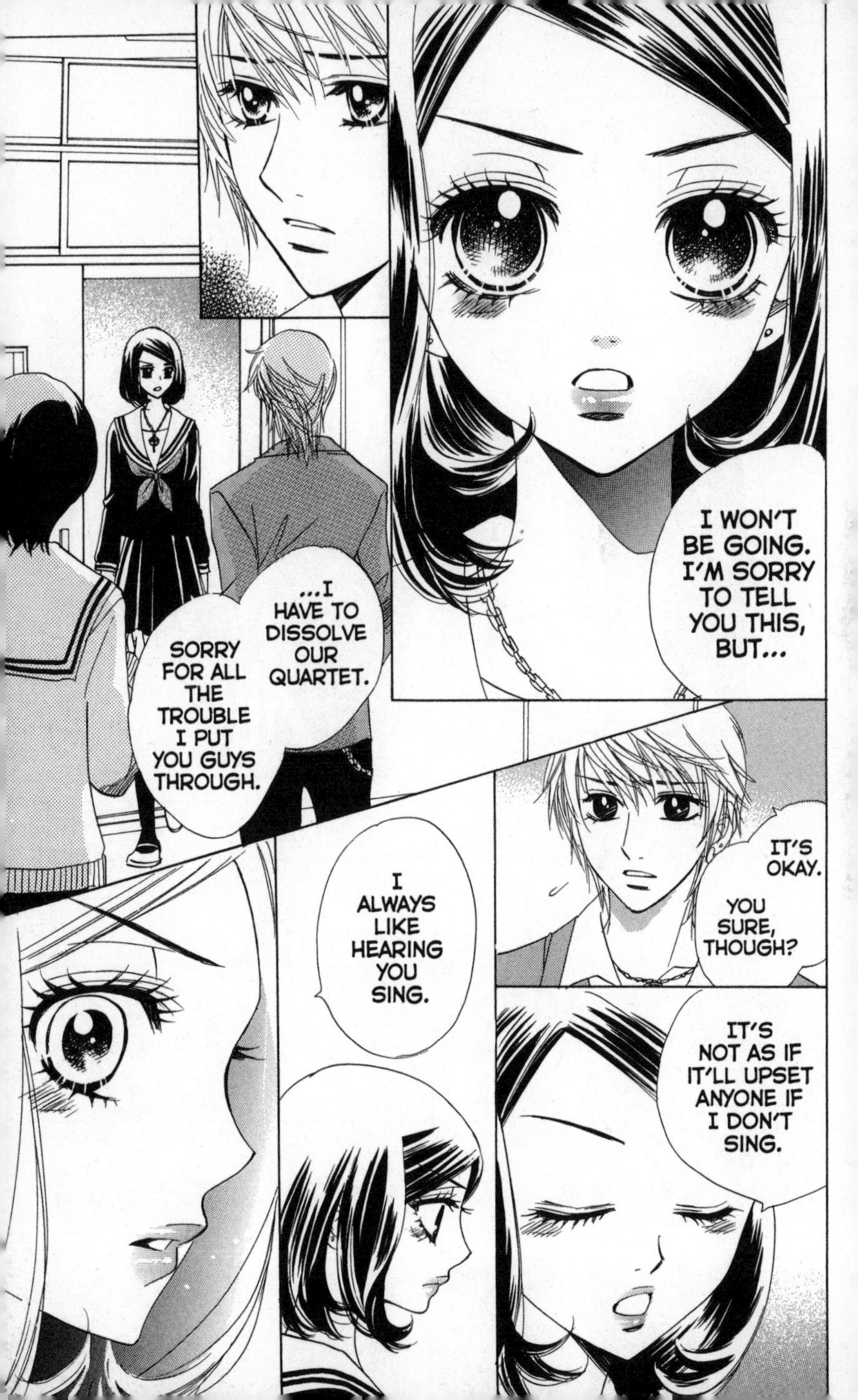
I WON'T BE GOING. I'M SORRY TO TELL YOU THIS, BUT...
...I HAVE TO DISSOLVE OUR QUARTET.
SORRY FOR ALL THE TROUBLE I PUT YOU GUYS THROUGH.
IT'S OKAY.
YOU SURE, THOUGH?
IT'S NOT AS IF IT'LL UPSET ANYONE IF I DON'T SING.
I ALWAYS LIKE HEARING YOU SING.

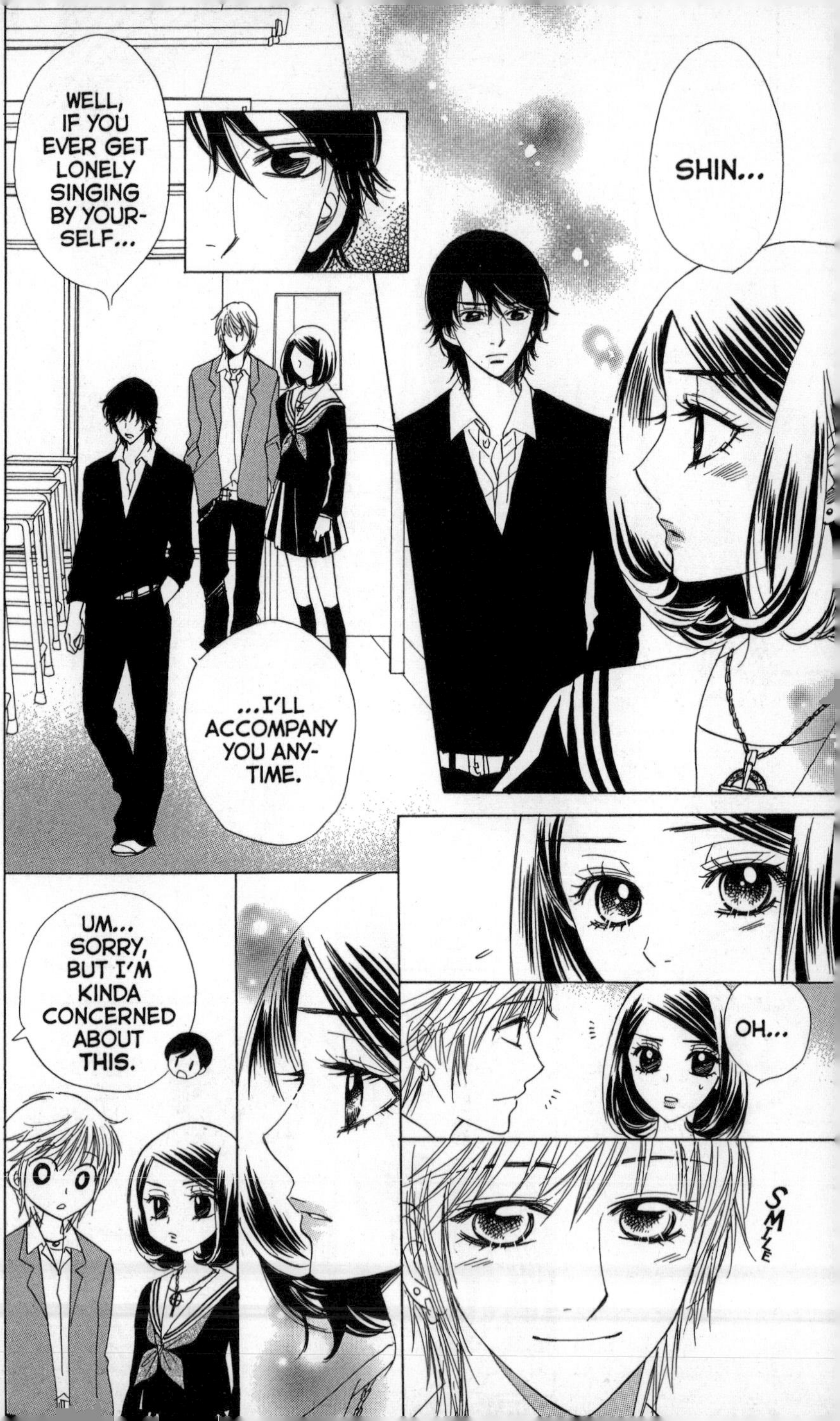
SHIN...
WELL, IF YOU EVER GET LONELY SINGING BY YOURSELF...
...I'LL ACCOMPANY YOU ANYTIME.
OH...
SMILE
UM... SORRY, BUT I'M KINDA CONCERNED ABOUT THIS.

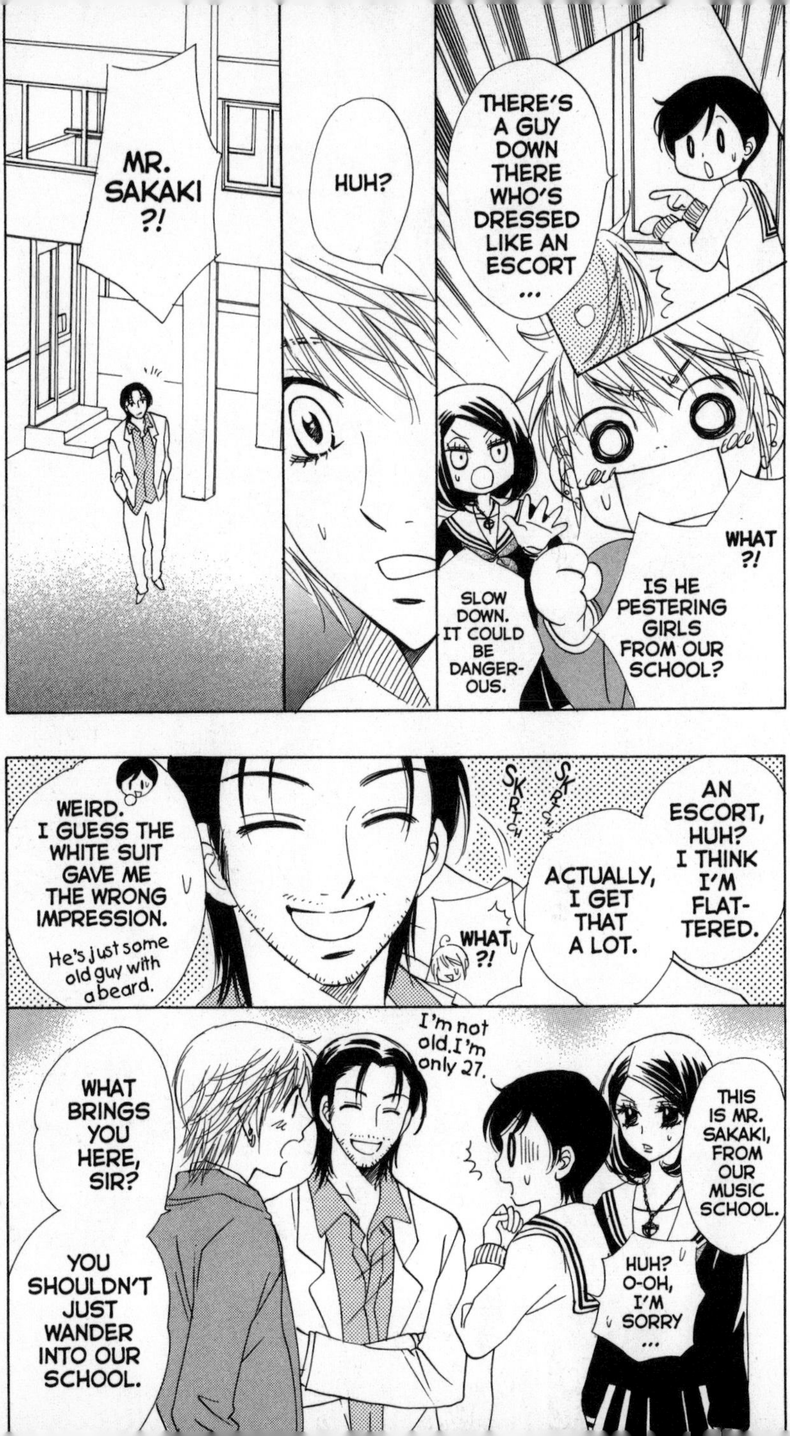
THERE'S A GUY DOWN THERE WHO'S DRESSED LIKE AN ESCORT ...
WHAT ?!
IS HE PESTERING GIRLS FROM OUR SCHOOL?
SLOW DOWN. IT COULD BE DANGER-OUS.
HUH?
MR. SAKAKI ?!
AN ESCORT, HUH? I THINK I'M FLAT-TERED.
SKRTCH SKRTCH
ACTUALLY, I GET THAT A LOT.
WHAT ?!
WEIRD. I GUESS THE WHITE SUIT GAVE ME THE WRONG IMPRESSION.
He's just some old guy with a beard.
THIS IS MR. SAKAKI, FROM OUR MUSIC SCHOOL.
HUH? O-OH, I'M SORRY ...
I'm not old. I'm only 27.
WHAT BRINGS YOU HERE, SIR?
YOU SHOULDN'T JUST WANDER INTO OUR SCHOOL.

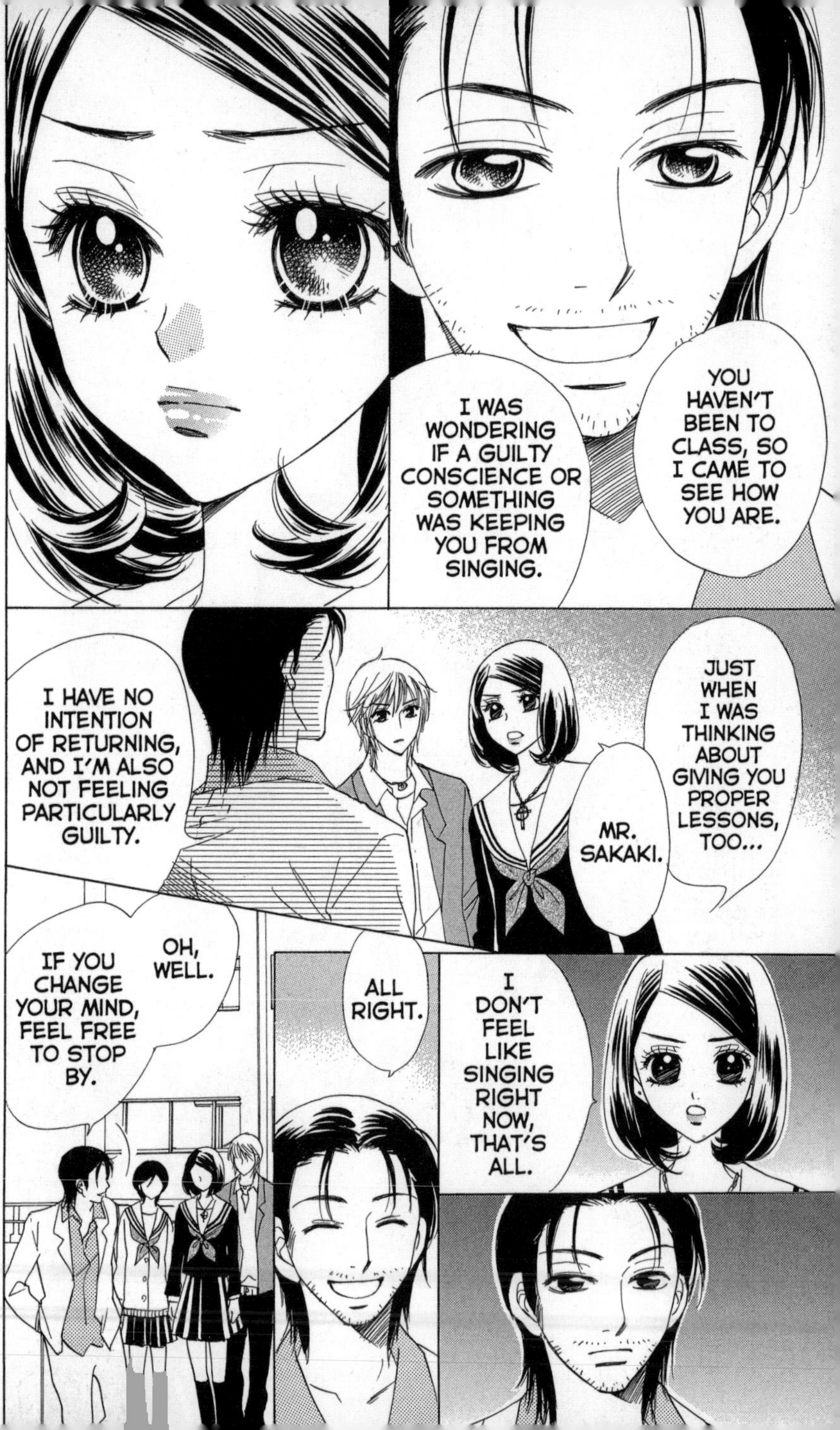
YOU HAVEN'T BEEN TO CLASS, SO I CAME TO SEE HOW YOU ARE.
I WAS WONDERING IF A GUILTY CONSCIENCE OR SOMETHING WAS KEEPING YOU FROM SINGING.
JUST WHEN I WAS THINKING ABOUT GIVING YOU PROPER LESSONS, TOO...
MR. SAKAKI.
I HAVE NO INTENTION OF RETURNING, AND I'M ALSO NOT FEELING PARTICULARLY GUILTY.
I DON'T FEEL LIKE SINGING RIGHT NOW, THAT'S ALL.
ALL RIGHT.
OH, WELL.
IF YOU CHANGE YOUR MIND, FEEL FREE TO STOP BY.

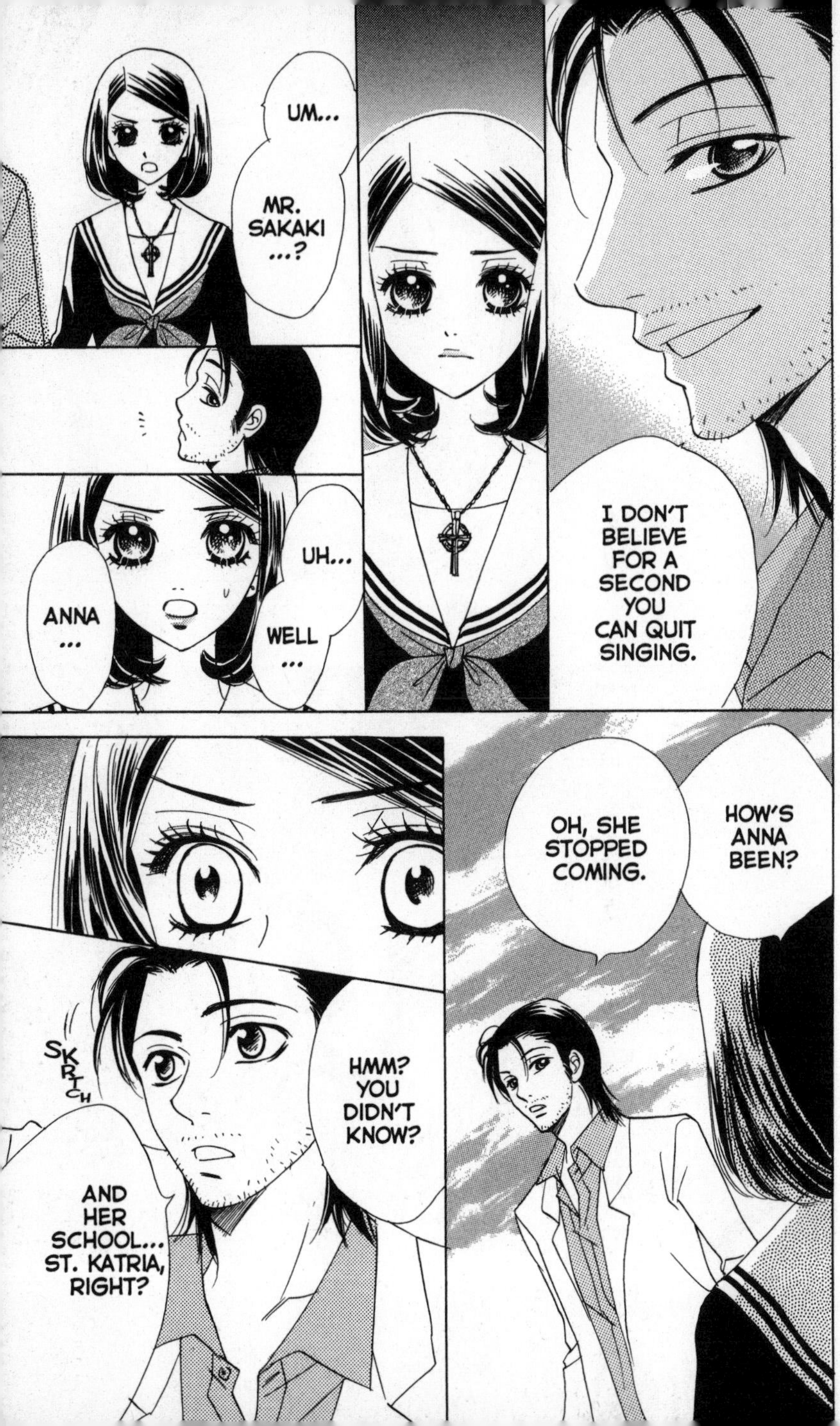
I DON'T BELIEVE FOR A SECOND YOU CAN QUIT SINGING.
UM...
MR. SAKAKI ...?
UH... WELL ...
ANNA ...
HOW'S ANNA BEEN?
OH, SHE STOPPED COMING.
HMM? YOU DIDN'T KNOW?
SKRTCH
AND HER SCHOOL... ST. KATRIA, RIGHT?

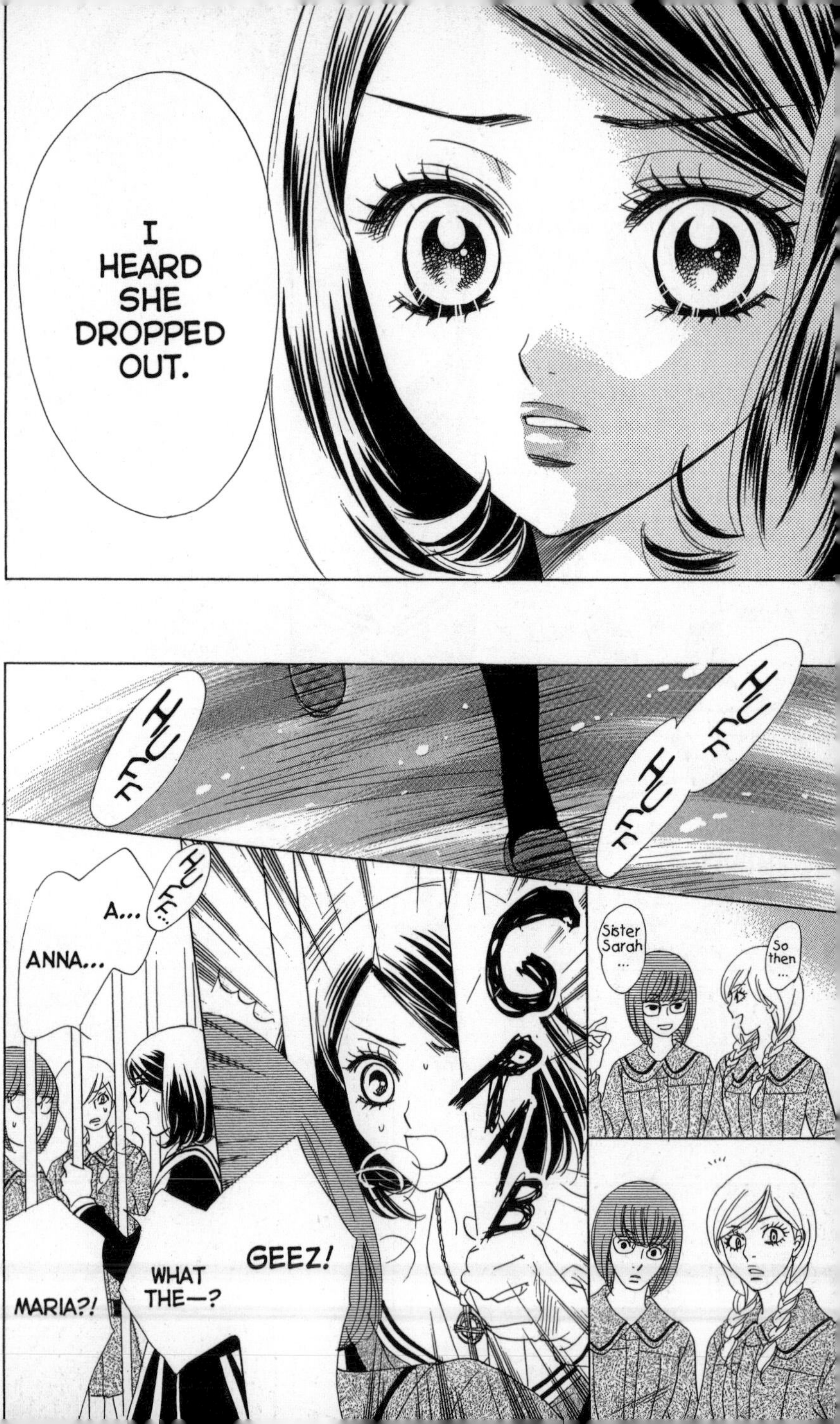
I HEARD SHE DROPPED OUT.
HUFF HUFF
HUFF
So then...
Sister Sarah...
GRAB
GEEZ!
HUFF...
A...
ANNA...
WHAT THE—?
MARIA?!

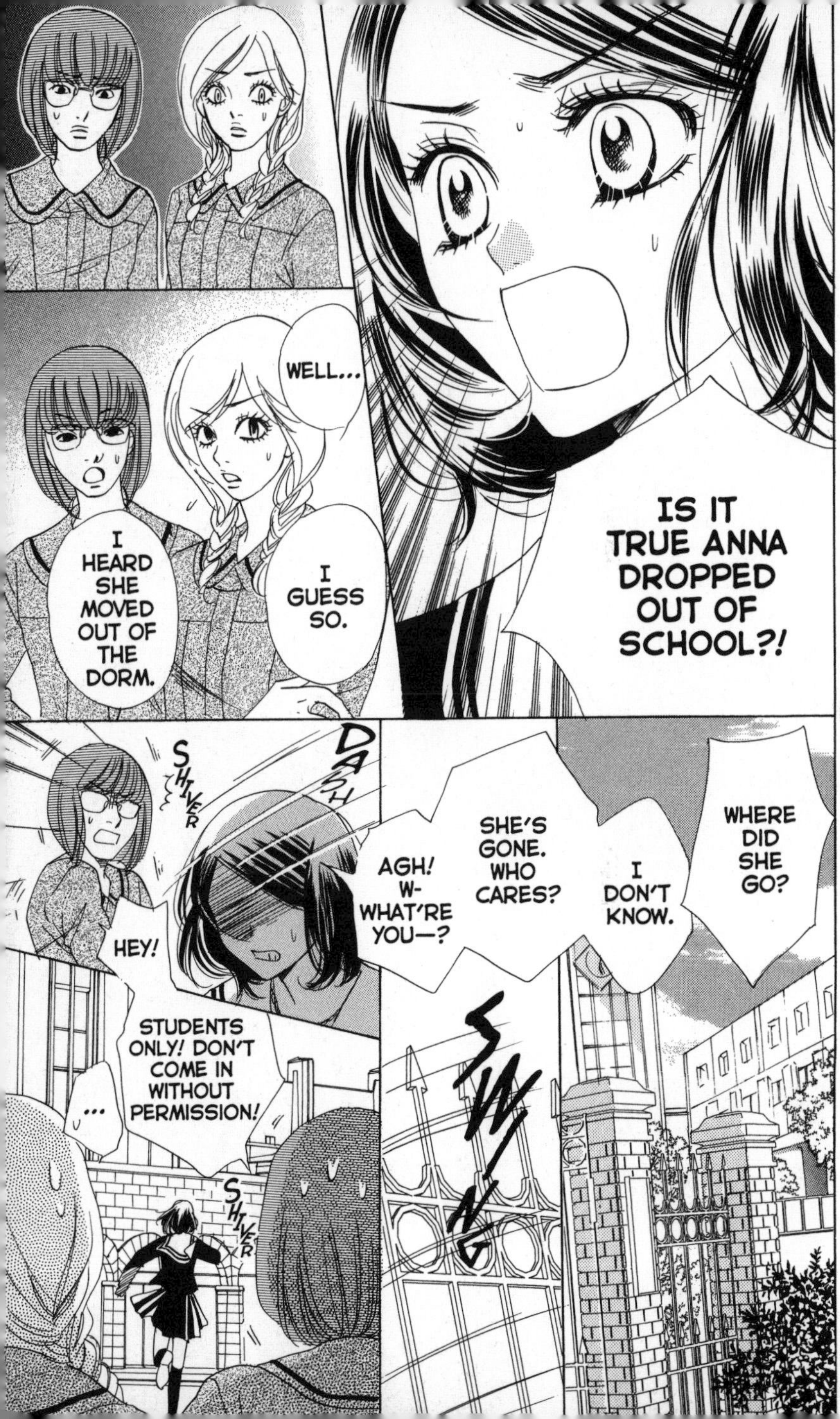
IS IT TRUE ANNA DROPPED OUT OF SCHOOL?!
WELL...
I GUESS SO.
I HEARD SHE MOVED OUT OF THE DORM.
WHERE DID SHE GO?
I DON'T KNOW.
SHE'S GONE. WHO CARES?
AGH! W- WHAT'RE YOU—?
SWING
DASH
SHIVER
HEY!
STUDENTS ONLY! DON'T COME IN WITHOUT PERMISSION!
...
SHIVER

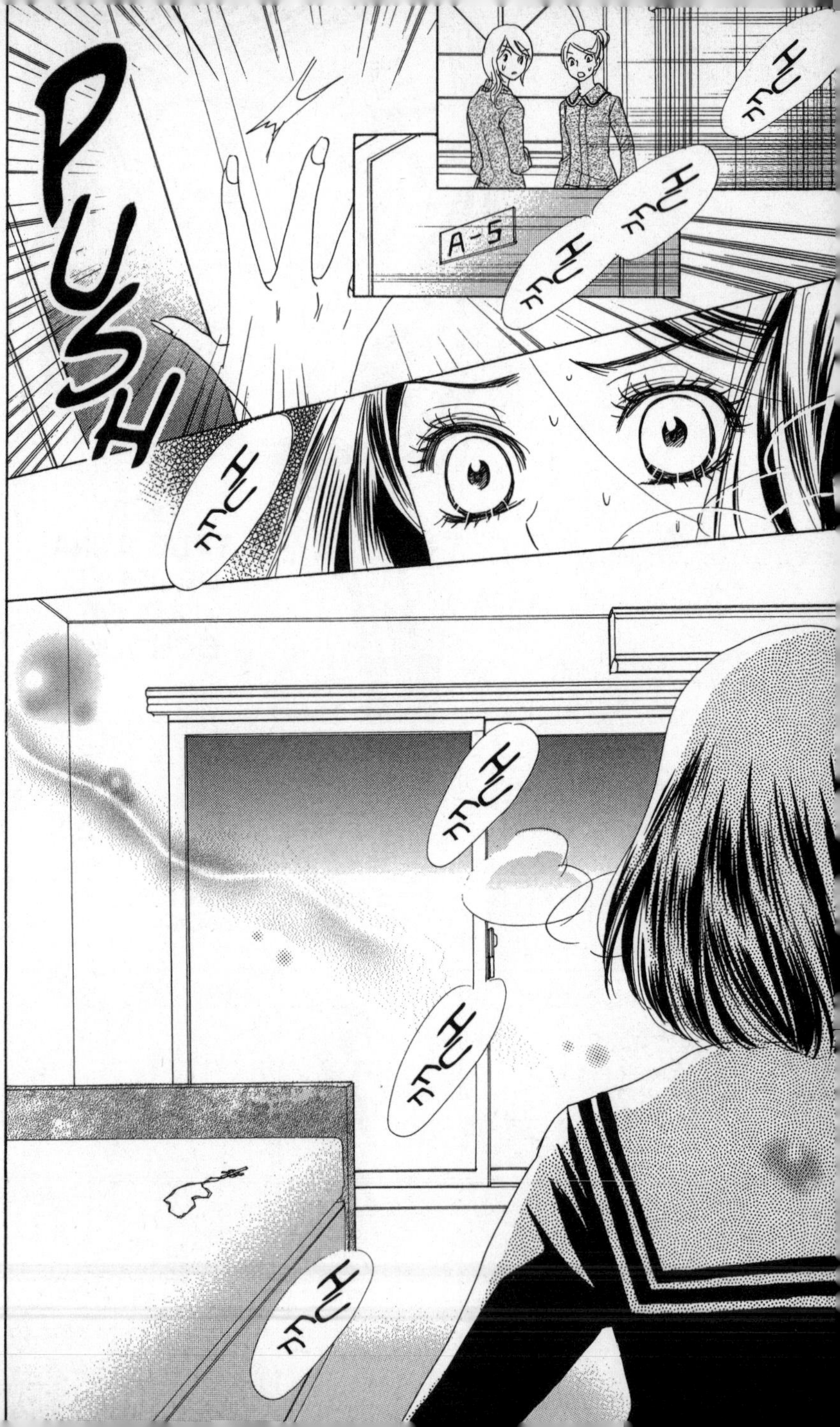
HUFF
HUFF
A-5
HUFF
PUSH
HUFF
HUFF
HUFF
HUFF

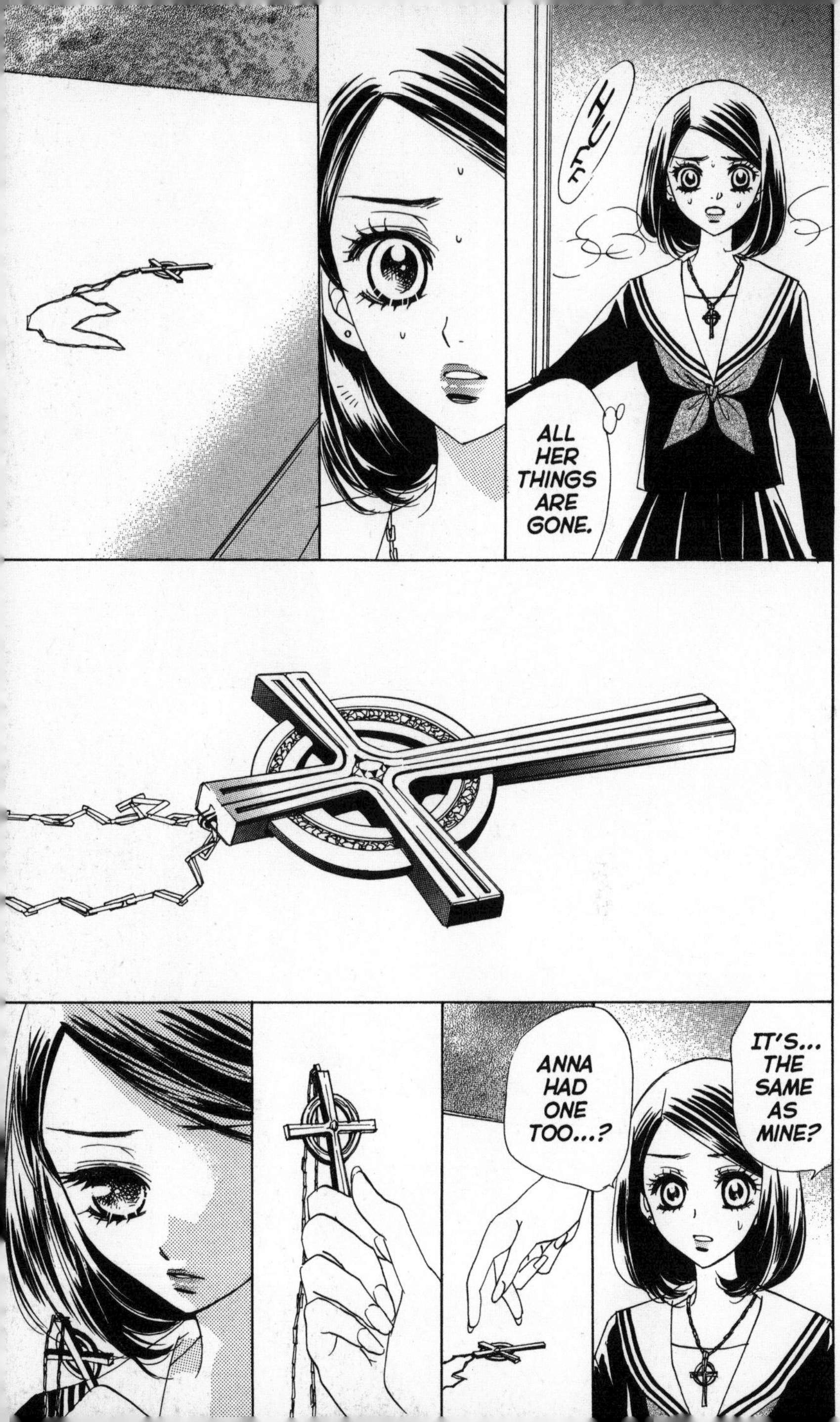
HUFF
ALL HER THINGS ARE GONE.
IT'S... THE SAME AS MINE?
ANNA HAD ONE TOO...?

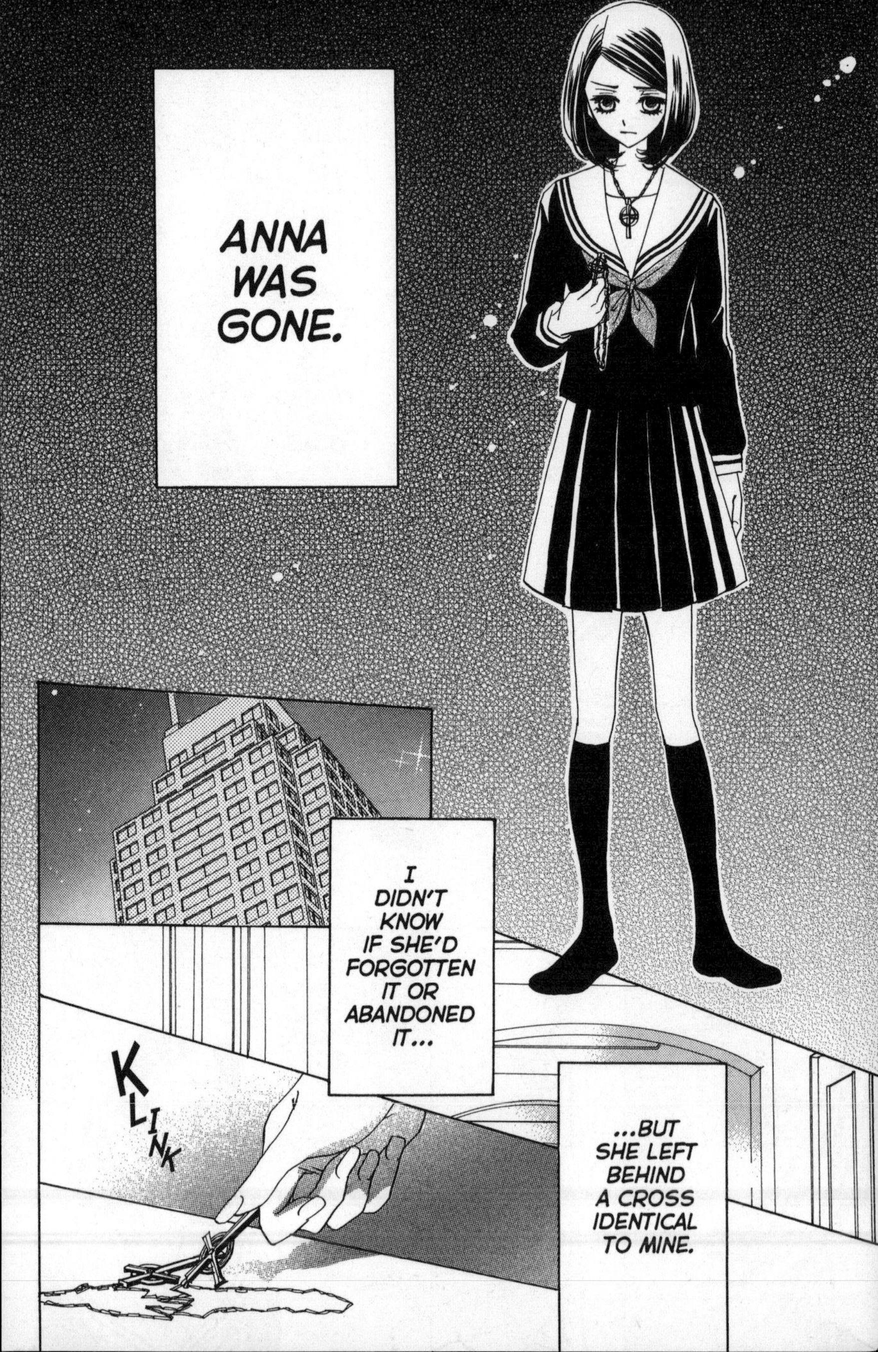
ANNA WAS GONE.
I DIDN'T KNOW IF SHE'D FORGOTTEN IT OR ABANDONED IT...
...BUT SHE LEFT BEHIND A CROSS IDENTICAL TO MINE.
KLINK

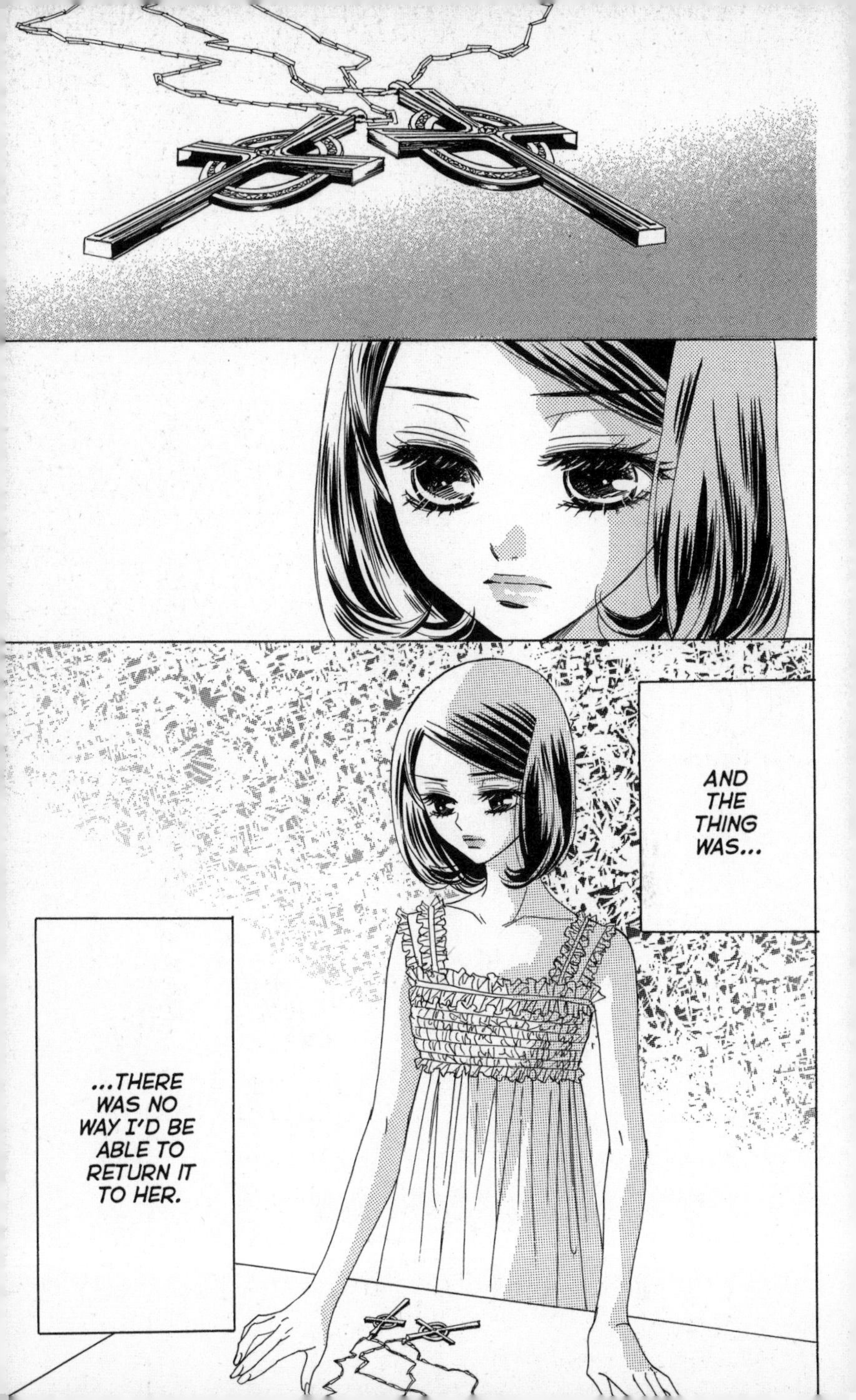
AND THE THING WAS...
...THERE WAS NO WAY I'D BE ABLE TO RETURN IT TO HER.

Continued
in
volume 8

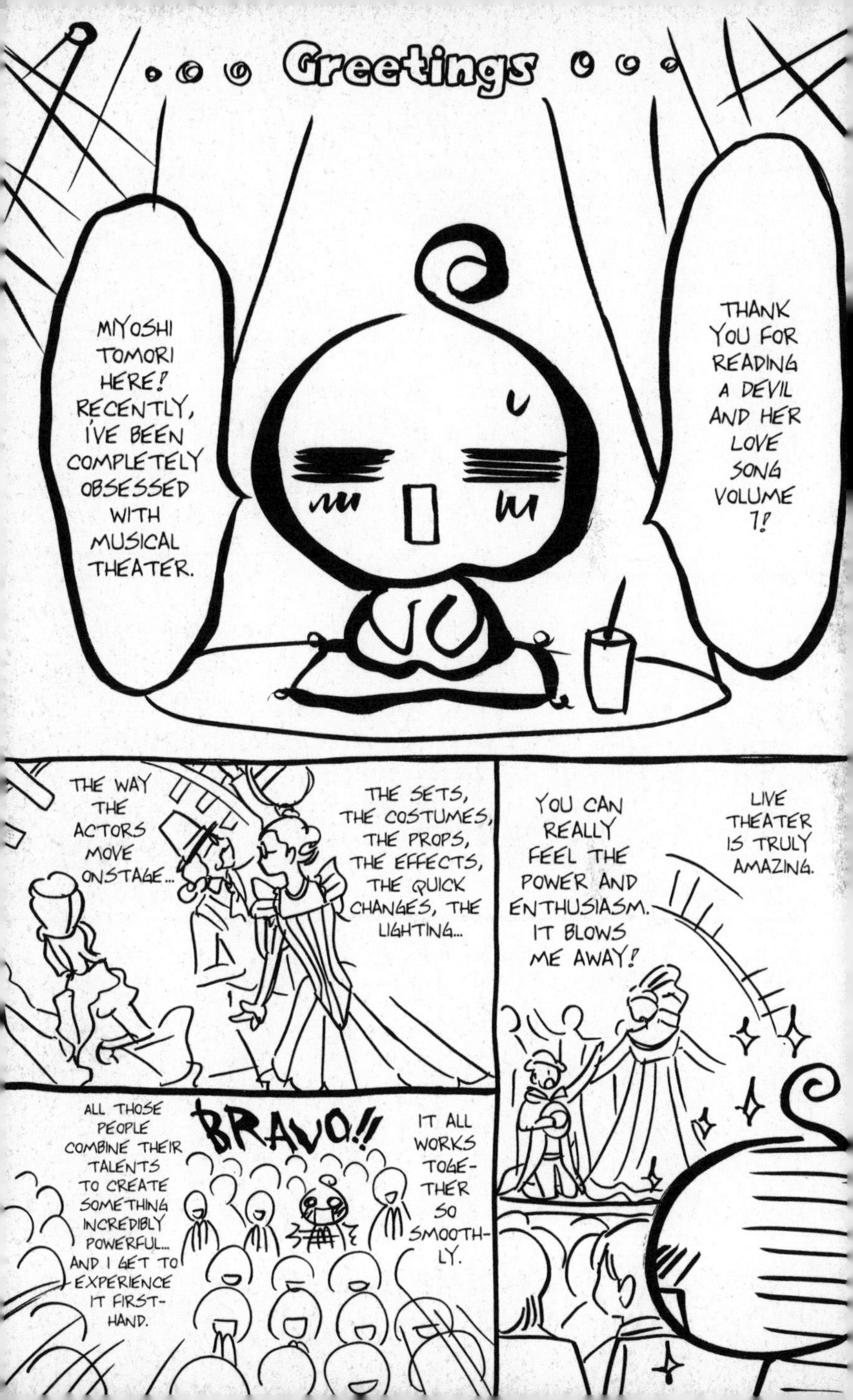
Greetings
THANK YOU FOR READING A DEVIL AND HER LOVE SONG VOLUME 7!
MIYOSHI TOMORI HERE! RECENTLY, I'VE BEEN COMPLETELY OBSESSED WITH MUSICAL THEATER.
LIVE THEATER IS TRULY AMAZING.
YOU CAN REALLY FEEL THE POWER AND ENTHUSIASM. IT BLOWS ME AWAY!
THE SETS, THE COSTUMES, THE PROPS, THE EFFECTS, THE QUICK CHANGES, THE LIGHTING...
THE WAY THE ACTORS MOVE ONSTAGE...
IT ALL WORKS TOGE-THER SO SMOOTH-LY.
BRAVO!!
ALL THOSE PEOPLE COMBINE THEIR TALENTS TO CREATE SOMETHING INCREDIBLY POWERFUL... AND I GET TO EXPERIENCE IT FIRST-HAND.

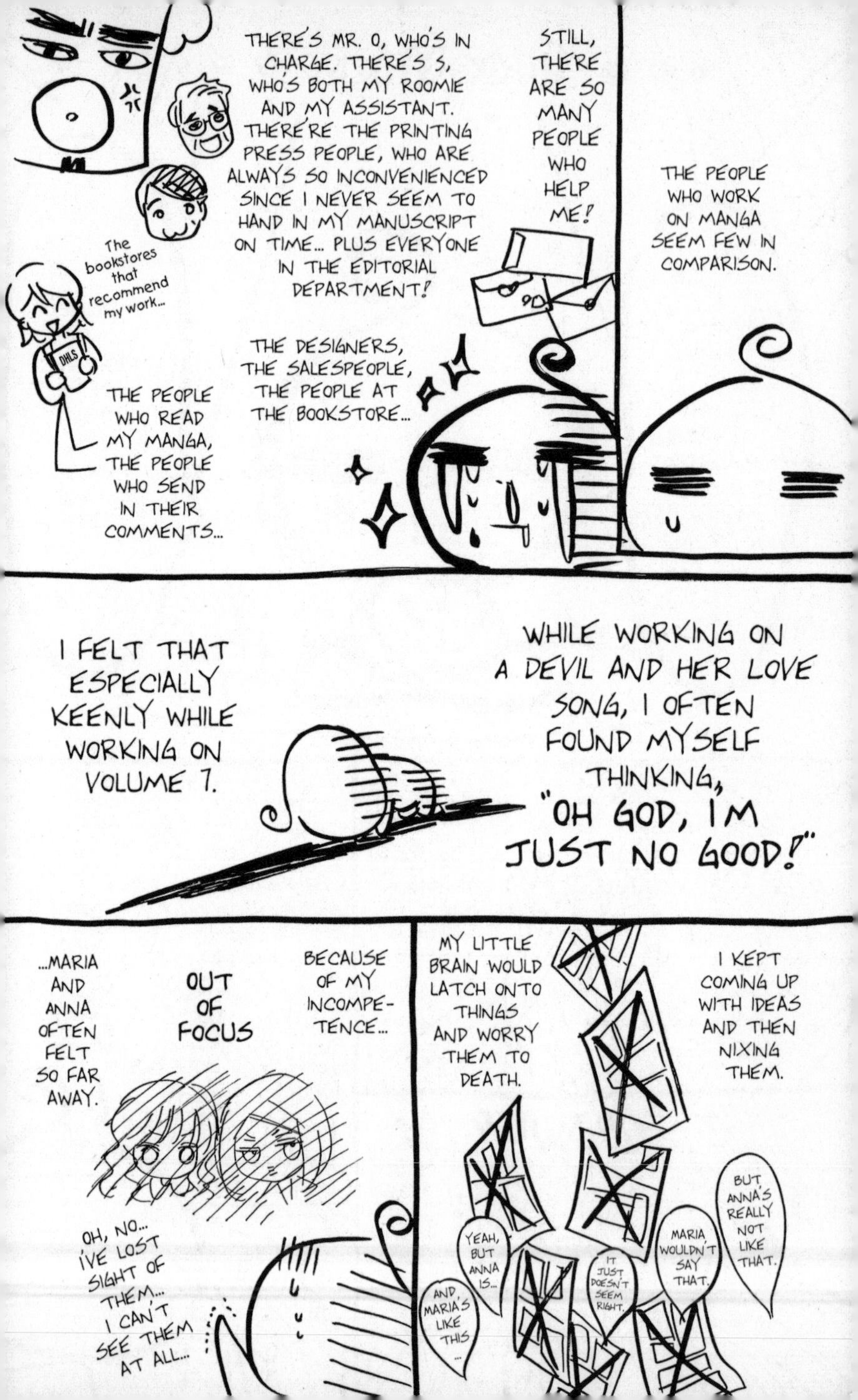
THE PEOPLE WHO WORK ON MANGA SEEM FEW IN COMPARISON.
STILL, THERE ARE SO MANY PEOPLE WHO HELP ME!
THERE'S MR. O, WHO'S IN CHARGE. THERE'S S, WHO'S BOTH MY ROOMIE AND MY ASSISTANT. THERE'RE THE PRINTING PRESS PEOPLE, WHO ARE ALWAYS SO INCONVENIENCED SINCE I NEVER SEEM TO HAND IN MY MANUSCRIPT ON TIME... PLUS EVERYONE IN THE EDITORIAL DEPARTMENT!
The bookstores that recommend my work...
DHLS
THE DESIGNERS, THE SALESPEOPLE, THE PEOPLE AT THE BOOKSTORE...
THE PEOPLE WHO READ MY MANGA, THE PEOPLE WHO SEND IN THEIR COMMENTS...
WHILE WORKING ON A DEVIL AND HER LOVE SONG, I OFTEN FOUND MYSELF THINKING, "OH GOD, I'M JUST NO GOOD!"
I FELT THAT ESPECIALLY KEENLY WHILE WORKING ON VOLUME 7.
I KEPT COMING UP WITH IDEAS AND THEN NIXING THEM.
MY LITTLE BRAIN WOULD LATCH ONTO THINGS AND WORRY THEM TO DEATH.
BUT, ANNA'S REALLY NOT LIKE THAT.
MARIA WOULDN'T SAY THAT.
IT JUST DOESN'T SEEM RIGHT.
YEAH, BUT ANNA IS...
AND, MARIA'S LIKE THIS...
BECAUSE OF MY INCOMPETENCE...
OUT OF FOCUS
...MARIA AND ANNA OFTEN FELT SO FAR AWAY.
OH, NO... I'VE LOST SIGHT OF THEM... I CAN'T SEE THEM AT ALL...

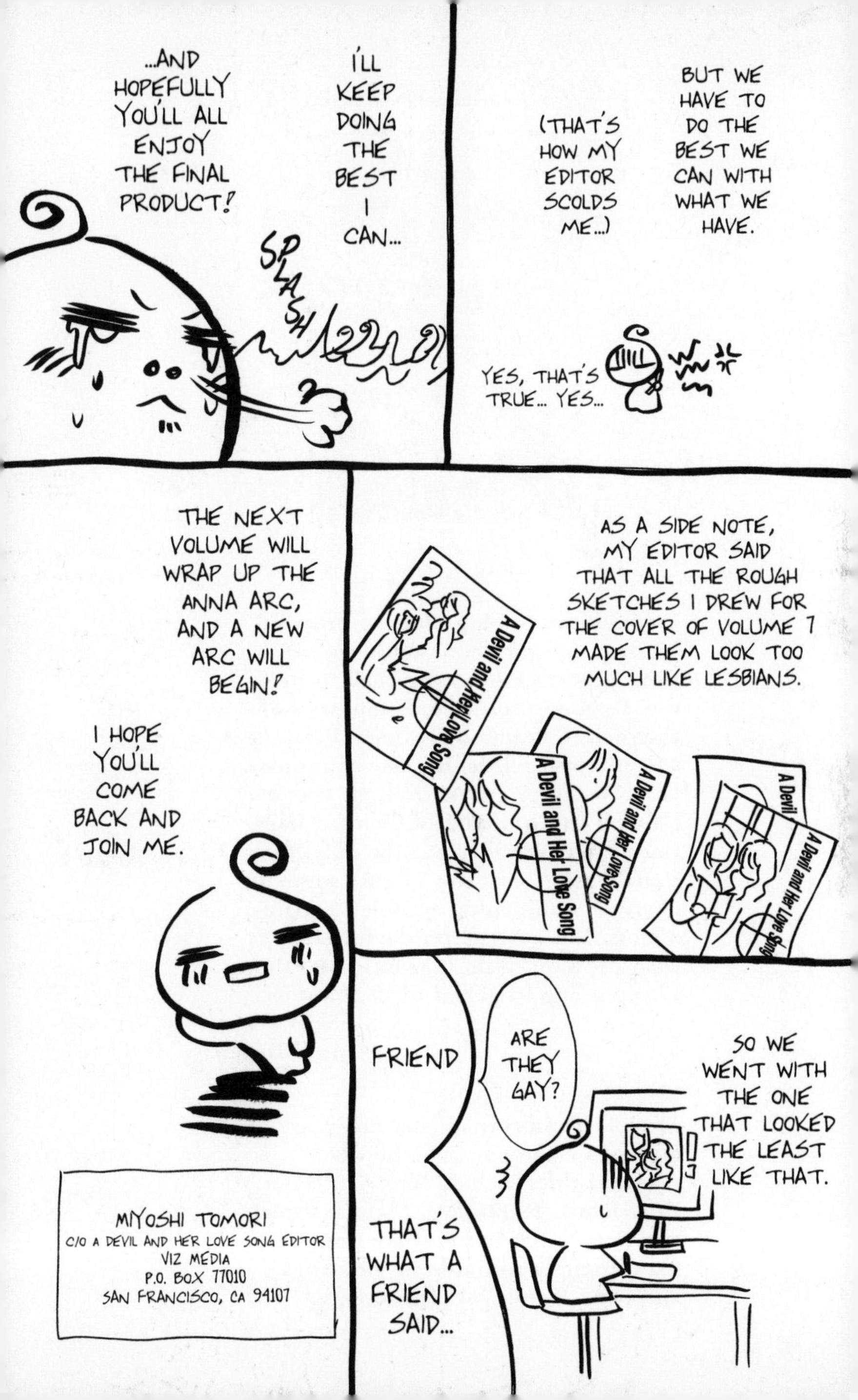
BUT WE HAVE TO DO THE BEST WE CAN WITH WHAT WE HAVE.
(THAT'S HOW MY EDITOR SCOLDS ME...)
YES, THAT'S TRUE... YES...
I'LL KEEP DOING THE BEST I CAN...
...AND HOPEFULLY YOU'LL ALL ENJOY THE FINAL PRODUCT!
SPLASH
AS A SIDE NOTE, MY EDITOR SAID THAT ALL THE ROUGH SKETCHES I DREW FOR THE COVER OF VOLUME 7 MADE THEM LOOK TOO MUCH LIKE LESBIANS.
A Devil and Her Love Song
A Devil and Her Love Song
A Devil and Her Love Song
A Devil and Her Love Song
SO WE WENT WITH THE ONE THAT LOOKED THE LEAST LIKE THAT.
ARE THEY GAY?
FRIEND
THAT'S WHAT A FRIEND SAID...
THE NEXT VOLUME WILL WRAP UP THE ANNA ARC, AND A NEW ARC WILL BEGIN!
I HOPE YOU'LL COME BACK AND JOIN ME.
MIYOSHI TOMORI
C/O A DEVIL AND HER LOVE SONG EDITOR
VIZ MEDIA
P.O. BOX 77010
SAN FRANCISCO, CA 94107

I would love to blog. But the minute I pick up my cell phone to do so, memories from grade school come back to stop me. During summer vacation, we were assigned to keep a daily diary. Every year, I would wait till the last day of summer vacation to try and write it all at once. (Well, it was more like a weather diary since the newspaper was the only thing I could refer back to.) I figure someone like that would never be able to write a blog. So I gave up on the idea. But then I'll want to do it again... And thus, I keep going back and forth about it.

-Miyoshi Tomori

Miyoshi Tomori made her debut as a manga creator in 2001, and her previous titles include *Hatsukare* (First Boyfriend), *Tongari Root* (Square Root), and *Brass Love!!* In her spare time she likes listening to music in the bath and playing musical instruments.

A DEVIL AND HER LOVE SONG

Volume 7
Shojo Beat Edition

STORY AND ART BY
MIYOSHI TOMORI

English Adaptation/Ysabet MacFarlane
Translation/JN Productions
Touch-up Art & Lettering/Monalisa de Asis
Design/Courtney Utt
Editor/Amy Yu

AKUMA TO LOVE SONG © 2006 by Miyoshi Tomori
All rights reserved. First published in Japan in 2006
by SHUEISHA Inc., Tokyo.
English translation rights arranged
by SHUEISHA Inc.

Printed in the U.S.A.

Published by VIZ Media, LLC
P.O. Box 77010
San Francisco, CA 94107

10 9 8 7 6 5 4 3 2 1
First printing, February 2013

www.viz.com   www.shojobeat.com

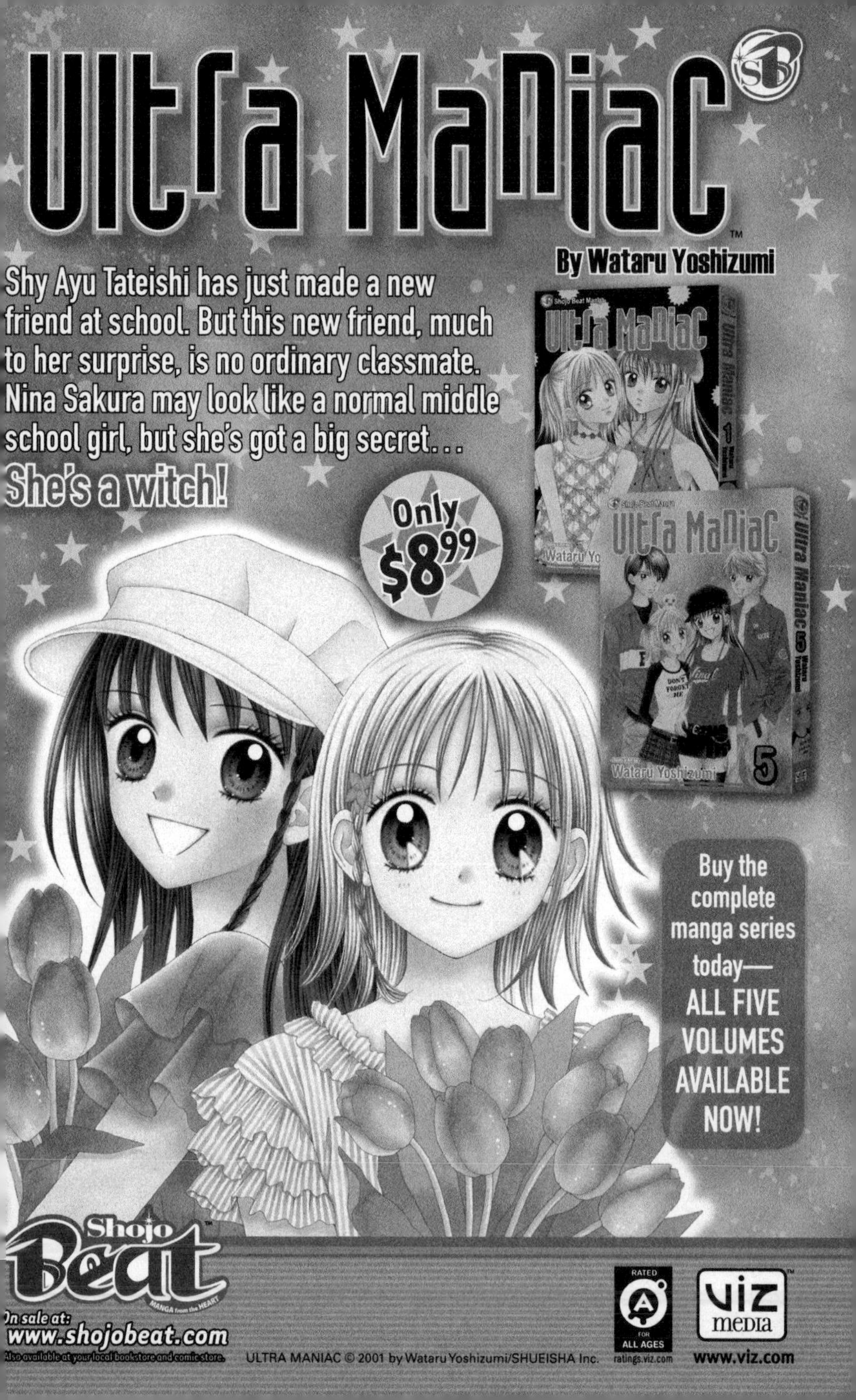

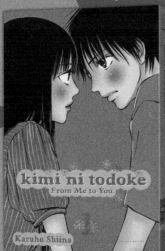

Surprise!
You may be reading the wrong way!

It's true: In keeping with the original Japanese comic format, this book reads from right to left—so action, sound effects, and word balloons are completely reversed. This preserves the orientation of the original artwork—plus, it's fun! Check out the diagram shown here to get the hang of things, and then turn to the other side of the book to get started!

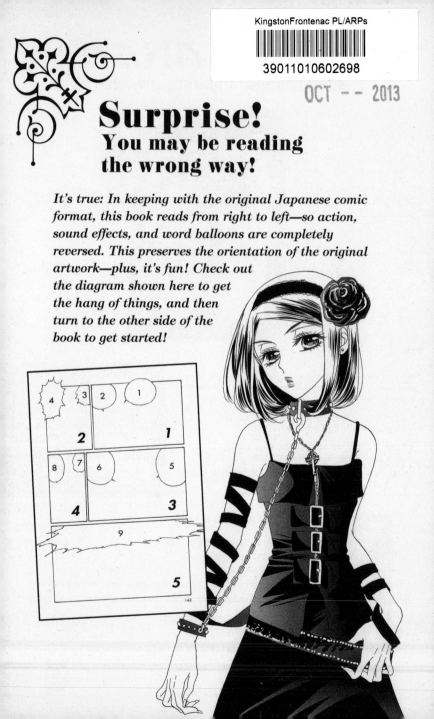